D1611739

The Peasant Marketing System
of Oaxaca, Mexico

The Peasant Marketing System of Oaxaca, Mexico

Ralph L. Beals

University of California Press
Berkeley / Los Angeles / London

University of California Press
Berkeley and Los Angeles, California
University of California Press, Ltd.
London, England

Printed in the United States of America

Contents

Acknowledgments

This report on the peasant marketing system of Oaxaca, Mexico, and the studies on which it is based, are the product of many persons and institutions. To name every individual who contributed to the research and writing is impossible, and to those whose names are omitted I extend my apologies and assure them of my gratitude for their help.

The greatest debt is owed to the villagers and traders who provided most of the information used in this report. In few places in the world are people so friendly to strangers or so cooperative and frank as in the region of the Oaxaca marketing system. As Bronislaw Malinowski wrote in the preliminary report (Malinowski and de la Fuente 1957:13–14) of his earlier study of the market system of the Valley of Oaxaca in 1940 and 1941:

> I am gratified to say, finally, that in no other field study—whether it be in New Guinea, in Melanesia, in Bantu Africa, or among the tribes of North America—have I found the actual ethnographic technique more pleasant, easy, and fruitful than among the Zapotecs of the Valley of Oaxaca. A certain number of informants whom I had the personal good fortune to discover, contributed more to success than all the methods and clever tricks of previous field work [my translation].

These sentiments are not overdrawn, and to the hundreds of people in Oaxaca who helped the staff of the project, many of whom became good friends, it is a pleasure to extend in the names of all of us, our warmest thanks and best wishes for their future. But for them this study would have been impossible. Had their assistance been less generous, the results would be far less.

Various officials in Mexico also provided invaluable aid. The late Eusebio Dávalos Hurtado, then director of the *Instituto Nacional de Antropología e Historia,* gave the project the official sponsorship of the institute, provided letters of introduction to officials in Oaxaca, and made it possible for members of the institute staff, especially Prof. Fernando Cámara and Dr. Ignacio Bernal, to attend a three-day discussion and planning Round Table at the end of the first year of field research. The late Dr. Alfonso Caso, director of the *Instituto Nacional Indigenista*, discussed the project with me at length and made it possible for various members of his staff to participate in the Round Table. These included Dr. Gonzalo Aguirre Beltrán, Dr. Daniel F. Rubín de la Borbolla, and Prof. Ramón Hernandez.

We benefited from the knowledge and advice of Drs. Bernard Siegel and John Hotchkiss, who also made available to us student reports from Stanford University's field training program in Oaxaca.

In Oaxaca the Governor of the State of Oaxaca, *H. Lic.* Rodolfo Brena Torres, through his secretary, provided letters of introduction for staff members which greatly facilitated acceptance of the project by various municipal officials. The rector of the University "Benito Juárez" of Oaxaca, *Lic.* Alberto Canseco Ruiz, provided facilities for the planning conference and later, as mayor of the city of Oaxaca, opened the municipal archives to us. The *Administrador de Mercados*, Carlos López, gave the project free access to the archives of the *Administración de Mercados*.

The necessary financing of the field research was provided by the National Science Foundation. The foundation also provided funds for secretarial help in organizing the extensive field data and research assistance for its analysis and the preparation of this manuscript.

Most of the data on which this report is based were collected by a dedicated staff of field assistants consisting of Richard Berg, Martin Diskin, Theodore Downing, Paul Steinberg, Charlotte Stolmaker, Ellen Waterbury, Ronald Waterbury, and Clyde Woods. Among them they spent approximately twelve years in the field. In addition three local Oaxaca residents must be mentioned. Federico Jiménez Caballero, a student at the University "Benito Juárez" of Oaxaca, was with the project for some two years, working not only as a field assistant to members of the staff but also conducting many interviews. His sister, María Dolores Jiménez Caballero, assisted at times by typing notes and copying documents. Miguel Ramírez Ochoa did much of the work of locating and copying documents and also made a survey of traders and artisans in the village of Mitla. The field notes, collected and collated in a central file, supplied much of the data used in writing this report. While specific credits are given to the field staff from time to time in the text of this report, this does not adequately reflect the importance of their contributions. Although the interpretations and the text in this report are primarily my responsibility, members of the field staff must be considered as major collaborators in the enterprise. Fundamentally this is their report more than it is mine.

Various researchers working in Oaxaca independently of the market study project were helpful. Beverly Litzler Chiñas, studying a community in the Isthmus of Tehuantepec, made many of her field materials available to us and participated in meetings of the field staff. Herbert Eder, working on the economic botany of Oaxaca, discussed many matters with us and made some of his unpublished materials available. Kent Flannery and Aubrey Williams discussed their research at length. Cecil Welte, head of the Office for the Study of Man in the Valley of Oaxaca, contributed freely of his knowledge of the Valley and made the resources of the institute, especially its excellent library, available to staff members. We are especially indebted for permission to use his detailed map of the Valley. To all those we express our gratitude.

Mention must be made of the part played by Ronald Waterbury in preparing the initial project proposal and getting the project started. The project had its genesis, in part, in a seminar I conducted on Latin American markets, but it took form principally in discussions between Waterbury and myself. In view of my impending absence from the country, Waterbury volunteered to undertake the onerous task of putting the proposal into shape for submission to the National Science Foundation. If my memory serves correctly, I wrote the initial plan in Los Angeles, the principal draft proposal in Buenos Aires in 1962, and signed the final papers in Kano in 1963. To these, Waterbury not only contributed many suggestions but did most of the tedious detailed work involved.

Acknowledgment must be made of the aid given by research assistants working in Los Angeles. These included Ellen Waterbury, Myrna Berg, Luanne Hudson, and Charlotte Stolmaker.

Two persons require special mention. Ralph C. Cassady, Jr., professor of marketing in the School of Business Administration at the University of California, Los Angeles, served as an unpaid consultant to the project from its beginning. He made three trips to Oaxaca and suggested many problems for field investigation. He also reviewed a draft of the manuscript for this report in great detail. Not only did he aid in clarifying much of the discussion of economic and marketing problems in the report but he made innumerable editorial suggestions for improving the manuscript as a whole. Charlotte Stolmaker served as research assistant for two years. She prepared many of the tables, organized and supervised the preparation of maps and figures, and not only made many suggestions for improving the organization and wording of the manuscript but rewrote numerous passages that I have incorporated with little or no change. She did much of the onerous work of checking bibliography and putting the manuscript in shape for the press. She could with justice be classed as a coauthor.

R. L. B.

1
Purpose and Nature
of the Study

BACKGROUND OF THE STUDY

This monograph summarizes the findings of a detailed anthropological study of an extensive traditional marketing system and its modern transformations. The major questions considered are (1) the scope and structure of the system, (2) its functioning, and (3) its responses to the relatively recent impact of a modernizing and industrializing national economy. The first of these questions involves identifying the geographic limits within which the system operates; the formal institutions, information networks, and conventional understandings, and the relationships among them, which constitute the system; and the range of goods and services handled by the system. The second question requires us to ascertain which goods and services enter the system through production and which through importation, and the extent and nature of the transactions by which they move through the system to the point of consumption or export. Here must also be identified the people who participate in the system, their varied roles as producers, intermediaries, and consumers, the alternatives open to them, and the kinds of decisions they make and how they arrive at them. The third question requires some minimal consideration of the national economy, particularly with respect to the new goods and services it makes available, the expansion of regional markets it provides, and modern forms of distribution, as well as adjustments and responses to these on the part of peasants.

The locale of the study is the eastern sector of the state of Oaxaca in Mexico, a region retaining a high proportion of Indian population. The society of this region clearly is market oriented and has been so for a very long time.[1] As the society and its culture are in considerable measure traditional and non-Western, consideration is given to the ways these affect the functioning of the marketing system and the economy that it serves.

A visiting economist surveying the traffic, color, and scale of exchange of the main Oaxaca City peasant marketplace exclaimed, "There isn't an economic theorist in the United States who has the faintest idea what goes on in a place like this!" If this remark be only reasonably true, then perhaps this study needs no other justification. With some exceptions, economists not only of the United States but also of Europe have been notably ethnocentric. Until recently, too, anthropologists usually have ignored the work of economists, whose treatment of indigenous economies has been superficial or lacking. In classical ethnographies, if economics is mentioned it generally is limited to a discussion of technology, with perhaps a few brief words about trade and division of labor. A noteworthy change was stimulated by the early work of Malinowski (1922), Firth (1939), and Herskovits (1940), and the past decade has seen several important studies of indigenous economies. Many of the studies have dealt with problems of the distribution of goods, that is, problems of trading and marketing, and the functioning of specialized personnel.

In Mesoamerica, the indigenous marketplaces and trading activities have attracted the attention of laymen and professional anthropologists alike since the earliest contact period.[2] Cortés described the marketplace of Tlaxcala in his second letter to the crown. Bernal Díaz del Castillo and Bernardino de Sahagún wrote of the principal marketplace of Tenochtitlán, the Aztec capital, and Sahagún (1950) delineated the various specialized traders in the marketplace. Sahagún and other chroniclers dealt with the special class of long-distance traders, the *Pochteca*. The principal significance of those early accounts for this study is the evidence they provide for the pre-Columbian existence in Mesoamerica of daily and cyclical marketplaces, specialized traders, and extensive marketing networks.

Numerous modern anthropological and geographic studies dealing in varying

---

[1] The term "market oriented" does not mean that all economic activities are controlled by the market. Rather, it means that the majority of the population involved are aware of market considerations and that this influences their economic decisions. Thus, in Oaxaca, a peasant who is engaged primarily in the production of foodstuffs for his own consumption usually does so as the result of an evaluation of the market and has decided that subsistence farming is the best use of his available time and resources. The discussion of multiple occupational roles and the patterns of production elaborate this point.

[2] The term "marketplace" is employed in this study in a specific sense discussed later in this chapter.

degrees with Indian or peasant economies in Mesoamerica are listed in the bibliography, for example, Beals, de la Fuente, Foster, Kaplan, Leslie, Marroquin, Nader, Nahmad, Parsons, and West in Mexico; McBryde, and Tax in Guatemala. Some of these offer data on marketing networks or systems, but the majority are village-oriented rather than system-oriented; for example, Tax (1953) described the market system of the Lake Atitlán region of Guatemala from the viewpoint of the village of Panajachel. The most noteworthy exception is the partially published study of the Oaxaca market system in 1940–1941 by Malinowski and de la Fuente (1957), although much of the data for it were collected in the city of Oaxaca and a few nearby marketplaces. (As yet unpublished notes and papers from this study, currently being edited by Ronald Waterbury, will contribute greatly to the analysis of recent changes in the system.) Marroquin (1957) described another market system in the state of Oaxaca, centering in the Mixtec town of Tlaxiaco. While this study has many merits, it is based upon a limited degree of field research, deals almost exclusively with Tlaxiaco, and uses a simplified and rather doctrinaire Marxist interpretive framework.

Among the economists, some have sought to cast their theories in universalist terms even in the last century, but the economic phenomena they knew were primarily those of the early industrializing economy of western Europe. Lacking a comparative perspective, they rarely recognized the extent to which the economic processes they discussed were embedded in and modified by the cultural values, traditions, and social structures of the societies in which they lived. Hence they were led to consider economics as an isolated system with its own internal dynamics. The major exception, Marx, saw the interrelationship of economics and society, but he drew upon the early anthropological works of Tyler and Morgan and accepted their evolutionary orientations uncritically. The state of primitive communism hypothesized by some early anthropologists of evolutionist persuasion became a basic element in Marxist theory. The efforts of evolutionary anthropologists to trace uniform stages of social development and to link these with stages of technological change undoubtedly influenced Marxist thought. Although Marx went beyond his contemporaries in perceiving the interrelations of economics and society and used the rudimentary anthropological knowledge of his time, his cross-cultural knowledge was second hand, and he did not test his theoretical conclusions against the realities of non-Western economies.

Modern economic theorists have tended to dedicate themselves to systems of model building within either a capitalist or socialist framework or some combination of the two, and to the extent that they have dealt with data they have applied themselves primarily to the macroeconomic phenomena of Western society. Studies of microeconomic phenomena and behavior have been limited. These deal mostly with the firm or with aspects of marketing behavior, again in the context of industrialized Western society. Until fairly recently few economists evinced any interest in non-Western economies, and of these, some either questioned the applicability of economic concepts to simpler situations or denied that indigenous economies had relevance to modern economics. An economist's plea for the study of indigenous economies is eloquently voiced by Polly Hill in the opening chapter of *Studies in Rural Capitalism in West Africa* (1970).

Economists may find in this book not only data useful for a variety of purposes but also evidence of the applicability of economic concepts in the study of a regional peasant economy that has long been relatively isolated from the main current of Western economic life. In some measure it builds on the work of Malinowski and de la Fuente, but it attempts to go further in depth and to examine the relations of the marketing system to the economics of village life. It is essentially an anthropological study, and its handling of economic theory and concepts, and the use of economic methods of analysis, leave much to be desired. For example, economists may be disappointed that no systematic attempt is made to test economic theories. Formal models in economics are not utilized, and technical methods of analysis found in economics are employed only occasionally, at best. There are many passages that invite reference to the substantivist-formalist controversies in which some economists and anthropologists have engaged, but there is no systematic discussion of the issues. Such comment was omitted not because the staff was unaware of the controversy but because, as the report indicates, it has limited relevance for the Oaxaca marketing system and economy. This is not to deny that gifting, reciprocity, and redistribution mechanisms exist in Oaxaca; they do, just as they do in all Western societies, and they have about the same importance. The main objective has been the analysis of a market-oriented economy and the way it functions within a non-Western culture and society in terms that have meaning for economists as well as anthropologists.

More specifically, the analysis gives at least some insights into the use of capital and credit, the nature of supply and demand functions and their influence on the formation of prices, the variety of economic alternatives, the nature of the choices made, and the extent to which choice-making is influenced by maximization principles or modified by noneconomic aspects of the culture and society. An important aspect is the understanding it may contribute to the workings of peasant marketing systems. Possibly, also, it may suggest ways in which more technical economic analysis might be applied, particularly in testing economic theories.

The choice of Oaxaca as the locale for the study of a peasant marketing system was influenced by several considerations. One was familiarity with the region as a result of an earlier study of one of its groups (Beals 1945) and extended, if unsystematic, observations of Oaxaca marketplaces beginning in 1933. A second important consideration was the prior study of Malinowski and de la Fuente, dealing with the traditional marketing system in the Valley as it was in 1940–1941, which could provide a baseline for the analysis of change. It seemed evident that (1) the traditional marketing system of the Oaxaca region retained great vitality and integrity and offered good opportunities for a study addressed to the nature and operation of the system, and that (2) since 1940–1941 the influence of the modern national economy had expanded enormously. Corollaries to these points were the significance of the adjustments that the traditional marketing system has made to the modern economy, and the relevance of these adjustments for enlarging our understanding of processes of modernization and for projecting the future of the traditional system. Any consideration of change and adjustment, however, depended upon knowledge of the nature and operation of the traditional marketing system.

Another factor that influenced the choice of the Oaxaca system was its extent and the number of inhabitants it embraced. The extent of the system is dealt with in chapter 3, but it may be noted here that, conservatively, at least 1,044 localities are involved, with a total population of more than 750,000, and that the minimum value of goods and services consumed annually is nearly a billion pesos.

PLANNING THE STUDY

Given the incompleteness of existing knowledge of the region, the formulation of initial plans for the study, which were necessarily cast in general terms, presented methodological problems. Some of the problems are inherent to any holistic or "systems" type of study, particularly when one is concerned with process rather than with the relatively obvious structural features of the system. As Cook notes (1971), our knowledge of such a complicated system will always be conditional and incomplete. Its processes would have to be studied segmentally since time, manpower, and funds were finite, and the results could be only a series of approximations of a reality that is dynamic and ever-changing. We would have to deal with innumerable transactions occurring in distinctive social and cultural contexts, with relatively differentiated production and supply subsystems, and a complex, culturally conditioned consumption subsystem. The first problem, then, was to identify the segments, aspects, or processes for the beginning of a systematic study.

Several basic questions had to be answered. These included the range of products marketed, where and by whom they were produced, where and by whom they were consumed, the routes they followed, the sites where they were exchanged, and the personnel involved at various points in the exchange process. The investigation of these questions could profitably be accompanied by the accumulation of specific materials relating to the marketing system, including not only its transactional aspects but also production and consumption. The studies of the total economy would include such matters as resource control; the roles of capital, savings, and credit; supply and demand factors; facilitating services; prices and price formation; the nature and conduct of transactions; restraints and available options in marketing; and the strategies employed by participants in the marketing system. At the same time data concerning cultural and social factors affecting the marketing system were gathered.

An associated problem was selection of the locations for data-gathering. An obvious first step was a replication of the Malinowski and de la Fuente study of the Oaxaca City marketplace. This central marketplace not only offers the widest variety of marketing situations but also draws products, vendors, and buyers from all parts of the system. Observation of products sold, interviews with buyers and sellers and, ultimately, precise counts of vendors selling each item, provided firm data concerning the variety of goods traded in this city and the number of vendors handling them, as well as information about the origin and destination of goods. This part of the study was conducted by Ronald Waterbury and Ellen Waterbury. Martin Diskin carried out a similar study at Tlacolula, one of the largest secondary marketplaces in the Valley, and Richard Berg studied Zoogocho, a small marketplace in the mountains north of the Valley.[3] Surveys were made of all the other large marketplaces in the Valley on their respective market days, and the smaller marketplaces were examined in varying detail. In those marketplaces that were intensively studied, special attention was given to their roles in the communities and in the areas they served.

The marketplace studies, supplemented by product surveys carried out in the northern Sierra, furnished information on the origin of goods and vendors and indicated the relative importance and distinctive characteristics of the various marketplaces. The results permitted us to ascertain the geographical range of the marketing system and the variety of products traded, and to identify types of traders and trading activities in the marketplaces as well as the ways exchange is conducted.

The investigation of the exchange system was further advanced by a series of village studies that demonstrated the varied character of villages' involvement in the market system, and suggested the extent of exchange activities that do not take place in the periodic markets. Field work also furnished data on production and consumption systems. Villages studied in some detail included Diaz Ordaz, a farming and weaving village (by Theodore Downing); the farming and metate-making village of Magdalena Ocotlán (by Scott Cook); the market

---

[3] The term "Valley" when capitalized refers to the valley of Oaxaca as defined in chapter 3. This conforms to local usage although various speakers may define the area involved slightly differently.

gardening and trading village of San Antonino Ocotlán (by Ronald Waterbury); the farming and pottery-producing village of Santa María Atzompa (by Charlotte Stolmaker); and the dairying village of San Lázaro Etla (by Clyde Woods). Cook had earlier and independently studied other metate-making villages, San Juan and San Sebastian Teitipac, and the Waterburys had spent some time in a farming and weaving village, Teotitlan del Valle. Separately financed, Beverly Litzler Chiñas carried on a related study of the town of San Blas Atempa in the Isthmus of Tehuantepec. The village of Mitla was investigated to discover what had happened to the intervillage traders of this community since Parsons's (1936) account. And virtually all villages in the Zapotec Sierra, including all marketplaces, as well as many villages in the Valley, were visited briefly.

With the cooperation of the Mayor and Administrator of Markets of the city of Oaxaca it was possible to examine the complete records of the market administration for recent years and such older records as we could locate in the municipal archives, dating back to 1938. Union officials assisted us in examining the records of the Federación de Expendedores de Mercados Públicos de Oaxaca (the federated unions) and some of its constituent unions, virtually since their founding. Data were also secured from records in state and federal offices.

PROBLEMS OF TERMINOLOGY

Many of the common terms that occur in this study are used in a specific regional sense and hence require definition. For example, the terms "village," "town," and "city" differ from the official census classifications. The term "city" is applied only to Oaxaca de Juárez, with a population approaching 100,000 at the time of the study. Although five localities in the isthmian region have populations between 10,000 and 20,000, none, because of the importance of farming, is classed as a city.

The term "town" is used in a more ambiguous sense. In the Valley and isthmian subregions I have applied this term to localities with secondary marketplaces (that is, those secondary in importance to the principal marketplace of Oaxaca City). Tlacolula, in the Valley, has a population of nearly 7,500; other secondary marketplace towns are smaller. For example, Zoogocho, a relatively important marketplace town, has a population of about 1,000 (1,083 in the 1960 census, 957 by Berg's observations); Yalalag's population in 1960 was 3,117. Marketplace towns also are the locations of civil administrative offices and services such as secondary schools; health, postal, and telegraph, and electricity services; and offices serving judicial, police, tax collection, and forestry control functions.

"Village" is even more loosely used. Generally the term refers either to a *municipio* (a political unit similar to the United States county) or to the principal settlement or *cabecera* of a *municipio*. In some *municipios,* all or virtually all of the population lives in a single nucleated settlement. In others, there are one or more smaller settlements subsidiary to the *cabecera*. Most *cabeceras* are larger than settlements recognized as rural communities by the official census classification. The "village" of Mitla, for example, in 1960 had a population in the neighborhood of 3,651, and the *municipio* of which it is a part numbered nearly 5,000 inhabitants. The Mexican National Census recognizes more than a thousand towns, villages, and hamlets for the region. The *municipios* of which they are a part, however, are more-or-less integrated social and cultural systems as well as administrative political units.

Although towns and villages are not clearly differentiated by size, they tend to differ in other characteristics. The populations of most villages are wholly or primarily Indian in origin and are engaged in farming, craft production or, to a varying degree, trading operations in the marketing system. Town populations often include a significant proportion of mestizos, and substantial numbers depend on marketing operations for all or most of their income. Towns with marketplaces also usually are centers of state and federal offices and services.[4]

Such terms as "market" and "marketplace" also are used with limited or special definitions. In this study the term "market" refers solely to the interplay of demand and supply at any given time or place. This differs from the usage frequently found in the literature for Mesoamerica where it refers to a place where goods are customarily interchanged. Technically, of course, any spot where a market transaction occurs is a marketplace, and the restricted meaning in this study must be kept in mind. Throughout, a "marketplace" (and what in much of the Mesoamerican literature is called a "market") refers to a specific area in a community where numerous (but not always the same) buyers and sellers assemble to exchange commodities on either a daily or weekly basis. It follows from this restricted use of the term "marketplace" that in Oaxaca not all transactions occur in a marketplace. Some goods are exchanged in stores or warehouses that are not part of the marketplace as here defined.

Many marketplaces have two components, for which the local terms *mercado* and *plaza* are used. (The Aztec word *tianguis* is sometimes used in place of *plaza,* especially in Oaxaca City.) The *mercado* is a permanent structure occupied primarily by full-time traders or vendors with fixed locations, operating on a daily basis. In contrast, the *plaza* is an open-air marketplace occupied primarily by

---

[4]   It is worth noting that a substantial part of the population of the city of Oaxaca also is of Indian origin or ancestry. Many of these people, although frequently employed as wage earners, essentially follow the life styles of the village peasant. A few farm on a small scale while others carry on household-based handicraft manufactures.

intermarket traders or producer-vendors, and is normally a weekly event. This distinction breaks down somewhat in the isthmian subregion, where *plazas* are daily although some of the personnel are irregular in attendance. It is also less clear-cut in villages with permanent buildings used part of the time by a few permanent vendors but fully used only on *plaza* days.

The term "marketplace district" includes not only the marketplace as above defined but also stores, depots, warehouses, and other enterprises clustered around the peripheries of the marketplace and depending in part for their custom on the buyers and sellers attending the marketplace. In Oaxaca City, for example, most of the coffee and chocolate mills are in an area occupied by the Saturday street marketplace. In that area are also cheap hotels, inns, saloons, and restaurants deriving most of their patronage from buyers and sellers in the marketplace. Around the peripheries of the district are the termini of most of the bus lines.

The term "marketplace area" refers to the cluster of villages from which a given marketplace draws most of its buyers and producer-vendors of local products. The majority of these come from nearby villages but the term is imprecise, for the marketplace area may differ with respect to particular products. Thus most buyers of cattle in the northern Sierra travel to Tlacolula in the Valley when they are in the market for such a large purchase, while vendors of deciduous fruits or lumber or other forest products may travel to distant marketplaces. Moreover, many villages, because of location, may be in the market areas of two different marketplaces.

The term "marketing system" refers to the interrelated and interdependent market activities and processes found in a regionally delimited group of villages, towns, and marketplaces. It includes those mediating social understandings specific to the market situation which enable diverse social groups to function and interact in it. The system is not completely closed but encompasses most of the economic transactions of the various components.

No distinction is made herein between marketing and trading. Paul and Laura Bohannan, writing on the economy of the African Tiv (1968:241), pointed out that the Tiv concept of marketing is to sell one's own products and buy one's own requirements, whereas trading involves the transport of goods for profit. This distinction was made by Marx in 1867 (1936:164), but he did not consider the two institutionally separable. The Oaxaca peasant is aware of this difference and distinguishes between the producer-vendor (*propio*), who sells his own product, and the trader (*regatón*), who buys and sells for a profit. Some of the differences in marketing behavior between the two types will be pointed out later, but the Oaxaca peasant pays little attention to them. In fact, the *propio* at times transports his own product some distance and sells in quantity, while some traders buy and sell within the same marketplace.

Throughout the study the terms "traditional" and "modern" have been used extensively. They are used here more specifically than in the general literature on development. Shils recently wrote:

> The terms "tradition" and "traditional" are used to describe and explain the recurrence in approximately identical form of structures of conduct and patterns of belief over several generations of membership or over a long time within single societies (with a more-or-less delimited territory and a genetically continuous population) and within corporate boundaries as well as over regions which extend across several bounded territorial discrete societies which are unified to the extent of sharing in some measure a common culture—which means common traditions (1971:123).

Shils further points out that societies that change relatively slowly or which explain or legitimate actions of authority by reference to the past are commonly called "traditional." Societies that undergo relatively rapid change or which seek to account for actions without recourse to tradition tend to be classed as "modern."

Shils's analysis has the merit of eliminating the directional quality found in much development literature that tends to measure modernity by the degree of change toward Western capitalist or Communist models (depending usually on the national affiliations of the writer). His approach admits the use of criteria internal to the society for measuring its modernity or traditionalism, without recourse to external yardsticks. As applied to this study, this means that the Oaxaca peasant society and its economy should provide the bases for evaluation, and when I have used the terms "traditional" and "modern" I have attempted to keep to these internal criteria. As applied to marketing in Oaxaca, the terms are used in a special sense that becomes clear in the following discussion.

What I have termed the traditional marketing system in Oaxaca is the system existing before the completion of the Pan American Highway in 1948, and such aspects of it as have continued into the present. It includes a broad spectrum of peasant producers, consumers, and traders, based primarily in rural villages within a definable region, who participate in an exchange system with minimal extraregional involvements. The system deals in products of farm, forest, and ocean, a wide variety of village handicrafts, and a few town or city products that are extensively used in villages. The limited consumption of urban products is underscored because some basic metal tools are still forged in villages. Much, but far from all, of the trading in the traditional system has taken place in marketplaces, most of them periodic, which serve for the assembly and dispersal of products. Most vendors are either peasant producers, or traders and middlemen of various types who also are usually peasants or have peasant antecedents. Likewise, the majority of retail buyers are village-dwelling peasants although, now as in the past, town and city dwellers also have acquired their provisions largely in the peasant marketplaces. This system is traditional in that it has a long historical background. While it has aboriginal antecedents (Whitecotton 1968), its basic patterns and relationships were modified in Colonial times. Changes have occurred over time but they were slow and relatively minor. Because of limitations of resources and time, little systematic effort has been made to trace the origins and development of the traditional marketing system. It is taken as a "given," to be examined as it exists now or in a recent past.

The term "modern" is at times applied in a general sense to the marketing system as a whole as it has developed since 1948. It thus covers both the contemporary peasant system and the local aspects of the national economy. More frequently the term "modern" refers to the marketing system of the modern economy characterized by stores, warehouses, wholesalers, and other essentially recent commercial types of establishments dealing largely in industrially produced goods from outside the region. In designing the project, the modern marketing system also was taken as a "given." I was not concerned with the origins and nature of the modern economy except as they affected the traditional marketing system and its adjustments in recent times.

The traditional and modern systems are noncompetitive to some extent, for they deal in different kinds of goods. They also interdigitate to a degree: modern products, formerly not available or available only seasonally, have a limited distribution through the traditional marketing system, while the modern commercial marketing system provides new outlets for some traditional products, especially external outlets. The line between the two systems is also somewhat blurred. For example, to exclude from the "traditional" category all fixed vendors in *mercados* and stores, and all trade in modern industrial articles or all extraregional trade, would be misleading. Stores and daily vendors have existed in most of the larger localities for a long time; some of the operators are peasants. Extraregional trade also has long been important, for example, the export of silk and cochineal in Colonial times and the importation of cacao even in pre-Columbian times. Industrial or quasi-industrial goods have entered the market on a limited scale for some time. Some of them, such as iron products, woolen textiles, leather and shoes, milled sugar, distilled liquors, and roof tiles, were of Spanish introduction. The quantity of goods imported was small. Until completion of the railroad in 1892 all imports reached Oaxaca on pack animals, and even afterward exterior commerce was limited.[5] Not only was the railroad an inefficient, high-cost line, but the demand for industrial products was small.[6] Only with the

___

[5] In pre-Spanish times transport was on the human back. Most long-distance trade hence was in highly valued and easily portable items, but there is evidence that at least some such items as salt and cacao were from the Isthmus and Chiapas, respectively.

[6] The rail line may have been subsidized, thus reducing freight costs. The point was not

rising industrialization of Mexico, beginning in the 1940s, and the opening of the Pan American Highway link from Puebla to Oaxaca City in 1943, did the flow begin to quicken. This was the "watershed" era that divided a regional economy dominated by a traditional marketing system from the massive introduction of a modern economy of national dimensions. Much of the expansion in Oaxaca was commercial, and it was dramatically symbolized by the opening of a Sears, Roebuck retail store in Oaxaca City.

In my terminology, then, what is "traditional" includes the categories of goods and services, the techniques and patterns of production, the kinds of consumption (both concrete and in terms of values and preferences), the modes of exchanging goods and services, and the various kinds of economic actions and interactions that the Oaxaca peasant has acquired as part of his cultural tradition. The term "modern" refers primarily to those goods and services, techniques and technology, and ways of responding to economic situations which represent modifications resulting from recent external contacts, pressures, and opportunities. In adopting these meanings I do not imply that all changes from the traditional are the result of external influences. The traditional market system has its own dynamics of change, and the Oaxaca peasant has been independently inventive in adapting to the new and the external. Nevertheless, because of their relatively important effects on the Oaxaca peasant, as well as for their more general significance for the problems of socalled developing societies, those changes are emphasized which result from the impact of the external industrializing economy. Such changes are considered to have begun at the time that external influences became numerous and change became rapid.

THE PEASANT CHARACTER OF THE OAXACA SYSTEM

In this study the traditional marketing system is referred to as a peasant system. Other writers have used the term "Indian" when discussing the traditional economies of Mesoamerica, or "Zapotec" when referring to the Oaxaca region. "Indian" is unsatisfactory because many of the component parts of the Oaxaca system are villages where no Indian language is spoken today. The term is much less commonly used in Oaxaca when compared with other parts of Mesoamerica. "Zapotec" is also unsatisfactory because, although the majority of inhabitants involved do speak Zapotec or did in the past, speakers of other languages such as Mixe and Mixtec are an integral part of the system, while "Zapotec" is applied to a cluster of at least six languages or dialects, in some cases mutually unintelligible. I

---

investigated. Although now converted to a standard gauge line, it is still unreliable and most freight moves by truck.

have used the term "peasants" to refer to those people locally known as *campesinos*—village-dwelling farmers, artisans, wage workers, and traders living in rural settlements that are usually nucleated, essentially endogamous, and partially closed communities. These communities exhibit similar social and cultural characteristics but may have distinctive local variations culturally, socially, and economically. They are involved in varying degrees in an economically interdependent system functioning through the market.

According to most of the rather vague typological definitions of the term "peasant," the Oaxaca country folk are readily identifiable as such, but they differ markedly from the peasants of Haiti or China or Medieval Europe. I do not intend to enter into the extensive and somewhat fruitless attempts to define peasantry. In this study the term conveniently identifies a rural, village-dwelling segment of a larger society which shows points of similarity to groups that have been classified as peasants in other parts of the world.

One point of difference requires clarification. I have characterized Oaxaca peasants as usually living in partially closed communities. Eric Wolf (1955) characterized Latin American peasantry, and peasantry in general, as consisting of either closed corporate or open communities. In so doing he was not dealing with polar opposites but rather with a continuum extending from "closed" to "open." The criteria he used were mostly economic: a closed community is one with no involvements in an external market. In describing Oaxaca peasant communities as "closed," I refer rather to their cultural and social characteristics, such as the existence of an internal prestige system, a degree of political and religious autonomy, restriction of landholding essentially to community members, and an essentially endogamous marriage system. Economically, however, in terms of the traditional regional marketing system, most Oaxaca peasant villages fall toward the "open" end of the spectrum. Only the regional economy viewed as a whole tends toward the "closed" end of the spectrum. The impact of the modern national economy has given a more open character to the present-day regional economy. It has enlarged the scope of the villages' economic involvements, and this has been accompanied by an increasing openness in other aspects of village life. I must reiterate that the data in this report demonstrate, to my mind, that economic interdependence and openness are characteristic of the village economies within the Oaxaca regional marketing system and that these characteristics do not depend solely upon involvement with Western economic systems.

Most discussions of peasants tend to emphasize the subsistence nature of their economy. Production of surpluses for the market either is considered minor or else is thought to be the result of pressure from the larger society. It is true that a great many Oaxaca peasants consume part of the foodstuffs they produce, and in this sense they have a subsistence economy. The data show, however, that few if any of them produce all the foodstuffs they consider to be part of their basic diet. Put another way, the Oaxaca peasant is dependent upon the market for part of his food and other consumption goods. Moreover, since many economic roles exist even within agriculture, farmers do not necessarily all grow the same crops, and those who do grow the same crops do not necessarily use the same cultivation techniques or harvest food crops at the same time. Most peasants control the knowledge and skills to occupy several different roles that offer profitable alternatives in the use of labor and capital, so economic decision-making is required. The subsistence aspects of the Oaxaca peasant economy make the collection of quantitative data difficult while the number of alternatives complicate structural analysis. This does not mean that the economy is different in kind from Western economies. Determination of differences and similarities between the two types of economies, and of the applicability of modern economic concepts to Oaxaca, are important goals of this study.

2
Making a Living
in Oaxaca

The Oaxaca peasant's view of economics is simple and pragmatic: economics is the means of earning a living. The initial response to a question concerning the goals or returns from his economic activities is, *"Ganamos la vida"* ("we make a living"). If he is very poor, he may consider that "making a living" means obtaining the minimum of food, clothing, and shelter necessary for survival. For most Oaxaca peasants it means earning enough in addition to secure some amenities and to be able to meet social obligations.

The overwhelming majority of Oaxaca peasants make all or part of their lving by farming. In this they resemble peasants everywhere, but they also present important differences. Most cultivators in Oaxaca supplement their incomes by other occupations and for a great many, farming is neither their primary occupation nor is it the main source of income. In addition, many Oaxaca peasants do not farm at all—they make their living by selling labor and specialized services, making handicrafts, or engaging in trade. The ways of making a living hence are numerous and varied.

The ways Oaxaca peasants farm also are varied. As is shown in chapter 4, Oaxaca cultivators differ in the kinds of soils they cultivate and the crops they produce. While most grow some maize, many specialize in other crops including vegetables, fruits, flowers, coffee, fibers, and the like. Even maize farmers cultivate different kinds of lands with a wide range of humidity and temperature conditions. The various situations and crops require specialized techniques and skills in production, and often different marketing practices. The term "cultivators" thus embraces many specialized activities; to shift from one activity to another requires possession of proper resources, acquisition of new skills, and awareness of market possibilities.

Within other occupations there is a similar degree of diversity. For example, the brief classification of actors or functionaries in the exchange system given in chapter 3 is a great oversimplification; not only are there many variants within these broad categories but there are also many other economic roles related to the marketing system. In comparison with many other peasant economies, economic roles in the Oaxaca production and marketing system appear to be unusually complex. This impression may simply reflect different emphases by investigators. The Oaxaca system, however, does seem distinctive in the following respects:

1. There is a high degree of specialization in production and marketing activities, and a considerable variety of roles involved in these activities.

2. Many individuals are engaged in production and marketing activities, often in both together.

3. Consistent role combinations resulting from individual options are few.

Here I am using the term "role" to denote an occupational activity. Use of the term in this sense may be questioned by some readers. "Role" most commonly is defined as the activity or performance associated with a status or position within the social structure, and often has hierarchical implications. Some of the occupations or clusters of occupations listed in appendix 1 are related to statuses in the society, but many are not. In fact, as we shall see, the occupational structure in this region is remarkably open. Considerations of class or status almost never impede entry into a particular occupation, although knowledge of Spanish is important in many segments of the exchange system, and higher-level white-collar employment may require a mestizo appearance. While all occupations require particular skills and abilities to meet acceptable performance standards, the requirements are technical rather than social. Social benefits may accrue, however, as some occupations have a higher status than others. For example, farmers are considered to have higher status than laborers. Some occupations are traditionally assigned on the basis of sex: women do little farm work (usually only during harvesting), and I have never seen a woman operate a broadloom or, except in Mitla, a man operate a backstrap loom. Nevertheless, most such ascriptions are not absolute.

The openness of the occupational structure does not mean that occupations are interchangeable. While economic roles are less clearly associated with statuses than are social roles, each occupation is discrete and specialized in its function. Yet most individuals are engaged in several roles either simultaneously or sequentially in very diverse patterns. (The term "simultaneous" means that in the course of a year the individual carries on two or more occupations; the term "sequential" means that over time, individuals learn new occupations.) The multiple occupations are combined in fairly random ways, which makes it difficult to discuss occupational patterns.

The major roles and subroles that define the economic activities of Oaxaca peasants are listed under their respective category headings in appendix 1. Their presence or absence in the traditional and modern systems, respectively, is indicated as is their changing importance in each. The roles are titled in English. For roles that are widely recognized, the generally used Spanish label is given in parentheses. No attempt has been made to give labels in indigenous languages, for these are too numerous. Some roles that lack Spanish labels are analytically derived by the ethnographer, but individuals who engage in these economic activities would readily recognize the distinctiveness of each. All the roles meet at least two, and usually more, of the following criteria:

1. The need for special knowledge or skills;
2. The need for access to particular resources (for example, land, raw materials, liquid capital);
3. Knowledge of special role-related strategies or tactics;
4. Participation in personal interactions appropriate to the role;
5. Distinctive function; and
6. Existence of role-related performance standards by which performers may be evaluated.

Mechanical application of the above criteria could result in almost infinite role multiplication owing to the considerable diversity within most economic activities. An example may be drawn from ceramics production. In the Valley of Oaxaca there are several types of pottery specialties, differing not only in shapes, sizes, and finishes, but also in production methods and suitability of the finished product for specific uses. Oaxaca City produces a serving ware, usually wheel turned, with polychrome glaze. The village of Atzompa is known for green-glazed ware, unglazed griddles, and some red-slipped [1] shapes for special purposes; pottery from this source is considered ideal for cooking over open fires. The town of Ocotlán and the village of San Marcos Tlapazola produce two different types of slipped red wares with differing shapes and qualities. A black ware from San Bartolo Coyotepec is unsuitable for cooking but makes excellent liquid containers. Except for the city-made ware, the vessels are hand shaped, although often with the aid of a hand-turned platform.[2] Each village uses different clays, tempering materials, slips, and finishes, and different firing techniques. The red wares are sold mostly by *propios* directly to the consumers. Most of the other wares are sold to *regatones* either at the place of manufacture or in the marketplace.

---

[1] A slip is a wash of fine clay in water, applied after the vessel is dry to give a smoother finish.
[2] A mushroom-shaped mold is used at San Andrés Ocotlán.

Turning to a single village such as Atzompa, one finds further distinctions. Roles of men and women, while not rigid, are clearly defined. Men always mine and transport clay, temper, and slip materials, usually pound and screen the tempering material, and grind glaze (if the glaze materials are not bought already ground and mixed). They do much of the polishing of dry pots before firing, cut or collect fuel, load the kiln, fire, and (with the assistance of the women) unload the fired pots, transport the finished pottery to marketplaces, and do most of the selling. Women form the primary shapes and usually add modeled decorations, if these are used, but it is principally the men who decorate by stamping or incising. Usually men, but sometimes women, apply the glaze. These distinctions between men's and women's roles do not necessarily apply to pottery-making in other communities. Nor are these the only role distinctions in Atzompa. Although all utilitarian ware is formed by the coiling technique, each woman tends to specialize in one or two shapes, for example: casseroles (*cazuelas*), open, flat-bottomed cooking vessels with interior glaze and often with exterior glaze as well; tubs (*apaxtlis*), red-slipped for use as laundering vessels or glazed for cooking; jars (*jarros*) with necks and handles, glazed inside and out; *ollas*, globular shapes with constricted necks, with interior glaze, for cooking or liquid storage; flattish griddles (*comales*) for baking tortillas, and the like. Today a few Atzompa potters specialize in figurines, miniature vessels (*juguetes* or "toys"), and other exotic ware primarily for the tourist trade. A potter usually will not attempt a form very different in shape from the one in which she specializes, and one who produces small *ollas* usually will not attempt a very large one. One reason for this is the need to develop specific skills. Moreover, the various types and sizes require different ratios of clay to tempering material,[3] different textures of tempering material (not only do the sources vary with the specific form, but also the size of the metal mesh used to sift temper varies), different wall thicknesses, and even different firing temperatures. Naturally, unit production varies with the size of the vessels produced, but some women work more rapidly than others; speed and quality of production are also variable.

The successful production of pottery in Atzompa thus requires specific materials, knowledge, skills, and often business relationships. Potters must know what clay and temper is appropriate for a particular type and size of vessel, the clay-temper ratio required, and the amount of water needed for mixing the clay. Potters must acquire the motor skills to form a particular shape and the necessary appendages (necks, handles, decorations) and to scrape and polish to achieve and maintain the proper wall thickness and learn to judge when vessels are properly dried for firing.

---

[3] Temper used in pottery making is a coarse material such as sand or decomposed rock to make the clay more ductile and prevent cracking of the shaped vessel during drying.

In addition to knowledge, potters must have access to the raw materials required (clays, tempers, slip, glaze, fuel), and possess the capital or credit to buy these and to maintain the household from one firing to another (an interval of one to two weeks).

Potters also must develop and maintain relationships with a supplier, if clay and temper are purchased in the village from resellers, relationships with buyers, if the pottery is sold to intermediaries, and relationships with kiln owners for firing ware. (While an unmarried woman can buy clay and thus avoid mining it, she would find it difficult to chop the heavy wood required for the glaze firing. Also, ware with exterior glaze must be unloaded quickly from the kiln after the glaze firing or it will stick together.)

Finally, the potter must meet market standards; if the potter chooses to sell to intermediaries, she must meet the requirements of the dealer for fineness of ware, shapes, sizes, finish, glaze quality, and reliability of delivery. Even if the pottery is sold directly to the consumer in the marketplace, it is expected that certain standards will be met. These standards are set not only by buyers but by potters themselves. Consumer-buyers and dealers usually tap each pot considered with a knuckle, producing a vibration that tells whether the vessel is whole or cracked. Chipped, warped, or cracked and mended vessels are not acceptable except at reduced prices. Some potters are more sought after by buyers than are others, but this usually is due to the superior appearance of their product; all makers of utilitarian ware are expected to produce pots serviceable for cooking over open fires.

Thus the occupational role of potter has a set of general requirements, a specific (but not rigid) division of labor by sex, and a division of labor, associated with special skills, by form and size of vessel. Other occupational roles listed in the table could be similarly subdivided.

The list of roles in appendix 1 hence is selective; the titles included are selected here for their usefulness, as in any typology. The further subdivisions of the potter's role, indicated above, would serve little purpose in a general study of the Oaxaca marketing system, although it is indispensable in an analysis of the economy of the pottery-making village and for any understanding of pottery production and sale in the region.

Although roles related to farming are present everywhere, many roles are of limited occurrence. In San Sebastian Teitipac, Cook (1968:101) found 49 named and recognized roles almost equally divided among primary, secondary, and tertiary occupations. These are shown in appendix 2. Only 10 are related to agriculture; but of the 356 male and female heads of households, 327 were involved in cultivation to some degree. In contrast, 297, including some of the female heads of households, engaged in nonagricultural occupations, usually in addition to farming activities. In appendix 3 are listed 34 occupational roles that Diskin (1967:144) found in Tlacolula: three in agriculture, 23 in crafts and services, and eight in trade. In Santa María Atzompa, Stolmaker found 50 occupations providing supplementary sources of income for potters' families, which are listed in appendix 4. The primary occupations in Diaz Ordaz are farming and weaving, but at least 31 other occupations are followed on a full- or part-time basis. In San Lázaro Etla, a small village where dairying is important, the major occupations are farming, animal raising, cheese making, and basket weaving. Some people practice more than one of these. In addition there are various sellers of prepared foods, firewood, and specialized agricultural products; there are laundresses, storekeepers, laborers, and a barber. For at least 21 people these occupations provide a major part of their incomes; for others they are secondary ways of getting a little money, as are equipment rental, ox team rental, and minor trading operations. These lists provide evidence of the variety of economic activities to be found in the villages, many of them not detailed in appendix 1.

Some households in the majority of villages depend on labor; in some villages many households have depended on labor for some time. Parsons (1936:63), writing of Mitla in the period from 1929 to 1933, indicated that 98 out of 371 men enumerated depended upon wage labor for some of their income. The number varies from village to village, and most peasants who give their principal occupation as laborer also have some *oficio* or other occupation. In Atzompa, for example, excluding 42 households with members working at steady jobs, nearly half (160 out of 392) of the household heads listed labor, principally farm labor, as a part-time occupation. There were only 2 full-time farm laborers at the time of the field census, however, and out of 22 self-declared part-time farm laborers in a sample population of 80 households, 4 had not worked as such in the previous year. Of the 92 households in San Lázaro Etla, 5 full-time and 23 part-time *jornaleros* or *mozos* and tractor operators were listed in a census.

While most Oaxaca peasants engage in several occupational roles, there are some exceptions. Some laborers (*jornaleros*) apparently do nothing else. But the cultivator (*labrador* or *agricultor*) becomes a vendor in the marketplace if he sells his own produce—a few kilograms of maize or a couple of chickens. Such selling requires a special set of skills in ascertaining the market price, attracting customers, and bargaining. In the transactional sphere, stallkeepers in a daily marketplace (*locatarios*), intermarket traders (*regatones*), and wholesalers (*mayoristas*) may devote all their time to these occupations. The *locatario*, generally a retail vendor, engages in a wholesaler's role when he supplies an itinerant vendor (*ambulante*), and if he sells foodstuffs, he may raise some of his own produce with the help of his family. The stallkeeper may even be a baker who produces bread at home and sells it in the marketplace as a *propio,* again with the help of the family. Illustrations of the latter types of role diversification are given in chapter 8 where marketplace vendors are discussed. In the villages role combinations are even more complex, as the village population may not support full-time enterprises. A person who is a storekeeper may also be a cultivator, an animal raiser, a baker, a butcher, a moneylender—perhaps several or even all of these. Following are a few examples of role complexity from actual village censuses.

Case A.   Farmer (*labrador*), hog raiser, *propio*, baker, storekeeper
Case B.   Farmer, metate (quern) producer, *propio*
Case C.   Farmer, basket maker, *propio*
Case D.   Farmer, goat raiser, *propio*
Case E.   Farmer, dairyman, ox team renter, *propio*
Case F.   Farmer, musician, metate producer, *propio*
Case G.   Farmer, storekeeper, *propio*
Case H.   Farmer, basket maker, baker, plow assembler, *propio*
Case I.   Farmer, blacksmith, plow assembler, basket maker, *propio*
Case J.   Farmer, dealer in the marketplace (*regatón*), *propio*
Case K.   Farmer with own lands, sharecropper, *propio*, buyer of standing crops for resale in the marketplace, traveling trader (*viajero*) between Mexico City and Tapachula, Chiapas.

Cases B through J are from one village, Magdalena Ocotlán, which was small enough to permit a complete census. Here Cook found 139 heads of households with independent or (in three cases) semi-independent economic status. Seven were headed by women, some of whom listed occupational roles such as midwife, tortilla maker, dressmaker, and landowner. Of the male heads of households, three were landowners but not active cultivators, and also listed nonfarming occupations of storekeeper, musician, goat and cattle raiser, and operator of a mill to process maize. Three men listed their primary occupations as sheep or goat raiser; one had an additional nonfarming occupation. Seventeen men were laborers with no other occupation; seven more laborers listed an additional occupation. Forty-eight were farmers with no other occupation, but 54 farmers had additional occupations. (The additional occupations included dairying and goat raising.) Many farmers who cultivated their lands with ox teams that they owned, also rented the teams to other farmers, usually with the owner's (or his employee's) services. Some farmers listed wage work as a secondary occupation, but others who did not list it may have worked as laborers irregularly. Farmers may be subdivided into *milperos*, those who grow maize almost exclusively, and *hortelanos*, those who grow vegetables or flowers. It is probable that all farmers are *propios*, at least occasionally, selling their own products in the marketplace. Other occupations listed for Magdalena Ocotlán included, in addition to those mentioned above, storekeeper, mason, tailor, and cowherd.

In Atzompa, Stolmaker found that out of 392 households, 348 produced pottery as a primary or secondary occupation. There were 236 landholders (211 of whom were also potters), and another 23 (of whom 19 were potters) received income from land through sharecropping. Of the 44 who did not produce pottery, five listed occupational roles related to pottery making, such as pottery *regatón* (one who buys for resale), miner and seller of clay, and owner of a manually operated glaze mill that is rented out to other potters. Of the families reporting pottery making, only 18 did not list some supplementary economic role.

Sample censuses and life histories from other communities in the Valley of Oaxaca and in the northern Sierra indicate that multiple roles are common, and from the Isthmus, near Tehuantepec City, Beverly Litzler Chiñas reports role diversification for both men and women in almost all economic pursuits. This is not to say that the multiple role pattern is universal. In the traditional transactional sphere one finds full-time *regatones*, both traveling traders and those operating in and between town marketplaces. Where permanent daily markets exist or industrial products from the modern economy are involved, the number of individuals occupying single roles increases. Among those peasants with access to land, where farming is carried on by traditional means, however, it is likely that only those with abundant lands can afford not to have a secondary occupation. Most farmers are also animal raisers, and almost all function as *propios* in the market system to sell their own products.

Life histories show advancement through sequential roles. A boy who begins as a helper (*mozo*) in a marketplace stall may in time acquire the enterprise and even go on to become a wholesaler. Having accumulated capital through the enterprise, he may branch out into real estate, open a small factory, become an officer in the Lions Club (the leading prestige club in Oaxaca), marry the descendant of a former high-status family, and drive a Mercedes Benz. This represents an actual "rags-to-riches" life history, although a very unusual one.

Similarly, a truck driver's assistant (*machetero*) may become a truck driver, and a driver working for a wholesaler or dealer may himself become a dealer or a wholesaler with his own fleet of trucks. The openness of the occupational role structure in both the traditional and, to a lesser extent, in the modern market systems encourages change and social movement. There are no ascribed roles and few entrance restrictions; anyone with the desire, knowledge, and capital to participate may enter any occupation—and some occupations require little knowledge or capital. The wage laborer in the village may seek wage labor in the city or even outside the region. In the city he can work as a porter (*cargador*) on *plaza* days. He can also become an independent itinerant vendor (*ambulante*); this requires at most ten pesos and the appearance of a good credit risk, so that a stallkeeper or wholesaler will give him goods on credit. Alternatively, the peasant's son entering the city or town labor force may become a helper in a marketplace stall or in a butcher or baker shop, learn the trade, and in time, with experience and a little capital, establish his own business.[4] Many helpers in the marketplace stalls and other business operations come to be regarded as family of the proprietor and often are given the opportunity to attend night school. With literacy added to business experience, opportunities expand in many directions. Oaxaqueños of rural origin do not consider present job status as permanent or confining but utilize opportunities to learn the skills and develop the abilities required by higher-level roles to which they are exposed.

Thus the marketplace offers individuals opportunities to observe and experiment with new roles and in this way functions to promote social and cultural change. It promotes change, too, by exhibiting new kinds of goods and services. In 1967, for example, at the patron saint fiesta in the important *plaza* town of Tlacolula, tractors were displayed in the town square. Thus the traditional market system and the traditional fiesta event were used to expose peasants to modern agricultural equipment.

In modern times occupational roles have changed, particularly in the production sphere. The *hacienda* system with its role of *peon* (often almost a serf) has virtually disappeared. The 1960 census shows 14 "*haciendas* and *fincas*" in the state, but agricultural estates theoretically are limited to 100 hectares of irrigated land. They employ labor and may have foremen or supervisory personnel as the large *hacienda* once had, but labor pay must conform to salary standards for the area. These relatively modern "farm firms" are owned mostly by mestizos or Spaniards and usually are near the city of Oaxaca or other large communities. Since the Mexican Revolution the number of small landowners has grown, and there has been added a new and significant classification of *ejidatario,* that is, holder of government-grant land that was once *hacienda* property. The creation of the *ejido* has involved peasants in a new government bureaucracy and a new local institution (the *ejido* committee) and has given them access to special credit facilities. Despite this, neither *ejidatarios* nor small landowners make much use of modern agricultural technology. Village industry has not increased appreciably, but there are a few new types of undertakings, and some traditional ones have increased in importance. For example, some artisans in handicraft villages now use hired labor: a weaver may own several looms and employ labor to operate them.

Most new roles are found in the modern sector of the economy, especially in auxiliary and service occupations and in modern transportation. The traveling trader has abandoned the burro for the modern bus or truck as a means of transport, yet he is superseded by the more modern trader who owns his own

---

[4] A few parents are reported to have placed their sons in enterprises where they might learn the trade, a form of apprenticeship.

truck. Bulkers and bulk breakers have increased in numbers and importance, reflecting the increased quantities and varieties of goods entering and leaving the region. The whole apparatus of bookkeepers, accountants, administrators, bankers, salesmen, and buyers, has expanded substantially. It is noteworthy that lower-level white collar posts are being filled by the sons and daughters of villagers.

Competition with the larger cities has affected local industrial and farm labor, forcing wages upward, rather substantially in some villages. In Diaz Ordaz near Tlacolula, as a result, landholders who depend upon wage labor are ceasing to cultivate some marginal or distant land. Instead, they invest labor and scarce capital in increasing the productivity of their better lands through leveling, terracing, irrigation, tractor hire, and experiments with commercial fertilizers. The influence of higher wages on aspirations is reflected in the strong preference for the role of salaried employee over that of trader, which Diskin found in Tlacolula.

Among the modern changes is a diminution in role diversification in the market system, especially in the permanent *mercados*. Wholesalers, stallkeepers, and some other types of vendors tend increasingly not only to give full time to their businesses but also to specialize in particular classes of merchandise. The licensing system and union organization have the effect of enforcing specialization; for example, dealers in perishables are limited to the handling of certain kinds of produce. The increasing complexity and volume of market transactions also encourages specialization. The *regatón* must know the market for his goods and also the best sources from which to buy, and both the market and the number of suppliers have grown in recent years. Even pottery dealers tend to specialize in the black ware of Coyotepec, the green-glazed ware of Atzompa, or the polychrome ware of Oaxaca City. Also, the modern economy has introduced new requisites. Whereas anyone can participate in the *plaza* at any level his capital and skills permit, participation in the *mercado* and in many activities in the modern sector requires permits and sometimes union approval. Many of the new roles call for education or considerable experience. But the same growth in the complexity of trade that promotes specialization and bureaucratic control also provides the traditional producer with increased opportunities, and sales channels have proliferated both for traditional goods and for new cash crops. Increased production finds a market, and the producer benefits.

In summary, the traditional production and exchange system serves to support a relatively large number of participants, many of them with a low level of living. Both the traditional and modern sectors of the marketing system contribute to cultural and social change by offering a wide variety of opportunities for learning new roles, for establishing a small trade or business with relatively little capital, and for expanding and diversifying one's economic activities to progressively higher levels. The individual is not limited by his birth or his family's tradition, although family transmission of skills may be an important determinant in his choice of occupations. The great variation in multiple-role patterns reflects individual appraisal of relative rewards, while the ways in which actors allocate and reallocate their resources to their different occupational roles reflect continuous reevaluation of the economic potentialities of each role as they vary with time and circumstances. Clearly, the rural-born Oaxaqueño does not function as a tradition-bound automaton but uses current economic criteria in his decision making. As a final word, it may be emphasized that the Oaxaca peasant does not hold a variety of undifferentiated jobs simply because he is poor; he selectively learns additional roles as he sees opportunities for improving his economic position.

3
Setting and Extent of the Oaxaca Market System

The Oaxaca market system extends through most of the central and eastern sections of the state of Oaxaca, Mexico (map 1). Its name, however, is taken not from the state but from the capital city of Oaxaca, the central point about which the market system functions. This region lies in the heart of the era culturally defined as Mesoamerica, which includes most of Mexico south of the Tropic of Cancer and a substantial part of Central America. Within the larger region the existence of extensive pre-Columbian trade is well documented archeologically and by the early Spanish chroniclers, and market systems similar to that of Oaxaca are known to have existed. These are referred to in chapter 1.

THE ENVIRONMENTAL SETTING OF THE SYSTEM

The environment of Oaxaca (as well as much of Middle America, a geologically defined area that includes Mesoamerica) clearly creates conditions favorable to trade and the formation of markets and plays an important role in the character of the present market systems. These conditions are conveniently summarized for Middle America in Volume I of the *Handbook of Middle American Indians*. The geographic setting has also been described by Tamayo (1950). This section draws in part upon a summary by Waterbury (1968).

The state of Oaxaca is characterized by extremely rugged terrain with great differences in elevation (map 2) and marked variations in temperatures, rainfall, soil characteristics, vegetation, and native fauna. It lies approximately between 15°

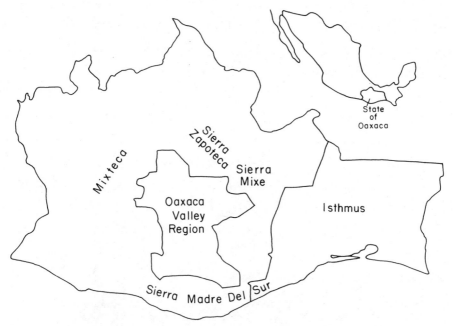

MAP 1. The state of Oaxaca and its regions

39′ and 18° 42′ north latitude and 93° 52′ and 98° 32′ west longitude, a total area of 95,354 square kilometers. A substantial part of the state is occupied by the Mesa del Sur or southern highlands, made up of the highly dissected Sierra Madre de Oaxaca and the Sierra Madre del Sur, but the eastern part includes much of the lowlands forming the Isthmus of Tehuantepec. Elevations within the area of the Oaxaca market system vary from sea level to 3,390 meters, the summit of Cerro Zempoaltepec (also called Zempoaltepetl), the highest point in Mexico south of the peak of Orizaba. In contrast, the highest elevations of the isthmian region are approximately 250 meters. Most lands in the area are steeply sloping. The major exceptions are a few basins, of which the Valley of Oaxaca is by far the most important, a few narrow Pacific coastal plains, and the lowlands of the isthmian region. In most of the area the Sierra Madre del Sur descends abruptly to the sea, often forming coastal cliffs, and the areas of coastal lowland are insignificant. In the Isthmus, however, extensive lagoons provide most of the marine products circulating in the market system. For reasons not yet understood, most of the Sierra Madre del Sur and the adjoining coastal lowlands of western Oaxaca seem not to have significant marketplaces or, until recently, to participate in any extended marketing system.

The largest upland basin is the Valley of Oaxaca, a down-faulted trench

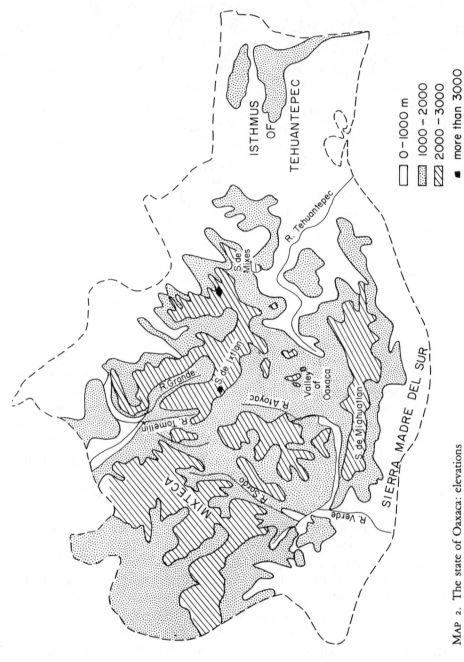

MAP 2. The state of Oaxaca: elevations

ISTHMUS
OF
TEHUANTEPEC

S. de
Mixes

R. Tehuantepec

R. Grande

S. de Ixtlan

R. Atoyac

Valle
of
Oaxaca

S. de Miahuatlan

R. Tomellin

R. Salado

MIXTECA

R. Verde

SIERRA MADRE DEL SUR

0 - 1000 m
1000 - 2000
2000 - 3000
more than 3000

extending about 95 kilometers in an approximately north-south direction, with a width of about 25 kilometers and with an average elevation of about 1,550 meters for the valley floor around Oaxaca City. Two subsidiary basins, Etla to the northwest and Tlacolula to the east, adjoin the northern end of the Valley and extend the area of flattish or rolling lands of the basin considerably. The Valley is one of the most densely settled rural areas of Mexico. To the north the Sierra Madre de Oaxaca rises abruptly to the continental divide. Eastward a rugged mountainous region separates the Valley from the Isthmus of Tehuantepec, while to the west is the elevated region locally known as the Sierra Mixteca. Southward the Rio Atoyac, the main stream draining the Valley of Oaxaca, turns sharply westward, flowing through deep canyons to join the Rio Verde. The Sierra Madre del Sur forms a high and rugged barrier between the Valley of Oaxaca and the Pacific Ocean. Not all writers define the Valley of Oaxaca in quite the same way. Some, for example, Flannery and his associates (1967), and Welte (1965), include the basins of Etla and Tlacolula but exclude the areas to the south around Ejutla and Miahuatlán, placing the boundary along the hills interrupting the valley floor between Ocotlán and Ejutla.

The face of the Sierra Madre de Oaxaca rises sharply along the north edge of the Valley of Oaxaca and the Etla and Tlacolula basins. The Sierra de Juárez, looming above the city, is the second highest peak in Oaxaca, and elevations of over 3,000 meters are common in the Sierra. West (1964:63) describes the Sierra as "a highly folded and faulted range of limestone and metamorphics" forming a formidable barrier between Veracruz and Oaxaca states. "There is little level land in this rugged mountain mass," he writes. "The hundreds of small torrential streams that drain the highlands have carved deep V-shaped valleys into the surface, creating a land of precipitous slopes and knife-edged ridges." Of the eastern part he says, "eastward from the valley are the Mije highlands, a complex rugged mountain mass of volcanics, granite batholiths, and folded limestone." Despite its inhospitable character, most of this region is closely tied into the Oaxaca market system.

As in much of Middle America, the irregular terrain creates great climatic differences within short distances. Three zones are locally recognized. *Tierra caliente* usually lies below 1,000 meter elevation, although individual villages differ in their definitions. Much of this zone is hot and humid. It is found in the northern lower slopes of the Sierra Madre de Oaxaca, the southward slopes of the Sierra Madre del Sur, the narrow Pacific coastal plains, and the lower elevations in some of the canyons within the Sierras. The isthmian region, although it also is *tierra caliente*, is hot but dry.

Most of the area is in *tierra templada*, between 1,000 and 2,000 meters. This zone is cooler, with more moderate precipitation mostly in the late spring and summer.

The varied topography, however, causes significant differences of rainfall in short distances. The city of Oaxaca, for example, is ascribed an average annual rainfall of 650 millimeters (Taylor 1972:9), and is classed as dry steppe with summer rains in the Köeppen system of classification. Officially, the western end of the Valley at Etla averages 662 millimeters (ibid.), but some localities in this area probably receive twice the rainfall that occurs around Mitla in the eastern end of the Tlacolula arm. The Ocotlán-Zimatlan area receives more than 720 millimeters.

Above 2,000 meters most lands are classed as *tierra fría*. Most of these are humid, but there are again important differences in rainfall. As a result of the differences in elevation as well as in air circulation, the mean annual precipitation with the region of the marketing system varies from little over 500 millimeters to well over 2,000 millimeters. Similarly, mean annual air temperatures at ground level vary from less than 15° to more than 25° C. These figures are all based on insufficient and sometimes unreliable data. Most meteorological stations are of recent establishment. From the standpoint of human occupation of the area, the frost and snow lines are important but are equally variable. Limited parts of the Valley of Oaxaca, for example, are briefly subject to moderate frost in January or February of some years. Snow is relatively rare in most of the area. It occurs occasionally as low as about 2,000 meters, but even at the highest elevations it is infrequent and soon melts.

The many differences, not only in temperature and moisture regimes, but in soil types, are reflected in extremely varied floral and faunal resources. The influence of man over several thousand years has been so heavy in much of the area that original conditions are difficult to reconstruct. The great variety of plants and animals found reflect the overlap in distribution of many families or genera occurring primarily in either North America or South America. The forest types vary from tropical rain forest or, at higher elevations, tropical cloud forest, to tropical thorn or xerophytic associations in drier lands, dry land oak and madroño associations, mixed oak and coniferous associations, and some moderately extensive and relatively pure stands of some conifers. Most, but not all of the latter occur at higher elevations. For some plants, soils rather than climate are primary determinants of distributions. In general, many plants in the associations found in higher or drier areas have North American affinities; those in lower and wetter areas tend to have South American affinities.

The same is true of the predominantly land fauna, with a mixture of species of Nearctic and Neotropical affinities. The northern whitetail deer and the southern peccary are two major food animals in the area (now relatively rare). The small brockets occur only in the tropical lowlands of eastern Mexico and penetrate Oaxaca rarely if at all. The northern gray fox, the coyote, and the intercontinental puma are present, but most of the cats are southern—the jaguar, ocelot, margay, and jaguarundi. Skins of the latter, especially of the jaguar and ocelot, were important items of ancient trade and tribute. The rattlesnake was associated with the rain cult, and its representations are prominent in religious art from central Mexico to Yucatan. Only one species is known from Central America south of the Isthmus of Tehuantepec, and in Oaxaca other species of the Bothrops group, including the fer-de-lance, are more numerous.

The main purpose of presenting this very abbreviated and superficial comment on the environment is to emphasize the great variations in the distribution of natural resources in areas located close to one another. Ideal preconditions for trade and exchange existed even for people at a hunting and gathering level. With the appearance of farming and the development of more complex sedentary cultures, new demands developed which could be satisfied only by trade expansion.

How early these exchange patterns began to appear is still uncertain. The Valley of Oaxaca was close to the center of maize domestication; indeed, the possibility still exists that the first cultivation of this basic American staple may even have begun in the Valley. Certainly premaize cultivation existed and the black bean, still prized in the area, probably was a local domesticate. Small black beans and squash seeds forming part of a premaize cultivation pattern were in use, although possibly in uncultivated form, as early as 7000 B.C. (Flannery et al. 1967:6). We may never know when chocolate (cacao) became an important import to the region, but it probably was early. By pre-Classic times, perhaps as early as 1000 B.C., sea shells from both the Caribbean and the Pacific were important raw materials for an active handicraft industry in the Etla Valley (Flannery et al. 1967:7) and prove the existence of extended trade. There is evidence that the use of money and the existence of regular marketplaces antedate the coming of the Spanish (Easby, Caley, and Moazed 1967; Flannery et al. 1967:8). Although what is called the traditional marketing system in this study undoubtedly was extensively reshaped in the Spanish Colonial period, there is little doubt that it rested on an aboriginal exchange system of considerable antiquity.

The differential distribution of resources in the Oaxaca marketing system area not only played an important role in the creation of the exchange system but still significantly affects its character. It is not the only factor operating, however. The character and distribution of the population, the way in which it is organized socially, and the mixed Indian-Spanish culture within which it operates are of at least equal importance.

DEMOGRAPHY

According to the census of 1960 (Direccion General de Estadistica [DGE] 1963) there were 1,727,266 inhabitants in the state of Oaxaca and a population density of 18.1 persons per square kilometer. Preliminary figures from the 1970 census show 2,171,733 inhabitants and a population density of 22.8 persons per square kilometer. This population lives in a surprisingly large number of local settlements, involving 3,694 localities. (The 1960 census uses the criterion "recognized by law or custom" for localities of Oaxaca State; this phrase is used for no other state. Other criteria for recognition of localities are: houses grouped in blocks or streets; inhabited permanently, periodically, or transitorily; and having a place-name.) These communities are organized into 571 *municipios,* each with an administratively independent main town or *cabecera* and often with several smaller dependent settlements. *Municipios* not only are more numerous than in any other state in Mexico but they also tend to be smaller in both area and population. In turn, the *municipios* are lumped together for historical and administrative reasons into 30 exdistricts, each of which usually bears the name of its *cabecera* or head town. The prefix "ex" is used because the Mexican Constitution of 1917 outlawed any political subdivision between *municipio* and state levels. Nevertheless, the state has retained the *distrito* unit for administrative and judicial purposes while officially maintaining that it no longer exists. Most of the principal towns of the *exdistritos* also have marketplaces.

Prior to the Revolution each *distrito* was headed by a *jefe político* appointed by the governor. In many places the *jefe político* became a powerful political boss (*cacique*) who often abused his authority and in some more remote districts even maintained a private army. The abuses of the *jefe político* system led to the establishment of the *municipio libre.* The *municipios* were to elect their own semiautonomous governments that would not be subject to district political bosses. This in effect legalized an earlier system of local self-government common in many peasant communities, and especially Indian communities, in Oaxaca as well as in other parts of Mexico. Some would-be reformers attribute many of the political problems in the state to the large number of *municipios,* but because of a strong sense of local community autonomy, efforts to consolidate *municipios* meet with fierce resistance, and indeed there are frequently strong local pressures to create more independent *municipios* rather than to reduce their number. Such pressures often involve tensions and even violence.

Most of the Indian and mestizo peasants of Oaxaca live in rural *pueblos* that adhere in varying degrees to Eric Wolf's (1955) description of "closed corporate communities," except in some economic matters, and have semiautonomous political systems or "civil-religious hierarchies" (Carrasco, 1961). Oaxaca has the largest number of speakers of Indian languages of any Mexican state. In 1960 there were 297,319 persons who spoke only one of ten or more Indian languages (17.2 percent of the population), while another 386,099 (22.3 percent) were bilingual. Thus a total of 683,418 persons (39.5 percent) of the state's population can be classified as Indian according to speech. It is important to bear in mind that many native languages are spoken in the state. Moreover, the Zapotecs, comprising the majority of the Indian speakers in the Oaxaca market region, speak several dialects, some of which are not mutually intelligible. Language, however, does not adequately define the peasant of indigenous origin. Santa María Atzompa, for example, may not be distinguished culturally in any meaningful way from other handicraft-farming villages in the Valley although it has been 100 percent Spanish-speaking for so long that inhabitants are uncertain whether their forebears spoke Zapotec or Mixtec (probably the latter). Similar situations obtain in other villages.

The 1960 census figures indicate that approximately 80 percent of the population of Oaxaca is engaged in agriculture. In keeping with this, the bulk of the population is rural. Census figures in this regard are misleading, for in Mexico as in the United States, residents of any locality with 2,500 inhabitants or more are classed as urban. Oaxaca City is the only settlement with a population of more than 20,000. Only five other communities have populations of more than 10,000, and all these are in the isthmian region. (These figures refer to *cabeceras*, not to the total population of the *municipios* in which they are located.) In fact, even in many larger places, most of the population is engaged in agriculture.

The population of the state of Oaxaca has grown substantially in the twentieth century, as follows (figures rounded to the nearest hundred):

1900	948,000	1960	1,727,300
1920	976,000	1970	2,171,700
1940	1,192,800		

The major growth has been in the last fifty years, and most of it has been rural.

Except for a decline during the Revolutionary period, the population of the *municipio* of Oaxaca follows a similar pattern. Population figures for the city of Oaxaca between 1920 and 1970 are as follows:

1920	27,792	1950	46,741
1930	33,423	1960	72,370
1940	29,306	1970	99,535

(All population statistics are from the official censuses except the 1950 statistic for Oaxaca City, which is taken from the 1956 *Encyclopedia Britannica*.)

Even with its growth, Oaxaca City remains primarily a center of commerce and administration. The greatest expansion has been in commerce; between 1939 and 1955 the number of licensed commercial enterprises in the state had increased around 1,500 percent, and the district containing Oaxaca City had 24.5 percent of them (Tamayo Lopez Portilla 1960:72). Some industries in the *municipio* of Oaxaca are directed toward the expanding tourist trade. Almost all are small scale family enterprises with little differentiation. There also has been great expansion in industries serving local needs, such as building materials and construction, automotive repair facilities, and bottling plants. The largest industry is a plywood plant employing about 300 people. The three soft drink bottling plants employ about 30 people each. Some production from these plants goes into regional distribution channels but little reaches national markets.

Most of this growth probably is associated with the opening of the Pan American Highway to Oaxaca in 1943, completion of its paving in 1948, and its extension to Tehuantepec and Chiapas where a passable road reached Comitán on the Guatemalan border by 1946 (Stewart 1957:99).

THE CULTURAL CONTEXT

Only the most salient features of the social and cultural aspects of the Oaxaca market system are treated here. Generally, the ethnography of Oaxaca has been neglected and most published studies on the subject are incomplete or focus on special problems. The nearest approach to comprehensive ethnographies are still those of Parsons (1936) for the Zapotec valley community of Mitla, and Beals (1945) for the Mixe. Others are a specialized study of Mitla by Leslie (1960) and a study by Nader (1964) of Talea, a village in the Sierra. Julio de la Fuente has published fairly extensively on Yalalag (1949) and more briefly on Choapan (1947), both in the Sierra.

Although in prehispanic times the Valley of Oaxaca was the center of a major regional form of Mesoamerican civilization, its history is less well known than that of Central Mexico or Yucatan. Until fairly recently most archaeological work centered on spectacular ruins such as those of Mitla and Monte Albán, while the documentary record at contact is far less rich than for the Valley of Mexico. An early horticultural economic base permitted the formation of village-type settlements that in varying form have persisted to the present (Flannery et al. 1967). These communities seem gradually to have been consolidated into larger political entities dominated by one town, and these in turn were at times merged into larger states. The dominant centers appear to have shifted through time, and external groups controlled or occupied parts of the Valley. The Mixteca from the west clearly dominated much of the Valley in the last Monte Albán period, and some villages in the western valley and adjoining mountains are still Mixtec speaking.

In the 1400s, the Aztecs established sufficient hegemony to collect tributes from the region, and a military garrison and trading center was located at or near the site of modern Oaxaca. These occupations do not appear to have altered significantly a stable stratified society with hereditary local ruling families, often allied through marriage. Probably, as in the neighboring Mixteca, many of these families could trace genealogies back through several centuries. The bulk of the population were farmers or artisans. Public, especially religious, architecture was well developed. Religion was elaborate. The religious patterns, although many had distinctive local characteristics, broadly resembled those of other high cultures of Middle America.

On the whole, early Spanish influence rested lightly on the area. The Zapotecs remained neutral in the struggle between the Spanish and the Aztecs and their allies, and after the fall of Mexico City accepted the Spanish as successors of the Aztecs, continuing to pay the customary tributes. Oaxaca City was founded in 1522, in part as a replacement for the military garrison settlement of the Aztecs. Most Spanish military activity, however, seems to have been limited to intervention in local disputes and protection of the Zapotecs from other groups. The second Spanish settlement in Oaxaca, San Ildefonso de Villa Alta in the Sierra, founded some years after Oaxaca, was a Spanish-Tlaxcaltec garrison to protect the western Sierra Zapotec region from incursions by the Mixe, a group bypassed in the Aztec conquests in Oaxaca. It appears from the data extant concerning *caciques* that these ruling families became Christians, were often rather thoroughly hispanicized, and long retained authority over local matters to a considerable degree.

Spanish labor demands through *encomiendas* and *repartimientos* were not excessive except around a few mining areas. But Oaxaca, although it had important placer gold areas near the coasts, contained no Taxcos or Pachucas, let alone competitors of the great mines farther north. Cattle raising, the second great wealth source of the Spanish, was early restricted in the Valley of Oaxaca and some of the surrounding area. Even the later *hacienda* system was relatively little developed in the area; villages retained some lands and a degree of local autonomy even though many were partly dependent on the *haciendas*. Some villages still retain archives dating back to the 1500s; for others there are evidently substantial but as yet unutilized records in the archives in Mexico City.

The city of Oaxaca nevertheless flourished during much of the Colonial period, and part of the time was considered the third most important city of New Spain. The prosperity and importance of Oaxaca in Colonial times lay first in its strategic location on a main trade route to southern Mexico, Guatemala, and Central America. In addition, much of the South American trade, especially with Peru, passed through Oaxaca to the ports of Tehuantepec. The second advantage was possession of cochineal, until the mid-1800s the most prized dyestuff in Europe. Cochineal, derived from a parasitic insect occurring on a species of cactus, was produced in several areas, but Oaxaca was by far the largest producer, and from

1745 to 1854 the bishopric of Oaxaca held a monopoly on production. The major center was the town of Miahuatlán in the southern valley (Dahlgren 1963; Rojas 1964).

The basic culture of the village or peasant populations of Oaxaca took shape and became stabilized during the Colonial period through an acculturative process drawing upon both aboriginal and Spanish cultures. In this process the Dominican order of friars played a major role not only in implementing some aspects of Spanish policies of directed culture change, but also acting as screening agents for the contact of the Indians with Spanish culture. They also introduced creative innovations such as the *Caja de Comunidad,* a community treasury for the payment of tributes and support of community enterprises. Lay Spaniards also played some creative part in culture change. For example, the introduction of silk production in the area is credited to the wife of Francisco de las Casas, *encomendero* of Yanhuitlan in the Mixteca (Jiménez Moreno and Mateos Higuera 1940:14).

Without examining the acculturative process in detail, some of the important changes were the introduction of Spanish farming and technology with the wooden plow and draft animals, together with a number of Old World plants. In Oaxaca the most important introductions from Europe were wheat and to a lesser extent other Old World grains, vegetables, fruits, cattle, pigs, sheep, and chickens. Some new handicraft technologies also were introduced. As a result, Oaxaca for a time was the major center of silk production in the New World, and still has a small local village production around Yalalag and Betaza in the Sierra. The broadloom partially replaced the aboriginal backstrap loom in textile production, and wool partly replaced cotton. The pattern of village specialization was continued and some populations were relocated to take advantage of natural resources not previously exploited by the local inhabitants.

In social organization Spanish practice encouraged the importance of the nuclear family. Whether this involved any significant change from pre-Spanish patterns seems unlikely. More important, the pattern of village government was standardized in ways common to much of Colonial Middle America. A hierarchy of municipal offices and public duties was established and closely interrelated with a hierarchy of religious responsibilities such as *mayordomías* (religious festivals). Modernly, offices in the hierarchy are based on the theory that an adult male owes service to his community, including the donation of labor and at times materials or money for community projects, and service in the lowest levels of the hierarchy. Progress through the hierarchy of offices or *cargos* to the top levels ultimately completes this duty. In theory this is expected of every man; in practice the number of offices is less than the number of possible candidates. In addition, the very poor may be unable to make the expenditures necessary to carry out the obligations of office and never complete their service. Status and prestige within the community depend primarily upon the positions attained in the hierarchy of offices.

The religious offices at first sight appear related to the Spanish *cofradía,* an association of laymen dedicated to carrying out religious activities, usually maintaining the cult of a specific saint. *Cofradías* (religious sodalities) of Spanish type existed in Spanish settlements in Colonial Mexico and survive in some mestizo towns. The term is sometimes applied in some Indian communities even today. The more usual form of religious service, however, is the *mayordomía.* In Oaxaca, as in most of Indian Mexico, the *mayordomía* requires the head of a household to maintain the cult of a saint for a period of one year. In both the *mayordomía* and the *cofradía,* various types of essentially secular activities are involved such as group dance performances, hosting feasts, and providing fireworks, in addition to caring for the image of a saint and arranging masses. Carrasco (1961) has suggested that the *mayordomía* also is partly derived from aboriginal antecedents. Certainly, the occupation of positions of authority in the organizations of Aztec merchants required the prior carrying out of various ritual obligations in a fashion very suggestive of the village civil-religious hierarchy system (Van Zantwijk 1970).

How the civil-religious hierarchy became established in Indian communities in Middle America is still inadequately researched. It is widespread and displays many common features. Yet it also is infinitely varied in details from town to town. In many parts of Mesoamerica it continues to be a major boundary-maintaining mechanism for Indian communities (Hinton 1961).

Of primary concern to this paper would be the history of the original formation of the traditional marketing system in Oaxaca. Unfortunately, little data exist, and for reasons of financial resources, time, and manpower, extensive historical investigation was excluded from this study. For example, the existence of systematic marketplaces in Oaxaca in pre-Spanish times is mentioned in a few early Spanish sources but descriptions are lacking.[1] We do have some archaeological

---

[1] Whitecotton (1968:93) translates Burgoa concerning the marketplace in Santa Ana, district of Zimatlán, as follows: "This place [Santa Ana] has been famous since aboriginal times because it is in the middle of a valley with an abundance of water and sufficient accommodations for food that from one [town] to the other they bring things to sell." Burgoa also noted that the market in Chichicapa was held every five days, the common interval in pre-Columbian markets. According to Whitecotton, Córdova's dictionary has Zapotec words for "fair or market" and for "fair or market held every five days." As to the character of these markets, it is of some interest that Burgoa always used the words meaning "to sell" and "to buy" and never the words for "trade" or "barter." Whitecotton also gives considerable evidence for extended pre-Columbian trade in specific commodities such as salt, cotton, and textiles.

Although writing much later than Burgoa, Gay (1950:I:100) considered the Aztec domination of

evidence of village specialization extending into the Formative period in Oaxaca as well as evidence of internal differentiation in occupations. In some strategic sites, extensive *plazas* not associated with religious structures have been interpreted as possibly having been marketplaces. There is also evidence of trade over considerable distances. But we do not as yet have evidence of the nature of the exchange system.

The Aztecs, we know, had a system of cyclical marketplaces or *plazas* as well as the great daily market in Tlatelolco-Tenochtitlan. The city depended heavily on outside sources for its provisioning (Calnek 1972). We also know that there existed highly organized groups of traders serving not only Tenochtitlan but also several other cities. Outside Mexico City a major garrison town, Tochtepec on the northern border of the present state of Oaxaca toward Veracruz, was the focal point of trade to the south and east, and two important trading centers were maintained at Oaxaca and Tehuantepec within the area of the present traditional Oaxaca market system (Van Zantwijk 1970). The presumption is reasonable that Oaxaca markets resembled those of the Aztecs.

It is an interesting fact that in Colonial times the Spanish administration regulated some aspects of existing markets; for example, they shifted cyclical markets from a five-day cycle to a seven-day cycle, and established Indian markets in Spanish towns both to insure a flow of foodstuffs and, in some cases, to control or monopolize the middleman's profits on some commodities. The location and nature of Colonial marketplaces in Oaxaca were certainly regulated. We do not know, however, whether this constituted a reorganization of an indigenous market system or a transference of the system from the Valley of Mexico and its environs. The probabilities are high that an indigenous market system existed in Oaxaca. Chronicles of 1579 and 1581 indicate that imported salt and cotton as well as other items were bought by villagers of the region from merchants in Antequera, as Oaxaca was then called, and that there was at that time a Saturday market in this town (*Relaciones* 1955:21; *Relacion* 1956:24). So far as our firm data go, what is

Oaxaca as too recent and insufficiently universal or complete to explain the prevalence of Aztec language and toponymy. Instead, he attributes it to a vast and sustained commerce:

Algunos explican este hecho, haciéndolo resultar de la dominación azteca en Oaxaca; pero por la historia consta que ni fué muy antigua, ni universal, ni completa, sino muy pasajera esa dominación, y por lo mismo, insuficiente para propagar tanto un idioma extranjero. Lo que se percibe con claridad es que un comercio vasto y sostenido ligaba a unos y otros, quienes tenían necesidad de entenderse para verificar sus cambios y contratos.

Although the town is on the border of Puebla State and not within the Oaxaca marketing system, the *Relación* for Teotitlán del Camino of 1581 (*Relación de Teotitlán* 1905:215) states that the people lived from their fields and from making *huipiles* (women's blouses), which merchants traded for cacao in Guatemala, Soconusco, Chiapas, and Suchixtepec.

considered the traditional market system in this report must be taken as a system of uncertain antecedents which took its present known form in Colonial times.

The Oaxaca City marketplace certainly was not important in early Colonial times. The city—and of course its marketplace—were founded by the Spanish. In 1544 the city had only thirty Spanish *vecinos* or heads of households. (Gay [1950:I:501] cites a letter written in that year by Bishop Zárate, ascribing the reduced number of urban residents to the growth of the surrounding Indian population to the point where the Spanish had no lands and had to buy everything from the Indians at high prices.) Apparently the early Oaxaca marketplaces often shifted location because, according to Portillo (1910:153), the first fixed marketplace was established in the middle of the seventeenth century when one Fernandez Fiallo purchased the "Plaza del Marqués" and dedicated it to the poor to sell their products. This was the area now forming the central garden *plaza* or *Zócalo* of the city, and it continued to be used as a marketplace until late in the nineteenth century. There are also early references to market activity carried on in the *Plaza de Armas* (now *Plaza de la Constitución*) and the small plaza in front of the cathedral now known as the *Alameda*. The population of the city was then around 3,000 or less.

Development of the present central marketplace began in 1862 when the municipal authorities obtained the old convent of San Juan de Diós for public use. The present building of what is now called the Mercado Benito Juárez was completed in 1894. The structure housing the Mercado 20 de Noviembre was constructed in the 1950s, occupying space earlier devoted to open-air sales.

The first secondary marketplace, Mercado Democracia, popularly La Merced, was established in 1861 in the atrium of the Merced Church, and the permanent building was constructed about 50 years later. The Mercado Sanchez Pascua, commonly known as El Cármen, was established in the 1870s in the *Plazuela Sangre de Cristo*. After several changes in location, the present building was constructed about 1910 (Portillo 1910:153–154). The other secondary markets came into being after 1910, two since 1940. None of this information, however, casts light on the development of the Saturday *plaza*.

NATURE AND EXTENT OF THE TRADITIONAL MARKET SYSTEM

The traditional market system of Oaxaca involves the subsystems of production, consumption, and exchange characteristic of the peasant population of a geographically limited region of the state of Oaxaca (see maps 3 and 4). As we have seen, it took its basic form during the Colonial period. This system has counterparts in other parts of Middle America but developed unique features of its own.

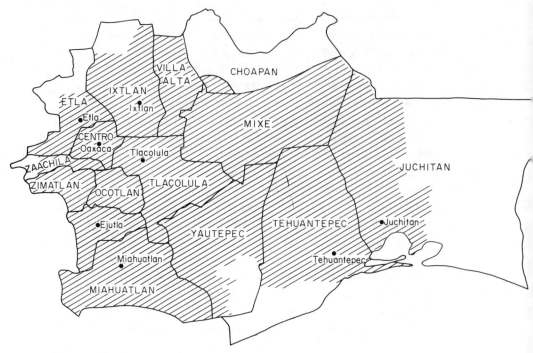

MAP 3. The Oaxaca market system

The Oaxaca market and its attendant marketing system exists in large part because of the specialized system of production (in its form-changing aspects) with the result that no village creates all the goods required by its pattern of internal consumption needs. To understand the marketing system, it is therefore necessary to examine the form-changing aspects of peasant production and the patterns of consumption or use of the goods produced. The unit of production and consumption, essentially, is the household, and within villages this should be the unit of analysis. Households exhibit differentiated patterns in both production and consumption and as a consequence there is in each village an internal exchange system. This type of exchange, however, is dealt with only tangentially in this report; a full understanding of it can only come through additional intensive studies at the village level, such as those made by Berg, Cook, Diskin, Stolmaker, Waterbury, and Woods for this project but still mostly unpublished. But because villages, viewed as collectivities, specialize extensively in production, they are an important unit of analysis for the study of the regional exchange system.

Before attempting to define the extent of the traditional system, a brief mention of the main channels of exchange might be helpful. They consist of the following:

1. Intravillage exchange either between households or between households and stores;
2. Village-to-village direct exchange not passing through cyclical *plazas;*

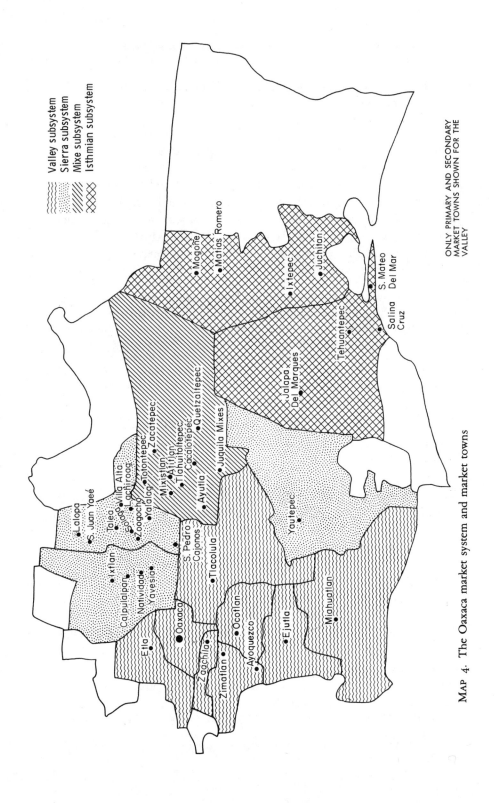

Valley subsystem
Sierra subsystem
Mixe subsystem
Isthmian subsystem

ONLY PRIMARY AND SECONDARY
MARKET TOWNS SHOWN FOR THE
VALLEY

• Mogoñe
• Matías Romero
• Ixtepec
• Juchitán
• S. Mateo Del Mar
Salina Cruz
• Tehuantepec
• Jalapa Del Marques
Juquila Mixes
• Quetzaltepec
• Cacalotepec
• Tlahuitoltepec
• Mixistlán
• Ayutla
Zacatepec
• Totontepec
• Yalalag
Zoogocho •
• Lachiroag
Villa Alta
• Talea
• Lalopa
• S. Juan Yaeé
• Ixtlan
• Natividad
Calpulalpan •
• Yavesia
S. Pedro •
Cajonos
• Tlacolula
Yautepec
• Ella
• Zaachila
• Oaxaca
Zimatlán •
• Ayoquezco
• Ocotlán
• Ejutla
• Miahuatlán

MAP 4: The Oaxaca market system and market towns

3. Village-to-village exchange passing through one or more *plazas;*
4. Inter*plaza* exchange of goods assembled in one *plaza* and distributed through another;
5. External exchange of goods passing out of or into the regional marketing system to or from other regions.

These channels of exchange are supplemented in the contemporary marketing system by various commercial channels such as stores and wholesale establishments. More detailed discussion of trade channels can be found in chapter 6.

Most discussions of peasant marketing systems tend to concentrate on the marketplace aspect of the exchange system. In Oaxaca, however, it must be borne in mind that, despite the importance of the *plaza* or marketplace, a significant amount of the exchange takes place through the other channels mentioned. Even exchange within the marketplaces is carried on by several types of actors or functionaries. The main types are:

1. Producer-vendors (*propios*) who sell their own products either directly to consumers or to intermediaries, both wholesalers and retailers;
2. Traveling middlemen or traders (*regatones* and *viajeros*) who go from marketplace to marketplace, or from *plaza* to village, or from village to village;
3. Fixed-location middlemen or traders, mostly resident in the market town;
4. Storekeepers selling goods not only to peasant buyers but also to town dwellers;
5. Itinerant vendors (*ambulantes*) who sell from a stock of small items, generally acquired from a trader or storekeeper, which they carry about with them and sell on the streets or from door to door.

Types of actors or functionaries in the marketing system are considered in more detail in chapter 6.

In defining the extent of the Oaxaca marketing system, several criteria are used. Some difficulties arise, because the Oaxaca marketing system is not closed. In other words, some goods exchanged are produced outside the limits of the system, and some buyers come from outside the system. In general I have defined the extent of the Oaxaca system in two ways:

1. A marketplace or *plaza* is part of the system if more than 50 percent of its inter*plaza* relations are with the city of Oaxaca, directly or through an intermediate *plaza* linked to the city. Usually this is no problem; generally the major links clearly are directly or indirectly with Oaxaca City.

2. A village is part of the system if more than half its external trade is directly or indirectly through *plazas* connected with Oaxaca. Usually this involves selling products and buying supplies in a *plaza* or, occasionally, through middlemen operating in connection with a *plaza.* Here the boundaries are less definite; particularly in border areas, many villages have more than one *plaza* available, and without actual study it is uncertain which *plaza* is the most important.

A few cases may illustrate the problem areas. The market town of Nochixtlán in the Mixteca Alta west of the Valley of Oaxaca has an important trade with the city of Oaxaca. Some inter*plaza* vendors centered in Oaxaca include the Nochixtlán *plaza* in their regular routes. Although we lack sufficient data for positive classification, we have excluded Nochixtlán from the Oaxaca system. Instead, we view it as an important exchange point through which goods from the Oaxaca system flow into the market systems in the Mixteca Alta and through which Mixteca Alta products flow into the Oaxaca system. The buyers in the Nochixtlán *plaza,* however, are almost wholly from surrounding Mixtec villages or *plazas* in other systems. Such markets may be viewed as "transit" markets, to borrow a useful phrase from Kwame Arhin (1970), writing on Ashanti markets in Africa.

Several of the villages in the Sierra are insufficiently known for me to be certain of their primary affiliation. I know, for example, that some Mixtecan villages in the Sierra west of the southern part of the Valley sell an important part of their production, mainly deciduous fruits and forest products (firewood, charcoal, and wooden artifacts) in the Oaxaca City *plaza* or in other *plazas* of the system or directly to villages. As these villages are poor, I suspect that they also buy most of their purchased goods in the *plazas* where they sell their own commodities. Nevertheless, some doubt exists as to whether they are affiliated with one of the Mixteca Alta *plaza* systems or with Oaxaca. There are similar problems with some Zapotec villages in the northern Sierra.

There is some uncertainty, too, concerning the isthmian region. The majority of villages in this area have not been studied and I have no data whatever on them. I do know from our study that most of the marine products (salt, dried fish, and shrimp), and such items as coconuts and pineapples and some cattle that reach the Valley and Sierra, come from the Isthmus, mostly passing through the major *plaza* towns of Juchitán and Tehuantepec, and that there has been a sizable flow of products between the Valley and these localities. Such data as are available on the isthmian region, principally the marketplaces of Juchitán and especially Tehuantepec, suggest that the market system there functions very much as does that in the Valley of Oaxaca and is closely interrelated with it. Therefore I consider it a subsystem of the larger Oaxaca market system.

Other subsystems may be identified. The northern Sierra region has a considerable amount of internal market exchange. This applies both to the Zapotec-speaking villages and the Mixe area. In the past the latter area also was involved with the Isthmus, through a triangular exchange carried on by intervillage traders from Mitla using pack animals. These traders carried Valley of Oaxaca goods to the Isthmus. There they bought marine and tropical products to carry into the Mixería, where they bought coffee to take back to the Valley. To a considerable extent this trade has persisted, but in different forms, since the opening of the Pan American Highway. Isthmian products still reach the Mixería, but they travel by truck from the Isthmus to Mitla and thence into the Sierra Mixe. A Sierra subsystem is therefore postulated. Perhaps it, in turn, should be subdivided into Sierra Zapotec and Sierra Mixe subsystems.

The Valley of Oaxaca, for which we have the largest body of data, may also be treated as a subsystem (see maps 5 and 6). It may be that the southern extension (as treated in this study) comprising the exdistricts of Ejutla and Miahuatlán will, on further examination, prove to be a separate subsystem.

Certain *plazas* have special importance in the system because of their relations with external exchange systems. The relations between Oaxaca and the Mixteca Alta through the *plaza* of Nochixtlán have already been mentioned. Miahuatlán, Ejutla, and Ayoquezco are important transit points with neighboring regions. Miahuatlán and Ayoquezco are entry points for products from the Pacific coast and intervening regions, a function that has grown considerably in importance since the building of roads to the coast. Miahuatlán and Ejutla also are transit points for the Sierra Madre del Sur, and Miahuatlán is a major collection point for the old but now rapidly growing coffee production in the Sierra Madre del Sur. The mechanisms of exchange with these regions are still obscure. Neither the Mixteca region of the coast nor the Sierra Madre del Sur seem to have cyclical *plazas*. The way trade is organized in this section is uncertain.

The Isthmus also has some as yet undefined relations with Chiapas and the Nahua-speaking area in the eastern part of the Isthmus. Historically, Chiapas and especially Tabasco have long been important as the major source of cacao.

With these comments in mind we can make some estimate of the extent of the Oaxaca system. The marketplaces or *plazas* are listed below, subdivided as to subregion and, for the Valley, classified as "primary," "secondary," and "tertiary" on the basis of size of their trading areas and amount of activity. The importance of tertiary *plazas* in the Valley varies markedly. *Plazas* at Atzompa, San Antonino, and Mitla, for example, although visited by some outside vendors, are primarily local affairs. Some are essentially local reflexes of the nearest secondary *plaza*. Others, such as San Pedro Apóstol and San Pablo Huixtepec, are large operations with some hundreds of vendors, attended extensively by people from several surrounding villages.

The problem of proper categorization is compounded by the presence of the *mercado,* which Waterbury has called the urban component of the traditional system. As indicated in chapter 1, the *mercado* is a daily marketplace consisting of more-or-less permanent vendors with fixed locations. It is best developed in Oaxaca City, where it is housed in two large public buildings and in neighborhood market buildings. Except on *plaza* days, most of the buyers are urbanites. Many vendors are of village origin but some are completely mestizoized and urbanized.

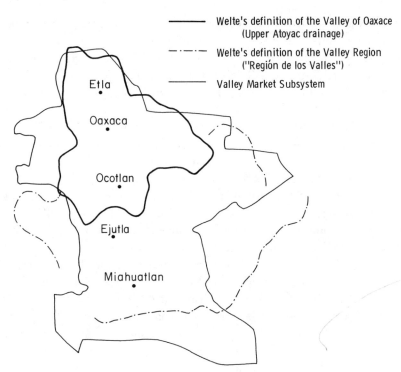

MAP 5. The Valley region and Valley market subsystem

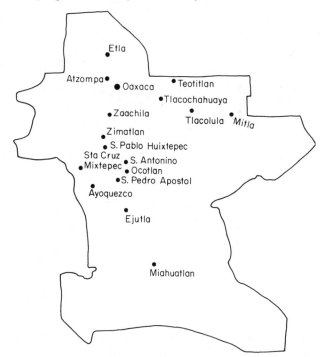

MAP 6. The Valley of Oaxaca and market subsystem, showing market towns

They occupy a low social status in contrast to the owners of larger urban stores and commercial enterprises. The vendors are specialized, dealing in distinct classes of merchandise, and are grouped in sections of the *mercado* with others selling similar commodities. Establishments selling nonfood items often seem to differ from the larger stores outside the *mercado* mainly in the variety of goods and size of stocks carried. Some buy directly from factory representatives and receive direct factory shipments. The products sold in the *mercados* include most local peasant foodstuffs, often acquired from peasant vendors, and some peasant crafts, but imported fruits and vegetables bought from wholesalers are also sold.

Most towns and villages with *plazas* (and a few without *plazas*) have permanent market structures but these vary in their character and use; the daily vendors in most towns are very few. The *mercado* is associated with the *plaza* and may be an outgrowth of it, probably related to increasing urbanization. In Oaxaca City its development goes back at least to the last century. As a contemporary form it may usefully be viewed as a type of market institution intermediate between the recurring *plazas* and the developing modern commercial system of distribution. Thus, when I speak of a *plaza* town or village, there is also an implicit reference to a daily marketplace whose size is more-or-less commensurate with the size of the community and which is thus largely of local importance. The movement of goods to, from, and between weekly *plazas,* in contrast, is far more intensive and extensive, and is of major significance to the regional marketing system.

Having ascertained the marketplaces within the network and the approximate boundaries of the system, identification of the villages from which buyers and sellers come is still difficult, particularly around the margins of the area covered. Although the major aboriginal linguistic group involved is Zapotec, not all present or former Zapotec-speaking villages participate in the framework of the system. Probably all Mixe-speaking villages and the surviving Huave-speaking villages are involved. In the west, some present or former Mixtec-speaking villages are clearly included, although the majority of Mixtec speakers are not. Some other neighboring language groups—Chatino, Pochutla, and Chinantec—may be excluded entirely. Some western Zoquean-speaking villages may be involved in the system, as are some Tequistlatec-speaking villages, at least in recent times. In contrast, mestizo communities, including the city of Oaxaca, are deeply involved in the traditional system even though many are primarily served by stores or *mercados* linked with the modern economy. A further criterion is whether or not a village is included as a supply source in the list of village specializations (app. 7, below).

The Valley subsystem is most clearly defined. It includes all the localities within the drainage of the upper Rio Atoyac plus a few beyond the limits of the watershed, such as Cuajimoloyas. Following is a list of the *exdistritos* of the region,

PLAZAS OF THE OAXACA MARKETING SYSTEM

	Plaza town or village	*Primary market day*
VALLEY SUBSYSTEM:		
Primary *plaza*	Oaxaca de Juárez	Saturday
Secondary *plazas*	Ayoquezco	Tuesday
	Ejutla	Thursday
	Etla	Wednesday
	Miahuatlán	Monday
	Ocotlán	Friday
	Tlacolula	Sunday
	Zaachila	Thursday
	Zimatlán	Wednesday
Tertiary *plazas*[1]	San Pablo Huixtepec	Sunday
	San Pedro Apóstol	Sunday
	Mitla	Saturday
	San Antonio Ocotlán	Sunday
	San Lorenzo Cacaotepec[2]	Sunday
	Santa Cruz Mixtepec	Sunday
	Santa María Atzompa	Tuesday
	Teotitlán del Valle	Wednesday
	Tlacochahuaya	Sunday
	Totolapan[2]	Tuesday
SIERRA SUBSYSTEM:		
Sierra Zapotec	Calpulalpan	Monday
	Ixtlán	Monday
	Lachiroag	Thursday
	Natividad	Sunday
	San Juan Yaeé	Sunday
	San Pedro Cajonos	Sunday
	Santiago Lalopa	Sunday
	Solaga	Sunday
	Talea	Monday
	Villa Alta	Monday
	Yalálag	Tuesday
	Yavesia	Sunday
	Zoogocho	Thursday
Sierra Mixe	Atitlan	Thursday
	Ayutla[3]	Sunday
	Cacalotepec	Friday

[1] The first two listed are more important than the others.

[2] Cacaotepec and Totolapan are listed by Malinowski and de la Fuente (1957), but from project observations their *plazas* are unimportant or nonexistent.

[3] Ayutla is the oldest and most important *plaza*. Most of the others in this group are relatively new or were formerly insignificant.

PLAZAS OF THE OAXACA MARKETING SYSTEM (cont.)

	Plaza town or village	Primary market day
	Juquila Mixes	Sunday
	Mixistlan	Wednesday
	Quetzaltepec	Sunday
	Tlahuitoltepec	Saturday
	Totontepec	Sunday
	Zacatepec	Thursday
ISTHMIAN SUBSYSTEM:	Ixtepec	Daily
	Juchitán	Daily
	Matias Romero	Daily
	Mogoñé	Daily
	Salina Cruz	Daily
	San Mateo del Mar	Daily
	Tehuantepec	Daily
	Jalapa de Márquez	Daily
	Yautepec	Daily

indicating which localities are probably within the limits of the marketing system centering on Oaxaca City.

Centro: All localities including the city of Oaxaca are included.

Tlacolula: All villages are included.

Ocotlán: All villages are included.

Etla: All Zapotec-speaking villages plus those Mixtec-speaking villages within the *exdistrito* to the west are included. Probably to be excluded are all those Mixtec-speaking villages in the northern part of the *exdistrito* lying outside the Atoyac drainage.

Zaachila: All villages are included except possibly two or three Mixtec-speaking villages in the western part outside the Atoyac drainage.

Zimatlán: All villages are included.

Ejutla: All villages are included.

Miahuatlán: All villages are included, although the participation of the more isolated villages to the west and in the Sierra Madre del Sur to the south may be very limited.

Sola de Vega: No *plazas* occur in Sola de Vega and there is no record of villagers from this region visiting other *plazas*. Many traveling traders from the Valley mention visits to Sola de Vega, and some handicraft products sold in the Oaxaca system come from this *exdistrito*. Most of the villages, except those in the western and southern margins, were once occupied by people who speak Valley or Logueche Zapotec dialects. For the present, however, Sola de Vega is excluded from the Oaxaca marketing system boundaries.

Juquila: The main town of Juquila is the site of what is probably the major annual pilgrimage fair in Oaxaca State. Many traders and thousands of pilgrims from the Valley visit it each year, but it is not included in the computations of villages and persons involved in the Oaxaca marketing system.

Pochutla: The boundaries of this *exdistrito* coincide almost exactly with the distribution of the Loxicha dialect of Zapotec but include a small enclave of Nahua-speaking Pochutla. The area lies wholly south of the summit of the Sierra Madre del Sur. It lacks *plazas,* and until the opening of the road to Puerto Angel it seems to have had minimal relations with the Oaxaca marketing system. It is not included within the boundaries of the system.

Yautepec: All present or former Zapotec-speaking villages are included. Tequistlatec-speaking villages are arbitrarily and perhaps incorrectly excluded.

Tehuantepec: All Zapotec-speaking villages are included, as is the town of Salina Cruz. The latter is essentially a modern town and has a *mercado* rather than a *plaza,* but it is visited by traders and supplied in part from the Oaxaca marketing system. Excluded are the communities west of Salina Cruz along the coast and in the Sierra Madre del Sur, formerly or presently occupied by Nahua-speaking Pochutla or Tequistlatec speakers.

Juchitan: Only part of this large *exdistrito* is included. Information about the eastern sector is lacking; although occupied presently or formerly by speakers of the Isthmian dialect of Zapotec, it is excluded from calculations.

Ixtlan: All villages are included except the Chinantec-speaking villages in the north, from Comaltepec northward.

Villa Alta: All villages are included.

Mixe: All villages are included.

Choapan: Information concerning this *exdistrito* is inadequate. The Chinantec villages in the northwestern part, from Latani northward, are excluded. Although speakers of the Bixanas dialect of Zapotec extend through the eastern part of the *exdistrito* and into Veracruz, they are geographically remote and inaccessible and are excluded from calculations. The village of Choapan itself is visited by traders from the Valley, and coffee from at least the western part has long flowed through Yalalag and Ayutla (of the Villa Alta and Mixe *exdistritos*).

With the exclusions indicated, the marketing system comprises approximately 255 *municipios*. According to the 1960 census these *municipios* contained 1,044 localities, of which at least 370 are villages with populations of 500 or more. The total population involved in 1960 was 741,481 (see appendix 5). Figures for the state from the 1970 census suggest that the population involved in the Oaxaca system on that date was on the order of 900,000.

Census evidence and field data indicate that the average number of persons per household in this area is little more than five; the minimum number of households would thus be about 180,000. Informants suggested 20 pesos a day as the minimum income needed to maintain a household with a "decent" standard of living (see chap. 5, below) including social and ceremonial obligations but not extraordinary expenditures as for major religious fiestas. Data collected on household budgets in the Valley support this approximate figure for families of five or six members who are adolescent or adult, although it may be somewhat lower in the more impoverished mountain subregion, for small or young families, or for those who are wage earners and have no operational expenses. In fact, the evidence in this report indicates that it was possible for a small, young family to make do with less than half this income at the price levels prevailing during our study. Nevertheless, there are many families that exceed the 20-peso estimate; and if this figure is taken as an average, I find that consumption in the region amounts to at least one billion pesos annually and probably more than 1.3 billion.

4
The Production System

Farming is the most important productive activity of the Oaxaca peasant and, like most peasants, Oaxaca farmers consume part of what they produce. Many peasants, however, do not farm and (as the next chapter on the consumption system demonstrates) no farmer produces all that he eats, let alone all the nonfood goods he requires. All goods the Oaxaca peasant can produce are salable, and some must be sold to meet all his consumption needs. Even the most dedicated farmer thus is aware of market conditions and is deeply concerned with prices. On the basis of this knowledge and concern, he makes many of his decisions as to how he will allocate his time and resources among different activities. If he is a farmer, this means that the market determines in part what crops he will cultivate and how extensively he produces them or instead engages in nonfarm occupations—decisions affected by his knowledge of prices and anticipated market requirements.

Considering production for exchange at the very simplest level, the Oaxaca peasant frequently takes goods to the marketplace to sell in order that he may buy other goods he needs for immediate consumption. In so doing, he first must estimate the price of the goods he wants and then the prices and amounts of the goods he has to sell. At a more complex level, he decides what to plant or how much time to allocate to a service or handicraft on the basis of expected returns. He is plagued, of course, because although he may be well informed about market requirements, he cannot know what the supply will be or what effect this will have on prices at some future time. For example, the horticulturists of San Antonino Ocotlán have found that in connection with the Day of the Dead there is a large and assured demand outside the Oaxaca market system for a flower known as *Cresta de Gallo* (an amaranth). The village has shipped as many as 120 truckloads of these flowers to Mexico City in one week. On some occasions the market is oversupplied by other growers, however, and prices are disastrously low. Other examples of complex economic decisions related to the anticipation of demand are discussed later in this chapter.

THE HOUSEHOLD AND ITS DEPENDENCE ON THE MARKET

The household is the locus of most productive activity by Oaxaca peasants. Although the nuclear family forms the basis of most households, it may be augmented in various ways. Most common is the presence of unmarried siblings or of one or more parents of either spouse. Less frequent is the presence of a single aunt or uncle, or nephew, or even an unrelated individual, usually a child or young person. More extended household units exist, consisting usually of two or more—rarely more—nuclear families, customarily headed by brothers or by fathers and sons. Households of more than one nuclear family usually are of a temporary nature and investigation may show that the families are separate household units occupying a common residential lot, eating separately and maintaining separate budgets and independent production activities.

Perhaps the most practical rule-of-thumb definition of a household is a group of people who eat together. This definition is sometimes inadequate, for occasionally we find related families or groups who eat together all or part of the time, but live separately and maintain independent economic activities except for sharing the labor and costs of meals.

Economic factors appear to predominate in native concepts of the household. For example, at San Antonino Ocotlán, Waterbury found that the local concept of a household was a "minimal budgetary group" maintaining separate accounts (*cuentas*). Thus an individual, for example, an elderly widow who owns lands that she gives for sharecropping, or a family fragment with independent sources of income which pays its proportionate share of household expenses, is considered a separate household. In accordance with this concept of the household as a significant economic unit, microscopic analysis of the household should be made in economic terms rather than in terms of residential or eating groups.

Households with more than one economically active member do have advantages. Rarely are the economic roles of each member identical, and such households are buffered to some extent from economic accidents or temporary reduction in income that may befall one role or the other. Very often the head of household considers himself in charge of all the family members with their respective roles, and in reporting his economic activities will list all of the occupations included in his household rather than just his own.

The predominance of the nuclear- or augmented-family household does not mean that more extended kinship is not important economically. Kinsmen do aid one another in many ways, including the rendering of economic aid. Such aid, however, is almost exclusively through short-term, interest-free loans of cash, food, or labor in emergencies. The conduct and control of production and other economic activities remain within the household.

The household is not only the productive unit but is also a complex budgetary unit. It operates with a considerable degree of economic rationality, and for some analytical purposes the household may be treated as a firm. Thus Berg obtained some interesting results by using the "firm" concept of the household in his study of Zoogocho and its environs in the northern Sierra (Berg 1968). Analogy with the firm as it is defined in the conventional economic literature concerning industrial societies nevertheless may be misleading. Perhaps a better analogy is with the family firm in preindustrial or emerging industrial economies, but even this comparison has limitations. The Oaxaca peasant household is indeed the locus of economic activities and decisions, but its economic character is quite complex. Production and consumption budgets are rarely separated. Frequently economic decisions are influenced by considerations other than maximization and pecuniary gain, important as these are. Economic means may be used for many noneconomic ends.

Investigation of the relations between household production and marketing is complicated because a significant portion of farming production goes into autoconsumption, that is, meeting subsistence needs of the producing unit. The factor of autoconsumption is illustrated by the most basic subsistence item, maize. Maize is grown in every village and is consumed by every family. Many villages, however, consume more maize than they produce and thus must regularly import maize. Some villages have a surplus in good years, but only a few villages regularly produce more maize than they consume. Among households within villages, we have encountered no village in which all households produce all the maize they consume, although such villages may exist. In most villages a variable percentage of households either do not produce enough maize to meet their needs or produce no maize at all. This probably has been true to some extent even in the past. For Mitla, Parsons (1936:54–55) reported that in the early 1930s a significant number of households did no farming, although everyone had access to land through sharecropping or cultivation of communal hill lands. In all villages, however, some households produce enough for their own needs and others produce a surplus. These facts would suggest that there might be substantial household-to-household intravillage trade in some villages, but in our studies we found that this generally is not done. A household with a maize surplus may use it to feed animals for sale or may sell the grain in the nearest marketplace, while households requiring maize usually buy it in the marketplace rather than from neighbors.

Moreover, maize production and consumption pervade and influence a wide variety of economic decisions. The household must decide how much land and how much labor time it will devote to the growing of subsistence maize as compared with other possible crops or handicraft or trading activities. Provision must be made for storing the maize, and the household must determine whether to market it, how much to sell, and when to sell, in accordance with its own need for cash and seasonal fluctuations in price. Even the household that is self-sufficient in maize, neither buying nor selling in the exchange system, has made a decision to be self-sufficient at least partly on the basis of its appraisal of market factors. The same is true of other products. The influence of market considerations on household production will become abundantly clear in later discussions of production and consumption.

A few categorical statements should be made and borne in mind continually in the discussion of household production:

1. No household in Oaxaca produces all the food it consumes, even foods regarded as indispensable.
2. Few households produce all their own clothing and none produce all the cloth, thread, and other items needed to make clothing.
3. No households produce everything needed for shelter, and most households must buy most or all of the materials and skills for house construction.
4. No household produces all the tools, implements, and other goods necessary to carry out its production activities or household functions.

Individual households may meet the deficiencies in their production through internal trade within the village, but in the main they must depend upon the external exchange system.

THE VILLAGE AS A UNIT OF ANALYSIS

Most of the statements made about the individual household may also be applied to individual villages. Villages tend to specialize not only in food production but also in other goods and services. In the past, for example, the village of Mitla specialized in trade and dominated most market transactions between the Valley and the Isthmus of Tehuantepec as well as much of the Sierra region between these regions and to the north. Macuilxochitl specializes in providing masons and stone workers, who have built many of the stone churches in the region. Four villages provide most of the handwoven textiles; four or five villages make most of the metates for the market region, and one village provides most of the mineral lime used for cooking maize. The degree of specialization is further documented below in appendix 7.

Some intervillage differences in the production of farm products and the exploitation of other natural resources may be accounted for by the environmental variations described in chapter 3. These almost certainly contributed to the early development of a market in the region, but they are insufficient to explain the present extent of differences in production. Far more important are the ways in which production is shaped by responsiveness to demand and to the influence of the market. In turn, specialization in production means that virtually all Oaxaca peasants depend upon the exchange system for at least some of the goods generally regarded as essential as well as for most of the desirable supplements and luxuries. These include foods, clothing and textiles, many raw materials used in the construction of housing, and most of the tools, equipment, and supplies essential to the functioning of the household and its productive activities. Most of the handicraft activities involve purchase of raw materials. Weavers, except perhaps those using the pre-Columbian backstrap loom, purchase their looms as well as most of their wool or mohair and all their cotton. The production system itself thus provides a market demand for some goods and services.

GOODS AND SERVICES PRODUCED

This section documents the production of goods and services for the market by peasant communities within the market region. The list in appendix 6 is compiled in part from published materials and from surveys in the villages, but primarily it is based on observation of goods sold in the various large marketplaces or carried by traveling traders. Some of the plant products are taken from a list supplied by Herbert Eder in connection with a continuing study of the economic botany of the area. The list is most complete for the Valley of Oaxaca and the Sierra Juárez to the north. It is less complete for the Isthmian region, but the omissions are few and relatively unimportant. The list also does not include important foods and raw materials such as cacao, or industrial goods produced outside the Oaxaca system. These will be considered in connection with extraregional trade in chapter 5 (appendix 19).

The items listed in appendix 6 differ markedly in importance. Some are important to everyone, while others are produced in very limited quantities and are found in the marketplaces only occasionally or seasonally. Some indication of relative importance is given in the discussion of consumption patterns in chapter 5, but adequate quantitative data can be obtained only by a very intensive study. A reasonably adequate quantitative study of the flow of goods into the Oaxaca City marketplace alone would require a trained staff of at least 40 people for an extended time period.

The relative importance of items, however, does not necessarily reflect their economic complexity. Pitch pine, for example, was at one time the only source of household lighting. It still is used to some extent for this purpose, especially in the Sierra, as well as for starting charcoal fires. For the last half century or more, its use has been declining as kerosene-fueled torches or lanterns, gasoline lanterns, flashlights, and in some places electricity, have become available. Despite the relative unimportance of pitch pine, Richard Berg (1968) found that approximately 80 typewritten pages were required to document its production, distribution, and consumption in the Sierra region alone, and to analyze the changes that have taken place as a result of the availability of new sources of lighting.

The items in appendix 6 differ in other characteristics. While the staple foods are largely indigenous, many of the food items listed were introduced in this region in Colonial times. Some cultivated products such as castor beans and alfalfa seed may be later introductions. The relative importance of some items has also changed in modern times. Production of cochineal, once the most important export of the marketing system, ceased completely in the nineteenth century and was replaced by coffee.

All of the items appearing in appendix 6 are produced for the market; they differ, however, in the extent to which they also are autoconsumed by the producers. Neither does the list suggest either the diversity of production patterns between villages or the degree of difference between productive activities of households within villages. In general, particularly at the household level within the village or settlement, the degree of uniformity of production and the amount of household self-sufficiency may have been exaggerated, not only in most studies of peasant peoples but in autonomous and nonfarming peoples as well. This suggestion has been made by Pospisil (1963), who found that among the Kapauku of New Guinea, an autonomous farming people, few households even approach self-sufficiency, even in foodstuffs. A few studies of nonfarming peoples likewise indicate that quite aside from sexual division of labor, not all individuals are equally skillful at all tasks and often may not know all the techniques necessary for survival. Over half a century ago McKern (1922) and O'Neale (1932) documented some types of specialization among California Indians, and more recently Graburn (1969) documented distribution patterns among the Eskimo of the northern Ungava Peninsula. Other examples could be cited, but in the main the ethnographic literature rarely describes in adequate detail the individual or household patterns of production or the ways food or other goods are distributed.

Oaxaca peasants consequently may not be as unusual as they appear to be in the variety of production patterns. In any case, the data strongly support the view that in peasant Oaxaca neither households nor villages are self-sufficient in any meaningful use of the term. Within the village, individuals and households differ in access to resources, skills, knowledge, and choice of economic activity. Villages differ from one another in much the same way and additionally show a marked tendency to specialize. Appendix 6 thus is not only a catalog of goods entering the market, it is also a catalog of potential production activities.

The only items in appendix 6 produced in every village are maize, beans (of the genus *Phaseolus*), squashes (of several varieties), and chickens and their eggs. Cattle and pigs are present in every village but are not bred everywhere. In most villages the cattle are draft animals, sold or butchered when old, while pigs are bought young and fattened for sale. While a household with a special ceremonial obligation may butcher its own cattle or pigs, most are sold to butchers or outside buyers.

Although maize is the most important item for autoconsumption, it also exemplifies the closest relationship between production and the marketing system. During their study in 1940–1941, Malinowski and de la Fuente (1957) found it to be the controlling factor in the marketing system. Fluctuations in the yield of maize were reflected in its abundance and price in the market. Price fluctuations were further affected by the operations of *acaparadores* (hoarders who bought maize at low prices and then held it to force up the price). Fluctuations in the abundance and price of maize affected the movement of all other goods in the market system and influenced their prices.

This situation has changed through modern communications permitting economical import or export of maize interregionally as well as its freer movement within the region. In addition, a system of government warehouses has been established since 1940–1941, and minimum buying and maximum selling prices are fixed annually. The differences between buying and selling prices are essentially limited to meeting operational costs of the government-controlled corporation, known as *Compañía Nacional de Subsistencias Populares* (CONASUPO). Actually, price controls are not complete in Oaxaca, for most maize imported into the region for sale by the government is of the new hybrid varieties that locally are considered inferior to local maize varieties, collectively known as *criollo*. Hence, local maize normally brings a modest premium above the price of maize from government warehouses, the amount of the price spread reflecting in part the annual or seasonal supply.

Although maize and its price appears no longer to dominate the Oaxaca market system, it still plays an important part, because both the state and the region are maize-deficit areas; that is, a variable amount of maize must be imported annually from elsewhere in Mexico to meet basic subsistence and livestock feed requirements. This is true even of the most impoverished subregion, the Sierra, where Berg estimates that around 40 percent of the minimum maize requirements of the subregion must be imported, despite the fact that this area has the poorest transportation system. Truckers and dealers in Mitla, a community once self-sufficient in maize, report that they import about 20 metric tons a month from the Isthmus and Chiapas alone. An undetermined amount of this maize is resold in the Mixe region (see chap. 11). The extent to which this deficit situation today results from population growth, or from shifts to production of more profitable agricultural crops, cannot be determined from our present knowledge. The existing situation certainly cannot antedate the modernization of transportation, for the costs of moving maize any great distance on the human back, with pack animals, or even with oxcarts is prohibitive. In the past when deficits occurred, people went hungry, and some starved or else migrated temporarily to places where food was more plentiful. Certainly this happened in the Mixe-speaking subregion in the early 1930s (Beals 1945). Even more recently, breakdowns of transportation such as occurred in the heavy rains of 1969 may cause fairly acute local or regional shortages even in the Valley.

The situation is more complex at the village level. Although every village grows maize, a substantial although undetermined number of villages never produce enough maize to meet minimum subsistence requirements. Only a small number of villages with relatively favorable population-land ratios regularly produce a surplus of maize for the market. In the Sierra exdistricts of Villa Alta and Ixtlán, only two out of 43 villages surveyed for this study regularly produce a surplus, while ten more produce a surplus in some years (Beals 1971). In the Valley probably not more than 25 percent of the villages produce a surplus in the best crop years. For other subregions of the market area information is lacking, but the Isthmus apparently exports some maize regularly to the Valley and elsewhere. In a substantial but unknown number of villages in the region, the total maize production may approximate subsistence requirements and in good years permit the sale of a surplus; in bad years they may have to import maize. In the Valley village of Diaz Ordaz, for example, the character of the available farm lands is such that maize is the most profitable crop, but in a very bad year there may be no surplus.

The intravillage situation is also variable. Although most Oaxaca peasants aspire to produce enough maize to provide minimum subsistence throughout the year, in all villages some households have no access to land, have insufficient land to produce enough maize for subsistence needs, or elect to concentrate on nonfarming occupations. Thus even a village with a regular maize surplus for the market includes households with maize deficits. Some households with inadequate maize production nevertheless may sell part of their crops to pay off debts or to meet emergencies. Later in the year they are forced to purchase maize in the market. Families on the borderline of self-sufficiency in maize may sell surpluses in the market in good crop years but become buyers in poor years. Surpluses sometimes are stored as a hedge against a drop in production the following year; the maize usually is damaged by insects in the second year and may become unfit for human consumption. It is not a total loss, for it may be sold for pig feed at approximately three-fourths the price of good-quality corn. Despite the possibility of this 25 percent loss, many households evidently prefer to store maize as insurance against later crop failure.

In addition to grain, fodder is a product of maize-growing, important for the maintenance of draft oxen. Normally the value of fodder is much less than that of the grain, but it is sufficient to warrant second plantings even when probability of failure of the grain crop is high. As with grain, some villages produce a surplus of fodder, others do not, and within the villages considerable differences between households are likely.

The other universally grown plants, beans (various varieties of the genus *Phaseolus*) and several varieties of squash, are of somewhat lesser importance. Beans are an essential source of protein in the diet and are grown by almost everyone able to plant maize. Squash (and the flower and tips of the runners, which are eaten also) are not critical elements in the diet; other plants including some wild "greens" may be substituted for them. In some villages where other vegetables are available, few squash are eaten. The flesh often is used almost solely as pig and cattle feed, but dried squash seeds are prized and sold extensively in the market for use as "snack" food or as an essential ingredient in a number of sauces. Relatively few squash reach the market.

Beans afford an interesting illustration of choice in the production process. Normally they are interplanted with maize. On favorable soils interplanting may yield an adequate supply, but on poor soils, particularly in the piedmont areas, the beans produced would be insufficient to supply the farmer's needs. In some places, for example, Santa Ana Zagache and neighboring villages, beans are grown as the sole crop in the field, mostly for the market. In contrast, the cultivators of nearby San Antonino Ocotlán, with similar soils, grow few beans, devoting themselves primarily to the cultivation of garden vegetables and flowers as cash crops; consequently they buy most of their beans and substantial quantities of maize as well. Beans are a relatively high-cost item, but as the quantity necessary for the diet is small, freight costs for a supply of beans are much less than for a household's maize supply for the same period, and it may therefore be considered more practical to buy beans than to grow them in sufficient quantity on lands where they do not produce well.

In addition to plants cultivated in every village, many more are cultivated in a limited number of villages, often as specializations. These special crops are listed in category II-A of appendix 6. They differ markedly in their importance, that is, in the extent to which they are grown. For each there is sufficient demand and they are salable in the weekly *plazas*. Part of the food crop is consumed in the household of the producer, but almost always it is planted with the intention of selling at least some portion of the harvest. It is impossible to generalize about the proportions consumed and marketed as these vary with the circumstances of each individual producer.

Early in this chapter the importance of price in making production decisions was mentioned; but many other factors affect the decision as to what crops to grow. Temperature, rainfall, the quality of lands and the possibilities for irrigation are limiting factors. In many instances the possession of adequate capital or special knowledge and skills are prerequisites. Outside these limitations, the estimate of relative profitability of alternatives is most important. Another important consideration is the relative amount of labor involved in growing different crops. A man with a good nonfarm alternative occupation (storekeeping or some types of handicraft, for example) may elect to grow only *milpa* (maize) rather than more profitable but more time-consuming crops. Also significant is whether the amount and quality of land available will permit growing at least some subsistence maize in addition to a cash crop; few landowners will devote all their land to specialty crops to the exclusion of all maize production. It is notable, however, that many farmers plant specialty crops even though this means they must buy part of their maize. The interval between planting and harvesting may also be important; to be assured of a constant income, some farmers growing specialty crops, especially fairly poor farmers without alternative sources of income, may choose to plant several specialty crops that mature relatively rapidly.

Specialty crops tend to be limited to particular villages or clusters of villages. As noted above, the village of San Antonino Ocotlán specializes in flowers, garden vegetables, and kitchen herbs. The major crop in the past was onions, followed by a considerable variety of flowers, garlic, and fresh vegetables. This pattern is changing. Cabbage, which requires less labor than onions, by 1969 seemed to be the more important crop, while garlic was on the way out. Apparently this shift was partly the result of the competition of imports from Puebla. Whatever the reason, instead of depending on two different varieties of onions for year-round production, the cultivators of San Antonino now tend to plant a single variety in the fall and winter. In contrast, flower growing showed little change or possibly was increasing. Some neighboring villages with similar environmental conditions follow the lead of San Antonino in these specializations; others specialize in black beans.

The village of Tlacochahuaya and its neighbors grow a great many vegetables— of which the tomato is perhaps most important—some flowers, and a few onions. Cuajimoloyas, high in the Sierra on the edge of the Valley, grows most of the local potatoes appearing in *plazas* as well as several varieties of flowers, of which the gladiolus is most important. (This relatively new village apparently owes its establishment to the discovery that potatoes do well there.) In the western part of the Valley near Etla several villages specialize in dairy products, mainly cheese, depending heavily on the proper soils and ditch irrigation for the production of alfalfa feed on a substantial scale.

A few other items merit special attention. The agave plant is cultivated only in areas of relatively low rainfall. It is planted either on lands unsuitable for other cultivated plants or on low-yielding maize lands. Several kinds of agave are recognized locally, but whether these represent species or varietal differences has not been determined. Some are cultivated primarily for ixtle fiber, and others for the production of mescal, a common distilled alcoholic beverage. Most agave for fiber is grown in the Cajonos region of the Sierra and adjoining villages to the west around Zoogocho where rainfall is too low to grow coffee. It is also important in other villages with dry lands such as San Pablo Guilá. Usually the fiber is hand-processed by the producers, but there are now a few owners of power machinery in the Valley who purchase leaves for processing from the growers. While there is some sale of fiber from producing villages, a great deal of it is converted locally into rope, cord, nets, hammocks, halters, cinches, and other items.

Agave for mescal manufacture is grown mostly in the drier parts of the Valley, especially in the east around Mitla. The bulk of the production is sold to industrialized mescal factories, but a substantial quantity is converted to mescal in household pot stills. Much of the latter production is clandestine, and the producer declares for tax purposes only part of what he actually produces. The untaxed production is sold secretly and is transported on burros over back trails. A tax collector estimated that 20 percent or more of the production of mescal in the Valley is untaxed.

Agave production is of special interest economically, for it is the clearest example of long-range economic calculation. The plants are grown from side shoots of mature plants, and for any sizable planting the grower usually has to invest considerable capital in buying young plants. The crop will not be ready to harvest for at least seven years. Moreover, much of the production for mescal in the Valley is on piedmont lands that may also be used for marginal maize production. For a few years some maize may be grown between the rows of agave plants, but the agave grower in this case must not only make an investment but also must face a reduction in income for the years while the agave matures. His rewards at the end of this time, however, are large.

A somewhat similar situation exists in the Sierra with coffee and avocado production. In both cases there may be some capital investment for young plants, and several years will elapse after planting before there is any significant production. Maize may be grown among young avocado trees but production clearly is reduced. But coffee and avocados often may be grown on land that is marginal for other cultivation. Nevertheless, in an era of perennial deficit in maize production, difficult decisions are involved.

Coffee growing began in the northern Sierra about 1875. It frequently was the only significant cash crop that could be grown. Because of its high value relative to bulk and weight, it could be grown and transported profitably on the human back or on burros. Avocados, in contrast, were grown commercially only after the opening of the roads in the Sierra. Even so, considerable quantities of avocados begin their journey to the market on burros that carry the fruit from the orchards to the nearest road point. The success of avocados has led to some experimentation with improved varieties of citrus and deciduous fruits. That this experimentation was undertaken by Sierra farmers rather than by government initiative is of some interest. As roads are improved and extended in the Sierra, there is a possibility that increasing amounts of land marginal for maize production will be converted to fruit production for the market, further increasing the maize deficit of the region.

The castor bean, like the agave, is grown mostly on piedmont lands that are marginal for maize production. Although extensively planted in the eastern part of the Valley, it may be found almost anywhere on piedmont lands or even on poor-grade alluvial soils. Some areas around Ocotlán and Ejutla, for example, have fairly extensive plantings of castor beans. The plants begin to produce much more rapidly than the agave but, as with the agave, maize is planted between the rows while the plants are small. Most castor beans are grown for the world market, and demand in that market has fluctuated substantially. Parsons (1936:9) notes that the oil produced locally in Mitla between 1929 and 1933 was used only for burning in votive lights in the church.

Tobacco, another purely commercial crop, was introduced recently in the Zaachila and Zimatlan region. Large tobacco companies have reportedly advanced money for seed and for purchase of irrigation pumps, provided advisers for the growers, and promised a minimum price for the product. Experience so far has varied. At least one peasant was encouraged to plant an experimental crop on soils too heavy for successful production. In another case, one company did not make it clear that the guaranteed minimum price was only for leaves in prime condition. It further expected the growers to string and dry the leaves properly, the first step in the curing process, which sometimes requires a heavy cash outlay for hired labor. Another company established a curing plant and bought undried leaves. Where experiments yielded poor results, tobacco growing was rejected by some villages. Where experiences were good, villages are now heavily involved in tobacco growing, notably Santa Ana Tlapacoyan, Santa Gertrudis, and San Pablo Huixtepec (as of 1970).

A relatively old crop, pecans, is grown successfully on the west side of the southern arm of the Valley. The trees are mostly scattered through maize fields. Another old crop, peanuts, is produced in the same region.

Alfalfa may have been cultivated on a small scale for a long time, although Parsons (1936:52) says that it was a recently introduced crop in Mitla in the 1929–1933 period. It can be grown only on humid lands or where ditch irrigation is easy or, more recently, where the motor pump is used for irrigation. It is the basis for almost all dairying. Most alfalfa is grown by dairymen to feed milk cows, but some is grown by farmers to feed pigs, oxen, and burros or to sell in bundles in the *plazas*. The amount of alfalfa fed to such animals depends partly on pasturage and other feed available. It is used more in the dry season when animals are worked heavily and pasturage is poor, but some cattle are fed alfalfa the year around. Since the opening of the highways, the Valley of Oaxaca has also become a major supplier of alfalfa seed in the Republic.

Although some animals are present in all villages, only chickens are bred everywhere. Of work animals, oxen are mainly instruments of agricultural production, while burros, horses, and mules are mainly for transport. Dairy cows are relatively rare in most villages except where dairying for the market is a primary activity of some households. Poultry are raised for household consumption and for sale in the market. Swine, among the most common animals, are raised primarily for the market. Such animals as dogs and cats (the latter very rare since the indiscriminate dusting of the state with DDT by the antimalarial program) have a minor economic function in the protection of property. All must be fed and in many cases there may be such incidental expenditures as breeding fees, medicines or veterinary fees, and inoculations. Animal raising and the production of animal products are closely interrelated and offer complexities that cannot be presented in tabular form.

Chickens are not only found in all villages but also are raised by most households. Most poultry are obtained through natural increase in the flocks, but some chicks are bought from neighbors while an increasing number of commercially bred chicks are bought in the *plazas* or from itinerant vendors. Chickens forage for some food with little care but turkeys, if they forage, tend to range farther and usually must be herded. Both are fed household scraps and usually some maize or *masa* (maize dough). Peasants usually consider that they raise chickens and produce eggs for household consumption, but households with more precarious resources are apt to sell most of their chickens in the marketplace for emergency cash or to buy maize. Although prices in the marketplace may fluctuate, there is always some demand for fowl. Egg production is relatively small and, especially near the larger towns, most eggs are sold in the market. In terms of relative nutritional value, families with marginal incomes find it more economical to sell eggs and buy beans.

Turkeys, although still regarded as a necessity for ritual events in many villages, usually are raised specifically for sale in the *plaza*. They require much more care than chickens and a substantial outlay for feed to bring them to a marketable condition. Turkeys are bred in the villages, but as with chickens, an increasing number of commercially raised turkey chicks are bought in the marketplace.

Pigs are raised in most, if not all, villages and by a high percentage of the households. Some brood sows are kept in the villages, but most pigs are bought as shoats or partially grown animals in the marketplace (or from a local pig breeder, if there is one) and fattened for sale. Also, owners of brood sows sometimes give shoats to fellow villagers to be raised on shares. If the modest initial investment in a shoat is to be protected, the animals must be continuously and adequately fed. Some pigs are slaughtered in the village—many specifically for fiestas—and the flesh, hide, and other products are sold there.

Many people view pig raising as unprofitable but see it as a means of forced savings. Zapotecs agree that they find it difficult to save cash and that they are apt to spend it on clothing, luxury foods, or other items that are not strictly necessary. The requirements of pig feeding absorb cash and often force the deferment of purchases other than those demanded for subsistence needs. The reward is a modest but (to the peasant) substantial sum of money. This also may be spent on luxury consumer goods but it frequently is invested in capital goods. Regardless of the economics of pig raising (see below), many peasants show great interest in it. Often they keep the pigs in brick or cement pens that are cleaned regularly, have some sophistication about breeds, and vaccinate animals against diseases.

Draft oxen and beef cattle, and to some extent dairy cows, are purchased. Most are bought in cattle markets. Oaxaca City butchers buy in one of the two cattle markets in Oaxaca City or in Ocotlán. City butchers are legally required to have their beeves slaughtered in the public abbatoir, where there is some inspection. (Elsewhere the butchers themselves slaughter the cattle they buy, in their house patios). The largest cattle market in the Valley, at Ocotlán, has been studied by economist Ralph Cassady, Jr., who will report on it separately. The one in Tlacolula appears to be the major source of animals for the Sierra. Cattle breeding is found to a limited extent in the dairying villages or districts in the northwestern end of the Valley as a byproduct of dairying, but the major sources for the Valley seem to be the district of Yautepec around Rio Hondo (between the Valley and the Isthmus of Tehuantepec), coastal Chiapas, Chahuites near the Chiapas border, and Sarabia in Veracruz.

Oxen are the most important draft animals, essential to most farming activities. Not all farmers own oxen; some hire them instead, usually with driver, when needed for plowing and cultivation. Dairy cattle are found only in a limited number of villages. Dairying probably has increased in recent years with easier access to the national market. Today many dairy farmers try to improve their stock by purchasing better animals in the markets and by artificial insemination, a relatively low-cost service provided by the government. Bull calves are sold either to be trained as oxen or to be slaughtered for beef. Over-age cows are also fattened and sold for beef.

Conversion of cattle into beef is mostly in the hands of specialized butchers. Meat prices are controlled in the city, and butchers blame the continuing problem of the low quality of beef on price ceilings that offer growers no incentive to improve the quality. Probably all villages have at least part-time butchers, but much of the meat consumed is purchased in the nearest *plaza*, often in the form of *tasajo* (dried beef). Cattle slaughtered in villages are usually over-age oxen that have been briefly fattened, and the quality of the meat is very poor. The beef sold in the plaza of Ocotlán, the town with the largest cattle market, however, is supplied by the butchers of the nearby village of San Antonino.

Of the equines, asses (*burros*) are found in all villages. Like cattle, they are usually purchased and apparently are bred only in a limited number. Throughout the area the burro population has dropped sharply since the building of roads and the expansion of modern transportation. Horses are rare and sometimes appear to be owned primarily for prestige. Horses do not thrive on maize fodder, and few owners feed them grain or alfalfa. Waterbury suggests that the peasants show economic rationality albeit with some cruelty in feeding their animals only to the extent of enabling them to perform the tasks for which they are used. Most horses are in poor condition, are badly handled, and probably short-lived. Saddle sores and galls on riding and pack animals are inadequately treated. The hardier mule is even rarer than the horse.

Goats and sheep, often herded together, are almost entirely confined to villages with fairly extensive rough pasture lands unsuitable for cultivation. Goats are milked for cheese production, which is primarily for the market. Both mohair and wool are peddled in weaving villages by producers or middlemen, or sold in the *plaza*.

The major objective of this discussion is to emphasize that such animal husbandry as this is generally not for subsistence but for the market. The goal is to obtain cash, not food. Most animal protein consumed by most households is bought in the regional *plaza*. In the Isthmus, except for marine animals, most animal protein is consumed at fiestas. This is probably true of families everywhere, especially in the Sierra, but in the Valley, at least, even very poor families consider small amounts of animal protein to be a necessity two or three times a week, and most Valley peasants seem to manage this. Impressionistically, the Indian peasants in the Valley eat meat more frequently than do most Mexican Indian peasant groups.

Returning to appendix 6, most of the processed foods listed are the product of household enterprises (category II-D). One exception is brown sugar produced in *trapiches* (with animal-powered cane-crushing apparatus) owned by operators who use hired labor and buy most or all of the cane from independent producers. The production of brown sugar does not meet regional demands. Local bakers are found in more villages now than in the past, but only a few villages have many bakers producing bread and other bakery products for sale in the markets or in other villages. Although tortillas are sometimes produced for sale in villages where women play a major role in handicraft production, especially pottery-making villages, most tortillas for sale are sold in the *plazas*. In Oaxaca City, women of three nearby villages specialize in producing tortillas for daily sale in the regular marketplace.

Exploitation of natural resources for income and consumption is uneven. Wild greens and grasshoppers, for example, are usually eaten by those collecting them, although some are sold in the *plazas*. Some raw materials such as ixtle fiber are processed before entering the market, while other raw materials do not pass through the *plaza* system at all. For example, clay may be mined by potters or bought in the pottery-making village from men who mine clay for sale. Some special clays such as one used for finishing (slipping) some pottery in Atzompa are imported to the village from longer distances. Tile, fired brick, stone, sand, and gravel also are purchased from producers at the point of production. Most of the extractive products, however, are found in varying amounts in the *plazas*.

Most processed raw materials are marketed through the *plaza* system and some go through the regular daily markets. Exceptions are some house construction materials or large pieces of furniture for which the consumer contracts in advance directly with the producer at his place of business. Most firewood is sold directly to consumers by woodcutters, especially in pottery-producing villages. Charcoal, a diminishing commodity since bottled gas and petroleum products became available, also is sold directly to consumers at their residences or, in the city, to owners of depositories. Although its production is supposedly illegal, charcoal is still sold openly in Oaxaca City, and burros bearing firewood or charcoal are now the only ones allowed in the central district.

Services are included in appendix 6 to emphasize alternative sources of income available to people living in villages. A few villagers devote full time to trading activities, just as there are those who live entirely from wage labor either within the village, or at some other place such as a mine, or working for farmers in other villages. But for most villages commercial activities, the exercise of special skills or the selling of unskilled labor are part-time activities. Probably no villager makes his living exclusively by being a barber or a musician. In a few villages (the most notable examples are Mitla and San Antonino), enough people gain such a very substantial part of their income from commercial activities that trading can be listed as a specialty of the community.

In appendix 7 specializations are indicated by village. The list is not complete, especially for the isthmian subregion. An agricultural specialization is listed only if the village concerned produces it primarily for the market or regularly produces a surplus for market sale. The list is based on surveys of villages and interviews with vendors in the marketplaces. It demonstrates again the importance of village specializations in the Oaxaca market.

PRODUCTION STRATEGIES

The purpose of this section is to review some of the problems faced by the Oaxaca peasant in his productive activities (in the narrow or form-changing sense), to suggest the economic nature of many of his decisions, and to show how these affect the marketing system. More detailed considerations of production problems will appear in village studies by various members of the project staff. The economics of production in the Valley also have been examined intensively by anthropologist Aubrey Williams but results are not yet published. Other independent studies are reported to have been made of specific handicraft production but these also are still unpublished.

The basic productive activity is of course farming. The differences between village environments have already been mentioned; there also are variations in land quality and availability of water for irrigation within the area of most villages. Especially in the Sierra, the lands of a community may be in more than one climatic zone. Within a village, households differ in their access to land. In most villages some households own no land. Landholding households may possess more than they are able to cultivate or may prefer to expend all or part of their available labor and capital in nonfarm activities. Landless individuals often gain access to these lands through sharecropping arrangements.

Control of land occurs at several levels. Most villages exercise some control over who may buy land, usually preventing purchase or use by nonresidents. This rule ordinarily is waived only for families who move into the village with the permission of village authorities and become permanent residents, assuming all the traditional obligations of membership in the community.

Most agricultural lands are held either in individual ownership or in *ejidos* (government-grant lands). Individually owned land may be inherited or may be purchased from other members of the community. Use of privately owned land may be granted for rent, either for cash rent or more commonly on a sharecropping basis. A few communities in the mountains retain ancient titles and hold all their lands communally; in such instances, villagers have only use rights to the land they cultivate. In others, again mostly in the mountains, villages hold nonagricultural lands, principally forests or pastures, in common, and a few villages own some agricultural land that is cultivated communally to provide income for support of town services, including schools or church activities.

The *ejido* is a relatively new type of land control dating from the Revolution. The land formerly belonged to *haciendas*. Title to *ejido* land rests in the federal government, but each *ejido* tract is administered by local *ejido* members through an elected administrative committee. Members of the group receive land allotments, the amount varying according to land type, the size of the *ejido*, and sometimes according to relative need. Allotments are held only as long as they are cultivated. They may be inherited but they may not be sold, and in theory may not be rented. Sharecropping on *ejido* lands is sometimes practiced clandestinely, but there is always the risk that the sharecropper may later claim the allotment in his own name. This is also true when sharecroppers are from another village. Stolmaker reports a case at Atzompa where sharecroppers from the hamlet of Los Ibañez attempted—unsuccessfully—to claim parcels they were cultivating for Atzompa *ejidatarios*.

The landless family, lacking special skills or control of some handicraft, occupies the most precarious economic position in the village. While the family head may farm as a sharecropper, he more usually works as a *mozo* or *jornalero*, most commonly as a wage laborer for a farmer who has more land than he can cultivate without assistance. In 1967 wages in the Sierra were commonly $7 (pesos) a day. In Diaz Ordaz wages had increased from $5 daily in 1960 to $10 daily by 1967, and there was a shortage of labor. In 1969 most harvesters in the village of Atzompa were demanding, and getting, payment in maize worth about $24 daily as against the prevailing wage rates of $10 to $12 a day; previously, payment in kind was a privilege accorded only to relatives and special friends. In San Antonino Ocotlán the going wage in 1970 was $10 daily, rising to $12 or even $15 in rush seasons such as the flower harvest before the Day of the Dead. Sometimes, however, a *mozo* might be hired for as little as $8 if two or more weeks' continuous work could be promised. To all these figures the costs of meals provided by the employer must be added. In contrast, a laborer in Oaxaca City might earn $20 or more daily, but without meals. (Throughout this book the dollar symbol [$] refers to Mexican pesos.)

Even at $10 daily, wages for *mozos* were only about half of what most peasants regarded as the minimum daily expenditure to maintain a "decent" scale of living for a family of five. Such a wage covered only minimum daily family food requirements. Moreover, such labor is usually intermittent. In addition to work in his own village, the laborer may find farm employment temporarily in neighboring communities, or offer his services as a porter at the weekly *plazas*. Some go to

Veracruz state for three months for the sugarcane harvest, earning $10 to $12 per metric ton cut or approximately $20 a day without food. Others seek a steady job in the city of Oaxaca or move to Mexico City or, before 1964, went to the United States as a *bracero*. Villages differ markedly in the way they respond to the various employment opportunities. In Magdalena Ocotlán, where many residents lack adequate land, seasonal labor outside the village is quite common, especially in the state of Veracruz. In nearby San Antonino, emigration is frequent but few seek seasonal wage labor outside the village. The *jornalero* or *mozo* is dependent on a labor market for his income, which is spent in the *plaza* system for his food and other necessary goods.

Grim as the situation of the laborer appears, his position is not entirely hopeless. Some, at least, find ways to improve their situation. The more fortunate perhaps are those who succeed in becoming sharecroppers. Sharecropping arrangements vary somewhat; often the tenant provides oxen for plowing and cultivating and labor, the landowner provides land and seed. The tenant and landowner each usually receives 50 percent of the crop.

Nonfarm occupations are also available; boys may be placed as apprentices to bakers, butchers, or others to learn a trade. Sometimes a permanent job can be found with a storekeeper or as an assistant to an intervillage or inter*plaza* trader. The assistant in the *plaza* may begin trading on his own account after he has "learned the ropes." The *jornalero*'s wife may raise chickens for market, do laundry, or make tortillas for wealthier families. The household may obtain a pig, fatten and sell it for a reasonable profit, and invest the proceeds in a burro or possibly in a young team of oxen to be rented out, thereby improving income and forming a capital reserve against the ultimate goal of buying a small piece of land.

The small landholder without other skills is also in a precarious situation. He has to work as a wage laborer part of the year, perhaps in the city, or as a seasonal employee in the cane fields. But his economic situation is slightly better than that of the villager without land. Moreover, it should be borne in mind (see chap. 2) that in those villages for which we have data, a majority even of the people who give day labor as their principal occupation also have some supplementary role or handicraft from which they derive part of their income; while more than one member of the household may have income. Incomes and expenditures are considered in detail in chapter 5.

Farming involves much more than access to land. With few exceptions the farmer must decide whether he will make a major capital investment in a team of oxen, depend upon hiring oxen, or—in a few villages of the Valley—hire a tractor for the major plowing. Wealthier families sometimes contract with poorer families to care for and train young oxen for two or three years in return for the right to use them. Ox teams can be rented out by their owners, and many cultivators exchange mature ones for younger ones (which do not put out as much work) every two or three years at a profit. The latter strategy presumably is profitable only if the scale of the farmer's operations does not immediately require mature oxen for extensive plowing and if he is willing to invest the extra time needed to plow with younger animals. There is risk in ox team ownership in that an animal may be lost through accident or disease. If the team survives and is held until no longer serviceable, part of the cost may be recovered by selling the animals for conversion into beef. As teams require replacement about every eight years, this type of expenditure is not regular and few farmers systematically plan for it unless they customarily exchange older teams for younger ones. When it becomes necessary to replace oxen, the farmer usually accumulates the capital by fattening other animals for sale and by selling maize or other farm products.

Tractor plowing and cultivating is increasing rapidly in some villages, and interest is widespread in the Valley. Cultivators are well aware that "when tractors aren't working, they don't eat." In San Antonino, tractor plowing now is the most common practice although only one small, aged tractor is owned by a village resident (and is not rented). Ownership of a tractor for custom plowing is becoming an increasingly attractive alternative for landless households. Tractor use may have long-term drawbacks. It eliminates the major source of fertilizer and on some soils may pack down the subsoil and cause drainage problems.

Farm operating expenses, which must be budgeted for on an annual basis, are rental of an ox team if one is not owned, or of a tractor; labor for planting, cultivating, and harvesting; and, if the farmer has no oxcart, rental of a cart, a truck, or burros to bring in the harvest from the field. A further cost may be hiring labor to cut and bundle the stalks to be used or sold as fodder, although this may be done by the family. Offsetting these expenditures, owners of ox teams or carts can rent them, although both represent considerable capital investment. Fuller discussion is given below (see "Economics of Production," below).

Differences in soils, moisture, and temperatures require different farming techniques, even for the basic crop of maize, and determine the range of possible alternative crops. Most peasants have some system of classifying lands from poor to good. These systems vary in detail from village to village. In general terms the lands in the Valley may be classed as mountain slopes, piedmont, and alluvial.

Most mountain slopes are too steep for cultivation, have poor soils or are too dry, and they ordinarily are cultivated only when they are of exceptional quality or the need is great. Areas sometimes are cleared or cultivated for a year or two, after which they must be allowed to return to brush and forest for several years before they can be cultivated again. Often they are too steep, rocky, or full of roots to be plowed, and the only implements used are a machete for cutting brush and trees, a sharpened stick for planting, and a *coa* (a curved steel blade on a wooden handle) for cutting weeds and piling earth around the roots of the corn plants. Even at best, the returns on seed and labor are small and few men consider them worthwhile. In the rainier mountains, however, there is a great deal of shifting or slash-burn farming.

Piedmont lands are the most abundant lands in the Valley of Oaxaca and consist of fairly gentle slopes or rolling terrain suitable for plowing. Soils are usually sandy and often contain varying quantities of small rocks or pebbles. Soils differ considerably in fertility and moisture-retaining qualities, and crop yields vary rather markedly from year to year depending upon the amount and distribution of rainfall. Where permanent or semipermanent streams emerge from the mountains, especially in the central, western, and southern areas of the Valley, some ditch irrigation is possible on nearly level land, resulting in better and more reliable maize crops as well as offering potentialities for other plants. Some imported nut and fruit trees will grow in favored spots in the piedmont areas, as do some native trees such as the *guaje* (which has pods with edible seeds). Most such trees are found in house yards or occur as isolated specimens in the fields.

The possibility of irrigating confronts the farmer with additional decisions as to how much labor he will invest in leveling or terracing fields. In Diaz Ordaz, as new water control measures expanded the opportunities for irrigation, some farmers abandoned their more distant and low-yield lands in favor of leveling, terracing, fertilizing, and irrigating existing fields to increase production. Some more important landowners who depended on the services of wage laborers also abandoned distant and poor lands because of the increase in wages for laborers as well as labor shortage owing to outmigration.

Maize is the principal crop on unirrigated piedmont lands. In the past some wheat was grown, which usually was ground locally either in metates or in water-powered mills for local consumption. At Mitla in 1930, all wheat produced was consumed in the village. Today all but two water-powered mills have ceased to function and one, at least, is reported to be grinding imported Canadian wheat. Whether consumer preferences or price have caused this shift is not known, although in Diaz Ordaz wheat growing is said to have become less profitable than maize growing.

In drier sections, piedmont lands may be planted to agave, or castor beans may be interplanted with maize. Where water is abundant, some gentler slopes may be irrigated. In the Sierra, even steep mountain lands may be plowed regularly for maize growing in much the same way as piedmont land, although fallowing for one or two years may be necessary after each crop.

Dark alluvial soils—flat, loamy, or clayey soils—are the most fertile in the Valley of Oaxaca and have high moisture-retaining qualities. They give the highest yields of maize but they also are suitable for many of the specialty crops grown. In some areas they will produce reliable and heavy maize crops without irrigation even in relatively dry years. Many are irrigated either through fairly elaborate systems for spreading flood waters from the main rivers, or by bringing water in ditches from mountain streams. Most of the specialty crops, however, are grown on alluvial soils where the water table is three meters or less and water may be drawn in pots from shallow wells for controlled irrigation of vegetables and flowers. All three methods of irrigation have been practiced in the Valley of Oaxaca for at least 2,000 years (Flannery et al. 1967). A noteworthy change in San Antonino since about 1960 is the great increase in power-driven irrigation pumps, replacing pot irrigation from shallow wells. Whereas in 1960 there were no pumps, by 1970 there were about 200 owned by 150 cultivators, and the number was increasing rapidly. Elsewhere the water is sometimes pumped from streams.

It is well to note that the foregoing land classification does not coincide with that used in most villages. Usually three, four, or five categories are recognized (even though not all occur within village boundaries). Some villagers make several finer subdivisions within the larger categories. Residents of San Antonino Ocotlán, for example, grade land on a scale of 1 (*primera*) to 5. Grades 1 to 3 are all dark alluvial in type, and no one so far has identified any type 4 lands in the *municipio*. San Sebastian Teitipac uses a four-class system, ranking most land as first-class and grading the remainder according to topography, attributes of the soil, annual crop yield, and the economic uses for which the land is suitable (Cook 1968:81).

The techniques and the knowledge necessary for success differ not only from one crop to another but also according to the types of soils and the availability of water. This is illustrated by an incident reported by Downing for Diaz Ordaz, where there is a rough three-class typing of lands. Most of the *municipio* consists of piedmont or mountain lands, but it also includes a small area of alluvial soils. The owners of these alluvial soils until recently farmed them in the same way they did the piedmont soils. One farmer realized that his neighbor across the municipal boundary line on similar soils was getting much better results, and several of the Diaz Ordaz farmers hired a farmer from Tlacolula to teach them how to improve their use of the alluvial soils.

Farmers of piedmont lands have several choices to make in growing maize. Often the farmer must decide whether to try for an early crop to increase his returns. An early crop may be a loss unless there is sufficient winter rain; unseasonable cold weather may retard it, and if the light spring rains fail completely, the farmer may get only a rather sparse crop of corn fodder. He also runs the risk that his summer planting may be delayed, especially if the summer rains begin early, and he may not get as good a summer crop as he otherwise would have. Finally, if he can harvest his summer crop early enough, he may in many locations be able to plant a hasty crop of garbanzos, if he judges that the soil has retained sufficient moisture.

Thus far this sounds very much like any farmer gambling on the weather. There are nevertheless many economic decisions involved. Even when growing *milpa* (maize), certain operations such as planting and harvesting are best done rapidly. In the past these were occasions for reciprocal exchange of unpaid labor involving a certain amount of feasting and drinking. In the Valley of Oaxaca this type of labor exchange in the fields is rapidly disappearing in favor of wage labor. While workers must be fed, the meals are not ceremonial in character ahd hence are simpler, there is no drinking, and the work pace is under the farmer's control. Only in the Sierra, where money is scarcer, does labor exchange persist to any extent.

The decision whether to try for a spring crop rests not only on the estimate of weather conditions; it involves a consideration of possible alternative uses of labor, for example, whether to engage in handicraft activities, or whether to utilize labor time and effort to prepare the ground early (for better moisture retention) or more thoroughly to insure the success of the summer planting. Similarly, at the close of the summer growing season, especially if he has a supplementary occupation, the farmer must decide whether to hire labor to harvest his crop quickly and hire help for cutting the fodder, tasks that might be done in more leisurely fashion by the members of the household. If he seeks aid in cutting the fodder, should he hire labor by the day or should he contract with someone to do the job at a fixed price? Finally, if his harvest is early enough, should he plant garbanzos, and will the returns on the garbanzos be worth the extra cost? Quite clearly there are differences of opinion on these matters, and in the same area some farmers plant garbanzos while some do not. The various input alternatives, costs, and possible returns are summarized in appendix 8.

In the northern Sierra somewhat different choices exist. As noted above, coffee has been a significant cash crop in the humid parts of this area since the latter years of the nineteenth century. In recent years coffee production has apparently increased with improved transportation and marketing facilities. The second Sierra cash crop, avocados, acquired importance only when truck transportation became available. The two may be grown together, with coffee planted in the shade of avocado trees. Moreover, they do not really compete with maize growing, for they can be grown successfully on lands that yield only very marginal maize crops. A third type of cash crop of some antiquity in the Sierra, increasing in importance through improved transportation, includes certain varieties of chile peppers that do well in the Sierra environment. Here decisions are more difficult, for chile requires lands that alternatively would give relatively high yields of maize.

Not all production decisions are equally sound. Some individuals are unduly apprehensive about the risks involved in the cultivation of new crops. Very few have precise information about costs, yields, and profits. Their somewhat intuitive estimates often turn out to be fairly good, but most decisions are made on the basis of inadequate information. Some errors are evident where considerable labor or capital investment is required for construction or upkeep of facilities. Terraces and water distribution systems established in Colonial times and used through the pre-Revolutionary *hacienda* period frequently have been allowed to decay, especially in the drier eastern end of the Valley, and lands are no longer in production. It may be that the local explanation has some truth to it, namely, that rainfall has declined cyclically in recent decades, but meteorological records are inadequate and contradictory on this point. It seems likely that failures to make the labor and capital investments to maintain the terraces and distribution systems is at least partially responsible for abandonment of some lands formerly cultivated.

The declining rainfall theory everywhere is invoked to account for a series of poor crops or declining fertility. Evidence is inconclusive for long-term changes, although there is some archeological evidence for prolonged drought cycles in the past. In the Isthmus, many fresh water lagoons, supporting a rich organic life, have disappeared in the last century, and older informants remember small lakes in the Valley. Certainly, annual variations in rainfall are considerable. The first massive migration of *braceros* to the United States, in the 1940s, is commonly associated with a very severe two-year drought, and many informants feel that most years in the 1950s and 1960s had inadequate rainfall. In 1969, however, after several years of normal or subnormal rainfall, considerable crop loss occurred from excessive rains and flooding. Agriculturally, the timing of rains may be more important than annual rainfall and may color memories about the weather.

Most farmers are aware that crop rotation, fallowing, and fertilization all affect yields. The majority use what animal fertilizer they have and some have experimented with commercial fertilizers. On the whole, most farmers are not very sophisticated or systematic about maintaining fertility. Considerable differences exist between villages, however. In some villages chemical fertilizers have been used without adequate information; either too little is applied to produce any discernible result, or too much is applied, which causes some crop damage. The most extensive use of fertilizer seems to occur in villages producing market crops, especially vegetables and flowers. Nearly everyone in San Antonino Ocotlán uses sulfate of ammonia. The practice was used successfully by one man and later was adopted by others. Sulfate of ammonia is now brought into the village in truckloads and can be purchased in local stores as cheaply as in Oaxaca. Possibly other high-nitrogen fertilizers would be better than sulfate of ammonia, but it does well on the slightly alkaline soils common in this village. It can easily be used in the cheapest way, that is, by applying small quantities near the base of the individual plant rather than mixing it generally with the soil. Other technical problems exist in the use of fertilizer, but the foregoing comments suggest that readiness for technological improvements is associated with production for the market rather than for direct use.

Readiness to experiment and efforts to maximize returns from land are not always associated with the possession of resources. A man with several hectares of land who owns a store or bakery or who has another profitable occupation such as butchering or trading may prefer to stick with traditional cultivation of maize on lands suitable for more profitable crops. Land is a safe investment and tends to increase in value over time. Conservatively farmed, it produces a small but relatively certain income. For the individual desirous of enlarging his income and living scale, other forms of activity seem more promising. It appears that those who are in the best position to experiment and to improve their technology for higher production often are the least likely to do so.

But the well-to-do are not the only conservatives. Very poor peasants with limited lands do not take chances either, and are apt to stick to *milpa* growing. Maize may be eaten, but it is difficult to feed an onion-growing family on onions if the bottom drops out of the market. Data suggest that the cultivators most willing to grow a variety of crops and to experiment with new technologies are those with a modest amount of land and with no income or limited income from nonagricultural sources. Even the more successful innovators would quickly leave cultivation if they could. As one successful and expanding small farmer remarked to Waterbury: "I'd leave here and go to Mexico City immediately if somebody could get me a job paying $1,000 a month salary."

Clearly, the degree to which individuals or households engaged in cultivation produce for the market, and many of the decisions they make about land use, choice of crops, or the undertaking of experiments or improvement in technology, are affected by the market or at least by the individual's perception of the market. At the same time, these decisions are also affected by the nonfarm aspects of the production system such as the availability of sources of income outside the production system. For the artisan-farmer, unless his handicraft is purely a spare-time occupation, decisions about farm strategies are also influenced by the profitability of his craft. Employment of farm labor and the hiring of ox teams or a tractor may be more attractive, and specialty crops involving extensive labor time may be avoided. Sharecropping to minimize labor input and losses in the event of a poor harvest may seem more sensible. Some of these alternatives and their advantages and disadvantages are given in appendixes 8 and 9.

In the case of a handicraft activity such as pottery production in Atzompa, where women play an important role in the production, there are other problems.

For example, should the wife make clothes or buy them? One woman, a successful potter, a widow, not only buys tortillas but hires a laundress, buys all her family's clothing ready-made or from seamstresses, and the family frequently eats its major meals with relatives, paying a share of the food costs. The potter's husband, if he has land, must allocate his time between cultivation and helping in pottery production. If he does not have land, he has the alternatives of working part-time as a laborer, participating in the pot-shaping process usually handled by the wife,[1] or dedicating a larger share of his time to marketing by selling not only the product of his own household but also the products of other households.

Quite aside from these decisions, many alternatives exist in the pottery production process itself. Examples are given in appendix 10, summarizing potters' alternatives in production and marketing, and in appendix 11, showing the actual distribution of alternatives used in procuring pottery materials in an Atzompa sample. Not all the decisions reached are purely economic in terms of higher income in the craft. A potter may decide not to mine clay himself because he believes his time may bring a bigger return if he invested in some other activity, or because mining clay is a disagreeable, dirty, and sometimes dangerous job that he wants to avoid.

Other handicraft occupations display similar problems. A yoke maker, too, may seek his own materials, but his time and skills may be better employed if he buys timbers from a woodcutter. Some other artisans have little choice but to purchase their raw materials; for example, weavers normally buy all their equipment and raw materials, and their outlay for capital goods may be substantial.

Sometimes the handicraft is viewed primarily as an occupation to be carried on when there is no need for work on the farm. This may mean a split day: oxen can be worked only about six hours a day without injuring animals, and the rest of the day may be devoted to the handicraft. A metate maker in Magdalena Ocotlán, who also owns a forge, often spends an hour or two in the morning sharpening and tempering tools for his neighbors, puts in six or seven hours in the fields, works until dark in the quarry, and spends two or three hours after dark finishing metates and manos (mullers) at home.

The demand for time for cultivating or manufacturing activities may also affect marketing strategy. Growers of specialty crops such as onions may elect to sell the crop in the field, the buyer undertaking the harvesting. If the grower prefers to take some of his products to the marketplace, he may in busy seasons sell them to buyers at the bus station or to a wholesaler in the *plaza*, returning home in time to put in a half day at productive labor. This is a favored choice of some farmers

---

[1] In Coyotepec, where black pottery is made, many men are potters. In the 1930s the industry here was in the hands of the men (Van de Velde and Van de Velde 1939:41).

during the period of heavy farm work. At other times, the grower may decide to sell his product at retail on the street, which brings a higher cash return but may take all day.

In a few handicraft operations there is some evidence of the kind of rationality associated with firms. In the serape-weaving village of Teotitlán del Valle, several weavers now own looms that are operated by hired workers. The master weaver may lay out the designs and supervise the work as well as make raw material purchases and carry on the sales activities.

ECONOMICS OF PRODUCTION

The preceding sections of this chapter have examined the variation in the production system at both the household and village level and presented data on the variety of options open to producers and the nature of some of their decisions. They have shown the close interrelations between form-changing activities and the market system. Underlying these discussions is the assumption that in general, the Oaxaca peasant makes his production decisions in accordance with economic principles of minimizing his inputs of capital, including cash and labor, attempts to rationalize his operations, and seeks to maximize his returns. Validation of this assumption calls for detailed economic analysis of all aspects of the production system. Unfortunately, the data for this are insufficient. Not all production activities have been studied in detail, and in general it is not possible to deal adequately with the differences between villages and producing households. In the following pages a few selected examples illustrate the problems involved and I hope will illuminate the economics of the production system.

Maize Production

Analysis of maize production faces three difficulties: lack of uniformity of measurements used; lack of common understandings of various measurements; and frequent tendency of informants to minimize or conceal actual production. Cook (1968:106) writes that in San Sebastian Teitipac,

> the standards employed in measuring corn output per plot are fairly uniform with the most accurate measure being in terms of the *almud*—a Spanish unit of measure equivalent in San Sebastian to four liters. However, when one asks a *San Sebastiano* how much corn a given plot yielded during the last harvest (or what his total corn yield was during a given harvest period), he will invariably make an estimate in terms of *carretas* (cartsful) of unhusked corn ears or *fanegas* (a Spanish bushel containing 24 *almudes*). Less typically the estimate is given in terms of *piscadores* or basketsful. A *carreta* holds anywhere from 30 to 50 *piscadores* of unhusked corn ears (the average capacity is 40 *piscadores*), with each 10 *piscadores* yielding 1 *fanega* or 24 *almudes* of grained corn.

Similar statements could be made for other villages. Unfortunately, however, not only are the measures used imprecise, but meanings of the terms used vary from village to village. The difficulties are evident from the following discussion of measures of volume and area. The most common volume measures are the *almud,* the *fanega,* and the *carreta.*

Almud. The *almud* is used both as a measure of volume and as a basis of land measurement. As a measure of volume it is no longer legally recognized in Oaxaca. According to Santamaría's *Diccionario de Mejicanismos* (1959), in the state of Oaxaca an *almud* may vary from 3 to 16 liters. Within the Valley of Oaxaca, however, an *almud* of maize is usually equated with 4 liters (in Tlacolula, 5 liters,) or, commonly, 3.5 to 4.0 kilograms by weight. The latter figure is particularly unreliable, for the weight of a liter of maize will vary according to the size of the kernels and the amount of moisture contained. Thus newly harvested maize typically weighs more per liter than well-cured old maize.

A common assumption is that an *almud* of maize weighs 4.0 kilograms. Malinowski and de la Fuente (1957) reported this figure for the best quality *maíz bolita* but only 3.75 kilograms for *maíz grueso,* and 3.50 kilograms for *maíz delgado.* For San Antonino, Waterbury reports 3.50 kilograms per *almud* for *maíz delgado* and nearly 4.00 kilograms for *maíz grueso.* Nahmad (1965:48) reports 3.50 kilograms per *almud* in the Mixería, presumably for local *maíz criollo.* These figures are if anything high. Imported *arribeño* maize we found to weigh only 3.00 kilograms per *almud.* The Oaxaca peasant is keenly aware of such factors as age and moisture content. Prices of *criollo* (local) maize vary, but much confusion exists regarding the precise relationship of weight to volume. Larger maize dealers in the marketplace sell exclusively by weight, but small dealers often have concealed an illegal *almud* measure for customers who prefer the old system.

Fanega. This old Spanish measure, often referred to as the Spanish bushel, is extremely variable. In Oaxaca, it usually is defined as 24 *almudes* or 96 liters, but some people define it as 25 *almudes* (100 liters), the latter figure given in the *Diccionario de Mejicanismos.* (According to the *Encyclopedia Americana* the *fanega* equals 2.577 U.S. bushels, but calculations based on a *fanega* of 24 *almudes* give 2.72 U.S. bushels; a *fanega* of 25 *almudes* would be equivalent to 2.84 U.S. bushels.) Malinowski and de la Fuente (1957:165) considered the 25-almud *fanega* to be characteristic of most of the Valley, with the 24-*almud fanega* confined to Tlacolula and Etla. Variations found in our study are given at the top of the next page.

Carreta (a cartload). Obviously this is a highly variable measure. Maize yields are usually given in *carretas* of unhusked ears. Actually, the measure is somewhat realistic as *carretas* are of approximately the same size and theoretically are loaded to a standard depth. The yield in shelled maize varies, however, with the size of the ears. As a rule of thumb, the Valley peasants seem to equate a *carreta* of

	Almuds *per* fanega	*Liters per* almud
Diaz Ordaz	24	4
Magdalena Ocotlán	25	4
San Antonino Ocotlán	25	4
San Lázaro Etla	24	?
Santa María Atzompa	24	4
Tlacolula	24	5

unhusked maize with 5 *fanegas* of shelled corn, but large ears are said to yield only 4 *fanegas* and some informants report as little as 3 *fanegas* of shelled maize to a *carreta*. Others report as much as 6 *fanegas* per *carreta*.

Among common land measures are the *hectare*, the *almud*, the *yunta*, the *surco*, and others.

Hectare. This official measure equals 10,000 square meters or 2.47 U.S. acres. It is accurate only where lands have been surveyed by instruments.

Almud. As a measure of land, it is the amount of land that can be sown with one *almud* of maize seed. The common rule of thumb equates 4 *almudes* with one hectare, but in humid lands more seed is planted than in *temporal* (seasonal) lands. Diskin reports the use of 6 to 7 *almudes* of seed per hectare for Tlacolula, depending on whether the land is dry-farmed or irrigated. From San Antonino, Waterbury reports 2.5 to 3 *almudes* of seed per hectare for *tierra delgada*, the least fertile type of land; 4 *almudes* for land called *grueso* or moderately rich; and 5 to 6 *almudes* for very rich (*muy grueso*) land.

Yunta. A *yunta* is the amount of land that can be plowed in one day with an ox team. The rule of thumb equates a *yunta* of land with one *almud* or about one-quarter hectare.

Surco or furrow. Fields often are "measured" by the number of furrows. Informants usually say furrows are 60 centimeters apart. Measured furrows in Atzompa were 53 centimeters apart. The latter figure also is indicated for an 18-meter-wide plot in Magdalena Ocotlán said to have 34 furrows.

Other land measures. Other measures of land include the *merga*, the *tabla*, and the *tramo*. The *merga* equals a *yunta* (in Magdalena Ocotlán). The *tabla* equals 4 or 5 *yuntas* (in Magdalena Ocotlán). The *tramo* is a plot of variable size in an *ejido* (Magdalena Ocotlán).

The imprecision in weights and measures makes it impossible, then, to make satisfactory comparative statements about costs and returns. In making decisions such as those listed in appendixes 8 and 9, the farmer is operating on the basis of his knowledge of local conditions as they relate to his experience with a particular plot or plots of land, but he generally uses local standards and seldom has accurate quantitative information, particularly if the crop is used for subsistence and not measured out for sale.

Inputs in Farming

In addition to alternatives in activities, appendix 8 gives some standard cost values and time inputs as well as expected yields in a particular village. Appendix 12 summarizes inputs reported by informants in whom we had confidence.

All farming involves some capital expenditures. A household producing its own maize supply for nine months would have an investment in land (some of which might be inherited) of $2,100 or more at current prices. Minor tools would surely include a machete, sickle, and *coa*. A team of oxen, if purchased rather than hired, would have cost between $1,700 and $3,500 during the period of the study (unless the animals were especially mature or of a specialized breed such as the zebu, which enhances their value). Associated equipment (wooden plow, yoke, and yoke straps) requires an outlay of approximately $130. A new oxcart costs as much as $2,500 and a second-hand one about $1,800, but more commonly transportation is rented as needed.

Time inputs for a hectare of maize are difficult to estimate because of differences in the length of working days at various steps in the crop production process. For example, plowing is usually regarded as a half day's work, but the hours may vary from five to six, depending upon the age and weight of the ox teams. In an emergency a team may be worked somewhat longer hours, but not on a regular basis. But detailed figures for each step as well as overall estimates by informants suggest that if ox teams are used, the number of whole or part man-days worked per hectare is between 50 and 60. If a tractor is hired for the major plowing, the number of whole or part man-days is between 30 and 40.

All farmers for whom I have data use some hired labor (although this probably would not be true of farmers with small plots). For three farmers we have detailed labor figures (see appendix 12). These, together with estimates, suggest that cash inputs may vary from $70 to $140 per hectare on different types of land when most work is done by the farmer with his own equipment, to between $350 and $390 per hectare if a tractor is used and considerable labor employed.

If the major equipment is not owned, the cultivator of the land must anticipate costs of hiring ox teams for cultivating, and a cart, truck, or burros to bring in the harvest. The evidence indicates that the budget for a Valley farmer who hires tractor, ox teams, and all labor could be as much as $600 or more per hectare for one maize planting, excluding the value of food provided for hired labor. These figures include land preparation, furrowing, sowing, weeding, hilling, harvesting, hauling, and cutting and tying cornstalks for fodder. They do not include any calculation of the labor cost of husking and shelling corn, usually done in spare time and not calculated by any informant. (In the one observed case of labor hired for maize shelling, the pay was $8.00 per *fanega* shelled.) Neither do the figures include the allocated cost of labor contributed by members of the household.

Costs clearly will vary not only according to the bookkeeping scheme utilized but also according to the type of land cultivated. Smaller variations may result from differences in weed growth or size of crop caused by rainfall fluctuations from year to year. Costs of labor also may differ from one locality to another. To the cost figures for households owning ox teams must be added the value of feed for the animals. The value of feed for a team may run from $6.00 to $20.00 daily in the dry season, although most of it usually comes from the farmer's own lands. While in the wet season many farmers can feed their animals by pasturing on their own or public lands, this may involve an expense of about $1.00 a day for a herder.

It seems fairly clear that if spread through the year, the minimum operational budget for a farmer working one hectare of land with his own ox team is at least $1,200 in the value of cattle feed alone, assuming that all labor is provided by friends or relatives on a reciprocal basis. With one hectare producing as little as $400 in feed annually, ox-team hire may be the wiser choice.

Maize Yields

Yields are at least as difficult to estimate as input, for they vary with land quality and weather. On very good humid lands, yields usually vary from 10 to 20 *fanegas* per year (and alluvial or irrigated lands may take two sowings per year); poorer lands will produce less. Such yields will give a net return somewhere between $800 and perhaps $1,900 per hectare per crop, including the value of both maize and fodder. With very good second-class land, one hectare can produce enough maize to feed a young family of four comfortably, but only if it is superior alluvial land can it produce a surplus for animal feed or sale. Most figures suggest two hectares as a minimum needed for both consumption and trade or sale for a household of five or six members, three or four hectares if animals are raised. Consequently, a farmer with one hectare of land clearly must have nonfarm sources of income such as a handicraft, service, or wage labor.

Despite the imprecision of the data, there is enough similarity between calculated costs and returns from records that were kept, and from the gross estimates of reliable informants, to suggest that the Oaxaca farmer has considerable awareness of the economics of his operations.

Animal Raising

Evidence concerning the economics of animal raising is somewhat contradictory. Most Oaxaca farmers raise pigs and most believe that they make money in this type of activity. The data suggest that most of them do not, at least, not directly. Examination of data relating to animal purchase, amount of feed, and selling price shows very wide variations. It would appear that some people report low buying prices and optimal selling prices and have a poor idea of what they actually feed their hogs. Precise figures for feed expenses are difficult to secure, especially for maize. While Oaxaca peasants have a pretty good idea of the household's daily maize consumption, they are often at a loss to say how much of it goes to feed animals.

Most pigs are bought by households when young. They are brought to maturity, fattened and sold or occasionally butchered for a household fiesta. Very young poor quality shoats may be bought for as little as $40, but most young animals bring between $50 and $70 each. A good three-month-old animal may sell for about $100. Prices quoted for one-year-old animals range from $200 to $700 and are most commonly between $400 and $500. Forced sales because of shortage of feed or the need to meet emergency medical expenses may be for less. One such observed sale was for only $150.

Feeding costs vary with the age of the animal, and not all owners feed their pigs adequately. Underfeeding is economically unsound; the best practice is to fatten the animals as rapidly as possible. In the forced sale mentioned above, the animal was being fed two kilograms of maize daily worth at least $2.00, or at the rate of $60 per month. Reported feeding rates range from four kilograms a week for a five-month-old animal to four kilograms a day for a six-month-old.

Specific cases illustrate the problem of pig raising. One Atzompa pig raiser reported that he buys partially matured seven- to eight-month-old animals for $150 each, feed them two *fanegas* of maize each (valued at $200) over a three-month period, and sells them for around $500, receiving an apparent profit of $150. The figures, however, are suspect. The quoted buying price for an animal of this age is low; most informants report prices of $250 or more for eleven-month-old animals. Probably this informant also fed his pigs alfalfa or other food in addition to the maize feed he reported.

In dairying villages, where the whey from cheese making is fed to pigs, pig raising appears to be quite profitable. An informant at San Lázaro Etla, a dairying village, bought a six-week-old hog for $60 and a seven-week-old animal for $70; spent approximately $220 to fatten them with maize (including the value of maize he grew himself), whey, and alfalfa; and sold them after 17 weeks for $200 each, leaving a profit of $50, or $25 each. (Feed data for the first few weeks were missing in this case and were estimated from other cases.) Another informant at San Lázaro was spending $14.80 daily for maize, whey, and alfalfa to feed three eight-month-old hogs and one year-old animal. Other San Lázaro informants reported that (1) two hogs, eleven and thirteen weeks old, were being fed at the rate of only $0.95 each daily; (2) two hogs aged five months were fed at the rate of $2.90 each daily; and (3) three piglets two and eight weeks old, and one twelve weeks old, were being fed at the rate of $1.07 per day per animal. The better profits reported from pig raising in dairying villages probably result primarily from the fact that whey, a by-product of cheese making, is an excellent pig food that would be wasted if it were not fed to the pigs. Profits from pig raising in such cases thus are, at least partly, indirect profits from dairying.

No doubt some peasants in nondairying villages make money raising hogs and a few have a clear idea of values and feeding costs. But they are almost certainly the exception. Most peasants do not have any accurate idea of the value of the feed they are using, since the maize is taken from the household's food supplies, and decisions are influenced primarily by the apparent difference between the buying and selling price of animals. In addition, some informants who admitted they lost money raising pigs defended the practice as a means of forced savings. The necessity of feeding the pigs helped them to avoid the temptation to fritter away small cash surpluses or to sell maize stocks in order to spend money on luxuries or recreation. Thus, despite apparent accounting losses, pig raising might be economically advantageous if accumulation of capital did result from this activity which would not have resulted without it.

The profitability of other animal raising is even more difficult to evaluate. The most optimistic estimate of income from a mature sheep is $40 per year from wool sold in Teotitlán del Valle (a day's trip with bus fares involved) for a top price of $10 per kilogram. The same optimistic informant claimed he paid $36.50 per sheep per year for herding, leaving an annual margin of only $3.50 per sheep. This seems inadequate to cover labor for shearing, marketing costs, and the possible loss from sickness of mature animals, worth at least $100 each. Any returns from sheep raising clearly must come from selling the increase in the flock, but I have no reliable data on this. In any case, relatively few peasants engage in sheep raising because they do not have access to the necessary pasture lands.

Raising turkeys requires a heavy expenditure, for these are heavy feeders. As an example, a large turkey may eat as much as a half kilogram of maize a day. When they are small, maize consumption is less, but six to eight large turkeys will eat about one *almud* (4 liters) of maize a day, which at 1968 prices cost $4.00 daily, more than the cost of feed for a moderately large pig. Some say that it costs $15 to $20 in maize to produce a salable turkey. At the time of the study a very good price for a good hen turkey was about $50 and for a tom turkey perhaps as much as $70. Prices are somewhat higher in November and December, and some turkey raisers try to have their birds mature at that period. Unless turkeys can forage for part of their food, however, and are sold promptly when ready for the market, it is unlikely that profits are significant, if they exist at all. This is perhaps the reason that few people have more than three or four turkeys at a time. Moreover, these fowl are delicate and mortality is high, particularly when they are young. In cold and humid climates they cannot be raised at all.

The profits of dairying and cheese making are similarly ambiguous. Summaries of several enterprises are given in appendix 13.

Handicraft Production

Data on handicraft production again suggest that the households involved in it often do not make enough profit for an adequate living. Appendix 14 summarizes some cases of pottery-making households. The data in the first case are taken from records kept by an informant; the remainder are derived from informants' estimates of expenditures and receipts. The data show considerable fluctuations in production and income, probably reflecting in part variations in market conditions. Some returns do not equal what could be earned by steady work as a *mozo*. In contrast, handicraft production is a higher-status occupation than that of laborer and gives greater independence. In most instances the household engages in complementary income-producing activities.

Service Activities

In contrast to handicraft inputs, most service occupations entail costs that are low and infrequent. A barber needs only scissors, comb, and perhaps a portable chair, although he also may invest in a cloth and perhaps a perfumed hair dressing. A mason needs a measuring tape, level, plane, plumbline, trowel, and a ball of string or thread; he might also purchase a hammer and chisel. These implements vary in quality. One mason estimated the cost of his tools to be "less than $100," another estimated the cost to be between $25 and $30. Such items need replacement only at long intervals.

Such data as are available on production activities suggest that most of them are only marginally profitable. Although Oaxaca peasants do consistently seek to minimize costs and maximize returns, clearly they often base their decisions on inadequate information. Multiple occupations are in part an effort to maximize the use of time that is not fully utilized by the primary occupation, and in part an effort to discover more advantageous ways of making a living. This search for "greener pastures" no doubt leads so many peasants to say that they would prefer a regular job with a fixed income, even though the wage might be relatively low. It also explains, perhaps, why they so rarely calculate labor costs. Man must work to live. He works at what he can or knows how to do. If it produces enough to feed, shelter, and clothe his family with some decency, and to meet his social obligations, then his economic activities are successful.

The discussion also indicates that an adequate idea of the economics of production requires much more carefully planned and detailed studies than the data gathering that was carried out incidentally in connection with the investigation of the exchange system. Such studies would require long-term, detailed observation of specific household activities; resources to undertake such a project on the scale needed were inadequate.

5
The Consumption and
Expenditure System

This chapter examines the nature of consumer wants in the context of the peasant village, the reciprocal relationships of peasant consumption and the traditional marketing system, and some recent modifications resulting from the effects of the modern industrial economy. It focuses on the common economic patterns and processes and suggests some of the range of variation to be found. Necessarily, such generalizing obscures somewhat the extent of variation between villages and between households within villages. A full understanding of consumption in the region would require more extensive sampling and more detailed studies of economic life in the various communities.

The term "expenditure" is included in the heading because "consumption" often is associated only with the using up of consumer's goods. The expenditures of the household—the primary consumption unit—involve much more than the utilization of consumer's goods; they involve all the ways in which people expend their resources of goods, labor, and money. As we shall see, the consumption system and the structure of demands that are concomitant to it not only are heavily dependent upon the marketing system for their satisfaction but also influence market activity and behavior to a significant extent.

Not all consumption can be viewed simply in household terms. The household is the major agency for meeting the basic survival needs of its members and also for providing those gratifications considered for cultural reasons to be necessary or desirable for a satisfying life. Yet meeting many of these cultural needs involves larger social units. And to the extent that villages vary in their cultural standards and demands, the village also might be regarded as a unit of analysis for consumption as it is for production. For the purposes of this discussion, however, village differences will be given minimal attention so as to focus on the more basic unit of consumption.

CLASSES OF HOUSEHOLD CONSUMPTION

For convenience household consumption and expenditure patterns are discussed under the rubrics of a subsistence budget, an operational budget, and a public and festive budget. Although these categories are not clearly recognized by the peasant, they form a hierarchy of demands for goods and services whose gratification depends upon available resources and responses to various goals. Demands may vary not only from household to household but also at various times within a single household.

To elaborate these categories, most households not only provide for the basic subsistence needs of food, clothing, and shelter, but they also consume goods or make expenditures related to production, to the achievement or validation of status and prestige, and to maintaining the social order of the community. The production of food and handicrafts requires the purchase of tools, raw materials, and at times labor. Most households sponsor public ceremonial or ritual events such as *mayordomías* and carry on household observances connected with the Day of the Dead, Christmas, and to some extent Easter, and also make expenditures for baptisms, first communions, weddings, and funerals. Public office holding requires expenditures of time, which is taken from productive activities, and in some communities requires validating ceremonials. Maintenance of community facilities traditionally involves labor time, provision of goods, and contributions of money. Modernly it may involve fees, assessments, and formal taxation.

For analytical purposes these classes of expenditures may be viewed as separate budgets. This is not a new idea. Wolf (1966) speaks of the peasant's "ceremonial fund" and "replacement fund." Nash refers to "the budgets of consuming units, the hierarchy and regularity of wants, and the savings and disposal of wealth" (1966:5), although he provides no breakdown of these. In suggesting the preceding classification, I emphasize that the classes are analytical artifacts, not categories to be found in the thinking of Oaxaca peasants. For example, few if any peasants think of public ritual or community activities and the attending consumption as being undertaken for purposes of status and prestige. Instead, they are commonly referred to as *servicios,* services to the community. Nevertheless, such services are frequently cited as reasons for according high prestige to members of the community.

The segments of the three-way classification are not mutually exclusive. The ethnocentric view of many observers, including most anthropologists, is that much of the public budget, especially the very large expenditures for some ceremonies, is a completely uneconomic dispersal of resources. Not only are there extensive cash outlays, it is argued, but household reserves of food are dissipated and cannot be sold for cash. The only possible returns often are seen by outsiders as status, prestige, or religious gratification.

This overlooks the fact that a large part of the expenditures serves to feed a substantial number of guests. For example, out of $7,543 in cash and goods spent for a *cofradía* (brotherhood) fiesta in Santa María Atzompa in 1968, $3,852 was spent for food, not including liquor. Out of $3,121 in cash and goods spent for a wedding (the figure does not include the cost of the bride's clothes, which is also the groom's responsibility), $2,538 was spent for food and its preparation. Of $1,672 spent for a one-day Christmas *mayordomía*, $730 was spent on food and food preparation. Food hence is a major part of most festive expenditures, and in some (perhaps all) villages it normally is provided in such abundance that guests bring containers to carry away food (and often liquor) that they cannot consume on the premises. Such behavior is expected; not to eat or carry away all that is served is an affront to the host.

The important point here is that this food is not destroyed or lost in some limbo. It is eaten. It is true that some of it is luxury food not commonly included in daily diets. For some poor households (and in the Sierra this might comprise most households), the fiestas may be almost the only occasion when essential animal protein is eaten. But the food eaten at fiestas does not have to be provided in the guests' own daily household budgets, which are thereby reduced.

This argument is somewhat weakened because guests often bring presents to the giver of the fiesta. Nevertheless, there is clearly a relationship between fiesta budgets and the food expenditures of guests. This relationship is not unimportant, for many people spend 30 or more days a year as guests in fiestas. Nor are the dishes or clothing bought by the hosts especially for the fiesta discarded thereafter. The only major "lost" expenditures are for music, liquor (depending upon one's viewpoint), fireworks, and the mass when one is required. Even in these cases, expenditures for the various nonfood items provide income for others, and often involve market transactions. Moreover, although the host of a fiesta has provided food to others, he may expect as a quid pro quo to be fed in turn by them in the future. A proper evaluation of these relationships would require a more intensive study of fiesta consumption and attendance than the project could undertake, and should extend over a period of years.

Subsistence Budget

Subsistence consumption is defined as that consumption necessary to supply the basic living requirements of the household unit. Most obviously, it consists of the food, clothing, and shelter necessary for the members of the household to survive and carry on life activities. In space-age terms it might be called the life support system. The system includes more, however, than mere food and shelter as these might be defined by minimal physiological needs; it also includes expenditures for things that are defined as essential by the villager's cultural background and training.

The subsistence budget hence is not to be viewed as merely providing adequate food and shelter but as providing satisfying amounts of the kinds of food and shelter people have come to desire and expect as the result of their cultural conditioning. It certainly includes meeting some minimal health requirements, for example, the services of midwives, herbal or magical curers, and, for growing numbers, resort to modern medical services and medicines. It may even be considered to include religious services necessary to maintain psychological well-being as well as maintenance of security through participation in the systems of prestige and status. The latter item, however, will be considered as a separate category.

The subsistence budget consists of several subsegments. One involves the essentially perishable or short-lived goods necessary to maintain life, that is, the food supply. These goods must be available on a daily basis and are used up. They are called *transitory* goods by some economists. A separable category may be termed semidurable consumption goods, that is, necessary nonfood items that, once acquired, may be used repeatedly over a relatively short but still substantial period of time before they require replacement. These include clothing, baskets, blankets and sleeping mats, and short-lived household equipment necessary to feeding the household, such as pottery. Often acquisition or replacement of these may be deferred on a short-term basis. For example, if resources are scarce, worn or ragged clothing may continue to be worn past what the wearers would consider the normal replacement time. A third category, durable consumption goods, consists of necessary household equipment that usually requires a fairly large capital expenditure and has a fairly long life. Such goods may be used over and over, once acquired. For example, a metate (quern), normally acquired as a wedding present, could last an entire lifetime although commonly it is used up and replaced once or twice during a lifetime. Wood and metal household wares, furniture, and the house altar and its furnishings (indispensable for most Oaxaca peasants), are among other items in this category. A house in which people live, in the Oaxaca context, may also be considered in part to be a consumption item as well as a capital good. Even the flimsiest house construction has a life of several years; a properly maintained tile-roofed adobe structure may last more than a lifetime.

The problem of measuring food consumption may be approached in at least three ways: one is to ascertain what foods are produced in the village and in what amounts; a second is to identify foods distributed through the market system; and a third is to examine actual food budgets. Each of these approaches has both qualitative and quantitative aspects. As in many other areas dealt with in this study, the quantitative aspect can be treated only suggestively, not definitively. This latter has two facets: the quantity of food consumed, and its monetary value. Among the subsidiary problems are the ways food is distributed, the extent to which consumption patterns are modified by variations in economic resources and fluctuations in supply and in price, the economic choices recognized, and the process of decision-making about foods to be eaten.

The food production problem is dealt with in chapter 4 and the important data are summarized in appendix 6. Production data have several shortcomings as a source of information about consumption. Some important items listed in appendix 6 are produced primarily for the market. Also, villages may differ markedly in the extent to which a locally produced item either remains in the community (e.g., is traded within each village because of household differences in production-consumption patterns), or goes into intervillage trade, supplying the town and city, or is exported in the interregional market system. As examples, avocados and coffee are produced in large quantities in some villages. Both go primarily into the interregional market. Although most villages probably consume some of these products, the amounts consumed are small even in the villages where they are produced. Avocados are not a particularly favored fruit in the producing area.[1] And even in many coffee production centers, little coffee is used locally.

If a village produces one of the basic foods (what these are is discussed later), we may be sure that local consumption will normally have first call upon the production. But in most such villages, some households either produce none of the basic foods or produce an inadequate amount of them for their own use. For example, cacao is essential for many ceremonial occasions, and in many Valley villages chocolate appears to be a preferred drink for those who can afford it; but except for a small amount of this product grown in the coastal Sierra, cacao is imported from Chiapas.

About all we can conclude from the production data is that the Oaxaca villagers consume a wide variety of foodstuffs. They tell us nothing about how universally these foods are used either in terms of villages or in terms of individual households, nor do they indicate the quantities consumed.

---

[1] In 1933 in the Mixe village of Ayutla, before the development of interregional trade in avocados, most of the crop of a large and highly productive native avocado tree on public lands rotted on the ground. Despite a very limited food supply and a diet that, to an outsider, can only be described as grim in its lack of variety and of fruits or vegetables, the avocado crop was used only occasionally in preparing a dish for fiestas. Most of the time during my work there in 1933, I was the only consumer and had to organize and constantly stimulate collection of the fruit.

Similarly, the analysis of foods sold in the marketplace and through other distribution mechanisms confirms that a wide variety of goods are used. For the purpose of analyzing village consumption, the goods offered in secondary markets, especially by small vendors serving primarily buyers from the villages, and the goods offered by local vendors or peddlers and by stores in the village, are more meaningful than the list of goods sold in the large daily markets of the city of Oaxaca. But again, these lists of goods do not tell us how general their use is, and they give us little more than impressions about quantities consumed. (See chapter 6 for discussion of distribution.)

The best source of information, of course, is data concerning what households actually consume (app. 15). The budgets constitute the most important body of data about food consumption both quantitatively and qualitatively, although other data are needed also if we are to understand food distribution. Such data include types of family economies (app. 16), data on food consumed in Valley villages (app. 17), also nonfood items (app. 18), and imported products (app. 19). A composite inventory of household items (app. 20) shows what items are actually used. The collection of household budgets, unfortunately, is a difficult and time-consuming task that yields only imperfect results. In the first place, truly random or representative information cannot be secured; the investigator is limited to those families or households willing to cooperate, and unless the investigator lives with a family intimately over a period of time and keeps the records himself, he is further limited to literate families. The best source of such data is a cooperative, literate family willing to keep records. Even so, the data ideally should be checked daily or twice daily by the investigator to prevent oversights and omissions. Nevertheless, a good deal of casual consumption by individual household members outside the house is certain to be overlooked or not reported. Children or adults may collect *guaje* pods in the fields or at roadsides and eat the beans; the odd few *centavos* of candy, cookies, or fruit purchased in store or market are apt not to be reported; meals taken at fiestas or weddings commonly are overlooked or, if reported, quantities are given in only vague terms and values are not even estimated.

From observation and from informants' reports, however, we can identify the following list of basic goods:

Food items:

Beans	Garlic	Onions
Beef	Greens (often but not	Pork
Bread	always squash greens)	Salt
Cheese	Herbs	Squash and squash seeds
Chile peppers (green)	Lard	Sugar
Chile peppers (dried)	Lime	Tomatoes
Chocolate	Maize	

Nonfood items:
    Fuel   Soap or detergent
    Matches   (soap root a possible
    Pitch pine or candles[2]   temporary alternative)

These consumption goods vary considerably in importance both qualitatively and quantitatively. Some are less "basic" than others in the sense that their unavailability for a time would not result in actual want. They are included as basic, however, because they occur in all the household budgets collected on a fairly regular basis, even for the poorest families studied. The quantities consumed and the cost of each item of course vary from one household to another and even within a particular household, over time. A few *centavos* may be spent weekly on garlic, and but little more on tomatoes, onions, or chile peppers. Nonfarmers may raise greens or herbs in the house yard or collect them along the roadside in a pinch. Chocolate may be consumed daily or only once a week or even less. (A few do not like chocolate or say it does not agree with them.) Chocolate may be purchased in prepared form, but if it is consumed regularly the family may prepare its own. An example of a 15-day supply for a large family consuming home-prepared chocolate fairly regularly gives the following expenses:

Cacao, 1 kilogram	$18.00
Almonds, 2 ounces	1.00
Cinnamon, 25 grams	2.00
Sugar, 2.5 kilograms	4.00
	$25.00

Not included is the cost of power-milling the first three ingredients (hand-milling is an alternative) and the value of the two hours' labor to mix ingredients and mold the chocolate into tablets. The tablets are shaped in a mold, and the residue that cannot be scooped up conveniently in the mold is rolled into balls. Households that prepare their own chocolate often sell part of each batch either to storekeepers or in the *plaza* for a small profit.

Only the consumption pattern of the major basic item, maize, will be analyzed in detail. The amount of maize consumed per capita varies somewhat with the amount of bread eaten. One point of special interest in the Oaxaca budgets is the

---

[2] This might be questioned as a "basic" item. Reliance on firelight might be possible, but in most villages fuel is very scarce. A very poor family might rely on leaves, dead shrubs, and similar fuel scavenged along roads, trails, and field borders, for enough fuel for essential cooking; but it would be difficult to obtain enough for useful lighting. Most cooking fires provide inadequate illumination even for food preparation. The alternative to pitch pine, candles, or other lighting is to limit drastically activities in the hours of darkness.

amount of bread consumed; contrary to some stereotypes about Indian diets in Mesoamerica, it is often eaten on a daily basis. Despite the relatively high bread consumption, maize remains the most inflexible item in household consumption. Exact figures for consumption are difficult to come by for two reasons: if the family has animals—and few do not have at least chickens—the maize fed to them is usually included as part of total household consumption; further, if some of the maize is produced by the household, the daily amounts are rarely measured or weighed. Informants' estimates from a sample of 80 households in Atzompa give a human dry maize consumption ranging from 0.26 to 0.80 kilograms per person per day, with an average of 0.51 kilograms. A calculation of human consumption for Diaz Ordaz gives 0.49 kilograms of dry maize. A figure for Zoogocho in the Sierra gives 1.1 kilogram of dry maize per person, but this may include animal feed. Also, much less bread probably is eaten in the Sierra, and consumption of animal protein is lower.[3]

For a household of two adults and two children 6 and 8 years of age (this hypothetical household is used as the basis for all estimates), it is estimated that the minimal annual maize consumption, based on a daily consumption of 0.5 kilograms per person, is 730 kilograms, costing between $700 and $800 at 1967 prices. (At $1.05 per kilogram the exact cost would be $766.50.) This figure is at or close to an absolute minimum for long-term survival. It represents the one item that must somehow be provided daily. Nevertheless, the annual maize intake is not greatly increased for households in better economic circumstances. The maximum consumption probably would not exceed 950 kilograms annually for such a family,

---

[3] The figure for maize consumption is difficult to establish although it is crucial to budget analysis. For the Maya, Cowgill (1971:55–56 and personal letter) estimated 636 pounds of maize per adult per year (0.80 kg. per person per day). This would approximate 1,154 kg. per year for a family of four adults. Lewis's (1963:192) estimate for a well-to-do family of four adults at Tepoztlan is 546 *cuartillos* or 1,021 liters; assuming a weight of 875 grams per liter, this amounts to about 893 kg. per year. Figures from Michoacan by four authors (Belshaw [1967] in Huecorio; Brand [1951] in Quiroga; Beals [1946] in Cherán; and Rees [1971] in Capacuaro and San Lorenzo, vary only slightly from the lowest estimate (by Rees) of 864 kg. annually for a family of four adults. In Veracruz State, Coe (1969) calculated a per-person range of maize consumption between 200 and 240 kg. per year at San Lorenzo Tenochtitlan—an average of 880 kg. for a family of four, or 0.60 kg. per person per day. Except for Cowgill's figure, all these estimates fall between my own estimated minimum (730 kg.) and maximum (950 kg.) annual maize consumption figures for the hypothetical Oaxaca household (app. 16), which, however, consists of two adults and two children.

Crucial as maize is to the survival of the household, its importance can easily be overestimated in relation to total expenditures for food. Beals (1946:85) estimated that maize comprised 9.3 percent of the total food budget for a family of five in Cherán. Foster (1948:158–162) estimated maize to be 11 to 20 percent of the budget for the well-to-do in Tzintzuntzan, as high as 30 percent for an impoverished family. Oaxaca peasants must have maize to survive but they do not live by maize alone.

although an additional quantity probably would be consumed by the household's animals. Usually, per capita consumption of maize is inversely related to household income, that is, the lower the income, the more maize is consumed. Increased economic resources normally result in increased expenditures for other foods, especially bread, rice, *pasta*, and animal protein, usually with an accompanying reduction in maize consumption. Similarly, bean consumption in poor households generally is higher than in more prosperous households. As the consumption of meat, fish, and cheese rises, bean consumption declines.

The estimated annual budget for food and essential food-related items for a landless family is minimally $2,122 (app. 16, Family Type A). This allows for no expenditures for sweets or refreshments, school expenses for children, medical costs, or participation in any social or ceremonial events. It also assumes that all maize is hand milled, although in the Valley few households grind maize entirely by hand. Such a household almost never consumes chocolate; and meat and cheese probably would not be purchased more than once or twice a week. As we shall see below, this still is not the minimum budget for long-term existence, for some nonfood items are essential. The important point here is that such landless families must secure all their food in the market or through intravillage trade.

Unlike the landless household, a family producing all or part of its maize and perhaps other food items is less directly dependent on the market for necessities, but the way it utilizes its own food production still is affected by market considerations. Even if the maize produced by a household is inadequate for its yearly consumption needs, some of it may be sold to get capital for carrying on a handicraft, for example, or to purchase animals, or for other types of capital expenditures. Such households then rely on selling wage labor or getting income from nonfarm activities such as handicrafts to buy maize later in the year. If a surplus of maize is produced, it may be sold; alternatively, such a surplus may be used to fatten animals, possibly to effect a larger return from ultimate sales; or it may be kept against a possible crop shortage the following year. Households producing some or all of their own maize usually will spend somewhat less in the market for basic foods, but normally they expand the consumption of other food items. it is estimated in our hypothetical budget that a family of four would still spend a minimum of $1,753 to $1,803 a year on food (excluding related necessities) in the marketplace or in intravillage trade (app. 16).

Even the poorest family in Oaxaca requires more than the essential foods to survive on a long-term basis. The minimum budget household requires some "soft goods." The minimum annual expenditure for clothing would be around $350 (app. 16). Any family that can afford to do so spends more than this. Other short-lived household equipment would have a value of around $200. Assuming an estimated 40 percent replacement rate annually, these goods would cost about $80.

The total minimum cash budget for a landless household, then, is at least $2,550 a year, of which food is the major item. In addition, such a household will have an investment in housing, unless it rents quarters, and a few durable items of household equipment such as a metate and mano, a trunk, and a machete or knife, valued at about $175. Unless friends or relatives have allowed it to live on their house lot, or it is able to "squat" on public or semipublic lands, such a family will usually own the real property as well. Such capital expenditures have not been taken into account in the minimum annual budget.

Once household subsistence budgets exceed the basic survival requirements, living levels rise. Budgets usually include some public consumption expenditures, and the lines between budget segments are less clear. Households operating permanently at the minimal survival level over any length of time seem rare in the peasant villages. Further consideration of subsistence budgets will be included in a discussion of living levels, below.

Operational Budget

Any family engaged in farming or handicrafts has an operational budget consisting of the expenditures required to carry on such production activities. As we have seen in the discussion of production, most peasants engaged in farming have need of some cash outlays for maintaining or hiring tractive animals or, in some cases, for hiring a tractor; for hiring labor in various stages of the cultivation process; for hauling and for marketing. Animal raising may require expenditures for animal purchases, feed, breeding fees, inoculations, medicines, or veterinary fees. Moreover, artisans must buy raw materials as well as make investments in equipment, and the craft occupation may influence their production and consumption patterns in other areas. If they are landowners, for example, they may elect to sharecrop the land or to engage in low labor-cost production as against other alternatives (such as raising garden vegetables as a cash crop) requiring a high labor input; and their wives may purchase prepared foods and manufactured clothing, lacking the time to produce clothing or tortillas at home, and even seek laundering services in other noncraft villages.

Similarly, some specialists make expenditures to carry on their activities. *Arrieros* (traders who use pack animals) are in the market fairly frequently for animal replacements, and all kinds of traders are constantly in the market to acquire goods for resale. For service occupations, however, operational expenditures are generally low and replacement costs so infrequent (see chap. 4, above) that they might be viewed as minor capital expenditures. The only Oaxaca villagers who lack an operational budget are landless laborers or employees who do not engage in any handicraft production or skilled occupation requiring expenditures for materials or implements. A landless schoolteacher or salaried employee may be in a favored economic position compared with fellow villagers not only because his income is regular and assured but also because he has little or no operational budget requirements.

Those who make expenditures to carry on production of goods or services rarely if ever make a clear distinction between the subsistence and the operational budgets and certainly do not keep them separate. A single purse is used for both, and the demands upon it require a constant balancing of needs with resources. Subsistence expenditures often are curtailed or deferred owing to production needs. Likewise, funds from productive activities supported by the operational budget are expended for subsistence.

Public and Festive Budget

In addition to the expenditures for household subsistence and for maintaining productive operations, all but the most poverty-stricken Oaxaca peasant households make expenditures for other goods and services. Most of these are related to the maintenance of community functions as these are locally defined. Analytically they may be identified as recreational or as establishing or maintaining status and prestige. Such distinctions are not ordinarily made by the peasants, however, who recognize as *servicios* or *cargos* those activities that a household owes to the community. The common factors in all these types of expenditure are that they involve persons outside the household as guests or participants and/or are undertaken because of informal public pressure.

One expenditure pattern that does not directly involve outsiders but is influenced by public opinion or outside pressures to some degree is the purchase of new clothing in connection with Easter and for some other major holidays such as the fiesta of the patron saint of the village. There is no direct public pressure to do this, but not to buy new clothes in a sense advertises the household's poverty. In many villages, indeed, an Independence Day parade of school children usually is marked by purchase of some new clothing—new trousers for one child, new shoes for another. Costumes are needed if children participate in dances or pageants at school graduation exercises, and usually a child graduating from school has a new outfit. Here some actual pressure probably operates, partly from the schoolteachers, partly from a desire to "keep up appearances" so the children will not be shamed. Moreover, many parents take a good deal of pride in the appearance of their children on such occasions.

On November 1, All Saints' Day, almost everyone buys flowers to place on the graves of deceased relatives and food for gift exchange with *compadres* (fictive kin) and friends. This holiday is also an occasion for buying new equipment such as chocolate beaters and pottery for household use. It is a period of quasi-ceremonial activity of great importance to the marketing system, the time of highest prices and greatest volume of sales.

In addition, from time to time most households buy objects for the household altar such as flowers, candles, incense burners, paper ornaments, and pictures or small statues of saints. At the sides of the altar or near it, secular pictures cut from magazines may also be tacked up. Most peasants take some pride in their altars, which occupy a prominent position in the houses of almost everyone but Protestant converts.

Far more important are the expenditures for parties of various sorts. In most villages there are a good many saint's-day (name-day) parties, especially in the more prosperous villages, accompanied by food, drink, music, and dancing. These may cost from $200 to $1,000. Music expenses (usually $50 a day for a phonograph with loudspeaker and records) are shared by *compadres*. No prestige seems to attach to these events; the prime motivation for them appears to be recreational. Attendance normally is by invitation; the guests are *compadres*, relatives, neighbors, and friends. It is good form for guests to bring a present of soft drinks, beer, or mescal. If a party extends through several days, the gift may be repeated each time the guest returns.

The most prestige-conferring expenditures are for the *mayordomía* or sponsorship of the fiesta of a saint, but there are many lesser events that also confer prestige. The less expensive (and less prestigeful) observances are the baptismal fiesta, reciprocated by the godfather at the time of the *sacamisa* or *sacada de misa*, and the first communion fiesta. Baptismal fiestas may be modest, requiring only a few hundred pesos' outlay, or they may be elaborate, with many guests, last for days, and cost a thousand or more pesos. The baby's godfather is required to purchase the baptismal clothes. A first communion usually requires, in addition to fiesta costs, an elaborate white outfit for the child.

A large funeral and *levantada de cruz* ceremony may be more prestigeful than a baptism or first communion, depending partly on the amount of money spent. A vigil of nine nights is held after burial; prayers continue and guests are fed. On the last night, the *cruz* or cross (a religious picture fashioned of mineral lime and other color elements), formed by a specialist at the home of the deceased, is scooped up by *compadres* selected for the occasion and carried off to the grave. If the family is poor, the ceremony is abridged: a simple cross is designed of lime at the time of the funeral and cast into the grave at the burial.

Weddings tend to be elaborate and to involve *guelaguetza*, a system of reciprocal exchange or loans that normally must be repaid in the same amount and kind at a future time (see Beals [1970] for a discussion of *guelaguetza* and other forms of gifts and loans). In one village, for example, a wedding involving a week-long *fandango* cost $3,335 in cash, if the value of the household's maize consumed is included. In addition, the family called for repayment of *guelaguetza* obligations that it had previously "planted" at fiestas sponsored by other households, in the amount of $348 in cash and $255 in goods. Also, guests provided or "planted" with the host $358 in cash and $271 in goods (new *guelaguetza* "plants" ideally are duplicated when the *guelaguetza* is "called"), to be repaid by the host at some future date. The number of guests did not exceed 51, but some of them brought *guelaguetza* contributions each day they attended. The apparent cost of this wedding, then, was $4,567. The figure does not include gifts to bride and groom by *compadres* and friends. Another wedding is reported to have cost $3,481; whether this includes *guelaguetza* exchanges or domestic food supplies is not certain.

More definitely in the category of public consumption in the view of the Oaxaca peasant is the *mayordomía*, involving a fiesta and other services for a particular local saint for a year. *Mayordomía* and *cofradía* festivals are generally considered necessary for the good of the community, and public pressure may be exerted on a household to accept sponsorship of an event if there are no volunteers. Frequently, however, the motivations of the sponsor are individual, for example, fulfillment of a personal vow made to a saint in time of sickness, or as a form of religious "insurance" to promote the future well-being of the family. *Mayordomía* sponsorship thus combines public service, achievement of prestige and status, and satisfaction of private religious needs.[4]

Such festivals usually involve major expenditures. A comparatively wealthy *mayordomo* in Atzompa spent $2,129 on a feast on the day of the saint; total expenditures for the year, however, were $4,266, including refreshments served to the *mayordomos* of other saints on conventional occasions during the year, flowers for the saint's niche, and so on. This figure does not include *guelaguetza* loans collected or "planted" at the feast. In the same village, a much poorer *mayordomo* spent only $1,672, not including reciprocal loans. The expenditures include payments for food, cigarettes, liquor, fireworks, firewood, music, candles, flowers, and the mass. Costs for a similar type of fiesta sponsored by a religious brotherhood (*cofradía*) totaled $7,543. In the generally poorer area of the northern Sierra, four *mayordomías* analyzed by Berg involved expenditures of $2,807.75, $2,466.00, $3,021.70, and $3,370.00. Field notes do not indicate whether these totals include reciprocal loans or household food supplies. The data suggest that *mayordomías* may cost from around $2,000 to nearly $8,000. Poor families usually do not undertake sponsorship of important *mayordomías*, although even laborers

---

[4] The *mayordomía* is a form of wealth redistribution and often is treated as if this was its only function. As the preceding paragraph should make clear, the *mayordomía* serves numerous other functions from the standpoint of the individual sponsor.

may sponsor one of the less costly affairs. In addition, even wealthier families increasingly are unwilling to undertake expensive *cargos*, preferring to use their resources for more economic ends or higher levels of living. Families that do not ever sponsor a *mayordomía*, however, are regarded with low esteem if they are poor and with some hostility if they are wealthy, as people who lack interest in community welfare.

In many villages the importance of public service has declined under the influence of modern ideas, but this is not always so. Writing of Mitla in the early 1950s, Leslie (1960:12) comments:

> The most obvious connection between Mitla's prosperity and its resistance to disintegration resides in the fact that the townspeople turned a significant part of their increased wealth into expenditures on mayordomías and other ceremonials. Whether this public spirit would have persisted if still more opportunities had existed for the profitable investment of savings is a question which must await further research into the history of the town.

Whether the festivity is for the household members alone or for a small group of friends, *compadres*, and relatives, or for a large group, special foods are expected such as the *mole* (chile sauce) dish that is served on most occasions of importance. While there is a steady market for poultry for everyday use in the towns, especially in Oaxaca City, the demand is expanded and general throughout the region for festive foods served during All Saints' week and the Christmas-New Year period. Fowl are considered appropriate for other special occasions too. For example, a leading weaver of Teotitlán del Valle invited many of his friends and regular customers to dinner on the occasion of the fiesta of the patron saint of the village. For this occasion he served turkey *mole*, for which he had bought several birds. Other villagers also had prepared special foods for chance visitors.

Holding certain public offices such as that of mayor, or member of the town council or of a special commission, is also regarded as public service and as conferring prestige, comparable to serving as a *mayordomo* for a ceremonial. Generally these public offices do not involve direct expenditures on the part of the officeholders, although in the more conservative villages, especially in the Sierra, officeholders are required to make some ceremonial expenditures. In contrast, in the Valley some officers may even be paid a nominal sum, often less than $1.00 per day. The main economic impact on the officeholder is loss of income. The time involved usually makes it impossible for him to maintain his normal level of production, and he often suffers a considerable loss of income for the year he holds office, especially in the case of the mayor (*presidente municipal*). As with *mayordomías*, for economic reasons some people today refuse to accept such offices or take them only under considerable pressure. They prefer to maximize their incomes as new consumption goals, such as the purchase of modern goods, replace the traditional prestige goals.

In addition to office holding, households are expected to contribute labor or hire a substitute for public works. The occasions for communal labor vary considerably from village to village but may include repairing streets or trails, repairing or constructing public buildings, or cultivating communally owned lands for support of town or school activities. In some villages contributions of materials, sometimes involving a cash outlay, or cash assessments may be levied for purchase of construction materials. In some remote areas, service to the village may require serving as porter or messenger. The Aztec term *tequio* (work) is still used for labor levies. In remote villages some coercion may be involved, including fines. Elsewhere, clearly manifested public disapproval of noncompliance usually is effective in securing service by the unwilling. Although this type of service does not directly involve consumption and only rarely involves cash expenditure, it does require expenditure of time and labor.

Almost everywhere taxes now are levied on businesses and private property. For example, taxes are collected on land and house lots. The amounts seem variable, and in villages with few external controls, collection is not thorough. In a few samplings, a *solar* (house lot) estimated by the owner to be worth $500 was taxed $15.00, and in another village, taxes on house lots ranged from $3.00 to $35.00 annually. In San Lázaro Etla, according to the local tax collector, most people pay only a nominal tax on their lots but he estimated that the tax on a $1,000 lot with a $10,000 house would be $165. Taxes on *milpa* (maize) land seem nominal or nonexistent. One owner reported paying $19.00 annually on four hectares. Storekeepers, butchers, and owners of phonographs for rent also pay business taxes. In San Lázaro, for example, municipal taxes on business enterprises were uniformly $3.00 monthly; state taxes ranged from zero to $40.00 monthly.

Two modern assessments in Oaxaca are for the installation of piped drinking water and installation of electricity. Part of the cost of installation is borne by federal and state agencies. Although arrangements for electricity appear to vary, for example, the federal rural electrification commission installs high tension lines to the edge of the town or village. Residents of the community are required to contribute about one-third to the cost of the distribution system within the village. This usually means assessments of from about $180 to $225 per household. If a householder elects to have electricity in his house he pays a further nominal charge. In some villages variable assessment scales apparently are used. In any case, collection of assessments often is a prolonged and rarely completed process. Additional assessments may be made later to improve, extend, or replace distribution lines or to drill new wells for potable water systems.

While water and electricity installation assessments are usually one-time charges, they involve further monthly charges against household budgets. Water must be pumped and the system maintained. The town council must raise money to pay for street lighting, and individual households must pay for private use. Electricity is not always metered, and charges sometimes are based on number of outlets, size of bulbs used, and equipment owned. Some households may refuse to use electricity, but for most villages where electricity has been installed, the majority of the households now pay a monthly fee for private use. Because of high initial assessments and continuing charges, some villagers may resist the installation of electricity. In the case of Diaz Ordaz, for example, installation of electricity was rejected for at least three years after the transmission lines had reached the edge of the settlement.

Not only does the character of public consumption vary from one household to another, but more secular forms of public consumption are growing at the expense of ceremonial consumption. The discussion, I hope, makes it clear that most households do make public contributions, and family members consider it a proper and expectable part of their expenditure pattern.

PLANNING AND SAVING

The foregoing analysis of consumption budgets by categories may create an illusion that the Oaxaca peasant engages in more precise planning of his consumption than is actually true. Clearly there is some short-range planning in food expenditures and in operational expenditures related to essential productive activities. There also must be careful planning and evaluation of potential resources before undertaking any major public expenditures. This is most obvious perhaps in the "planting" of *guelaguetza* obligations, sometimes years in advance of an anticipated wedding or *mayordomía* responsibility. There may be considerable medium-range planning to make some important investment such as in a lot, house, lands, or ox teams, but except when specific goals have been determined, savings in the abstract are not budgeted. Most informants freely confess that they find it very difficult to save cash.

Consequently, unexpected lawsuits or sickness usually precipitate economic emergencies. The evidence available suggests that the major economic disaster for Oaxaca peasants is a serious illness of a household member. When either a legal or medical crisis occurs, a household may be completely impoverished in a short time, having mortgaged or sold all its capital goods and exhausted its credit.

Also, impulse buying is not uncommon. On a small scale this may include purchases of mescal, luxury foods, surplus clothing, or recreational services. On a larger scale it may mean spending substantial sums on anything from furniture to radios which would not be justified in terms of a rational projection of future daily consumption needs and probable income. Sometimes items are purchased on credit. Waterbury reports a case of a man with sizable outstanding debts who, finding himself with a fair amount of cash, bought a phonograph outfit for $3,000 despite the fact that he had to go further in debt for part of the purchase price. It is possible that the man will be able to rent the phonograph outfit for weddings and other events, but he did not mention this as part of his motivation. His explanation was that he had some money, saw the outfit, wanted it, and bought it.

Recognizing these difficulties, most peasants who wish to save do it by investing any momentary cash surplus in some productive activity, of which by far the most important is animal raising, requiring the investment of both purchase price and feed costs. Thus, chickens can be sold to meet short-term emergencies; two pigs can provide most of the value of a young ox; burros can be rented and readily sold when cash is needed; ox teams can be rented and sometimes can be sold after a year or two at some profit, and a team may provide the principal payment for a small piece of land. Traders in the *mercado* report some savings through the purchase of small-denomination government bonds and even the use of savings banks. A few prosperous peasants may use these means also. Savings banks, however, seem to be used for rather specific long-range purposes such as more advanced education for children, rather than as capital for productive or income-producing enterprises. The institution of insurance is virtually unknown.

Some Oaxaca peasants also borrow money to meet emergencies or to finance major purchases. Members of *ejidos* may collectively obtain loans from the *Banco Ejidal* for purchase of equipment or animals. More generally, peasants use moneylenders or on occasion pawn lands or houses to fellow villagers.[5] Even traders in the *mercado* prefer borrowing from unlicensed moneylenders, from whom funds are instantly available on a simple note, to the red tape and delays involved in securing loans from banks. As will be shown, some traders in the modern sector also depend heavily on credit terms from suppliers, but with few exceptions (mostly handicraft producers) peasants do not make use of this form of credit.

Rates charged by moneylenders are relatively high. The lowest recorded was 2 percent per month; the highest, 25 percent per month, with the majority of moneylenders charging 5 to 10 percent per month. The variation apparently reflects to some degree the length of the loan and the credit standing of the borrower. Moneylenders are found in many villages as well as in towns and in the city. As a phenomenon they antedate the modern period, although there are no data on their antiquity. A considerable proportion of peasants use them. At Santa María Atzompa, 20 out of 80 informants stated that they had borrowed from

[5] Pawning land is common in Mexico. The lender takes possession of the land and farms it until the loan is repaid. The returns from crops are in lieu of interest.

moneylenders. Moneylending, in turn, provides an investment for a villager with spare cash, and considering the interest rates charged, it would appear to be a lucrative business.

The uses of credit involve a mixture of personal, social, and capitalistic type goals. It is used to meet personal emergencies such as illness and lawsuits; to pay the bus fare of a household member who has been offered a job in Mexico City (or, formerly, for fare to the point where U.S. *bracero* contracts might be obtained); or to maintain the household pending sale of an asset or receipt of income. It is sought for social obligations such as *mayordomías*, weddings, and other obligatory fiestas. It may be needed to complete the purchase of a capital asset such as an ox team, a truck, or a piece of land for which cash on hand is not sufficient; or to obtain or increase working capital for farming, handicraft, or marketing operations—for example, to pay costs of planting or to buy supplies for handicraft production. Savings and capital accumulation are pursued for similar purposes. It may be argued that some of these are noneconomic ends. This assumes that there *are* purely economic ends from the individual standpoint, an assumption questioned by some economists. In any case, although differing in some details, the use and purposes of credit, savings, and capital accumulation are similar to those found in the most capitalistic societies.

There are some other, less frequently used devices available to the peasant who would like to invest in income-producing activities but finds his resources inadequate. A few cooperatives have been formed to establish enterprises such as maize mills or to market handicrafts. Partnerships, usually between related households, are reported for the purpose of buying trucks and tractors (in such cases, bank credit or time payment facilities are also required), or of splitting operating expenses. Temporary associations have been formed to buy tracts of land larger than could be managed by individual households, the land subsequently being divided among association members.

LEVELS OF LIVING

The discussion of subsistence budgets dealt primarily with the basic survival needs of the household. As has been suggested, most peasant families consume more than the bare minimum required. The majority not only have operational and public budgets but also buy some luxury foods, and most families from time to time make various capital investments. It seems useful to consider different levels of living to which households might aspire.

A hypothetical bare subsistence budget set forth in appendix 16, Type A budget, amounts to around $2,550 a year, or a little less than $7 a day. It does not include some things considered essential by most families; informants in the Valley area generally estimated an average of $10 a day as the minimum income for a family of average size (5 or 6 members) in 1967–1968. This figure may be less in the Sierra, where living levels appear to be somewhat lower. Our reports indicate that even households producing part of their own maize considered $10 a day necessary for supplementary food and other items bought in the market system. Most informants questioned placed the minimum daily monetary requirement at $20 a day, if all food is bought in the market system, to provide an adequate or acceptable level of living for a household.

That most peasants do not live at the bare subsistence survival level is indicated by responses of a limited number of informants in several villages. Of 80 household heads in a sample census of Santa María Atzompa, only one, an irregular wage laborer, indicated that if he had more money his first choice would be to spend it for food; only one other mentioned food, as a second choice. (Two wives, however, mentioned food in their responses.) In Magdalena Ocotlán, a fairly poor village, only one of eight persons questioned mentioned food, as a second choice. The alternative hypothetical budgets and the list of products consumed (app. 17) suggest that most Oaxaca peasants consider themselves rather adequately fed, and in fact may actually be fairly well nourished if the diet be examined objectively, free from ethnocentric food prejudices. The varied diet of families above the basic survival level is further indicated below in the discussion of market relationships of the consumption system.

If most levels of food consumption meet the standard of wants or felt needs, in what ways *do* the living standards of Oaxaca peasants exceed their actual living levels? The several groups of interviews dealing with preferences (what informants would buy or invest in if they had more money) are revealing, even though the number of informants is limited and thus may not be representative of the total population. As we have seen, food does not rank high in this regard. Neither, evidently, do informants aspire to any increases in public consumption of any type, not even ceremonial consumption.

In the largest survey, Stolmaker's sample census of 80 families in Santa María Atzompa, respondents were asked how they would spend any surplus cash received. Of 69 families living primarily by pottery making, 22 listed as first choice either buying or building a new house or buying a new house lot. Ten more listed this as second choice. Moreover, farm land purchase was first choice for 8, second choice for 13. Of the 69 pottery-making families, 47 gave a high priority to housing or land acquisition or both.

Modern equipment was listed as first choice by 9 (bed, bicycle, motorcycle, truck, steel plow, irrigation pump, sewing machine), and as second choice by 8 (radio, bed, kerosene stove, sewing machine, truck, tractor). Other items receiving first priority by would-be buyers were house improvement (4), cows and ox teams

(8), other animals (8), clothing (1), more occupational supplies (1), musical instrument (1), and investments in income-producing services such as storekeeping and pottery dealing (6). Significantly, ox teams and other animals ranked high as second choices, 16 out of 55 giving these as second choices. One elderly couple had no wants.

Of 11 farmers and wage workers, 7 listed land purchase as first choice and 1 listed house improvements. Four wanted house improvements, a new house or a house and lot as second choice. Five gave animal purchase as first or second choice. Modern equipment ranked low in this group. None emphasized food.

In San Lázaro Etla, a dairying village, Woods asked 9 persons what they would spend money on if they "found" $5,000. As first choices, 4 indicated that they would buy animals; 2 would buy land; 1 each listed investment in a store, construction of a shelter for animals, and a house. Other choices included purchase of an ox team, house, irrigation pump and well, and an automobile (a fourth choice). In Magdalena Ocotlán, Cook asked 9 people what they would do if they had $5,000. Six listed oxen or other animals as first choice and 3 listed these as second choice; 2 would set themselves up as moneylenders. Only 1 listed a house and lot, as third choice. Land was listed as second or third choice by 2.

These somewhat inadequate data suggest that the biggest gap between living levels and living standards is in housing. This is particularly true of Atzompa, where there is a regular, if limited supply of cash from pottery sales. Only in this town were durable consumer's goods mentioned, and it is significant that many of the items mentioned are industrial products. Much more significant is the fairly high priority given to capital investments that might improve income. Land and farm equipment appear to be important for farmers, and animals rank high in all groups.

Some further insight into living levels is afforded by household inventories of equipment and durable goods. A composite of such lists is given in appendix 20. The lists suggest to some degree the influence of modern industrial goods now available in the market. Most of them reveal the use of some more modern form of lighting than *ocote* (pitch pine) splinters—for example, candles, kerosene or gasoline lighting, and electricity. Transistor radios rank high among modern items, and beds, flashlights, and sewing machines were mentioned frequently. Also found on the lists are modern wardrobe closets, chairs, dishes manufactured by modern methods, and metal cooking utensils. But also present are various traditional items such as metates, low stools, saints' portraits, and village-produced pottery for cooking or as vases on household altars. If we may judge by the preferences discussed above, however, only supplies of modern goods are felt to be inadequate for levels toward which these families aspire.

The inventories do not necessarily reflect the wealth of a household or even its interest in modernity. As indicated above, most people would prefer to buy land or animals or better housing when they have extra cash. This is not to say that they may not buy such items as radios, but they show relatively little interest in the gamut of modern paraphernalia. A man who holds 7 or 8 hectares of prime land—a wealthy farmer by Oaxaca peasant standards—may sleep on a palm-leaf mat raised on planks and may choose not to have electricity in his house even though it is available. Moreover, some families today invest cash in higher education for their children, an item that does not show in the preference lists, rather than spend the money on modern equipment. As a minimum this requires payment of a school activity fee, if not tuition, the purchase of suitable clothing, a considerable outlay for books, and usually some expenditure for board and lodging in Oaxaca. It is notable that children from many villages have become schoolteachers or skilled technicians or engineers.

The foregoing discussion indicates the importance attached to capital and durable goods expenditures by Oaxaca peasants. Such expenditures tend to occur irregularly, and many do not show up in consumers' budgets. Some, such as expenditures for land, have also been considered in relation to production costs in chapter 4, but as production budgets are not kept separately from household budgets they may properly be considered here as well. Lacking specific reporting on them over a longer term, it is possible to give only a rough idea of their importance.

Housing and Land Investment

The large item most closely related to subsistence problems is housing, which the preference lists show to be important. Housing may be erected on a borrowed lot or on common lands of the village, but even landless wage laborers often own a lot they have purchased or inherited. Lot prices are variable from village to village and are said to have been inflating rapidly.

Two lots in Atzompa each sold for $850 some years ago (one of them in 1961); one was small and near the main street, the second was fair sized and faced directly on the main street. In 1968 the owner of a small lot about a block from the main street valued it at only $500; a slightly larger lot on the same street recently sold for $800. The owner of a small lot on the main street with a large whitewashed structure suitable for a store refused an offer of $3,000 for it. An informant at San Lázaro Etla sold his lot for $2,000 (presumably with some dwelling on it) and bought a vacant lot for $1,000; another man valued his house and lot at $4,500. A lot without structures at Magdalena Ocotlán was sold in May 1968 for $1,100. In household inventories for Atzompa, values for three lots without their construc-tions were given at $400, $400, and $1,000, respectively, while four lots were valued with their constructions at $3,300, $3,000, $5,000, and $5,000. In January

1970 a strip of a lot 9 meters by 2 meters just off the main street in Atzompa was bid for by the owner's neighbor; the asking price was $400 and the buyer's counteroffer was $300, a square-meter price of $16.67. An informant in the relatively wealthy horticultural village of San Antonino Ocotlán set a value of $40,000 on his lot with a house measuring 736 square meters. The house had cost more than $13,000 to build and was exceptionally well appointed (glass windows, cement flooring, bathroom with toilet, electricity, store, and tailoring shop).

Another type of evidence is the cost of house building. A peasant and his family may live in a cane hut (*jacal*) that costs as little as $300 to $400 to build (costs reported from Santa María Atzompa and Magdalena Ocotlán, respectively), and has a life of only 10 or 12 years. But most Oaxaca peasants live in a tile-roofed adobe house that, with a little maintenance, may have a life of many years. A house of this type in Atzompa measuring 10 meters by 4 meters (a common size) cost $1,500 or more to construct, including a minimum mason's fee of $350 plus another $150 for a mason's helper. This figure does not include food for the mason or his helper. If a porch is added, the construction cost is said to double. This seems excessive, but a record made by Cook of the cash expenditures for adding a large porch 30 by 8 meters to an existing house in Magdalena Ocotlán in 1967 totaled $4,035.50. In addition, the owner fed the workers for four weeks and held a costly dedication ceremony at the conclusion of construction, slaughtering three turkeys and a sheep, which brought total expenditures to about $5,000. To finance the construction he sold a mature ox team for $4,500 and bought a younger one for $3,000; sold 10 *fanegas* of maize for $1,125, and used $1,500 in savings from past sales of fattened animals and maize.

In another case, materials for an adobe house cost $1,440; with mason's fee and helper's wages, the total (estimated) expense came to $2,300. In yet another instance, the receipts from sale of animals to build a house were $2,350, most or all of it presumably spent for construction. The family having such a one-room adobe house may do its cooking in a small *jacal* costing several hundred pesos more. Some houses are much more elaborate than those discussed; they may consist of several rooms and have cement floors and plastered exteriors. A laborer's family, then, may have an investment in housing of around $2,500, while more prosperous families may have investments of $5,000 or more in house and lot.

Chiñas reports that a Tehuantepec family spent $20,000 to build a new house. This household farmed 5 hectares of unirrigated land, and the wife contributed 50 percent or more of the family income from profits as a *viajera* (traveling trader).

If a family has animals, there often will be supplementary structures such as cement-floored, adobe-walled pig pens and sheds for oxen and burros. If milk cattle are kept, there may also be a cement-floored, tile-roofed dairy building.

An important consideration from the standpoint of the market is that, except for adobe brick in some instances, most house-building materials are purchased. Adobe bricks may be made by the family or, more often, with labor hired for the purpose; or they may be bought from adobe brick makers in the village. Items such as tiles, beams, stringers, door and window frame materials, and the doors and windows themselves are usually bought in the marketplace. Thatching materials and the canes used in some roof and wall construction may be produced locally but must be purchased by most builders. Appendix 16 gives further details on house construction costs.

Landowning farm families have additional large investments in land. These capital costs are not borne by sharecroppers or farmers working *ejido* or common lands. Farm lands vary considerably in value according to quality of land and whether it is irrigated or not. High-quality unirrigated lands around Atzompa cost a minimum of $4,000 per hectare in 1968, and prices were rising. Reports from San Antonino indicate that similar high values prevailed there. As most estimates indicate that it takes two hectares of land to support a moderately large family, plus another hectare to feed animals, including some production for the market, such a prosperous land-owning family living primarily by farming will have an investment in lands of around $12,000, plus a house and lot worth at least $2,000—a minimum real estate investment of $14,000, and for a substantial number of households the total investment may reach $20,000 or more.

Ownership of real estate is the primary criterion for wealth ranking. At Diaz Ordaz, Downing undertook a ranking of family wealth for a selected sample of households using a team of raters from the village. His most meticulous rater divided 26 households into 16 wealth levels (consolidating levels 5 through 14 into one group), as follows:

Level	Number of cases	Basis of rating
1	1	Valuable house, lot, and lands
2	1	Valuable lands but less valuable house
3	1	House and many goats, but no lands
4	1	Average house, lot, and lands
5–14	18	House and lot but poor, very poor, or little land
15	1	House but no land
16	3	No house of their own and no land

Other raters made fewer distinctions. Raters who were poor tended to lump the wealthier families together, whereas those who were more well-to-do tended to lump the poorer families together, but agreement in ranking was high among all raters.

Shifts to Industrial Products

What appear to be shifts in living standards through adoption of new or more industrial products may in fact be shifts that result in greater economy. Except in the Sierra, where firewood is often still abundant, kerosene or gasoline stoves are increasingly popular, replacing firewood or charcoal as fuel. Butane gas now is beginning to replace kerosene and gasoline stoves, especially in cities and towns. Although detailed studies are lacking, it appears that newer forms of heating may be cheaper as well as cleaner and more convenient than the older methods. Improved lighting, too, has nearly replaced the use of *ocote* (pitch pine). In the Valley, pitch pine is more or less a luxury item for starting fires for the relatively few people who still cook with charcoal. (For changes in the *ocote* trade in the Sierra, see Berg 1968:44–49.) The sequence of changes in lighting seem to be from *ocote* to candles, then kerosene flares, kerosene lanterns, gasoline lanterns, or, in stores, butane lamps, to electricity.

It may be noted that improved lighting permits carrying on household or craft activities after dark, while the now nearly ubiquitous flashlight facilitates nighttime outdoor activities. According to a study made by Downing, electricity may save the village money once the initial installation cost is paid. The $3.00 monthly street lighting assessment he found to be less than the usual expenditure for flashlight batteries, while the flat-rate charge for a 40-watt electric light is less than the cost of the two candles burned each night by most families, and produces much better light. Once electricity is installed, however, few families are content with a single bulb, and other appliances begin to appear, especially the electric iron. Here again there may actually be savings. Old-fashioned flatirons are not very cheap and they are difficult to heat cleanly without charcoal braziers. While the data are inconclusive, they suggest that modernization is not always more costly than traditional equipment, just as farmers are discovering that tractor plowing is better and sometimes cheaper than ox-team plowing.

MARKET RELATIONSHIPS OF THE CONSUMPTION SYSTEM

Peasant consumption patterns frequently are given little attention in the study of marketing systems. Peasant systems often are regarded as primarily subsistence economies, each household in large measure feeding itself. Such autoconsumption may be regarded as irrelevant to the marketing system, and peasant-produced goods passing upwards through the system are considered to be consumed by urban buyers only, and hence are not followed beyond their entry into the marketplace. In Oaxaca, as we shall see, such assumptions are far from correct. Not only are there landless households in all the villages studied which do not feed themselves, who depend upon the marketing system for all their food, but in addition many farming families do not produce enough even of the basic staple, maize, let alone other foods, to feed themselves through the year. Even when the quantities and values of purchased items are small, the household's consumption is definitely oriented toward the market. Moreover, as has been indicated in more detail above, even families that produce some of their requirements may still utilize those goods in market terms, especially maize.

Some households, especially in villages with special types of lands, may deliberately forego the production of subsistence maize because other crops are relatively much more profitable. In other words, the consumption pattern may be manipulated or altered and choices made which both depend upon the existence of the marketing system and also exercise some influence upon it. The extent of the Oaxaca peasant's involvement with the marketing system varies with the village's and the household's production specializations and with the commodity considered, but it is clear that at the household level some people produce none of the basic commodities consumed, while at the village level no villages produce all of the commodities essential to existence. Consideration of total consumption patterns is therefore essential to understanding the marketing system.

Restricting the discussion to villages in the Valley of Oaxaca, only 7 of the 17 food and food-related items listed in appendix 17 as basic necessities are produced in every village. These are maize, beans, squash and greens, beef, pork, and herbs. Often village supplies are inadequate to meet the minimal needs of its residents, and some households do not produce any of the items. Another 8 of the basic items and some pork products are not produced in all Valley villages; in most communities, households must buy part or all of their supplies elsewhere. Three of the basic items are supplied in part from other subregions of the marketing system and 7 are supplemented from outside the system. Refined sugar comes entirely from outside the Oaxaca system.

Two examples illuminate alternatives in procurement. Households short of herbs or greens may collect some along the road and field boundaries, but usually people prefer the superior quality of herbs and greens available in the marketplace. Similarly, although corn cobs, twigs, and trash gleaned from public lands may provide enough fuel to do essential cooking, in many villages everyone who can afford to buys firewood or uses kerosene or gasoline stoves, both available in the marketplace.

Turning to items frequently consumed by some people in the Valley villages—and many of these items are consumed by most people in the villages—we can identify 48 additional food items. In most villages these items are produced only if they are village specialties for the market (in which case a portion may be consumed locally). Of these 48 items, 31 are produced wholly or in part in some Valley villages, 9 are produced or supplemented from production in other subregions of the market system, 7 are supplemented from outside the Oaxaca system, and supplies of 10 items come entirely from outside the system.

Seven items on the list are considered to be particularly desirable at certain seasons or for special occasions. Of these, only 3 are produced in the Valley. Two are obtained partly or wholly from elsewhere in the system, and 3 more come entirely from outside the system.

Finally, I can identify some 42 items that are consumed occasionally or are considered luxuries to be consumed when consumer-buyers can afford them. Of these, 18 are produced within the Valley, although for some supplies are inadequate for total local requirements. Other subregions of the system supply some or all of 17 of the 42 items, and 13 are supplied wholly or in part from outside the system.

Turning to nonfood items, 39 of these, excluding animals, originate in various Valley villages (app. 18). Few if any of these are produced in every village. Supplies of many are supplemented from outside the Valley. Some of the items, however, are regarded as indispensable by most households. Approximately 13 items or classes of items are produced in the city of Oaxaca, and 40 items or classes of items are produced outside the Oaxaca system.

The foregoing discussion and the lists in the appendixes give some idea of the variety of goods that flow through the market system. Our data give little idea of the quantities of goods involved or, except for a few items, the relative importance of village consumption in relation to the total flow of goods through the marketing system. Yet an overall estimate of the monetary value of the goods peasants obtain in the market is possible.

In the discussion of household budgets I arrived at a minimum subsistence budget, for a landless laborer's household, of about $2,550. A few households living in poverty may not spend this much, and most farm households are able to reduce their cash budgets by consuming some of the goods they produce; but they tend to use these "savings" to vary and expand their diet and to buy more clothing. If my hypothetical budgets approach reality, most peasant families produce a significant part of their food and nevertheless spend between $4,000 and $5,000 annually in the market, again without considering public expenditures or capital investments. The hypothetical budgets are extremely conservative, but to be ultracautious we will assume that the annual expenditure per household is a minimum of $2,550.

In chapter 3 it is suggested that the value of goods consumed in the region might well exceed one billion pesos. If all of the approximately 180,000 households in the region are assumed to be living at the economic level of $2,550 per year, in accordance with our hypothetical minimal budget, the value of all subsistence goods consumed would be about $460,000,000. How much of this is represented by autoconsumption is uncertain. In our minimal hypothetical budget for the household of a landless laborer, maize, which is normally the major item of autoconsumption, represents about 30 percent of the total budget, but in this case it is all purchased. In the hypothetical budgets for households with enough land to produce all the maize they consume, for example, Family Type D (app. 16), the value of the maize consumed is 20.6 percent of the total budget. For the Sierra, where autoconsumption is higher than in the Valley, Berg (1968:111) estimated that only 44.5 percent of the maize consumed was self-produced. These figures would suggest that less than 50 percent of the value of the subsistence goods consumed is produced by the consumers; for some subregions it may be substantially less.

The negative contribution of autoconsumption to marketplace exchange, however, is balanced by the relatively few households that live at such a minimal level. A very large proportion have cash outlays that amount to $4,000 to $5,000 annually, excluding monies expended for capital goods, for operational or public budgets, and for emergencies, and excluding goods that are autoconsumed. All these considerations suggest that cash purchases by peasants in the regional markets amount to at least $720,000,000. Turning to another line of evidence, if we accept the statements of many informants that a decent level of living requires a daily cash outlay of $20 per family, then the figure escalates to $1.3 billion annually. Although the $20-per-day figure probably includes some expenditures for emergencies, recreation, and luxuries, as well as for operational and public expenditures, it probably does not include any major public ceremonial expenditures, any large part of the operational budgets, or capital expenditures. Considering these omissions and the conservative nature of our various assumptions, it seems likely that the monetary value of the consumption or demand aspect of the peasant market in this region is well over a billion pesos annually and that a major part of this passes through the marketing system.

EFFECTS OF CONSUMPTION NEEDS ON MARKET BEHAVIOR

A final minor note must be added to the foregoing analysis on the effect the consumption needs of the peasant have on behavior in the market. It is quite obvious, of course, that the peasant seeks to buy at the lowest price. To this end he shops around or haggles (more on this behavior in chapter 9). Peasant knowledge of market prices clearly has a bearing on how effectively this is done. Although there is considerable variation in individual knowledge and sophistication, generally the peasant in Oaxaca is extremely conscious of prices and of supply-and-demand factors. This is perhaps more true of the Valley peasant than the peasant of the Sierras. Some mestizo market vendors, especially sellers of clothing and textiles, tend to act as if the peasant, particularly the peasant from the Sierra, is stupid, and often take a bullying attitude toward him. Privately, the more perceptive vendors admit that usually even the Sierra peasant drives a shrewd bargain.

The peasants' determination of what and when to sell in the market is often conditioned by immediate consumption needs. This "target marketing" is particularly evident with storable grains and in the sale of animals, especially chickens. The peasant with only a limited amount of maize to sell frequently does not sell his surplus at the time when prices are best. Rather he hoards it to sell in small quantities to meet emergencies when cash is short for immediate consumption needs. Thus he takes to the marketplace for sale only the quantity he thinks he can sell for the amount of cash required to buy other goods he needs, for example, meat, chiles, lard, or a garment for a child in a school event. This limits the quantity he brings to market and may affect his pricing strategy. If the market is slow, he may reduce his asking price. Peasants who eat eggs normally may sell them when cash is needed for other purposes. Chickens very frequently are sold to buy food for a couple of days when cash is temporarily in short supply. The time when a pig or a yoke of oxen is sold may be determined by the opportunity to make a larger purchase. A couple of pigs may be sold quickly to buy a yoke of oxen; a yoke of oxen may be sold quickly to take advantage of an opportunity to buy a house or a piece of land or to meet major ceremonial consumption needs.

Handicraft producers also may cut prices as the *plaza* day advances, to clear out all their stocks. To some extent the price may be reduced because it is too costly to take unsold goods home or store them. Nevertheless, the seller's behavior may also be determined in part by his subsistence needs or by the need for cash for the operational budget that supports his productive activities.

6
The Structure of the Marketing System

The geographical scope and limitations of the marketing system and the system of cyclical marketplaces centering on the city of Oaxaca are discussed in chapter 3. Chapters 2, 4, and 5 examine production activities and consumption patterns viewed as subsystems of the marketing system. In this and subsequent chapters the nature of the marketing system is examined in more detail. This chapter examines the way goods and services move through the marketing system, the kinds of actors participating in it, and the characteristics of the marketplaces.

CHANNELS OF EXCHANGE

Most of the goods and services exchanged through the traditional peasant marketing system originate in the peasant village and are consumed in other peasant villages. Some goods also originate outside the traditional system; although not large in volume, some are essential to the traditional consumption patterns. In modern times additional goods from outside the system have become important in village consumption, and an increasing number of industrial products are being consumed in the peasant village. Many of the latter are distributed through the modern commercial exchange system rather than through the traditional market exchange mechanisms. The same is true of some local products exported from the region. Consequently some data on the modern marketing system are included in this chapter. The origins of various kinds of goods and services entering the marketing system and the ways they leave the system are extensively treated in chapters 4 and 5 and are not dealt with further in this chapter.

The following are the major kinds of channels through which goods flow:

1. Intravillage exchange occurs directly between producers and consumers residing in the same village. This constitutes a minor part of the market transactions within the system. Some of the intravillage exchange, such as gifting and ceremonial distribution, is only marginally related to the marketing system (see chap. 7). More clearly market oriented is the buying or selling of goods and services between households within the village. An important characteristic of this exchange is that the seller does not solicit buyers; rather, buyers with needs seek out vendors. There are exceptions, however. A barber may set up a chair in the central *plaza* on Sunday or a fiesta day. Women may offer small amounts of produce or prepared food for sale on the *plaza* or in the market building, if there is one. Small quantities of eggs or staples such as maize or beans may be offered to a local storekeeper by the producer, usually in exchange for store merchandise by barter. But most transactions are initiated by a household with a specific need. A farmer needing hired labor or rental of a team of oxen seeks out the individuals whose services he needs, while a household wanting maize may try to buy it from one known to have a surplus. Even these transactions seem relatively rare: both buyer and seller would rather deal in the nearest *plaza,* where more buyers and sellers may be found and current prices may be discovered. In emergencies between *plaza* days, borrowing from kinsmen or neighbors is favored if possible.

Village stores usually are owned by villagers, most of whom have other sources of income as well. Many villages have bakers or butchers who produce primarily for intravillage consumption. Maize-grinding mills usually are locally owned. There may be specialists such as masons, carpenters, barbers, or traditional curers to serve local needs. Some villages still have marriage arrangers or speakers, a traditional type of specialist probably less common now than in the past. Part-time local blacksmiths are found in some villages, especially where there are special needs as in metate-making villages.

In summary, there are some essentially market-type transactions at the intravillage level, particularly with respect to services, but they are relatively minor.

2. Village-to-village transactions. Relatively few goods move from villages directly to other villages. They consist mainly of specialized farm products or raw materials. A few examples may be mentioned: vegetables and beans produced in Tlacochahuaya are peddled door to door or offered in the central square of nearby villages. Firewood is brought almost entirely by vendors from San Felipe Tejalapan to Atzompa for pottery firing, or potters may go to firewood-producing villages for supplies. Pottery may be bought in Atzompa by villagers from elsewhere. Wool is

sometimes sold to weavers in Teotitlán del Valle by vendors from producing villages. In most cases these transactions account for only a small part of the sales of the producing village and only a small part of the needs of the receiving village.

3. Village-to-*plaza* transactions. These constitute a major category of exchanges. Farmers and artisans in villages take their products to the nearest *plaza* or, in some instances, to more distant ones, where they sell them either at retail or make bulk sales to dealers of various sorts. For storable products such as maize, often only a small quantity is taken for sale to secure cash for immediate consumption needs, but large surpluses may be transported and sold in bulk at one time. In retail sales the village seller in the *plaza* again waits for buyers to approach him, but in bulk sales the peasant often approaches dealers. For a few commodities such as coffee, pigs, and in a few areas, cattle, dealers from the market towns go to the villages to seek out sellers, transporting their purchases then to a *plaza* or market town. This type of buying seems to be increasing as the use of trucks becomes more common. Villagers growing perishable crops such as vegetables or flowers may be regular vendors in a *plaza*. Growers of seasonal products such as deciduous fruits may sell in a *plaza* only a few days a year. Producers of handicrafts also may be regular sellers in a *plaza*.

4. *Plaza*-to-village transactions. These also constitute a major category of exchanges. They involve most kinds of goods produced in villages as well as many types of town-produced or industrial products. Peasant villagers purchase from other peasant vendors or dealers in the *plaza* mc of the foods and handicrafts they do not produce for their own consumption, to take back to the village. They also make many purchases from stores in the market towns. Some traveling traders also carry goods from *plazas* to sell in villages.

5. *Plaza*-to-*plaza* transactions. These involve all types of goods and consist of purchases of goods in one *plaza* for resale in another. Many of the traders are full-time operatives. Some are peasants with headquarters in a village, but many are town-based mestizos.

6. Subregion-to-subregion transactions. These differ from items 3, 4, and 5 only in that the goods move across lines from one subregion to another.

7. Region-to-region transactions. These involve movement of goods into or out of the Oaxaca system into other regional systems or into the national market. Most of these transactions take place through modern commercial channels but some goods, especially near the limits of the Oaxaca system, flow through more traditional avenues. Some traditional items such as cacao are still transported by peasant traders although they may use modern transport.

TYPES OF BUYERS AND SELLERS

The significance of these categories of transactions and the flow of goods through them may be illuminated by examining the types of actors involved. It should be borne in mind that the various categories of actors or functionaries discussed are not mutually exclusive. For example, most buyers are also sellers, but the two activities are discussed separately.

Buyers

Peasants living in villages are the largest group of buyers in the marketplace and probably account for the major volume of sales. The peasant buyer commonly is a producer who purchases in the market those subsistence items he does not produce, but laborers, specialists, and others may not be producers in the usual sense. The peasant also buys raw materials for any handicraft activity he cannot obtain by his own efforts, or which he prefers to buy, possibly because such materials are not available in his own village or because he considers this more economical than taking time from production activities to seek them out. Most purchases of durable or semidurable goods and implements also are made in the marketplace.

Most of the goods bought are produced in villages, but there is a growing demand for town-produced or industrially produced items. Examples of the latter include processed foods such as groceries, mainly regarded as luxuries; soft drinks and beer; cloth or dry goods and factory-made clothing; modern building materials such as cement, roofing paper, or corrugated roofing panels; and, in some villages, pumps for irrigation, trucks, and occasionally even automobiles. Although the peasant may have a variety of sources of supply, he makes most of his purchases in marketplaces.

Urban or city buyers frequently are peasantlike in their buying behavior, especially if they are engaged in essentially handicraft types of production. A majority of the urban buyers, however, are wage workers or salaried employees or are engaged in service activities (including some types of government work) or in commercial activities. While the urban buyer purchases some of his foodstuffs from the traditional market *plaza,* he may also buy a significant proportion in the daily *mercado,* and he is the primary patron of urban shops and stores.

In addition to buyers who make purchases primarily for meeting consumption needs or for carrying on handicraft activities, there are a large number of what might be described as commercial buyers. These are of several types. Associated primarily with the traditional marketing system is the trader or *regatón* who buys for resale at a profit. The smallest type of *regatón* is the *ambulante* or peddler with no fixed place of business who buys a small stock of goods that he peddles in the streets. Most of these are found in the towns and especially in the City. Similar in their scope of operations are the operators of *changarros,* small stands that are inside house doors or in patios, usually offering a small stock of a few kinds of goods. These are found not only in the towns but also in the larger villages. A third important type, especially in the City, are *locatarios* who buy goods for resale from fixed stalls in the *mercados* or from small stores. Village storekeepers may be considered their rural counterparts.

Included in the category of *regatones* are individuals, usually operating on a part-time basis, who buy goods for resale in a variety of patterns. For example, many villagers visiting a *plaza* buy more goods than they need for their own use and sell the surplus in their home villages. As another example, the vegetable producers of San Antonino Ocotlán often buy the crops of people in neighboring villages for resale in the Oaxaca marketplace or may make trips outside the region either to buy or to sell. Other buyers purchase goods in the marketplace for resale in other *plazas.* Many of these are full-time operators and have their base in the City, but there are also many village-based traders of this type. Many truckers fall into this category, although often they have less regular routes than the usual inter*plaza* traders.

Another important type of buyer usually found in the City is the wholesale buyer or bulker who buys village products primarily for export. The most important example of this type is the coffee buyer. A specialized modern type of buyer is the butcher who visits villages with trucks to buy animals, mainly pigs. Some buyers are agents, usually storekeepers in villages, who buy coffee for brokers in Oaxaca City or castor beans for processors in the City. A few buyers now come from outside the system, most notably buyers of avocados. They usually have agents in the producing villages but send their own trucks from Mexico City and hence tend to bypass the *plaza* system. Finally, for completeness, one may note a few buyers of raw materials for industrial processes. These are few and relatively small scale. They include the castor oil producers and a few industrial or semiindustrial producers of mescal and maguey fiber.

Sellers

Vendors in the market system also fall into several categories. One major type is the producer-vendor or *propio,* most often a village-based peasant. Essentially the *propio* is a seller of the products of a household, whether these be farm products, handicrafts, or marine, forest, or mineral products. Some of the products sold by producer-vendors are sold within the village or in neighboring villages but most are sold to various types of buyers in the marketplaces. Within the marketplace the *propio* operates in a variety of ways, in part depending upon the product he has to sell. Mainly he sells at retail to the consumer from a location in the *plaza,* or he sells to some type of *regatón* or trader, perhaps a traveling trader engaged in either retail or wholesale trade. Occasionally he may sell in the village to traveling buyers of various sorts as described in the preceding paragraph.

A second major type of vendor in the market system is the trader or *regatón* whom we have already mentioned as a buyer, who seeks to resell at a profit goods purchased. Some traders occupy other roles as well, at times producing some of the farm products or handicrafts they sell. The vegetable producers of San Antonino Ocotlán have already been mentioned. Another example are some pottery makers of Santa María Atzompa who, in addition to selling their own product, may buy from their neighbors for resale. The majority, however, are essentially full-time buyers and sellers.

A significant number of *regatones* are based in villages. The outstanding known group are the traders of Mitla in the eastern arm of the Valley (see chap. 11). Similar groups are based in San Antonino Ocotlán, at Yalalag in the Sierra, and in Tehuantepec and Atempo in the Isthmus. The more important traders, at least in volume of transactions, are based in marketplace towns, especially Oaxaca City. Although a few specialized traders such as pottery *regatones* may buy part of their stock at the point of production, most buy in one *plaza* and sell in others. They buy in fairly large quantities in the *plaza* and sell at retail, following the cyclical *plazas* in other towns.

A third type of vendor is the storekeeper found both in villages and in towns and cities. In the village the storekeeper may have other sources of income such as farming, but in larger locations, especially market towns and the City, they are full-time operators. Similar to these are operators of permanent stalls (*locatarios*) in towns with enclosed *mercados*. Storekeepers deal primarily in nonperishable goods such as groceries, dry goods, and occasionally some industrial or semiindustrial products such as soft drinks, candles, kerosene, matches, and the like.

Larger-scale vendors are wholesalers, usually either bulkers (*acaparadores*) or breakers (*mayoristas*). *Acaparadores* buy in relatively small transactions and sell in bulk, mainly outside the system. Their former activities in hoarding to manipulate the market have already been mentioned in chapter 4. Breakers, in contrast, are in the main a fairly recent development. Generally they specialize either in perishable or nonperishable goods bought outside the region which are resold at wholesale to small-scale *regatones,* although in a few instances they may sell in quantity outside the system, in Chiapas.

Salesmen or order takers form another small but relatively important class of functionaries. Generally they seek out dealers in groceries, dry goods, and other types of industrial products, and essentially are order takers for goods that are delivered later through public transportation. Some agents penetrate into smaller towns, often carrying enough goods with them to fill small orders immediately.

Related to these, and also of fairly recent development, are peddlers who carry goods from market towns to the villages and who sell on credit. An item they commonly sell is ready-made clothing, and the operations are most successful in handicraft villages with fairly regular sources of income. In pottery-making Santa María Atzompa, for example, Stolmaker reports that 62 percent of the 80 potters interviewed were buying some item on installments.

The way in which these various actors participate in the market system and conduct their business transactions is examined in more detail in chapters 7 and 8. Here it is enough to say that these various types of actors differ from one another in the extent of their market participation and ways of doing business. Many idiosyncratic ways of doing business in the Oaxaca market system may reflect not only personality differences or variations in the life situations of the individual actors, but also individual evaluations and decisions of an economic nature. The economic choices made are mainly conditioned or limited by the nature of the goods involved, by the position of the functionary within the system, and by characteristics of the system itself.

THE MARKETPLACES

Despite the variety of ways in which goods may flow through the Oaxaca market system and the various kinds of transactions and levels at which they may occur, the overwhelming majority of economic exchange activities occur in connection with the marketplaces. This is true whether one considers the number of transactions, the quantity of goods exchanged, or the number of people involved, and whether one is dealing with traditional or industrial goods or with transactions between villages, between subregions, or with interregional trade. These marketplaces, as has already been pointed out, are in the various towns and the city of Oaxaca, where there are peasant-dominated *plazas*. Except in the Isthmian region, the *plazas* are periodic or cyclical in nature and usually occur at weekly intervals. A minor although significant exception concerns the fairs held in connection with religious festivals, especially the festival of the patron saint; these are also cyclical in nature although the interval is annual instead of weekly.

Oaxaca City

Despite Oaxaca City's great development of modern commercial establishments and involvement in the distribution of industrial products, the Saturday *plaza* dominates the rhythm of activity, not only for most residents in the City but for people in the surrounding villages. While this is primarily true of economic activities, the influence of the *plaza* permeates many other aspects of daily life. In a market town the day of the *plaza* is the time when government offices are busiest, political activity is greatest, and many churches have their largest attendance. The *plaza* often affects the rhythms of household life. In the City the *plaza* day is the time when, even in upper-class households, the mistress (usually accompanied by a servant) may participate in large-scale family shopping, storekeepers do their largest volume of business, buses from the villages run more frequently and carry more passengers, and pedestrian and automobile traffic are at a peak.

In the villages, household activities are also affected by the rhythm of the market. Except in the urgent planting season, farmers schedule their work activities in accordance with their needs to visit the *plaza* to purchase consumption goods or dispose of products. Handicraft producers gear their production to the *plaza* cycle. From some villages the poor or needy may visit the *plaza* in hope of employment as porters.

The rhythm of the *plaza* is evident even to the casual observer in the city of Oaxaca. On Monday following the Saturday *plaza,* street traffic and business are at their lowest point. In the central market area there are still some trucks completing the loading of goods for transit to more distant places, but otherwise the streets are clear of vendors and even inside the *mercado* business is slack, for many customers still have not used the perishable goods they bought in the Saturday *plaza.* Through the week, until Saturday, the rhythm of activity in the central part of the City gradually increases. In the area about the central *mercado* there is sometimes traffic congestion from trucks from long distance transport companies delivering goods from Mexico City or Puebla to shops and stores in or near the *mercado* buildings.

Friday the rhythm of activities accelerates markedly. Truck traffic increases through the day and into the night, bringing goods for the Saturday *plaza.* Most wholesalers dealing in perishable products from outside the system also try to schedule their trucks to arrive back on this day, preferably in the morning, and make most of their sales to operators of stalls in the *mercado.* Many peasant vendors with goods in quantity, hoping to sell in bulk to traders early Saturday morning, arrive in the city on Friday; by noon piles of goods begin to appear on the sidewalks and some people spend the night beside them. Smaller *propios* and intermediaries arrive toward evening and leave their goods at the bus depot or take them to inns where they spend the night. The inns, hotels, and *mesones* and the two "burro parks" west of the marketplace fill up. Eating places and bars do a flourishing business. The *locatorios* from the *mercado* who will sell in the street market on Saturday begin setting up their stands in the afternoon, and food stands catering to the marketplace personnel appear. Late Friday afternoon the streets immediately around the two market buildings are closed to automotive traffic in order to accommodate street vendors.

Saturday, activities begin before dawn. On most Saturdays twenty blocks of streets in the *plaza* area are closed to automotive traffic, but at designated places along the fringes the sidewalks are lined with trucks belonging to bulk buyers, either local or from out of town, some belonging to independent truckers hired by vendors or buyers to carry their goods. In a few spots trucks are permitted to sell loads of oranges, pineapples, and sometimes other goods. Most of the trucks cannot move until the streets are cleared Saturday night. Temporary stands are erected in the streets or vendors spread their goods on mats, and canvas shelters against sun and rain are erected. The latter vary from squares of canvas over a light frame supported by a single pole to larger canvases suspended by ropes or over frames covering a temporary wooden stall. Although many vendors are in place very early in the morning (see map 7 for locations of the various products), others continue to arrive as late as ten or eleven o'clock, while the erection of shelters may continue even later, depending somewhat on the weather.

Buyers appear soon after daylight also. In the earliest hours most are traders or wholesalers buying their goods in bulk; the few early retail buyers are mostly from the City. The great throng of buyers builds up as hundreds of crowded buses come in from the villages. From about eight o'clock until some time after noon the passageways in the streets between the vendors' displays are packed with village and City shoppers going from place to place, porters bearing goods on their backs or on hand trucks, ambulatory ice cream and soft drink sellers, peddlers of plastic bags or plastic sheets suitable for rain capes, peddlers of notions and other small items, and in the later hours of the market, women vendors offering bargains in onions, fruit, or other perishable products who have taken to the streets to sell the last of their stocks at bargain prices. For several hours foot traffic is slow and difficult and at times almost impossible.

By midday many vendors who have sold out their stocks may begin to leave, making their own purchases in the marketplace before going home. By midafternoon the number of small vendors has visibly diminished, and some of the temporary stall operators, particularly those selling clothing and dry goods, begin to pack up their stocks of goods. In the afternoon, as the crowds begin to thin, there is a secondary surge of buying by urbanites and some late peasant shoppers.

By Sunday morning the *plaza* is virtually depopulated and streets are open to normal traffic. Most of the refuse left by the street market has been cleared away. A few sidewalks may still be partially blocked with bags or boxes of goods where trucks complete their loading. On the one hand, activity in the central *mercados* is rather light, for most City buyers have satisfied their needs in the *plaza*. On the other hand, some of the secondary marketplaces in the City such as Merced, Cármen Alto, and El Marquesado are more than normally active with small street markets on nearby sidewalks and open spaces. Most of these street vendors have moved from the Saturday street market in the central district. Some of them are peddlers and other vendors who did not succeed in selling out all their stocks on Saturday.

The continuously varying number of both vendors and buyers in the central district during *plaza* days virtually precludes any precise field count of either category, and the hourly variations described, although based on prolonged observation, remain impressionistic. A fairly accurate measurement of total attendance by day, week, and month over the years is provided by the records of the Market Administration, summarized in chapter 10. Another source of information is a series of vendor counts made by the Oaxaca market study staff. As only three investigators were involved in that survey, the counts were taken on different dates and at different hours for various sections of the street plaza; and because the numbers of sellers and buyers change not only from week to week but from hour to hour on a single *plaza* day, totals are not strictly comparable. Sample data are given in appendix 21. Waterbury (1968:68–85) gives the results of a street-by-street count of vendors taken in 1964 and 1965. He estimates that on an average Saturday there are around 2,000 street vendors and perhaps 30,000 buyers crammed into the streets of this relatively small district. The busy and colorful scene has intrigued many visiting anthropologists and constitutes one of the most important tourist attractions of the City.

For the permanent *mercados* in the City, data are thought to be more reliable since there is a fairly permanent group of vendors involved. Censuses of these were made by the project in September 1964 through August 1965, which can be compared with a census taken by the *Banco de Pequeño Comercio* in December of 1965 (see app. 22). The Bank census shows a total of 1,930 *mercado* vendors; the census by the project shows a total of 1,797 for all *mercados* except the one called Venustiano Carranza. Neither of the censuses take into account the two livestock marketplaces near the central district.

In the Benito Juárez and 20 de Noviembre market buildings, stalls or *puestos* occupy most of the interior open space. These may have some storage space beneath counters which may be locked, but most of the sellers of foodstuffs in the Benito Juárez market simply cover their stocks with canvas at night. The building is locked from 7:00 P.M. to 7:00 A.M. and guarded by night watchmen provided by the market administration. The construction and size of stalls is also more-or-less standardized, and most stalls are now permanent structures built by the Market Administration. About the central area as well as facing the street are *casetas*. Most of these are enclosable, usually with wooden shutters, although some facing the street are small stores with display windows and doors. In addition, some permanent locations are found in the street; usually these are occupied by classes of vendors who have been unable to find adequate space inside the market building, such as butchers and vendors of hardware, sheet metal and tinware, and leather and

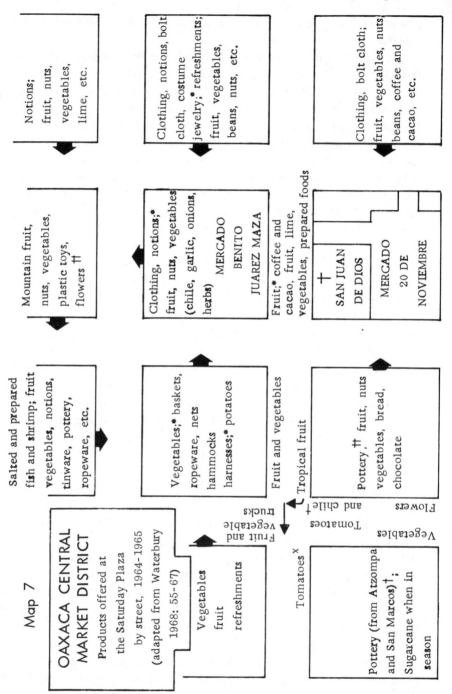

MAP 7. The Oaxaca central market district: products offered at the Saturday Plaza, by street, 1964–1965

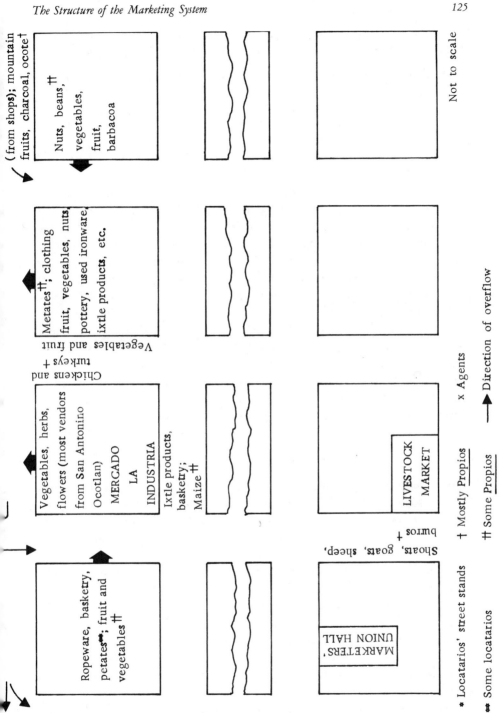

(from shops); mountain fruits, charcoal, ocote†

Nuts, beans,†† vegetables, fruit, barbacoa

Metates††; clothing fruit, vegetables, nuts, pottery, used ironware, ixtle products, etc.

Vegetables and fruit

Chickens and turkeys †

Vegetables, herbs, flowers (most vendors from San Antonino Ocotlan)

MERCADO LA INDUSTRIA

Ixtle products, basketry; Maize ††

Ropeware, basketry, petates**; fruit and vegetables ††

Shoats, goats, sheep, burros †

LIVESTOCK MARKET

MARKETERS' UNION HALL

Not to scale

x Agents

→ Direction of overflow

† Mostly Propios

†† Some Propios

* Locatarios' street stands

** Some locatarios

rubber findings for making huaraches. Finally, there are a number of permanent kiosks scattered through the business district of the City, which are usually located on sidewalks, licensed by and paying rent to the *Administración de Mercados*. Many of these specialize in such things as newspapers, cigarettes and matches, or soft drinks.

Some of the major classes of merchandise in the central open part of the Benito Juárez *mercado* are: fruit; vegetables (with specializations in such vegetables as tomatoes, onions, potatoes, fresh chile peppers and dried chile peppers; beans, and related products such as garbanzos); eggs; milk; cheese; flowers (now mostly moved outside); fish; dressed poultry (live poultry is sold in the streets, primarily on *plaza* days); walnuts, pecans, and peanuts; and refreshments (unbottled soft drinks, custards, gelatins, and ice cream). In *casetas* facing the open part of the market, or in the corridors of the building, the types of enterprises represented include groceries; hardware; sheet metal work and tinware (now mostly outside the market building); sandals; hats; cloth; ready-made clothing; rebozos; perfumes, soap, toothpaste, and related products; beef and pork and their products. A large part of the 20 de Noviembre market is occupied by small restaurant stands or *fondas*. Here also are found almost all the sellers of *barbacoa* (grilled meat, mostly mutton or goat, usually eaten on the premises), bread, brown sugar, and prepared chocolate. The exterior *casetas* of this market building are occupied primarily by shops selling pottery or *jarcieria* (maguey) and palm fiber products. Other maguey product vendors and sellers of maize and baskets are in the *Mercado Industria*. More detailed data are given in appendix 23 for the two main market buildings. As in the street *plaza,* similar merchandise tends to be located together.

On the basis of official records and counts by the Waterburys, the total number of separate enterprises in the Benito Juárez *mercado* seems to have varied in recent years between just under 800 to nearly 900. An exact figure is difficult to give because some transient sellers permitted in the aisles and entrances sometimes are included in counts. In addition there is a constant fluctuation as stalls are abandoned, change hands, or are temporarily vacant, while during the period of the study, parts of the market building were being remodeled.

For the 20 de Noviembre market, a count by the Waterburys gave a total of 416, including 147 *fondas*. For neither market were the many transient tortilla vendors counted; their number fluctuates from hour to hour as well as from day to day. The total number of separate enterprises of all sizes involved in the central *mercados* is certainly not less than 1,200 and more probably approaches 1,500.

Located in other buildings outside the market structures of the central district are permanent businesses closely linked with the *mercado* or the weekly *plaza* or both. Most wholesalers of fruits and vegetables are located close to the permanent *mercado* buildings and several are across the street from them. In addition are depots specializing in maize, other grains, and dry foods including peanuts, dried fish, nuts, and similar products. The fruit and vegetable wholesalers function primarily to import fruits and vegetables for resale to *regatones* from within the system or from Chiapas. A few offer second-grade, overripe, or bruised merchandise at retail, at bargain prices, but otherwise make little effort to sell good produce at retail. Dealers in dry foods function partly as buyers from peasant producers and sell principally to *regatones*. Other businesses closely related to the market include milling establishments specializing in grinding coffee, chocolate, or dry grains.

Modern commercial enterprises face the market area. For example, the smallest of the three "supermarkets" is across the street from the Benito Juárez *mercado*. Large grocery, hardware, and dry goods stores are close to the market area and do their biggest business on *plaza* days. Many of these are also wholesale establishments selling to *regatones*. It should be observed, however, that most of the larger stores catering to the City population and to tourists are outside the central market district. In addition, there are many small neighborhood businesses, mostly grocery stores with specialized or limited stocks, scattered through the City and the outlying *barrios*. Some are tiny and resemble the *changarros* found in villages, consisting of a table with a small collection of fruits or soft drinks or other common food items.

Little can be said about the number of *ambulantes* or peddlers, most of whom sell outside the market district. A few types of small vendors such as those who sell tortillas tend to be in fixed locations in or near *mercado* buildings but are not charged a market tax. At a guess there are rarely fewer than 25 tortilla venders in the larger Benito Juárez marketplace on weekdays between the hours of 10 or 11 A.M. and about 3 P.M., but there are 100 or more *ambulantes* on Saturdays. These figures do not represent the total number of vendors of this type, for as some sell out their stock, others take their places. A few offer tortillas even into the late evening near the barbecue stands in the 20 de Noviembre market building. Neither is any estimate possible of the number of porters transporting goods through the central district.

Secondary Valley Plazas Outside Oaxaca City

The secondary and in some cases the larger tertiary market towns in the Valley to some extent duplicate the variety of goods offered for sale in Oaxaca City. They differ from the City marketplace primarily in the lesser variety of industrial products, the relative unimportance of *mercados,* and the smaller numbers of vendors and buyers in the weekly *plazas*. Stores are fewer and smaller, and there are few wholesale dealers. The latter usually are semijobbers selling to consumers at retail, and at wholesale to intervillage traders or to *regatones* based in villages who resell in their home communities. Other storekeepers, acting either independently or as agents for Oaxaca enterprises, may buy local or subregional products, thus acting as bulkers.

Each secondary and tertiary market town is the primary service area for a cluster of surrounding villages, with the difference that village dwellers in the tertiary market area may alternatively visit the nearest secondary market town. This is especially true of sellers. The metate makers of Magdalena Ocotlán, for example, always sell their metates in Ocotlán although the tertiary market town of San Pedro Apóstol is only a fifteen or twenty minute walk. Zimatlán and Zaachila draw vendors and buyers from the nearby mountains to the west, many of them from Mixtec villages. Ejutla is in part a "transit" marketplace, an exchange point for part of the Sierra Madre del Sur. In this respect Miahuatlán is even more important and also is one of the major points for assembling coffee, a rapidly expanding crop in the Sierra Madre del Sur. In addition, it serves in part as a point of entry for goods from the coastal region to the south. Ayoquezco has become more important since it became the head of the pavement on the road to the coastal port of Puerto Escondido and to Sola de Vega, a region lacking *plazas*. Etla, in the western arm of the Valley, has one of the smaller secondary *plazas*. Much of the activity there takes place in the courtyard or otherwise unoccupied sections of a central market building or in the *plazas* and streets surrounding it. Also within the market building are stores operating on a daily basis. Although Etla is close to the mountains of the Mixteca, it does not seem to draw many buyers or sellers from that region except from the closer villages. It is in the heart of the principal dairying region of the Valley, but few dairy products are offered for sale there; most are sold by Etla producers to permanent operators of cheese-vending stalls in the Oaxaca City *mercado,* to buyers on the trains to Puebla and Mexico City, or in a few instances by direct shipment to these larger cities.

Ocotlán, located south of the City in the midst of the most fertile and densely settled part of the Valley, is the largest secondary marketplace in terms of numbers of vendors. For some commodities such as metates, it apparently serves an extended area to the south. It also has the largest cattle market in the Valley, which supplies most of the cattle butchered in Oaxaca. Tlacolula is a major service point for a large part of the Zapotec Sierra of Villa Alta, the Cajonos region and the Mixería. People in the distinctive costumes of those areas are more frequently seen in Tlacolula than in Oaxaca. The Tlacolula cattle market is the major one for the people of the Sierra. Tlacolula, Ocotlán, and Oaxaca City receive almost all the metates made in the region, and each has a distinctive distribution area. Tlacolula and Miahuatlán are important assembly points for coffee, but all Tlacolula coffee goes on to Oaxaca while some Miahuatlán coffee is shipped direct by sea through Puerto Angel.

The locations and schedules of the secondary and tertiary markets are given in chapter 3. Each of the secondary market towns in the Valley was visited several times by project staff members on *plaza* days, and three or four complete censuses by products sold were conducted for each. The results of these censuses are shown in appendix 24. Only Ocotlán had more than a thousand vendors for the week of highest activity, just before the Day of the Dead.

All the secondary marketplace towns have *mercados* with permanent market structures. None of these, however, is fully occupied during the week. The number of daily vendors is relatively small and the variety gf goods is limited. Selling by producers is almost entirely confined to *plaza* days.

Tlacolula marketplace. The market town of Tlacolula was intensively studied by Martin Diskin. Diskin mapped the marketplace and observed it systematically in some detail for nearly a year. He also mapped the town, took a census count of the community, and conducted an extensive survey from a large sample. Part of the results of this study are available (Diskin 1967), and here I will only summarize a few characteristics of the marketplace.

Tlacolula, about 18 miles southeast of the city of Oaxaca, has the most important secondary marketplace in the Valley of Oaxaca (although Ocotlán has more vendors on most *plaza* days). It is connected with the city by a spur railroad and is traversed by the section of the Pan American Highway which connects Oaxaca City to Tehuantepec. In recent years roads have extended from Tlacolula into the mountains to the north as far as Yalalag.

Tlacolula is an essentially mestizo town of about 7,500 people. It has many stores and some small, mostly handicraft, industries. The largest enterprises are a mescal factory and an establishment for mechanically processing maguey fiber. Other occupations are given in appendix 3. In its commercial role Tlacolula serves as primary marketplace to about thirty villages and is an important distribution center for the northern Sierra.

Most market activity in Tlacolula takes place in a large space south of the church and on some adjoining streets. Half of this space is surrounded by a group of permanent public buildings called *galeras*. The open space between these buildings has a fountain and trees, and some attempt has been made at gardening. The unenclosed space is barren ground in which trucks sometimes park to sell goods on *plaza* days. On weekdays from 78 to 148 vendors sell in the *galeras*. Their activities apparently are geared to the daily needs of local housewives. For example, maize is sold in one *galera* in the evenings, presumably so housewives may buy a supply to prepare for the mill the following morning.

The weekly *plaza* occurs on Sunday. This is the only time the *galeras* are filled with *puestos*. So, too, is the open space they enclose. The open space outside the *galeras* is rarely completely filled but its use fluctuates markedly with the seasons.

Diskin estimates that the average number of *puestos* on *plaza* days is about 700 but that the number may fluctuate seasonally by as much as 200 to 300. He estimates an average of 100 *ambulantes* in addition. The main fluctuations are geared to the ritual calendar when some people are accustomed to make purchases of certain goods for the entire year, for example, of metates, clothing, and cloth. Another source of fluctuation is the seasonal character of some perishable goods, for example, watermelons and papaya. Consequently there are some vendors who are present practically every week while others sell on a part-time basis and probably have other sources of income. Many of the *regatones* selling regularly in the *plaza* are traders following the weekly cycle of *plazas;* others, mostly based in Tlacolula, sell only in the local *plaza.*

In general, through the year the relative locations of vendors of each type of goods in the marketplace do not change. For example, most pottery is sold in the interior part of the marketplace area by *regatones* who are present on a fairly regular weekly basis. The pottery of San Marcos Tlapazola, however, is sold by makers on a rather irregular basis, and vendors are to be found outside the area of the *galeras.* San Marcos is a poor village, and it might be expected that pottery sales would be an important and more regular supplement to their income. San Marcos pottery, however, is a thick, polished redware, inferior for most purposes to ceramic products from elsewhere. It is not widely distributed and is rarely if ever handled by *regatones.* The *regatones* in the interior of the market *plaza* handle higher quality wares from other Valley towns such as Atzompa, and a few offer small quantities of "luxury" glazed wares from Puebla and Guanajuato which are in some demand for eating dishes on special occasions.

The following data selected from an inventory made by Diskin on September 12, 1965 show the origins of vendors and the type and source of a variety of goods. They make clear the specialization involved for regional productions. Generally, vendors of a single type of goods have adjoining *puestos.*

FLOWERS: 9 *propios* from Tlacochahuaya.
                    15 *propios* from San Lucas Quiavini and San Bartolome Quialana.
                    16 *regatones* from Tlacolula who bought flowers in Oaxaca.
                    Not counted were women from Oaxaca City with lilies and gladiolus.
DRIED FISH: 15 *regatones* from Tlacolula selling fish supplied by truckers.
                    4 *regatones* or *propios* from the Isthmus.
FRIJOL (BEANS):   8 *propios* from San Marcos Tlapazola selling *frijol delgado* and *frijol grueso.*
                    4 *regatones* from Tlacolula with larger and more varied stocks.
MECATE (IXTLE FIBER PRODUCTS):
                    75 *propios* from San Pablo Guilá.

7 *regatones* from Tlacolula.

(Surprisingly, there are no *propios* from the Cajonos region in the nearby Sierra.)

TOMATOES: 41 *propios* from San Bartolome Quialana.

6 *regatones,* selling other goods as well, from Tlacolula.

VEGETABLES (MAINLY ONIONS, GARLIC, STRING BEANS, HERBS):

13 *propios* from Tlacochahuaya.

ONIONS: 6 women (status uncertain) from San Antonino Ocotlán selling both wholesale (by the hundred) and retail. Each woman had several *piscadores* or harvest-size basketsful delivered by truck.

OCOTE (PITCH PINE):

15 *propios* from San Miguel del Valle.

POTATOES, OCOTE, AND GLADIOLUS:

15 *propios* from Cuajimoloyas (the only producer of potatoes in the region).

CHILE PEPPERS: 5 *regatones* (assumed to be *regatones* because they are regular visitors) from the Mixería.

In his field notes Diskin suggests that the number of vendors of particular commodities in the various secondary markets is in part a reflection of the specialized production in the nearby villages. San Marcos pottery has already been mentioned as having a special place in the Tlacolula *plaza*. Except for a smaller number of *propios* encountered most weeks in the *plaza* at Oaxaca, this pottery is not regularly sold elsewhere. Diskin also notes the very large number of vendors of *mecate* or ixtle fiber products and attributes this to the close ties with the Cajonos region in the Sierra to the north, where ixtle production is very important in local village economies. On the surface, this is borne out by the 75 ixtle vendors in his 1965 census, but in fact all of these vendors are from San Pablo Guilá, located in a rather small ixtle-producing area in the hills at the southwestern extremity of the Tlacolula arm of the Valley. Diskin further notes that most of the same vendors seem to have been present for several weeks. It is unlikely that this predominance of vendors from Guilá and the absence of vendors from the Cajonos towns is because of seasonal factors or that the seven *regatones* from Tlacolula handle all the Cajonos output. At present no satisfactory explanation can be offered. This points up the need for additional detailed studies of particular commodities such as Cook has done for the metate industry.

Tertiary Plazas

The tertiary *plazas* are understressed in the study. Some, such as that at Tlacochahuaya, are considered to be relatively unimportant reflexes of larger nearby secondary marketplaces. Most of the vendors at Tlacochahuaya appeared to be local residents who had bought goods in Tlacolula for resale to fellow villagers who were too busy or whose wants were too small to warrant the trip to Tlacolula. Most of the goods offered are foodstuffs, primarily perishables. Some of these are not important; Tlacochahuaya is itself a major vegetable-producing area.

Other tertiary markets are much larger and merit more detailed study. Their importance was not recognized until late in the field work study period. An example is San Pedro Apóstol, a few miles south of Ocotlán. There the *plaza,* held on Sunday, takes place in the town square. In many ways it reproduces the secondary *plazas* in terms of the variety of goods offered, and for most goods sold there are several competing vendors, although for most products they are fewer than at Ocotlán, the nearest secondary *plaza.* Neither do buyers form dense crowds as in the larger markets. Judging the origins of those who participate on the basis of their dress, there appear to be fewer buyers and sellers from a distance at San Pedro than at Ocotlán, although some *propios* bring highland products from the Mixteca Sierra to the west.

Like the larger *plazas,* San Pedro Apóstol is visited fairly regularly by buyers from a number of surrounding villages. But whereas the nearest secondary *plaza,* Ocotlán, may draw buyers from twenty-five or thirty villages, San Pedro Apóstol seems to draw from only some ten surrounding villages. Most of those who attend the San Pedro *plaza,* moreover, are also within a reasonable distance of Ocotlán and sometimes visit that *plaza* as an alternative.

Yet, as is the case with many larger *plazas,* San Pedro Apóstol has some special features. About the central square are found grocery and dry goods stores, some of them at least as large as many in the larger market towns. In addition, the *plaza* offers perhaps the largest selection of wooden building materials of any *plaza* in the Valley. One block-long side of the square is occupied by carts offering beams, plates, rafters, stringers, and planks. Why this should be so was not discovered; San Pedro is not as close to forested mountain areas as are some other *plazas.* It may be that this smaller market is not so often visited by forestry officials and tax collectors. Diskin notes that the few vendors of forest products at Tlacolula are located on a back street, and the number of sellers fluctuates. He suggests that most of them operate without forestry permits.

Another similar *plaza* is said to be held at San Pablo Huixtepec, a town located about $2\frac{1}{2}$ miles south of Zimatlán and connected with Ocotlán by an east-west road that runs about 5 miles north of San Pedro Apóstol. This *plaza* was not visited. It is reported to be a major *plaza* on the occasion of the fiesta of the patron saint, drawing large numbers of buyers and sellers from considerable distances on this occasion. Most of the year, however, it seems to be comparable to San Pedro in importance.

Enough observations have been made to indicate that the lesser secondary *plazas* and the tertiary *plazas* in the Valley operate on much the same basis as those studied more intensively. Perhaps the major differences are in the extent to which towns have permanent *mercados,* how large these are, and the number and size of stores. The principal factors contributing to the importance of market towns seem to be the size of the community, adequacy of transportation in the area, and the nearness of satellite villages, some of which may be near enough for frequent visits. But Mitla, although it is a highly commercial town with intensive intervillage and inter*plaza* trade and stores that are exceptional in their number and size, has virtually no *plaza.*

Sierra Plazas

In the Zapotec Sierra, Berg has studied the *plaza* of Zoogocho in the *exdistrito* of Villa Alta both intensively and over a substantial period of time, and visited all other *plazas* in the area at least once. The physical arrangements of most Sierra *plazas* are modified by the rugged terrain that prohibits any sizable level area. If due allowance is made for the sloping terrain, however, the *plaza* vendors are as close together as is practicable, and vendors of similar goods tend to be grouped together just as in the Valley. The major distinguishing features include some modification of the kinds and relative quantities of goods offered, which is a function of different consumption needs and limited local production of some items. Zoogocho is the primary marketplace for 14 other villages, but altogether they have only 825 households. Generally the population is poorer than are similar populations in the Valley. The rugged terrain about Zoogocho limits the number and size of villages within reasonable travel distance of the *plaza.* Similar conditions throughout the Sierra result in a larger number of small *plazas,* relative to the size of populations served, than occurs in the Valley.

Some description of the Zoogocho market is found in Berg (1968). The major *plaza* in the Mixe area of the Sierra, Ayutla, is discussed in chapter 10, below, and in an earlier work (Beals 1945).

In conclusion, despite differences in size and spatial arrangements, the marketplaces throughout the marketing system show recurring characteristics:

1. A number—often large—of vendors selling the same items;
2. A high degree of specialization of vendors who usually limit themselves to one product or a group of related products;
3. Vendors selling the same type of product in adjacent locations;
4. Both producer-vendors and professional traders in the same marketplaces; and
5. A large selection of various items from which the buyers can choose.

Finally, although the bulk of goods distributed in the region passes through marketplaces, it should be borne in mind that there are alternative distributional arrangements that bypass the marketplaces.

7
Dynamics of the Marketing System: I

Chapter 6 identified the different locations of marketing activities, identified the various types of actors involved, and examined the organization of some of the marketplaces. This chapter examines in some detail how goods flow through the marketing system and the ways in which various kinds of sellers carry on their marketing activities. Two types of such actors or functionaries are generally recognized in Oaxaca, the *propio* or producer who markets his own product, and the *regatón* or middleman who buys and sells goods produced by others. The two categories are not entirely distinct, for some individuals engaged primarily in production may at times act as *regatones,* while some *regatones* may be engaged in some productive activities. Thus at different times an individual may be classed either as a *propio* or as a *regatón* depending upon the origin of the goods he is selling.

The way goods flow through the marketing system and the manner in which various actors participate in or respond to market situations vary with the characteristics of different commodities, with the level or scale of operations, and with the types of actors involved. There are several ways of approaching the functioning of the marketing system. One approach, emphasizing the production aspect of the system, traces particular commodities from their creation in the production process through the various steps until they are consumed or discarded by the ultimate consumer or are transformed through intermediate steps into more complex consumer's goods. The character of the Oaxaca peasant production process has been examined in general terms in chapter 4. Some studies, notably those by Scott Cook and certain aspects of the studies by Charlotte Stolmaker, have emphasized the production of specific handicraft commodities (metates and ceramics) and their flow through the market from producer to consumer. Cook's study, covering all metate supply sources, shows that each supply source serves a different market in different ways, while Stolmaker's study of a single village shows the numerous ways pottery may be distributed. Details are given in appendixes 25 and 26.

Another approach to understanding distribution is from the opposite end of the chain of marketing transactions, that is, consumption. In chapter 5 consumption in peasant Oaxaca is presented in general terms, but the examination of the marketing system from the consumption standpoint is not so detailed as the special studies from the production standpoint. Consumption-oriented studies as well as more production-oriented studies no doubt will amplify, and in all probability modify, the general comments on the functioning of the marketing system presented in this chapter. This section is oriented toward the market transaction and the conduct of business, and must be understood as providing only a partial view of the marketing system.

The village, as has been made clear, is an important unit for the study of production and consumption in the Oaxaca marketing system; within it, households are the loci of most production and consumption activities. In addition, the village is an important scene of exchange transactions and is the residential location of the producer-vendor or *propio,* clearly recognized as a special type of actor in the marketing system. Among the important questions relating to the village's role in the marketing system are the extent to which the village producers act as *propios,* marketing their own products to consumers or to intermediaries; and the degree to which market principles operate within the village and how they affect exchange. Also, how much of the production is for household or intravillage consumption? Can exchange transactions within the village be viewed as market transactions or do they involve other kinds of exchange such as reciprocal gifting? Only partial answers to these questions can be given at this time, pending further analysis of village data. Further village studies also are needed, for the evidence suggests that our sample of village studies is too small to cover the range of variations existing.

AUTOCONSUMPTION AND INTRAVILLAGE EXCHANGE

It is characteristic of peasant economies that the household consumes part of its own production. The discussions of production and consumption (chapters 4 and 5) suggest that in Oaxaca the amount of this autoconsumption is relatively small. But for the 15 Sierra villages involved in the Zoogocho primary *plaza* network,

Berg (1968:273) identified 516 products or classes of products (for example, he listed ixtle products as a single item) consumed. He found that 63 percent of all items consumed either were produced by the household or were procured directly from other producing households without the involvement of intermediaries. Some of these items also were available through the *plaza*, the *tienda*, or other types of market-oriented mechanisms. The relative quantities of these items that are autoconsumed, acquired through intravillage exchange, or purchased in the store or *plaza* are difficult to ascertain. Yet some perspectives may be obtained from Berg's estimate (1968:111, and chap. 5, above) that in the Zoogocho system only 44.5 percent of the maize consumed by the average household is locally produced, a figure that probably applies to the Villa Alta region as a whole. This means that 55.5 percent of the most basic food is obtained through the marketing system.

For the Valley, the larger scale of the market has not yet permitted quite such detailed information at the household level, but the percentage of goods autoconsumed by the household or procured in interhousehold trade would seem to be lower than in the Sierra. Not only is farm production more specialized in Valley villages, but there is also a much higher production of handicrafts with concomitantly lower food production, and in many villages a large landless labor force exists which produces none of its own consumption goods. Also, in contrast with the Sierra, a larger percentage of Valley peasants depend on trade for a livelihood; the number in such villages as Mitla and San Antonino Ocotlán is substantial. Moreover, in the Valley much of the secular household-to-household intravillage exchange recorded appears to be in the form of temporary loans of cash or consumption goods. By and large the village household in the Valley, as we have noted, prefers to buy or sell in a marketplace where there is more information about prices.

Whatever the degree of autoconsumption may be, it seems clear that all peasant households in the Oaxaca region are in some degree involved in exchange transactions. Put another way, all households dispose of some good or service in order to secure other goods and services. It does not automatically follow, however, that all peasants are *propios* involved in the marketing system. From the standpoint of the system, the *propio* is most clearly defined in the *plaza* as an important type of vendor. He differs from other vendors in that, in his case, goods potentially may pass directly from producer to consumer without any intervening transactions or functionaries. Especially within the village, it is conceivable that market principles do not operate in some of these direct exchanges. A brief examination of interhousehold and intravillage exchange hence is in order.

Intravillage Exchange

Barter clearly occurs in the village (and sometimes also in the *plaza*). Much of this barter, however, occurs within the context of the market price of the goods exchanged. This introduces the element of bargaining, which may easily lead to disagreements disruptive of the smooth operation of social relationships within the village. Moreover, often it is difficult for parties in such barter transactions to match their respective needs. For both these reasons it is suspected that short-term loans of goods are preferred by both parties to a formal exchange transaction even at the barter level. There is also some reciprocal labor exchange in the intravillage situation, more in the Sierra than in the Valley, but generally, the greater the cash flow, through selling of farm products or handicrafts in the market, the more wage labor replaces labor exchange. The explanation usually given is that wage labor is less costly and more efficient, for the farmer has more control over the level of work activity and less expense for feeding the work force. All information from the Valley indicates that the use of wage labor is definitely responsive to market conditions and that wages for farm labor increased on the order of 100 percent in the decade of 1960–1970.

The important issue from some theoretical discussion is the extent to which reciprocity replaces market operations in the Oaxaca peasant village economy. As Beals (1970) has pointed out, true gifting occurs when goods (or even cash) are bestowed on others in a variety of secular and ritual circumstances for which no formal reciprocity is expected. Goods are given to promote some social relationship without expectation of repayment in kind or of equal value. Most of the gifts are of food or drink. The most massive gifting is on All Saints Day and involves only food. It is true that continued gift giving often depends on some kind of reciprocation, which may be little more than the support of the donor's social position by the recipient, and it is also true that there is a diffused expectation that the gift giving will balance out in the long run even though there may be no equation between donors and recipients; but there is no formal time interval or expectation that goods in return gifts will be equivalent either in kind or value. This is very far from representing a consistent and economically important method of exchanging goods.

Much more pertinent is the formal exchange known as *guelaguetza,*[1] the "loaning" of cash or goods on ritual occasions, the loans to be repaid by the recipient in kind, but without interest, when the donor has some similar ritual obligation. Such "loans" are clearly distinguished from gifts, although the latter also occur on the same occasions. In *guelaguetza,* if goods are involved, values are precisely calculated and returns in the same kind and of the same value are expected and socially required on the demand of the donor. Most *guelaguetza* is solicited, mainly from friends and neighbors. Individuals, however, may volunteer *guelaguetza* to establish credit against an anticipated future need. Although this

[1] This is the common term used in the Valley; other terms are used in some subregions.

may be viewed as reciprocity, as Beals (1970) has indicated, it may be regarded equally as a noninterest system of savings and credit in which the recipient gains assistance for extraordinary ritual obligations and the lender establishes savings or credits toward the time when he must meet similar obligations. From the very nature of the institution, *guelaguetza* is not a systematic means of meeting day-to-day secular consumption needs.

Although these types of intravillage exchange, as well as the distribution of goods through the ritual and ceremonial system, are only marginally related to the market, they cannot be ignored completely. On the one hand, exchanges and reciprocation result in goods being withheld from the market. On the other hand, gifting and distributions in ritual and ceremonial contexts may involve expanded purchases by gift-givers through the market system. In all cases economic decisions are involved.

OPERATIONS OF THE PROPIO IN THE MARKETING SYSTEM

The foregoing discussion is presented as a general background to the way the producer-vendor operates in the marketing system. Any examination of how specific goods move from the producer's household will show that the problems and the ways in which these problems are met differ markedly with the product. In addition, although in local terminology all producer-vendors are classed as *propios,* there are marked differences between individuals within the class, depending upon the degree to which behavior in the marketplace is affected by various kinds of consumption needs.

As used locally, the term *propio* refers essentially to an individual who sells something he has produced, including not only the raw products of farm, forest, and sea but also household-produced handicrafts. Analytically, although not in the local usage, the class might be extended to include the landless *jornalero* or laborer in the village or the purveyor of some specialized service such as the musician, barber, or *curandero.* In the abstract all are alike in that they can determine whether a particular commodity or the segment of the supply that they control enters the market or not. In fact, they are less than free agents in this regard, for they also are driven by inescapable consumption needs that continually force them to dispose of some portion of the commodity they control. Even for farmers, as has already been emphasized, these consumption needs usually include basic subsistence commodities, for even those who produce an adequate supply of maize for household consumption do not produce all the types of foodstuffs generally regarded as essential. In addition, the producer-vendor is driven to reliance on the market by other needs. He may require cash to carry forward production activities such as the rental of oxen for plowing or the purchase of raw materials to continue craft production, or to meet some social obligation.

The selling activities of the *propio* may appropriately be considered simply as a terminal part of the production process (in the utility-producing sense). This is especially true of those sales made at the point of production. The choice of alternatives in the sale of products, however, depends in part on the conditions of the marketing system and the options it offers. And once the producer decides to sell outside the village, he becomes involved in some of the same problems that face other types of traders, including questions of capital and transportation, the selection of marketplaces, and the alternatives of selling at retail to consumers or at wholesale to *regatones*.

Capital considerations in the *propio*'s operations are either lacking or very small. Yet even a small-scale fruit vendor from the Sierra must own nets or baskets, usually purchased, and generally must either own or rent burros, unless he uses trucks or buses and is situated near a road. If he travels with burros, he must spend money for "parking" fees (unless he has a charitable friend in town), for fodder, possibly for lodging for himself as well as for meals and market fees. Some of these costs may be avoided if he sells his goods promptly at wholesale.

Finally, time considerations may be important in reaching decisions. In many discussions of peasant economies it is assumed that time spent in marketing is of zero marginal utility. This may be true in some seasons. It is not true of all peasants generally, and it is never true of the handicraft producer. All these considerations affect decisions about the place of sale, that is, whether to sell in the village or outside. At however low a level, then, all *propios* are involved in some variety of decisions with respect to the marketing system.

Farming Propios

For the *propio* selling in the marketplace, there are still many alternative opportunities and also substantial differences in options according to the type of goods involved. Even among producers of foodstuffs, the difference between the marketing of perishable fruits such as apples, peaches, cherries, or quinces from the Sierra and the vending of perishable vegetables and flowers from, say, San Antonino Ocotlán, is quite marked. The producer from the Sierra may be selling in the market only a few days a year. The San Antonino producer may sell weekly in the market, possibly as a *regatón* part of the time, reselling goods he has bought. Although he appears to be selling to retail consumers, often the bulk of his sales is to dealers who buy in quantity. The same is true of some other *propios*, for example, pottery vendors. In the Oaxaca *plaza* such vendors make most of their bulk sales by 7 or 8 A.M.

At first sight it may appear that many *propios* selling the basic staple, maize, are selling a surplus in the market to get cash to buy some needed supplementary foodstuffs or other goods. In fact, this may be true but only in a very limited sense. The maize-producing *propio* may have a surplus of maize at a given moment but may well not have enough maize to meet his needs until the next harvest. Traditionally, the Oaxaca peasant likes to have enough maize from his own production not only to carry him over to the next harvest but also, if possible, as a reserve against a poor crop the following year. Nevertheless, he may sell some of his maize to make purchases of other goods he wants or needs at a given moment. Thus the *propio* maize vendor of today may be a maize buyer next month or six months from now. Such a *propio*'s method of operating in the market may be entirely controlled by consumption needs. Normally he will offer for sale in the market only that quantity of maize that he estimates, from his knowledge of prices and demand, he must sell to buy the particular goods he wants. These wanted goods may range from vegetables such as tomatoes and onions, or spices, coffee, chocolate, candles, or kerosense, to clothing for a school graduation, medicines for a sick wife, or a piglet to fatten. More rarely, he may sell larger quantities on a speculative basis: he estimates that maize prices may be lower at some future time when he will enter the market as a buyer. More probably, if he has no immediate needs he will feed the grain to animals, especially pigs, thereby using it as part of an investment that will yield a lump-sum return when the pigs are fattened and sold. Or the maize may be sold to obtain cash for some other profit-making activity, for example, to pay for ox-team rental or tractor plowing or for some piece of equipment that enhances the peasant's agricultural productivity.

These various motivations do not exhaust the complexities of the market operation and the kinds of choices the *propio* may make. A small quantity of maize may be sold to the village storekeeper or else sold retail in the *plaza*. A larger quantity of maize is apt to be sold in the market town to a *regatón*, in this case either to *agencias* or bulkers who sell wholesale, or a *puesto* operator specializing in selling maize retail.

Similar patterns of operation exist for such nonperishable food staples as beans, garbanzos, or dried peas, as well as for poultry and eggs. Although poultry is often said to be raised for autoconsumption, most fowl, especially chickens, are perhaps more commonly sold to meet other urgent consumption needs. A substantial number of the chickens entering the *plaza* are in this sense forced sales, usually providing funds for a week's food supply purchased from *plaza* sources, although some may be sold to meet emergencies of other sorts. The main point of emphasizing these types of motivations for selling on the part of the *propio* is to make it clear that in some sense the transactions are responding to forces other than the full free play of market supply and demand. Demand is always present in the sense that there are always people who are prepared to buy at some price, but the *propio* is not a free agent in negotiating for the most advantageous price or in withholding his product until prices are more favorable. Another point of importance which I have already made is that the *propio* does not ordinarily seek out buyers in local households but sells either to consumers in the *plaza* or to an intermediary of some sort.

With perishable vegetable food products the *propio* also has limitations but they are not the constraints imposed by selling to meet immediate consumption needs. Rather they are the constraints imposed because goods, once matured, must move quickly to the consumer before they deteriorate. The producing household may consume some such products, but the main production passes through the market system to the consumer. The possible time lapse between harvest and consumption differs with products; onions, for example, permit much more flexibility on the part of the *propio* than do tomatoes or flowers. Onion or potato harvests may be delayed for a week or so in response to unfavorable market conditions. Actually there is little evidence that this is frequently done. But the goods may be held by the vendor and particularly by intermediaries for several days. In contrast, if they are to be sold to consumers in the local market, they must be timed so that they are reasonably mature when they reach the ultimate consumer. Once ready for sale, they must be moved promptly to avoid losses. Again constraints are placed on the freedom of the seller to bargain or hold out for higher prices. Another constraint or condition affecting the movement of perishables is the availability of transportation.

Most *propios* selling fruit in Valley marketplaces come from the Sierras to the north and west of the Valley. The main exceptions are a few producers of citrus and bananas who are mainly from the southern arm of the Valley. Sierra producers sell mostly deciduous fruits or avocados. Usually they are maize farmers who have a limited number of fruit trees producing several varieties of peaches and apples or, less frequently, pears, quinces, and cherries. These are inferior traditional varieties grown with a minimum of arboriculture, with little pruning, cultivation, irrigation, or fertilizing. The fruit tends to be small, and except for a distinctive flavor, is generally inferior to modern varieties now available from outside the region.

Fruit-selling *propios* not only deal in a seasonal and fairly perishable product, they also travel fairly long distances. In addition, they usually have deferred consumption needs, which they try to meet in the Valley *plazas* to take advantage of lower prices. This further limits the time available for selling. Much of the fruit is offered at retail. If all of the vendor's stock is not sold at retail on a *plaza* day, what remains may be sold to *regatones* or, in the City, the *propio* may stay over a day and try to retail the remainder of his stock on Sunday in small street *plazas* outside neighborhood *mercados.* Or, if opportunity offers, he may sell all his stock to *regatones* early in the day.

Sierra fruit is packed in large carrying nets lined with leaves to protect the fruit. Two or three of these are a normal burro load, although single nets may be carried by a man. In the past burros were the common means of transportation. They still are often used to get the fruit to a bus route, and some *serranos* still travel to the Valley with burros. But most fruit in the major marketplaces today arrives on buses or, less frequently, by truck. Oaxaca City is the major market for this fruit, for it has by far the largest population of potential consumers and is also the most important redistribution center for other *plazas;* some sellers, however, go to other *plazas* such as Tlacolula or Zaachila.

Almost all of the fruit is sold at retail, and in the Oaxaca *plaza* in the fruit season a sizable area on the east side of the *plaza* district is occupied by *propios* from the Sierra. People from the same village tend to cluster together, each selling about the same variety and quality of fruit. Each vendor's stock is small, perhaps four to six nets on the average, crowded into the smallest possible ground space in order to pay the lowest possible fee to the market collectors. The fruit is laid out in small piles or *montones* with standard prices. Bargaining by buyers is confined almost wholly to discussions of quality and size of the *montón* (see chap. 9, below). As the vendor makes only one to three or four trips a year to the *plaza,* there is little or no question of stable or preferential buyer-seller relationships.

Some bulk sales do occur but the processes and subsequent distribution chains are obscure. The larger wholesalers do not handle Sierra fruit; neither do the permanent stall holders in the *mercado* in Oaxaca City. The only bulk transactions observed were in Zaachila on *plaza* days when some purchases of entire nets were made by the larger vendors of other fruits. The sales were subject to bargaining and the fruit was transferred to baskets used for transport.[2] Some undoubtedly goes ultimately to villages or outlying areas of Oaxaca City for sale by sidewalk or doorway small vendors.

The problem of price is minimal for the visiting Sierra fruit vendor except for bulk sales. For retail sales he can see the size of the *montones* being offered by others and witness the reaction of potential buyers. The vendor's main problem is to dispose of his stocks within a reasonable time, preferably before the end of the *plaza* day, to avoid the direct expense of staying over an additional day either to dispose of the last of his stock or to make purchases. His main problems are consumer demand, the competing supply, and theoretically the competition of

---

[2] Baskets commonly used for transporting goods are of a standardized wicker type known as the *piscador* because it is used to harvest maize (*piscar*).

other types of fruit such as the imported modern varieties. The quantity the market will absorb seems to be relatively stable. Variation in supply results from factors beyond the producer's control, involving mainly insect damage and weather. The individual vendor usually brings to market what fruit his trees have produced to the extent that he can transport it.

The Sierra fruit producer-vendor is rather minimally involved in the market, then. His choices are limited. He may, on a long-range basis, increase his production, but most fruit is grown on a very limited basis and is a minor crop for the producer. His short-range considerations seem to be: (1) whether he has enough fruit to make the selling trip worthwhile; (2) at which *plaza* he should sell; and (3) whether he should sell retail or in bulk (the latter option apparently is not always available). The producer must also reckon with the labor cost of harvesting the fruit (a family enterprise), the cost of carrying nets, and out-of-pocket outlays for transport, market permit, and usually some food purchased in the *plaza*. Despite the low level of participation, the Sierra fruit vendor supplies fairly definite requirements, and his small income from sales may be a major source of cash income for purchases of clothing or similar items.

Despite the number of Sierra fruit vendors in the Valley, only a small fraction of the fruit produced reaches the marketplace. Berg (1968:55–56) has identified 25 fruits grown in the Villa Alta region. Of these, only coffee and avocados are disposed of commercially, the latter often being sold directly or through agents to Mexico City wholesalers. Most of the other fruit is autoconsumed, mostly by children. Berg estimates that only five or six percent of the more than three million bananas and only about one percent of other fruits produced in the *barrancas* in the Sierra ever reaches the *plazas*. Much of this is consumed by buyers on the spot in the *plaza*. Evidently only producers within reasonable distance of major Valley *plazas* and with enough fruit to make the trip worthwhile ever attempt to market their fruit outside the Sierra.

Somewhat different patterns are followed by the producer-vendors of animals (other than poultry). Driving animals any distance is difficult, and reduces the market value of fattened pigs. Hence many are sold in or near the village of origin. Fattened pigs and beef cattle are often sold to butchers in or near the home village, but modern transportation has opened new avenues. Single sheep and goats often are transported by bus; larger animals may be transported by rented truck to major *plazas*. Many of the beef animals as well as young draft oxen for the Valley and the Sierra come from the Yautepec district or the Chiapas coast and are offered in the animal markets of Ocotlán, Tlacolula, or Oaxaca City. Some vendors are *propios* who have transported their animals by rented truck. Clearly the *propio* again is at some disadvantage. If he does not sell his animals on the *plaza* day, he may have to try to peddle them to buyers in the neighborhood, but if he has brought his animals from some distance most probably he will have to wait another week. The high value of these animals makes this a possible solution but it does increase expenses and reduce profits. Again there are pressures to cut prices to avoid delays.

With pigs, which are more widely fattened for market, the problem is somewhat different. Some animals are sold to butchers within the village or in a nearby village. Others are conveyed to a *plaza,* but increasingly in the Valley intermediaries with trucks tour the villages buying animals. To some extent sale in the village reduces the *propio*'s power to seek the best price; as a result, he may continue to feed the animal, hoping for a better offer from another visiting buyer or local butcher. The *propio* may also sell if pressed to meet an unexpected emergency, and most of the unusually low-priced sales of pigs recorded apparently are forced.

Handicraft Propios

Rather different patterns and alternatives exist with handicraft production. Virtually all the product goes to the *plaza* or to dealers in the distribution system; little or none is autoconsumed or consumed within the village of production. Essentially, the possible alternatives for the *propio* include: sale to an intermediary (local or from the outside) or inter*plaza* trader who transports the product to the *plaza;* transport by the *propio* to the *plaza,* where he sells to inter*plaza* traders, exporters, or operators of shops or *puestos* in Oaxaca City, or at retail; or some combination of these. To some extent the importance of these possible means of disposal varies with product. For some products, where tourist goods have become important business items, other ways of selling have appeared. Tourist shops in Oaxaca City often have special arrangements with village suppliers and may commission specific products. Bulk buyers or agents have appeared from outside the area and both they and some retail tourist customers have penetrated the village of production. In at least one textile-producing community, a large fraction of the production is controlled by a single entrepreneur who not only buys from producers and hires weavers to work on his own looms, but also obtains a large supply of the product by making cash advances to weavers.

Often, however, the handicraft *propio* is as limited in his market options as is the farmer, because of his lack of capital and the fact that his handicraft business is linked with the household budget. The handicraft producer ordinarily cannot withhold his product from the market even for a week or two because of ongoing expenses for the maintenance of the household, the purchase of raw materials to keep the handicraft operation functioning, and, in a few cases, the payment of wages. He may on occasion get short-term credits from relatives, from storekeepers, or even more rarely from suppliers. But the producer who continually is in debt is apt to wind up contracting his output to a dealer at a reduced price in return for a needed cash advance. In addition, some handicraft producers are faced with seasonal fluctuations in demand which may affect prices.

Restrictions on Propio Operations

The *propio,* then, has access to a free market with numerous alternatives. He may select a number of possible sites for disposing of his goods (including, of course, sale at the point of origin). His only restrictions on location are the requirement that he pay a fee to sell in a *plaza,* and the restriction to a particular section of the *plaza* which he shares with others selling similar merchandise. The fees are too small to constitute a serious obstacle, and the locational "restrictions" are shared by his competitors and may even be advantageous by ensuring exposure to a maximum number of potential customers. Under these circumstances, simple supply and demand factors theoretically should operate in the local *plaza.* In fact, other possible constraints exist. While supply or demand may be essentially local for some goods, at least within the limits of the market system, other goods may face competition from outside the system. This is true even of perishables. Not only does the producer have a seasonal production, but if prices rise or supply becomes limited, wholesalers may import goods from outside. This is manifest in the market for tomatoes. During the season of high production within the Valley, wholesalers do not import tomatoes, but as soon as production fails to meet the local demand or prices rise above a critical point, wholesalers will import this fruit. With more storable farm products or handicrafts, the producer still may be constrained to sell rather than to hold for expected higher prices, because of his own consumption needs. In addition, once some goods are conveyed to the *plaza,* it is too costly to take unsold remainders back to the point of production. It is here that the wholesaler or shopkeeper in the market town serves an important function for the producer: although he purchases at a lower price, his activities do help stablize the market and minimize losses by the producer.

The *propio* also is at the mercy of fluctuations in consumer demand which he is unable to predict except on the rather inaccurate basis of past experience. Some of the problems of price formation and the way prices are negotiated are discussed later. Here the most important point perhaps is that the decisions the *propio* makes not only are partly controlled by his own needs as a consumer but are also controlled by the effectiveness of his participation in the communication network. This latter factor helps to explain why two of the most absorbing subjects for conversation among most people in the area of the Oaxaca market system are prices and *movimiento,* that is, the numbers of people or the amount of activity at *plazas.*

MIDDLEMEN OR REGATONES

The term *"regatones"* (literally, "hagglers" or "bargainers") is the common Oaxaca term for all people who buy goods from others and sell them for a profit. Storekeepers and wholesalers, however, are sometimes distinguished by these terms from other *regatones;* they receive special discussion later. Within the usual category of *regatones,* several types can be distinguished analytically by the way they conduct their operations. All function wholly or in part within the traditional marketing system.

Village-based regatones. A common type of village-based *regatón* is a *propio* who carries on some trading in connection with the marketing of his own product. Such traders may buy additional goods similar to their own from fellow villagers or in nearby villages to sell in a *plaza,* or may buy goods in the *plaza* for resale in the home village. Some traders combine these two activities. The scale of their operations varies considerably. For smaller operators the trading activity is more-or-less incidental to marketing their own products. For others, trading may be a fairly important activity even though part time or seasonal.

For the small operator, little capital outlay is required and it is almost immediately recovered. The trader operates at whatever scale he can afford and in accordance to his estimate of demand and the possibility of profiting through price differentials. Larger-scale operators may also market some of their own products, but much of their trading is more systematic and important even though production activities may take a substantial part of their time.

Several men from Santa María Atzompa are pottery *regatones,* selling one or two days a week in one or two *plazas.* Most are basically *propios* selling their own household production, and most of the large-scale *regatones* are also farmers. Case histories indicate investments of $200 to $400 a week in pottery for resale. Around All Saints Day their investments in stock may go up to $1,000 a week. Most estimate their usual gross margins from pottery trading at around $100 a week. Informants' estimates of weekly expenses are given at the top of the next page.

These estimates suggest a weekly net profit of the order of $50. Purchasing goods, transportation, and selling probably require two days a week, giving a return of $25 a day for the time spent, not enough to support a family for a week unless there are other sources of income. Some of the larger *regatones* also own trucks, thus reducing transportation costs, but the primary function of trucks is to make a profit from hauling goods for *propios.*

Similar types of traders have been identified in other villages. Some producers in San Antonino Ocotlán specializing in the growing of flowers, onions, and other vegetables, buy from neighbors in the same village, or often from nearby villages

Plaza	Transportation cost, weekly†	Storage space rental cost, monthly
Case 1 Ocotlán	$43.75	$20.00
Case 2 Ocotlán	$35.00	$20.00
Case 3 Oaxaca	$20.00	$40.00
Case 4 Tlacolula	$12.00 to $25.00	$12.00
Case 5 Tlacolula, Zimatlán	$16.00 twice weekly*	$25.00, $15.00

† Fare for the trader is not included here, but this does include freight costs for his own pottery as well as the merchandise bought for resale.

* Probably an understatement. Another informant reported hearing the trader say he spent $30.00 for transportation and $10.00 a week for porterage on trips to Tlacolula.

growing the same products, and resell in the *plaza*. Some even go to Mexico City and Chiapas. An example of expenses and profits for this type of operation follows.

In December of 1966, HG of San Antonino bought a field of onions consisting of 32 rows, from which he anticipated a crop of 6,000 kilograms. He paid $5,500 for the field or about 91.5 *centavos* per kilogram. When the onions were ready for market, he could get only 90 *centavos* per kilogram in Oaxaca City. He then considered the alternative of sending the remaining onions—4,000 kilograms—to his sister in Tuxtla Gutierrez to sell in that Chiapas market, where onions were bringing $1.30 per kilogram. For the 4,000 kilograms, then, he expected a total sale of $5,200; 20 percent of the profit after expenses would be his sister's commission. He thought that trucking expenses would amount to approximately 10 *centavos* per kilogram, or $400. He estimated that his net profit would be about $894:

Gross profit		$5,200.00
Expenses:		
Cost of 4,000 onions	$3,667	
Labor to cut onions, approximately	15	
Freight costs to Tuxtla Gutierrez	400	4,082.00
Net profit		$1,118.00
Less commission		223.60
HG's receipts		$ 894.40

San Antonino apparently is one of the most important centers for village traders today. It is being studied in more detail by Waterbury.

Locally based *regatones* who buy from local producers are found in the metate-producing villages. Most commonly they buy "blanks" or partially finished metates from neighbors who operate quarries, finish, and market them. In Teotitlán del Valle some *regatones* either buy from the weaver or take serapes on consignment to peddle in Oaxaca or in other *plaza* towns. If on consignment, the weaver usually sets a minimum price and the *regatón* must sell for more than this to realize any gain and to pay for transportation and food. Unless goods are carried on consignment, considerable capital may be required for both metates and serapes as these have fairly high values per unit. Most Oaxaca vendors of Teotitlán serapes obtain them from one large buyer who maintains a warehouse in the village and another in the City.

Another type of village-based trader buys products from his own neighbors for resale in nearby villages that do not produce the same goods. Such traders are few, and most of them seem to be older women. Examples of such women traders were observed in Diaz Ordaz and Teotitlán del Valle. The women bought small stocks of vegetables and beans, food not produced or produced in short supply in these villages, in their home village of Tlacochahuaya, carried their stock on their backs, and either peddled them from house to house or offered them in the small *mercado* buildings at Diaz Ordaz and Teotitlán. The capital and costs involved are minimal; so also are the profits.

Yet another identifiable type of village-based *regatón* is the trader who buys and sells in villages other than his place of residence but who does not buy or sell in the *plaza*. As examples, pottery *regatones* from San Lorenzo Cacaotepec buy pottery in Atzompa for resale in the area villages nearby, although some go as far as Tomellín in the Cañada. A *petate* (mat) vendor from Teozacualco buys mats in Yutanduchi in the Mixtec region and sells them in Valley villages, picking up local specialties in their village of origin for resale in Yutanduchi. Such traders differ from the *viajeros* or traveling traders described below mainly in the scale of operations, distances traveled, and the fact that many *viajeros* also buy or sell in *plazas.*

Viajeros. Of considerable interest is yet another type of village-based *regatón:* the long-distance trader, usually called a *viajero,* who does not deal significantly in the products of his home village, but in goods passing through *plazas* or stores. Most of these seem to be concentrated in a few villages such as Mitla and San Antonino Ocotlán in the Valley, and Yalalag in the Sierra. Characteristically they both buy and sell at locations outside their home villages. The best known are the traders of *viajeros* of Mitla, often known as *arrieros* because they conveyed their goods in the past, and to some extent in the present, on trains of pack animals. Their operations are described in chapter 10.

Viajeros from the Isthmus, mostly women, represent a new class of trader. Some are older women without families, but many are younger women with families who supplement the family income. Most of the latter claim they would prefer to be simple housewives if the family income permitted. Some of the Isthmian traders are seasonal, making trips to the Valley during the mango season or when other fruits are available in the Isthmus and returning with Valley products to resell in their home marketplaces. Others make trips throughout the year, carrying marine products they buy from the Huave fishermen on the coast to take inland, mostly to the Valley, where they may purchase fruits and vegetables from Valley *propios* at low prices to resell to the Huave villagers. Local products are purchased by some Tehuantepec *viajeras* at wholesale prices, on credit, in their *plaza* for resale in remote population centers, for example, a construction site in Chiapas and an oil refining camp in Veracruz. Some carry Tehuantepec jewelry in addition to foodstuffs, and a few specialize in such merchandise, usually taking it on consignment from craftsmen who may be relatives. Most of the Isthmus traders have small-scale operations (seasonal *viajeras* are primarily producer-vendors), but a trader may accumulate a large capital, buy a truck, and engage in buying and selling truckload quantities of certain goods over a wide area.

The importance of this type of village-based trader is that it reveals a sizable marketing activity that is not entirely related to the *plaza* system. Some do buy goods from *plaza* vendors or from wholesalers in marketplace towns, or from local storekeepers who also act as wholesalers, and selling trips may be timed to take advantage of *plazas* and major religious fiestas when this is convenient; but much of the selling is quite independent of the occurrence of *plaza* days. Thus these traders represent a significant segment of the marketing process which could be entirely missed in a study confined to the marketplace towns.

Interplaza traders. This class of traders follows fairly regular circuits, selling in weekly *plazas* as a full-time occupation. A few village-based *viajeros* fit this description, but most inter*plaza* traders live in towns with *plazas* where they spend two or more days a week "resting." In the Valley many have their headquarters in Oaxaca, and if some originally were villagers, they no longer identify with their home villages. Most of the inter*plaza* traders in the Valley confine their activities to that subregion, although a few regularly visit the *plazas* of Nochixtlán or Tlaxiaco in the Mixteca and some make occasional speculative visits to other *plazas* or to large religious fiestas. (Probably there is a class of traders that specializes in religious fiestas, especially vendors of religious goods, but these have not been studied.) In the Sierra, inter*plaza* vendors have headquarters in one of the *plaza* towns of that subregion. Some may visit Oaxaca or Tlacolula to buy goods, but project notes contain no examples of traders who follow a regular circuit involving both Sierra and Valley *plazas*. In part this may be because of greater time investment that such a trading route would require, but conditions of marketplaces as well as language problems may play a part.

Before the introduction of modern transportation it was possible for inter*plaza* traders in the Valley to visit a different *plaza* every day. Both the timing of the weekly *plazas* and the distances between them are such that, by traveling at night, a succession of *plazas* could be visited even using burro transport. Even with modern transportation, however, most inter*plaza* traders today find this too arduous. Few visit more than five *plazas* a week; the majority probably visit three or four. In the

Sierra, travel times are longer and trails more difficult; the number of *plazas* visited in a week are correspondingly fewer.

The majority of the inter*plaza* traders deal in nonperishable goods purchased in *plazas* or from stores. The more perishable goods present greater transportation problems and cannot be stored between *plaza* days. Traders also tend to be specialized, dealing only in one class of commodity. A dealer in dried chile peppers, for example, may handle more than twenty different kinds of chiles, all produced in different places. To replenish stocks, pack, unpack, and arrange for display, keep in mind costs and prices, and make intelligent appraisals of demand when buying stock, is a complicated business. As another example, not only do pottery *regatones* tend to handle pottery exclusively, but they tend to specialize in the pottery either of Atzompa or Coyotepec or in Oaxaca polychrome ware. Some, especially those who handle Oaxaca polychrome, may also have small selections of imported wares from Puebla. Few handle the other local wares from San Marcos or Ocotlán. As yet another example, dealers in dry goods rarely handle clothing or vice versa, while *rebozo* dealers are a separate category. Specialized dealers are also found for *jarcieria* (articles of ixtle fiber), hardware, notions, palm-leaf products, coffee and cacao beans, peanuts and walnuts, and the like.

Inter*plaza* dealers in pottery usually replenish their stocks in the Oaxaca *plaza* rather than in production centers, buying either from village-based *regatones* or from *propios*. A few buy some of their goods in the village of origin, but unless they have arrangements with village producers, this is much too time consuming. Not only must the buyer seek out makers with pottery to sell, but he must locate several suppliers to have an adequate range of stock, because potters specialize in forms and sizes. Some inter*plaza regatones* also state that in the village they have much more difficulty ascertaining market prices.

The inter*plaza regatón* must arrange transportation of his stock from one *plaza* to another, usually by public transport or hired truck. Because pottery is bulky and the risk of breakage considerable, many dealers arrange to store unsold stocks of goods in each of the larger *plaza* towns, renting a room or a space in a house. The increase in inventory costs and the expense of rent they consider to be offset by the lower breakage rate. The *regatón* normally must pay cash for his supplies; the producer usually has no margin to permit credit sales. Hence operating capital is substantial. The *regatón* also often tries to accumulate some stocks against the rise in demand and the higher prices that prevail prior to All Saints Day. At least one *regatón* even borrows high-interest money from moneylenders to accumulate stocks for this high demand season.

Operating expenses for the inter*plaza regatón* are relatively low, involving transportation on bus, truck, or railroad, *plaza* fees, storage fees, and meals. By railroad, the cheapest means of shipment, a large basketful of goods sent from

Oaxaca to the farther points of the Valley may cost $3.00 to $5.00 in freight charges (not including porterage charges at the destination). The *puesto* fee for one day in a large *plaza* is usually $2.00. A good-sized storeroom rents for $30.00 to $40.00 per month.

A large-scale interplaza *regatón* interviewed by Diskin started out in business with a capital of $250. He handles not only pottery but also a variety of other products that he sells in the *mercado* of Oaxaca and the *plazas* of Ocotlán, Etla, and Tlacolula. From February through September of 1965 his monthly investments in pottery alone averaged $2,550, and in April he invested some $3,000 in a large shipment of metates, mortars, and pestles. With such a large, bulk and difficult-to-transport stock, he *must* maintain storage facilities at the *plazas*. Occasionally, when his capital is depleted, he buys stock on credit.

Regatones who handle compact, nonperishable and nonbreakable products such as dry goods, clothing, fiber products, notions, dried chile, and the like, may be able to carry their stocks with them daily from *plaza* to *plaza* with a corresponding reduction in investment in stock. In a few instances dry goods and clothing dealers interviewed owned light trucks or vans that facilitated transport and permitted them to attend more *plazas* during the week than they could otherwise, or to visit more distant *plazas*. A vendor of bolt cloth interviewed by Diskin covered Tlacolula, Miahuatlán, Ayoquezco, Etla, Ejutla, Ocotlán, and Oaxaca with his small truck, spending a day at each *plaza*. An important difference between dealers in industrial goods and pottery dealers is that the former can buy from wholesalers in Oaxaca on short-term credit. As noted above, however, at least one pottery *regatón* sometimes buys pottery and other items on credit, from *propios* as well as other *regatones*.

The inter*plaza regatón* and the *propio* are the heart of the *plaza* system. Not all street vendors on *plaza* days are necessarily of either type. Residents of the *plaza* town also become small-scale *regatones* on *plaza* days. This is particularly true of vendors of some prepared foods and small-scale vendors of other food items. In Oaxaca City, for example, on some of the approach streets to the *plaza* area, one finds numerous women with small stocks, usually of fruits in season. They often obtain their stocks from permanent stall holders in the *mercado* (who may in turn have bought their stocks from wholesalers). In some cases these vendors obtain all or part of their goods on credit. Others buy from inter*plaza* truckers who sell in minimum quantities. It is not uncommon to see one or more trucks of oranges or other fruit lined up on a *plaza*. The trucker is reading a newspaper between deals, while a few feet away is a line of women retailing his commodity. In scale, these small *regatones* differ little from the *changarros* or small retail operations in villages which offer small stocks at house doors. Except that they have fixed locations, they differ little from *ambulantes* (see below). Frequently their stocks, although small, are well selected, and many of the sales are in small quantities to town or city residents for immediate consumption.

Other *plaza*-day street vendors on a larger scale than just described are not in fact either *propios* or inter*plaza regatones*. Rather, they are holders of permanent *puestos* or stalls in the *mercado* who on *plaza* days maintain a second place of sale on the street, if family manpower permits, or they close down the stand inside the *mercado* to sell on the street, paying the usual $2.00 fee for street vendors as well as their ongoing rental in the *mercado*.

Ambulantes. *Ambulantes* are persons with small stocks that they can carry about with them, and are characteristically found in the larger *plazas*. The numbers present especially on *plaza* days are substantial, but no quantitative figure is possible, for many pay no fees. Some, at least in Oaxaca City, may operate on a daily basis, selling in streets away from the market district. For this reason their relation to the *plaza* is ambiguous. They are essentially town-based. *Ambulantes* are most active on *plaza* days, although relatively few operate within the *plaza* area. Those most evident within the *plaza* area are vendors of plastic bags, plastic sheets (used widely for rain capes), bags of detergents, and a few similar items. Many of these are boys who sell on commission for some storekeeper who, for example, buys 100-kilo bags of detergent, packages small quantities of this in plastic bags and gives them to vendors to sell in the streets. In this type of operation *ambulantes* are not unlike the innumerable boys selling *chicles* (chewing gum) or candies on the streets. Most of them get their stocks from one or two dealers in Oaxaca City, often partly on credit. Few of the *ambulantes* make a living from their activity, but there are some exceptions. An *ambulante* selling notions can obtain a stock with a capital of as little as ten pesos. Once known to the supplier (storekeeper or wholesaler), he may get larger stocks on credit. This is an easy way for a village-born migrant to the city to break into the commerical activities of the city, but in 1966–1967 the number of *ambulantes* in Oaxaca had increased to the point that no one, including the regular dealers in *mercería* (notions) in the *mercado,* was making much money, and one of the market unions was seeking ways to limit the number of *ambulantes* selling notions.

A number of other characteristics of the *plaza* are of interest. One is its self-regulating quality. The local authorities (in the City, the Administration of Markets) may set some rules as to what goods are to be sold in each street or part of a street, or may insist that goods should not spread out too much, that passage be left for entry into stores or *mercados*. Occasional disputes may arise between vendors over encroachments on their spaces. In theory, no street vendors in the *plaza* have continuing rights from one week to the next for particular locations. In actual fact, persons who sell regularly on the street on *plaza* days have the same locations week after week and their rights are generally respected. But they must occupy their spaces by a reasonable hour in the morning. If not, it is assumed that the vendor is not coming that day and the space may be occupied by someone else.

This self-regulating quality occurs in part because vendors of similar goods either are from the same village or follow the same *plaza* cycle. They hence know each other well; they need to get on with one another. Often, indeed, vendors may leave their goods in charge of a neighbor for short periods of time. In some cases, the occupant of a neighboring location may even make sales in the absence of the owner. A neighbor almost never interferes or comments during the course of another vendor's transaction with a customer. Only if the prospective customer breaks off a transaction may the occupants of adjoining locations attempt to attract his attention. While inspectors from the local authorities may pass through the streets, the almost total absence of police in the crowded *plaza* areas is quite striking.

As indicated earlier, occupation of space in the *plaza* is not as random as the foregoing might suggest. Local authorities designate areas for vendors from particular locations. This is best studied in the Oaxaca City *plaza* where the *Administración de Mercados* exercises general supervision. Street assignments are modified from time to time; either changes are passively accepted, or a delegation may visit the administrator seeking to negotiate new assignments. The most formalized arrangement is the reservation of one street exclusively for the vegetable and flower vendors of San Antonino Ocotlán. Vendors from this village are organized and belong to the Oaxaca Chamber of Commerce. In 1967 the San Antonino vendors felt their street was overcrowded. When requests for additional space were not heeded, they gained the support of the Chamber of Commerce, and as a result, part of an adjoining street was reserved for those San Antonino vendors dealing exclusively in flowers. The previous occupants were relocated elsewhere.

Provision is also made for *propios* who do not attend the *plaza* regularly. After a certain period of time in the morning, some move into spaces left by regular vendors who have not occupied their customary spaces. Some other areas are flexible, usually toward the margins of the *plaza* area. *Propios* selling deciduous Sierra fruits, for example, attend the *plaza* irregularly and seasonally. A special area is set aside for them; sometimes it is crowded, but at seasons there may be no *serrano* vendors. When there is room, vendors of other goods may move in from less desirable or overcrowded locations.

8
Dynamics of the
Marketing System: II

Thus far in our examination of the dynamics of the marketing system I have focused primarily on the more traditional kinds of marketing activities related to the village and the periodic *plaza* and to the various kinds of traders involved. In this second chapter on the Dynamics of the Marketing System, attention is centered upon the intermediate and more modern kinds of exchange in the *mercados,* stores, and wholesale establishments, primarily with reference to Oaxaca City. Even more than in the first of these two chapters, attention is given to the variations in trading activities related to differences in the classes of goods handled, and extensive use is made of summaries of selected case histories.

VENDORS OF THE MERCADO

Vendors in the *mercado,* it may be recalled, occupy fixed locations—an open stall or a small *puesto* or enclosable place of business—within or around the outer periphery of a permanent market structure. Normally they are open for business seven days a week, although on *plaza* days some stall operators may close their stalls inside the *mercado* and set up temporary stalls in the streets.

In this section the various ways in which business is conducted by various types of stall holders are examined. Depending upon the type of goods handled, dealers in perishables may buy part of their products from *propios* from the villages. Many sell to village buyers, although their major sales are to urban dwellers. Some, such as bakers or tinware merchants, sell their own products or the products of family handicraft.

Among the few general statements that can be made are the following: (1) all are more or less permanent daily vendors in the *mercado;* (2) except on the *plaza* day, the majority of the customers are town residents; (3) all operations are family enterprises; (4) most vendors are retailers but some also do some wholesale business. Many transactions may involve price negotiations; the major exceptions are groceries, where fixed prices are customary, and meat, the maximum prices of which are fixed by governmental authorities, leading to some "black-market" sales. Otherwise, depending upon size and the class of goods handled, the businesses are conducted in rather different ways. A few examples from the Oaxaca City *mercado* which follow will give some idea of the variations.

MR, tomato vendor.[1] MR conducts his business from a stall in the Benito Juárez marketplace in Oaxaca City. He deals primarily in tomatoes but also handles a variety of chile peppers, garlic, potatoes, and small quantities of beans. He sells home-grown vegetables and raises flowers. His entire flower production is bought for resale by his wife's mother at a fixed price of $200 per month. He does all buying for his business and also acts as commission agent for tomato producers in Huitzo and Cuicatlán, receiving a flat $3.00 per crate of tomatoes sold. His wife, two young children, and a 12-year-old *mozo* (a servant; he is unrelated but treated as a member of the family) tend the marketplace stall most of the time. Even the 5-year-old daughter is able to wait on customers, calculate prices, and make change, and is occasionally left in charge of the stall of her paternal grandmother (who has the adjoining stall) for short times under the watchful supervision of her mother. The *mozo* is given food, clothing, and spending money but no wages. During the day he helps open and close the stall, assists the husband with gardening, and then goes to night school.

Both husband and wife were born in Oaxaca, have worked in the *mercado* all their lives, and have relatives in the *mercado* who are also *puesto* operators and one in an administrative post. They regard themselves as Mexicans, that is, they identify with the nation rather than with a village, region, or tribe. They own property at the edge of town where they grow their flowers and vegetables, having installed a pump and pipes to irrigate with water from their well. Five years before our study, MR and his wife had borrowed $20,000 to buy the land and build a two-room house, paying 5 percent per month interest;[2] the $4,000 balance owing

---

[1] This is one of the most carefully studied vendors for whom we have data. Repeated interviews and more casual conversations covered 18 months. Hundreds of transactions were observed, and the field worker often spent entire days in the stall.

[2] Such interest rates are not uncommon in Oaxaca. Short-term, high-risk loans may bear as much as 20 percent per month interest.

was paid off at the time of the study, and house improvements (a new window, laminated roofing) were begun. Eventually they will add a bathroom and buy new furniture. Their level of living is indicated by household expenses itemized in appendix 27. Living costs and capital investments are taken out of earnings; accounts for household and business are not separated. The regular household expenses for food, clothing, and entertainment are paid from *puesto* earnings while house payments, improvements, and equipment are paid for from the husband's income as commission agent.

Capital involved in operation of the *puesto* is minimal. The original construction of the stall cost about $1,000 in materials and nothing for the labor, which was supplied by MR and his wife. The value of their stock on hand was estimated at approximately $1,000.

The owner-operators consider themselves to be primarily tomato dealers. They carry three varieties of tomatoes (*guajitos, bolas,* and *criollo*) as well as husk tomatoes (*miltomate*). *Guajitos* come in three grades based on size, and *bolas* in four grades of which only the first two are carried. Husk tomatoes come in two grades, large and small, and both are carried. Thus, eight classes of tomatoes are handled ordinarily. In addition to tomatoes, MR handles two varieties of garlic (white and purple), two varieties of potatoes (the best are from Puebla State, the others from the northern Sierra), both black and white beans, dry oregano, fourteen types of chiles (mostly dried), and four sizes of paper bags (bags are sold, not given to customers). Garlic, local potatoes, and black beans are also differentiated by size. Occasionally MR may add onions or squash to his offerings if a regular tomato supplier brings them. He and his wife hence keep track of supplies and buying and selling prices for about 40 items without written records.

The principal risks exist in the tomato business. Tomato prices fluctuate rapidly. For example, five crates of tomatoes may be bought on Monday at $40 a crate which are retailed at $3.00 a kilogram. On Tuesday the wholesale price may drop to $20 a crate and competitors begin selling at $2.00 a kilogram. Our informants then must drop prices to cost or below, to move their tomatoes before they spoil. While they may lose money under these circumstances, they may just as often be on the other side of the price swing, and they count on this to make up for losses. They also have some loss from spoilage. The amount depends on how ripe the tomatoes were on purchase and the length of time it takes to turn over stock. Some of this loss is recovered by cutting out spoiled parts from tomatoes and selling the remaining parts to restaurant and *fonda* operators for making sauces. Tomato prices also fluctuate markedly by season. Costs per crate may range from $15 to $60 for *guajitos,* from $30 to $105 for *bolas,* and from $20 to $110 for *criollos.* MR will not buy when the price goes over $90 a crate because of customer price resistance to retail prices over $4.00 a kilo. Prices of other goods fluctuate much less. Often MR buys a year's supply of some of the dried chiles, keeping surplus stock at home, with little fear of a serious price decline.

Retail prices are said to be based on three factors: cost of goods, current wholesale or supplier's prices (which may not be the same as cost), and the going retail price in the *mercado.* Ideally, MR feels, prices should rest on cost plus a reasonable markup. For purposes of our study actual markups were calculated for most items, based on cost data. They range from as little as 9 percent to 200 percent, with an average markup of 43.2 percent of cost price. (Unfortunately, tomatoes could not be included; they are bought by the crate and sold by the kilogram, and no standard or average weights per crate were calculated. Price spreads on home-grown produce also were omitted.) The prevailing retail prices in the *mercado,* however, place a ceiling on the prices MR can obtain and, as this enterprise is operated, also place a floor under prices. MR and his wife believe that cutting prices does not produce enough additional trade to make it worthwhile and results in resentment from fellow *puesteros.* MR's wife, who conducts most sales, never bargains with customers; she may reduce her asking price for everyone in accordance with market conditions but she rejects lower offers. But the husband, who often sells in the late afternoons, may accept lower price offers for tomatoes if the stock is in danger of spoiling.

Although price competition is almost lacking, the wife especially feels that she competes effectively with other vendors. Competitive advantages, she believes, come from superior location (based on the number of potential buyers passing the stand), offering an attractive variety of merchandise, reputation for offering good quality merchandise, and treating customers courteously and pleasantly. Actually, although courteous and pleasant, the wife is not particularly friendly or cordial. She never is disagreeable to difficult customers as some vendors are, but neither does she joke and laugh with customers as do some other vendors.

Buying is perhaps more complex and requires greater skill than does retail selling. Goods are bought from three main types of sources:

1). *Propios* who come to the stall or with whom MR has more-or-less regular arrangements. Their prices usually are lower than those of other sources. Some *propios* at a distance may ship goods; otherwise they deliver their purchases at the stall.

2). *Regatones* who offer products at the stall. Our informants do not know whether the *regatones* have bought from *propios* or from other types of *regatones.*

3). *Mayoristas* or local wholesalers who maintain warehouses. All wholesalers are said to carry about the same goods at the same prices. Therefore our informants have no regular supplier but shop around for quality and availability of goods. This statement is modified by a comment that they prefer to buy from a particular wholesaler who will give them up to a month's credit without interest. The produce bought comes from a large number of localities and sources of supply vary decidedly with the seasons. For some months of the year, for example, most or all of the tomatoes handled come from wholesalers who buy outside the region.[3]

Characteristically, MR and his wife do not distinguish their business and household budgets and have no clear idea of their overall costs and profits. They are very conscious of purchase and sales prices on each item they handle and know whether they are selling below cost or not. On the business as a whole they count total daily receipts and assert with some confidence that their average gross income from the *puesto* is $100 a day. From this they must replenish stocks, maintain the household, and pay the small operating expenses. The latter include the daily rent to the *Administración de Mercados.* At the time data were collected, before completion of remodeling of the market, they paid $1.00 daily. Another variable item is payment to porters for transporting goods from the house, from wholesalers, or from bus or truck stop. This amounts to $0.50 per crate for tomatoes or similar loads. Although vague about variable costs, the family was able to give fairly precise figures about household expenses.

As with many household budgets collected, on the surface MR and his family appear to spend more than they make from their business. The total of household and personal expenses appears to be at least $17,919 annually. This figure is undoubtedly low; several items are conservative estimates, and some items such as ready-made clothing, replacement of kitchenware and implements, and children's toys are not even estimated. Other cash outlays include possibly $2,400 annually for interest on the house loan (in lieu of rent), and $465 in business expenses for rental of the market stall and insecticides and seeds for production of flowers and vegetables (the latter figure does not include fuel costs for the irrigation pump or the costs of porterage mentioned above), or a total of $2,865. The average daily expenditure for replacing stock in the stall is estimated at $70 or $25,550 annually. The total of these expenditures is $46,334. Against this, the gross income from the market stall is estimated to average $100 daily, or a total of $36,500 annually. An additional $2,400 annual income is estimated from the sale of flowers, giving a total of $38,900 or a deficit of $7,434.

The figures (p. 159) do not cover all types of expenses or income. Repayments made on the house loan and improvements on the house and grounds are said to be covered out of the income of the husband acting as a commission agent at a flat rate of $3.00 per crate of tomatoes handled. MR tended to discount this activity and would give no estimate of his income, indicating that this was a declining

---

[3] In addition to goods bought from suppliers, the stand also sells some vegetables grown by MR on his house lot. Paper shopping bags, sold as a convenience to customers, are bought from a manufacturer's agent.

Summary of expenditures and income

Income
Gross income from stall operations	$36,500.00	
From sale of flowers	2,400.00	
TOTAL:		38,900.00

Expenditures:
Household and personal expenditures	$17,919.00	
Interest	2,400.00	
Business expenses	465.00	
Investment in goods	25,550.00	
TOTAL:		$46,334.00
Deficit:		$ 7,434.00

business. In the year prior to the study, however, he had paid off at least $2,400 of the principal of the house loan and paid $2,900 for irrigation equipment, a total of $6,300. This suggests that he handled at least 2,100 crates of tomatoes on commission, or on the average around six crates a day, not an improbable figure although the business is seasonal. In the year of the study he paid off the final $4,000 of the house loan from his commission earnings, indicating that he handled at least 1,300 crates.

At least two possibilities exist to account for the apparent deficit. The most likely one is that gross income from the stall is underestimated. From other case histories it would appear that this is almost a reflex action on the part of peasants, and in this Oaxaqueños are no exception. A second possibility is that MR's commission income is better than double the amount estimated, from his known expenditures against this source of income. A third possibility is that the expenditure period may have overlapped a period when their stall was located in the street while the interior of the *mercado* was being remodeled. While in the street, they estimated their gross income doubled to $200 daily, and expenditures may have risen in response to higher income.

MR and his wife would be considered as upper working class in the local social classifications. In dress, speech, and manner (and perhaps in income as well), they certainly equate with many who, because of their occupations, would be regarded as middle class.

JL, fruit vendor. Before reconstruction of the marketplace began, this vendor conducted her business from a stall in the 20 de Noviembre building (opposite the Benito Juárez building) except on Saturdays, when she sold on the street to take advantage of the greater traffic. During the reconstruction she was temporarily located on the street throughout the week. In contrast to MR, she has concluded that street vending does not have any advantage over vending within the enclosed marketplace, particularly as there is the extra *boleto* fee to pay.

Capital investment consists of her storage boxes and display boards, a *puesto* cover, and a weighing scale. The value of stock, most of it obtained on credit, was estimated to be between $800 and $1,000. Other expenses include the rental fee, $2.00 daily, and portage from the wholesale houses, $0.50 per crate.

The stall offers a wide range of fruits: oranges, mangoes (five varieties), plums (four varieties), apricots, apples (three varieties), watermelon, cantaloupe, papaya, pineapple, bananas (three varieties), and a local fruit called *jiotilla*. Much of the fruit comes from Cuicatlán, north of the Valley. Pineapple originates at the border with Veracruz State, and the apples are transshipped from Mexico City. Seven of the 27 products handled originate partly or wholly in the Oaxaca region. JL's suppliers include both *propios* and wholesalers. *Propios* are the lower-cost source, but wholesalers are usually given preference since they allow credit for up to four days, during which period most of the goods may be sold. Markups for items whose buying and selling prices can be compared average 23 percent. Price-cutting may be necessary to undersell nearby competitors; but the vendor knows that lowering prices may force her competition to do likewise and that beyond a certain point it is not feasible. She is well aware of the costs of purchase and porterage as well as the dangers of spoilage, although she is unable to give precise figures.

Among her customers are itinerant vendors (*ambulantes*) to whom she accords wholesale prices (about $0.50 per hundred below her retail prices) and a day's credit as well; they buy in the morning and pay her for the merchandise in the afternoon. Credit is allowed to no other customers.

JL has been selling in the marketplace since she was a child, as did her mother before her. Her mother still sells fruit in the marketplace, aided by two other daughters. JL had left the marketplace when she married but was forced to return to vending to maintain her household. She in turn has two daughters helping her, one of whom takes sewing lessons at night. Another daughter earns $300 monthly as a clerk, and a young son who lives with another family in the capacity of servant earns $50 a month and the costs of his schooling. Four other children are too young to work. The husband is employed as a potter but contributes little to household support.

MJD, bean vendor. Normally this vendor maintains a centrally located *puesto* among the bean vendors in the Benito Juárez marketplace, which she has occupied for 42 years, but during the reconstruction of the marketplace she was given a location in the street at the end of a row of bean sellers, that is, away from the main point of entry. She complained to the vendors' union and to the Market Administration, and after several trips to both offices she obtained a space that had been vacated by a tomato vendor at the beginning of a row. She places considerable emphasis on the importance of location in selling.

MJD is a childless widow. Born in the city, she achieved some degree of literacy during one year's schooling and entered the marketplace very young as a seamstress to vendors of ready-made clothing. Afterward she became an itinerant vendor of beans in Oaxaca and traveled to Etla, Ocotlán, and Tlacolula to buy and sell, before taking a permanent *puesto* in the Oaxaca City marketplace at the age of 30. Her capital consists of a wooden table; an awning; a scale; various containers of pottery, glass, tin, and fiber; a wooden storage box on legs; a plastic cover for the stall; a rag, and newspapers for wrapping. Her *puesto* fee is minimal, $0.50 daily, and she is able to manage without porters as she herself transports stock purchased from wholesalers, and the *propios* with whom she deals deliver the goods they sell her to her stand.

She believes that variety of merchandise attracts customers, and she stocks as many types of merchandise as is possible with her small capital. She handles primarily large and thin black beans (the thinner ones are said to be better flavored and more desirable), white beans, ground black beans, ground chick-peas for human consumption and for bird feed, broad beans, and several spices. The large black beans (*frijol grueso*) come in two grades, as do the chick-peas. Most of her regular stock originates in the Oaxaca region (some of the thin black beans, *frijol delgado,* come from Chiapas State), but she also sells a type of bean (*frijol amarillo*) that originates in the Mixteca and another type (*frijol vayo*) that is shipped from Mexico City. One type of large black bean harvested in the Valley in the fall is priced lower than the others. But the vendor claims that quotations for the other Valley beans do not decline with increased supply at harvest time because the farmers prefer to hold them until prices rise again. In fact, prices for her goods are quite steady throughout the year.

The beans are usually purchased from *propios* from some ten villages. At one time MJD traveled to the villages for a better price but she is no longer strong enough to do this. The *propios* do not accord her special treatment although she has dealt with most of them for many years. She also buys from middlemen who purchase from *propios* at bus stations and inns. She purchases chick-peas and other goods from wholesalers at their warehouses, shopping around to get the best prices and the variety of stock she wants. But she does not buy in large enough quantities to be eligible for lot prices or for credit. Wholesalers of these dried foods will not bargain as *propios* do, yet their prices may be lower than the *propios'* because of their large turnover. Occasionally a middleman who knows MJD will leave merchandise on consignment and return at a later date for the money and the unsold stock.

Disfigured, spoiled, and insect-eaten beans are sorted out and sold for pig feed. The remainder is either displayed or stored in bags, and if properly cleaned can last a year without spoiling. Once a week the vendor prepares ten kilograms each of beans and chick-peas for grinding, toasting them at home and taking them afterward to a mill. A calculation based on her estimate of the costs of fuel and milling showed a gross profit for this amount of only $11.60. For a time before her street location was improved she was preparing these for sale only once a month, as sales were low and ground beans and chick-peas are not storable for more than two weeks. When she resumed preparing them weekly, she raised the price for the ground *frijol* by $0.50 the kilogram.

MJD's prices are about the same as those of other vendors offering the same products of the same quality. The difference between her buying prices and retail selling prices would seem to allow a gross profit of $0.20 to $0.25 per kilogram, but there are substandard beans to consider, which sell for $0.50 the kilogram (some are given away) instead of the usual retail price of $2.50 to $3.00 the kilogram. She will not bargain. She cannot afford to give credit, and in fact sometimes takes payment in advance for the beans and chick-peas that customers want ground. The only consideration she gives customers is courteous treatment and the service of storing bundles for them while they take care of other business.

From this small business she grosses about $50 inside the *mercado* on a good day, with minimal sales on a bad day of $20 or even $10, but while she was selling on the street, sales reportedly had been poor. As she has no dependents, MJD's expenses are low. The major expenses are for food ($4.00 daily), housing ($50 monthly), *puesto* rental ($15 monthly), payment of ongoing loans as well as 5 percent interest on them ($10 daily), and $10.90 weekly for toasting and grinding beans and chick-peas. Incidental expenses include union dues ($1.00 per month) and an unspecified amount for daily bus transportation between home and marketplace. These expenses amount to approximately $530 per month. MJD claims that her stock replenishment comes out of the loans, but the loans would cover only a small portion of this, as the principal can be only $286 monthly, while gross income and markups indicate a monthly investment of at least $900, and expenses covered by profits suggest that the stock investment probably amounts to about $1,225 monthly.

GAM, tinware vendor. This vendor is a 22-year-old unmarried woman whose family produces tinware. Her mother, who helped to set up GAM's stand in the Benito Juárez marketplace in 1957 and taught her to sell the tinware, has been a vendor for the family's production most of her married life and now sells at the Tlacolula, Etla, and Zaachila *plazas* as well as in Oaxaca City on Saturdays. GAM's father and five brothers operate the family workshop. Another brother is employed by a manufacturer of wrought iron products, and a married sister also operates a tinware stand in the marketplace. The sister does not buy from the family workshop since it cannot produce enough wares to supply two vendors.

The father has another source of income as a guitarist and leader of an orchestra that performs at social functions in the City. Also, the family's rent is reduced (from $225 to $100 for three rooms) since they manage and care for the group of apartments, which is owned by the father's sister. GAM and her brothers who work in the shop are considered to be their father's dependents and are not wage earners.

GAM manages her stand quite alone. Her capital equipment consists of the *puesto* structure and its corrugated tin covering, a shelf, two padlocked crates and a bin for storage, two chairs, and display battens. The stock, valued at about $4,000, is largely tinware manufactured by the family from raw materials originating outside the region. Galvanized items such as buckets are bought from a wholesaler who imports them from Mexico City; he gives a good discount—$0.10 to $0.20 per piece—and credit without interest up to 15 days. A few items such as braziers and needles are bought from producers who offer them at the vendor's stalls. The variety of items carried by GAM is extensive, including galvanized buckets; galvanized tubs; containers for kerosene, water, and powdered milk; volume measures; molds for making chocolate and ices; strainers and colanders; larger sugar spoons; covered butter dishes; braziers; tongs; bird cages; wire holders for irons; candlesticks; grates; graters; watering cans; water-carrying tins; enema tins; funnels; cups; simple kerosene lamps; and even cloth strainers and used glass jars. Most items are offered in several sizes. If the different sizes are considered, the number of items carried total well over 100. Sixty-eight of these are produced in the family workshop. Understandably, GAM is able to undersell the competition. She finds that her stand on the street (on Saturdays, and during reconstruction of the enclosed marketplaces) is more advantageous than the one inside the *mercado* since she is now grouped with other tinware vendors, so that her lower prices are more obvious.

Since villagers make up the majority of GAM's clientele, her sales fluctuate with the agricultural seasons: business is slowest during the cultivating season and best at harvest time. Gross income ranges from $80 to $200 daily inside the marketplace; an average day yields $125 to $150. On Saturdays, when GAM leaves her mother in charge of the stand indoors and takes a second stand on the street, the combined income reaches $450. Cost-selling price margins from the purchased galvanized ware are as little as 4 percent and never higher than 18 percent, but the family's products render a profit of 33 percent to 150 percent.[4] Prices are firm (the vendor bargains only between the asking prices and minimum selling prices established by her father for all items), and credit is never extended to customers. While there is a considerable concern with price, GAM claims that the daily income is not recorded. All income from the stand is given to her father; none is retained as wages, nor does GAM receive any percentage from sales.

---

[4] How costs are determined for household-produced goods is not clear. I suspect the cost figures given represent a more-or-less arbitrary minimum selling price set by the head of the household.

HD, baker. HD came to Oaxaca from his Mixtec village because there was not enough family land to divide among all three brothers. From an early age he worked as a cowherd, field hand, and mason's helper in the Mixteca. In Oaxaca he worked as a mason's helper and porter before becoming a baker's apprentice. Although he sent money home to his parents, he succeeded in saving enough to set up his own bakery, with credit arrangements and the help of his former employer. His parents and two brothers have remained in the village; four sisters went to Mexico City but their occupations are not known. His father is bilingual in Mixtec and Spanish and wears traditional village dress even when visiting Oaxaca. Although HD's wife is from the village, he speaks only Spanish. Their Oaxaca home is a five-room house of which two rooms are used for living quarters for the couple and their four children, and three rooms are for baking and flour storage. Most of the bread produced is sold from a *puesto* operated by HD in the 20 de Noviembre *mercado.*

Capital equipment at the bakery consists of a brick oven, boards for carrying bread and wooden racks to set them in, a wooden mixing trough, and paddles for moving the bread into and out of the oven. Ongoing expenses, totaling $10,450 annually, include the house rent ($500 per month), stall rental at the marketplace ($2.00 per day), business tax ($10 per month), social security payments for the family and hired workers ($300 per month), and an unspecified daily cost for porterage.

First-class flour is purchased from a wholesaler who has it brought in from a mill in the state of Puebla and delivers it to the bakery. HD buys 50 to 100 sacks at a time at a fixed bulk price of $75 the sack. He still occasionally buys on credit, paying about 5 percent of the billed price for this privilege. Four workers are employed in the bakery, who in 1964 were earning $15 each per day. They work in relays of two, six hours off and six hours on. Costs of egg bread production during the 24-hour work day are as follows:

2 sacks of wheat flour	$ 150.00
1,600 eggs	800.00
6 kilograms butter	30.00
6 kilograms lard	60.00
24 kilograms sugar	36.00
Salt	1.00
Yeast	6.00
Wood for fuel	20.00
Labor (2 workers)	30.00
	$1,133.00

As $1,200 worth of egg bread is sold during the day, one batch in the morning and one in the afternoon, gross profit (considering only the ingredients and labor) is

$67 per day. A type of white bread also is produced every half day, bringing returns of $200 per batch or $400 for the day's production. Costs are the same as for the egg bread except that the eggs and butter are omitted while an extra kilogram of lard is required for each batch. The gross profit on this "white bread" is $77 for the 24-hour workday. Thus, total gross profits for the day may reach $144 if there is no spoilage, and, assuming no days off, annual gross profits would be $52,560. The household also makes chocolate for sale but costs and income for this product were not given.

After baking, the bread is carried to the marketplace by porters where it is sold by HD with the help of his wife and 14-year-old son. (The son also assists with the baking.) Prices are said to be fixed and uniform among the bread vendors and reportedly had not changed in six years, at the time of the study. Although the informant claimed that there is no price rise for holidays and that higher prices merely reflect larger size, it appeared that for the All Saints holiday the bread vendors did charge more than normally. Even if they did not, their income would rise at that time since the volume sold increases during the All Saints season.

HD sells some of his production to middlemen, who travel to other towns and even to other states, at a discount of approximately 10 percent. Through these traveling vendors his bread reaches Veracruz, Puebla, and Mexico City.

VF, maize vendor. VF and his wife conduct business from a *caseta* or enclosable stall that they themselves constructed in the Mercado de Industria on land that they rent from the *Administración de Mercados* for $1.50 per day. They are concerned exclusively with the retailing of maize. The husband is from the village of Tlalixtac de Cabrera, where he still owns land on which he grows maize. The wife is from Santo Domingo Tomaltepec in the Central district. They have been selling maize in Oaxaca for 20 years but they retain a command of Zapotec (the husband tends to reply to questions in Spanish, although he understands Zapotec), and most of the business is carried on in this language. They own a three-room house that they share with a married son and daughter, their spouses, and four grandchildren. Both are illiterate.

Most of the maize sold is either *criollo* (grown in the Valley) or Chiapaneco. The latter is not all from Chiapas, and it is not clear from the notes whether this simply is to be equated with the maize sold from government warehouses. In any case the two main sources of maize purchased are local growers or, occasionally, middlemen and the government warehouse in Oaxaca. Maize *chiapaneco* (and from other observations, government maize) cannot be used for *atole* or *tejate* (maize drinks) and produces tortillas of inferior color and taste. "Government" maize is sold at fixed prices, although the base price may vary from year to year. At the time of the interviews the price was $99.00 per 100 kilograms plus $1.00 delivery charge in warehouse trucks. In addition, because government maize is "dirty," that is, mixed with fragments of maize cobs, a *mozo* is paid $1.00 per 100 kilograms to clean it, with a loss of about 1 kilogram of trash per 100. The retail selling price at the time was $1.05 per kilogram or $105.00 per 100 kilograms, a gain of fractionally less than $4.00 per 100 kilograms. Maize *criollo,* in contrast, sold at an average of $1.20 per kilogram but, as will be seen, this quotation is not very meaningful.

Transactions in maize *criollo* involve complex considerations. Maize *criollo* differs almost from village to village. The valley of Tlacolula produces good quality maize *criollo* but all this apparently passes through the *plaza* of Tlacolula and does not reach Oaxaca City. Oaxaca maize *criollo* comes mostly from the districts of Zaachila, Zimatlán, Ocotlán, Ejutla, and Miahuatlán, that is, the southern arm of the Valley of Oaxaca. As examples of variation, San Juan Chilateca produces a long-grained maize, heavy for its volume. The adjoining village of San Martín produces a round-grained maize known as *maíz bolita,* which is much lighter. Some consumers, however, prefer maize *bolita.* Ocotlán and some other communities produce maize *negrita.* The heaviest maize per volume is a yellow maize from Zimatlán. Heavy maize produces more tortillas for its weight than other maize. A further variable is the amount of moisture retained, and the age. Low-moisture "old" maize also yields more tortillas per weight and the flavor is superior.

Much of the maize *criollo* is purchased from producers by the *almud,* a traditional measure by volume. In examples observed, the dealer-buyer and the seller first bargained about the price. This tentatively agreed upon, the dealer then carefully examined the maize to ascertain the moisture content and whether it was "new" or "old" maize, before concluding the transaction. On other occasions, when stocks of *criollo* maize are low, late in the afternoon on *plaza* days, the dealer visits small retailers (*propios* or small *regatones*) on the third block of Zaragoza Street, tells them that he is buying maize, and indicates the price he will pay. Many street vendors, when the selling day is almost over, dispose of their stocks to the *caseteros* at a lower price.

Another way of getting *criollo* maize is through loans to growers. The price agreed upon is based on current prices and is unaffected by differences in price at the time of delivery. The contracts are oral but according to the dealers are scrupulously observed by both parties. Such loans are not always sought out of immediate necessity. In one case observed, the seller already had some maize sufficiently advanced to be harvested and consumed. Instead, however, he sought an advance and then bought "old" maize for his own consumption. His explanation was that the new maize would produce only half as many tortillas, which would be less "filling" than tortillas of old maize. He hence preferred not to "waste" his new maize but let it continue to mature and season on the stalk before harvesting it.

Retail prices vary with the class of maize sold (except for "government" maize). Most sales are by the *pesada* or four kilograms. Theoretically, this equals the old and outlawed measure of one *almud*, although in fact the weight of an *almud* varies according to the class and quality of maize. The vendors have usual asking prices and minimum prices they will accept after bargaining. For example, for *maíz larguito arribeño* one dealer observed asked $4.50 a *pesada*, sold fairly readily at $4.40, and would go to $4.20. If the client were very persistent, he might even sell at $4.00. If so, however, he managed to short weight the client of about half a kilogram of grain by clever manipulation of the scales (this was observed as well as admitted). Yet for regular customers who have agreed on a "good" price, most dealers add a little maize after the weighing is completed (this was not observed with this particular informant). At the same time $4.80 was asked for maize *criollo* and some sales were completed at $4.40. For the most part, the vendor was courteous with clients, helped them lift heavy purchases to their heads or backs, and spoke the usual courteous words of farewell. The majority of the clients of this vendor are Indians from villages and the transactions are in Zapotec, although in cases of hard bargaining husband and wife might talk together in Spanish.

Sales of maize are normally for cash. The exceptions are tortilla makers who are well known to the vendors. Tortilla makers might receive as much as 24 kilograms of maize on credit, which they repay within one week. In an observed case, a girl recommended by a steady customer was given 6 *pesadas* on credit. The following week the girl's mother appeared to pay for the maize and requested another advance of 6 *pesadas*. The vendors demurred, saying the girl had been directly recommended but they did not know the mother. They finally agreed to advance the 6 *pesadas* at $4.80 a *pesada*. The woman objected that at his price, plus costs of milling and bus fares to and from her village, she would not make any profit. The vendors finally agreed to a price of $4.50 but then managed to short weight the buyer by a half kilogram for each *pesada*, or a total of three kilograms.

These vendors keep receipts from the current day's operations separate from those of previous days. Current receipts are drawn on for the daily payment to the market administration; accumulated receipts from previous days are drawn on for other expenses. No general statements could be obtained about total purchases or sales. Indeed, the informants probably do not know these. One source of uncertainty is the use, still, of the *almud*, especially in purchasing. One producer from San Martín Tilcajete brought 40 *almuds* of white maize *bolita* to town on the bus. Because he arrived at 1:30 in the afternoon, there were no collectors and he avoided payment of the import tax. He had intended to sell retail but because of the lateness of the hour, the slowness of the *plaza* that day, and his need to return home on other affairs, he paid a porter $1.20 to carry the maize to our informant's *caseta*, where he sold it for $4.00 the *almud*. The buyer weighed the maize and found it totaled 150 kilograms, making the price just under $1.07 a kilogram, a relatively high figure for a dealer to pay.

STORES

This classification covers a wide variety of essentially retail enterprises occurring in villages, towns, and the City. They differ widely in size and scale of operations. All are specialized to some degree and, especially in the City, can usually be easily identified in terms of major products carried such as grocery stores (*tiendas de abarrotes*), dry goods stores (*mercerías*), hardware stores (*ferreterías*), and similar terms. Most can, in local terminology, be called *tiendas,* but very large establishments may be called *casas de comercio* or *almacenes.* Small enterprises located on the streets or in market buildings may be called *casetas.* Stores differ from stalls and from some *casetas* in the *mercado* primarily in the kinds of goods offered and the conduct of operations. Larger stores often also carry on some wholesale business, supplying village stores and inter*plaza* traders. At the opposite extreme are *changarros,* often little more than a vendor and a table with a little merchandise situated in a house doorway. In addition, there are numerous small neighborhood stores, very similar to the small stores in villages.

Open stalls and many enclosed *casetas* in the *mercado* are in a sense an intermediate form between the modern distribution system and the *plaza.* They handle primarily peasant food and local handicraft products or goods that have been locally transformed (for example, meat, bread, tinware), although some imported products may be sold regularly or seasonally. Proprietors buy either from peasant producers or wholesalers. Stores and shops, in contrast, deal almost exclusively in industrial products. The principal exceptions are stores and shops specializing in peasant handicrafts and catering to tourists. In contrast to the stall holder, who may buy from local producers but usually is heavily dependent upon wholesale suppliers, the store gets supplies not only from wholesalers but also directly from manufacturers through agents or traveling salesmen.

The village store sells almost entirely to peasant buyers. Some City stores cater in part to peasant buyers, but many of the customers are urban dwellers. The importance of peasant buyers to a particular store is roughly correlated with location. Stores in or near the *mercado* area of the City usually have peasant customers. Even one of the three "supermarkets" in the City—essentially a self-service grocery store that carries no local perishable products—is located across the street from the Benito Juárez *mercado.* But the largest retail store, Sears, Roebuck and Company, dealing primarily in furniture and household appliances, is several blocks from the *mercado* area on the far side of the modern business district. It is doubtful if it ever sells its relatively high-cost goods to a peasant. A second large commercial enterprise, the Singer Sewing Machine agency, is ambivalently located on the main *plaza* a block from the Benito Juárez market, a reflection perhaps of the importance of the sewing machine among peasants. To the extent that they cater to peasant trade, the stores are the major channel for the flow of industrial goods into the peasant economy, just as the stalls in the *mercado* compete with the *plaza* vendors in the sale of peasant products to the City dwellers.

Except for a few types of *casetas* in the *mercado,* no attempt was made to study the operations of City stores in detail. Small retail sales by City stores almost always are on a cash basis, but expensive items such as radios, phonograph-loud-speaker systems, stoves, bicycles, or trucks, usually are sold on installments. "Special sales" are sometimes used to attract customers, but the "special offer" and "loss leader" are almost unknown. Negotiated prices are common in shops in the *mercado* or nearby that deal in such things as rebozos, clothing, and dry goods, while single-price policies are the rule in grocery, hardware, and shoe stores, although exceptions occur. In small grocery stores, for example, when a customer hesitates after being quoted a price, the owner may say, "But I'll offer a special price." The reduction usually is very small and there is no offer-and-counter-offer procedure as in negotiated price situations. Storekeepers, like most *mercado* vendors, believe that location, size and variety of stocks, quality of goods, and courteous treatment of customers are the main factors in attracting and retaining patrons. Except that they are less aggressive and less sophisticated in merchandising methods, most urban stores operate in ways that would be familiar and predictable in "capitalistic" societies. Most stores pay state and federal taxes, and keep more elaborate books than do stalls.

Most urban stores differ from stalls in the *mercado* in their larger capital investments in furnishings and equipment and in stock on hand, although there is a wide range of difference, depending on scale of operations and type of goods carried. Stores receive the usual credit facilities from suppliers, generally 30 days after delivery of goods. Indeed, credit terms and discounts offered strongly influence choice of suppliers. For long-term credit, small store owners make use of the moneylender but usually pay only about 5 (*sic*) percent a month; larger enterprises use banking credit facilities offering lower interest rates.[5] With the exception of a very few corporate enterprises, such as Sears, Roebuck and Company

[5] Interest on commercial bank loans was not studied, but at the time of the study banks advertised payment of rates of 8 to 10 percent per annum on savings accounts. The Banco de Pequeño Comercio, a government-sponsored institution, however, charged only 9 percent interest per annum (¾ percent a month) on loans to business enterprises. According to the manager, the minimum sized loan was $300, with the average sized loan falling between $5,000 and $10,000. As the maximum loan to any enterprise was 30 percent of its capital value, many small enterprises in the *mercado* would not qualify for loans. Others were unable to obtain the required cosigners.

and Singer Sewing Machine, all stores are family owned and managed. Larger stores have paid employees, although preference may be given to relatives. Smaller stores also are family operated. Some may employ a boy as a *mozo* but usually he is treated as a family member. Small store owners, like stall holders, usually are regarded as essentially working class and often resemble the latter in dress, speech, and self-image. Owners of larger stores commonly are middle or upper class in the local social hierarchy. Usually they are urbanized mestizos, and a few are Spaniards.

Stores in villages are more relevant to the traditional marketing system, although few traditional goods are stocked. Such institutions, however, are a relatively recent development in most villages and are virtually absent in smaller communities in remote areas. It seems likely that some small stores were present in larger communities in the more distant past, but data from informants suggest that the main spread of stores into the villages began after about 1920. Atzompa apparently had five stores in 1920; today it has 22, including 7 minor operations. In the Mixería, Ayutla in 1933 had only one tiny store and most Mixe villages at that time had none. Today they are numerous. The presence of stores in a community is partly a function of its size and prosperity, but the spread of stores recently is also associated with the extension of the secondary road network.[6] Early village stores often were run by mestizo immigrants but today they are mainly owned and operated by local residents.

Inventories of stores in Atzompa and Magdalena Ocotlán showed the following to be the most common items: soft drinks, beer, mescal, sweets, cookies and/or animal crackers, kerosene, matches, cigarettes, chewing gum, lard, sugar, salt, common remedies (mostly Alka-Seltzer and Mejoral), paraffin and wax candles, candles in glass containers, canned sardines, canned chile, and coffee. Less common items are: maize, beans, bread, cheese, charcoal, soap, pasta (mostly noodles), rice, spices, hair oil, fresh tomatoes and chile, fresh fruit, fresh meat (including a type of sausage called *chorizo*), herbs, firecracker wheels, eggs, brown sugar, rope, string, thread, starch, school supplies, camphor balls, wine, chocolate, and rubbing alcohol. Stores in Diaz Ordaz also carried nails, batteries, talcum, gasoline, and gasoline and kerosene lamps.

Price comparisons of stores in the Valley villages suggest that retail prices are about 30 percent above prices for the same items in Oaxaca City stores. Apparently even in villages with fairly good bus service to the city, the convenience of local buying makes the price differential acceptable as well as justifiable. Not only does it save time and bus fares but it also fits in with the widespread habit of buying frequently rather than trying to store foods in the house. A further attraction for many is the availability of short-term credit in the village store.

[6] Many secondary roads are primitive truck trails. Storekeepers often promote their construction but discourage improvement of them in the hope that casual competitors will not use them.

The conduct of the village store is rather different from that of the City store. Many village stores are simply front rooms in the operators' residences; therefore, rent is not an out-of-pocket expense. Long-term capital investment involves construction of counters, bins, and shelving, and is not extensive. Operating capital depends on the size of stocks, the amount of credit extended by the storekeeper, and the amount of credit obtainable from suppliers. The latter is of considerable importance to the individual starting a new store. Goods are mostly bought from wholesalers in the City, usually at higher prices than those paid by urban storekeepers who buy in large quantities or may buy directly from manufacturers. Often the storekeeper himself travels to the City and transports his goods back by bus or truck, although beer and soft drinks are delivered by the wholesale distributor in many villages.

Price data collected for several village stores indicate an average markup of a little over 35 percent of cost on most items and 38 percent on soft drinks, beer, and mescal, often the best-selling items. The storekeeper is almost compelled to buy some local maize or beans from customers who lack cash, but the amounts involved are small. In addition, success usually is dependent on extending credit to retail customers. Unless the storekeeper is skillful in identifying families to whom credit should not be extended and in placing limits on the credit he does extend, he will usually fail.

Once a successful store is located in a village, others often find storekeeping an attractive way of supplementing income. Often the major question to some would-be store operators is whether a suitable room is available to convert to this purpose. As a result, many villages have more stores than they can support. Very few storekeepers do not have some other source of income.

Following are a few examples of village storekeepers, their backgrounds, and their operations.

The largest store in the pottery-making village of Atzompa is owned by a widow and operated by her two unmarried daughters. Until about 1950, pottery-making was the principal source of income for the family, supplemented by the cultivation of government-granted land (*ejido*). In the early 1940s one of the sons was among five village boys encouraged by their primary schoolteacher to pursue the career of schoolteaching. He was allowed to work his way through secondary school in Oaxaca and completed teacher training by correspondence after he began to teach. His success led another son and a daughter to follow his example. Meanwhile, the husband accepted employment as caretaker of an archaeological site above the village, at a small salary that subsequently increased to $700 net per month. Upon the husband's death, the Instituto Nacional de Antropología e Historia gave the job to the youngest son, who also supervises cultivation of the family's *ejido* holdings. A fourth son has been employed in a white-collar position at the Oaxaca museum and recently received a diploma in accounting; he lives in a house owned by the family in Oaxaca City and contributes part of his salary to the village household.

The initial investment in the store (for shelving, display cases, counter, scale, ice bin for soft drinks, two wooden chairs, and stock) was made with a $5,000 loan obtained by one of the schoolteachers in 1964 at the behest of the elder of the unmarried girls. Since the store had a good location, being the only one in that sector of the village and also near the bus stop, it prospered. The elder girl acts as manager and does all the buying, traveling by bus to Oaxaca twice a week and to Zaachila once a week for the *plaza*. Menial labor for the household and store is provided, when needed, by a related family on the next house lot. When the store was established, pottery-making was discontinued entirely.

The store extends credit to very few customers. During observations over a period of a year, no customer was seen to ask for or receive credit. (Most of the customers are children, some of whom barely reach the level of the counter, sent on errands by parents.) A wide range of merchandise is carried: white sugar, salt, lard, brown sugar, cigarettes (six brands), tinned chile, noodles, cinnamon, maize, rice, coffee, mescal, soft drinks, beer, wine, two varieties of local black beans, sweets and cookies, chewing gum, hair oil, kerosene, charcoal, rope, firecracker wheels, school supplies, wax and paraffin candles, tinned sardines, common medicines, and a small supply of fresh foods (fruit, meat, vegetables) mostly from the Zaachila weekly *plaza*. Prices for the first eight items were compared with Oaxaca retail prices and were found to average 28 percent higher in the village store. Prices for soft drinks, the item sold in the greatest quantity, were somewhat higher, based on a 50 percent markup over wholesale buying prices, which include delivery. The markup decreased slightly when wholesale prices rose in 1968. The retail price of charcoal, bought from itinerant vendors, was 25 percent higher than in Oaxaca, involving a 100 percent markup over cost.

This family seems to make a good living. "Everything comes out of the store," said one of the young women, referring to the new television set and osterizer. Some of the family's assets, however, including real property it owns in and near the city of Oaxaca, are probably attributable to a life insurance settlement made by the government upon the demise of the husband, an INAH employee, in the amount of $45,000.

A more recently established store in the same village was set up in 1967 with $1,400 received from the sale of three pigs. This storekeeper has a good location, at a fair distance from other stores. His stock replenishment amounts to about $300 weekly for groceries alone. He brings merchandise purchased in Oaxaca by bus, and also buys eggs, cheese, and herbs from local people and itinerant vendors. His stock consists of soft drinks, mescal, beer (two brands), second-grade sugar, bread, cheese, candles in glass containers, paraffin candles, salted crackers, sweets, animal crackers, cookies, pork sausage, salt, tinned sardines, tinned chile, Alka-Seltzer, soap (two brands), and firewood and liquid glaze for pottery-making. A comparison of his buying and selling prices (see app. 28) shows an average gross margin over cost of 27.9 percent for 23 items. Before the rise in producer's prices of soft drinks and beer, it was a little less than 30 percent. Despite a large sign in the store which proclaims "I do not give credit," credit is extended to selected customers and is not as limited as in the store discussed above.

While the household has given up its government-grant (*ejido*) land, it continues to produce pottery that nets about $80 weekly or $4,160 annually, and in 1969 installed a billiard table with equipment costing $3,000 second hand, which is used by village boys who pay $1.00 each per hour. An unmarried daughter does some dressmaking, charging from $4.00 to $15.00 (depending on the fabric) for sewing. Raising pigs and fowl provides another source of income. Total net income from the regular activities of grocery vending, firewood vending, and pottery-making, amounting to about $26 per day, comfortably supports the husband and wife, their unmarried daughter, and also the small child of another daughter and son-in-law. The latter live in the same household but have a separate budget, dependent entirely on pottery-making.

All storekeepers pay taxes to the *municipio* and to the government in Oaxaca. The Atzompa *municipio* collects $4.00 to $5.00 monthly from storekeepers and the state collects a like amount. (Stores at San Lázaro Etla reported paying only $3.00 monthly.) Additional taxes are collected by both agencies for commercial phonograph operation.[7] The sale of mescal requires a $50 permit and is taxed by the state at $15 monthly.

Discrimination in the extension of credit is crucial to making a profit from storekeeping. A storekeeper in the village of Magdalena Ocotlán, in the southern end of the Valley, allowed unlimited credit and within three months of establishing his store had a credit list of 115 customers whose total debt amounted to $478.60. His initial investment in the store had been $600 for preparing a room, this amount obtained by selling a calf for $550 and some of his maize production for $50, and $425 for stock, taken from the proceeds of the sale of 15 head of sheep which had netted $700. His dislike of farming and lack of household personnel to pasture the sheep contributed to his decision to sell the sheep and open a store.

This storekeeper was fortunate at the outset since he bought his stock from a

---

[7] Phonograph music, "broadcast" over a loudspeaker, is "dedicated" for a fee to individuals such as friends or godfathers on their saint's days—a substitute for the older tradition of a serenade by paid musicians. Phonograph-loudspeaker outfits also are rented to provide music at household fiestas. Such outfits, with a stock of records, cost from $1,000 to $1,500 second hand.

store in the nearby *plaza* village of San Pedro Apóstol which, although it did not extend credit for his purchases, advised him how to price his goods for resale. This favor was accorded him because his mother had been a customer there. Also, the informant noted the prices his nearest competitor charged and attempted to undersell him by a few centavos on some items. He claims, however, that he was forced both to barter for locally grown products such as maize and eggs, and to give credit. He did not want to refuse customers who cannily picked up merchandise as if they intended to pay and then requested that the latest purchase be added to the list of debts. He has come to realize, however, that credit must be limited to those who have demonstrated a willingness to pay. As a result of the large amount he has been unable to collect, and also because of a poor crop year at the time of the survey, he was about to request repayment of a $1,000 loan made two years before, surrendering the piece of land he had taken in pawn as security. The money was needed to pay the two laborers who were farming his $4\frac{1}{2}$ hectares of *ejido* and to continue to invest $300 to $350 weekly in store merchandise.

The fastest-selling items in this Magdalena store are mescal, lard, cigarettes, kerosene, soft drinks, beer, and white sugar. Buying and selling prices for some of the items carried are given in appendix 29. Cost of stock on hand at the time of the interview amounted to $137.20.

In addition to farming, this villager used to derive income from lending money at an interest rate of 10 percent per month but had found it more advantageous to put spare cash into a shoat for fattening. He usually sold the pig when maize prices were low and bought maize to resell later when the prices rose seasonally. His estimated profit on the maize was $0.50 the *almud*, and gross profit on a pig, not considering the cost of feed, was about $200.

As another example, a storekeeper in the nearby village of San Antonino buys his merchandise in the large *plaza* town of Ocotlán. He started in 1928 with the assistance of an Ocotlán storekeeper for whom he had clerked and with credit from Oaxaca and Ocotlán stores. Subsequently his creditors limited the term of credit and he was forced to reduce operations. He then sold a piece of land to buy his stock for cash and now buys only beer on credit. His fastest-selling items are sweets and cookies, medicines, salt, soap and detergents, sugar, beer, soft drinks (mostly Pepsi Cola), and tamarinds purchased from San Antonino vegetable growers who go to the Isthmus to sell their products and bring back the fruit. The informant lives with his wife and a married son who will soon separate from the parental budget. For household expenses the wife receives an allowance of $8.00 daily from the store as well as any store merchandise she needs. In addition, home-grown products are at her disposal to use or sell. The latter include maize and alfalfa from 8 hectares of sharecropped lands, eggs, and wool.

Thus it may be seen from the several cases summarized that virtually no village storekeeper depends for his livelihood exclusively on the store. Most hold land or there may be income from some secondary activity such as dressmaking or animal raising, or a member of the household may be a salaried employee of a business or government agency. Some storekeepers are also butchers or bakers. One storekeeper interviewed in the Sierra town of Zoogocho had, in addition to a grocery store in the main square of the latter town, a small store in his home village of Yatzachi el Alto, as well as fields at Yatzachi where he raised chile. He and his wife took turns tending both stores.

Because the husband of a storekeeping family is often busy with farming and other secondary activities, much of the selling in these small stores is done by women and children.

The village store is clearly an intermediate type of marketing enterprise. It is an innovation not truly part of the traditional system, yet it is embedded in the system because most of its customers participate primarily in the peasant economy. Moreover, although the store deals principally in goods from the modern industrial economy, it is not the only channel by which these products reach the peasant. Some are sold by *plaza* vendors and *viajeros*.

BUSINESS STRATEGIES OF MERCADO VENDORS

Many small storekeepers and stall operators in the *mercado* say their businesses are easy to learn. The facts suggest otherwise. Analysis of censuses of *puesteros* in the City for 1960 and 1961 indicate, for example, a turnover of about 13 percent in one year. Most of those retiring from the *mercado* almost certainly failed for one reason or another. Inadequate knowledge or skill undoubtedly play an important part in the failure rate, a conclusion supported by the relatively specialized character of most *mercado* enterprises. Vendors must have a knowledge of alternate sources of supply, be able to evaluate quality differences in goods, have a good sense of current prices both from suppliers and among competitors in the market, know how to manage stocks (especially for perishable goods) and how to maintain and use operating capital and credit, and be able to deal with various types of customers.

Buying skills, especially in perishables such as fruit and vegetables, involve much more than knowledge of sources and comparative prices. In buying tomatoes, for example, the merchant must know what variety is involved, and from a fairly cursory inspection class them according to size, quality, and ripeness, decide whether the price is fair in comparison with prices of other suppliers and with respect to the state of the market. In addition, he must make a judgment as to how many he can expect to sell before the goods deteriorate or spoil.

Selling strategies also may be complicated and vary by product categories.

Bargaining is common, although many fruit and vegetables are bought without haggling and a few vendors in 1967 were experimenting with posted prices. Buyers of fruits and vegetables are more apt simply to shop around if they are not satisfied with a quoted price, in some instances returning to the first vendor approached if his price and quality are equal to or better than the others.

Most vendors try to deal impersonally with buyers in the transactional situation. Almost universally vendors state that unlike the situation in many cultures, they give no special consideration to kinsfolk or *compadres*. This is supported by interviews with buyers who are equally unmoved by considerations of real or of fictive kinship. Yet the vendor does hope to have some steady customers, and many do. Nothing exists resembling the semiformalized *suki* relationships described by Davis (1969) for the Baguio market in the Philippines, but both with suppliers and with buyers, *mercado* retailers have some similar but informal long-term relationships. For suppliers, these seem to be based on mutual respect and confidence that both parties recognize fair prices and that the supplier is honest about the quality of goods. To the extent that this is practiced, the supplier is assured of a fairly steady market for his goods; the dealer is assured of a fairly reliable supply. On the retail side, the vendor is assured of some fairly regular customers while the buyer is assured of fair prices and reliable quality. Despite the existence of some such relationships, however, most transactions in the *mercado* are casual.

A second aspect, even of the fairly regular trading relationships, is that although the transactions are marked by courtesy and respect, there are no social overtones or relationships outside the *mercado*. The vendor may be of service to the supplier or retail buyer, especially if he is from a village. For example, a villager may ask a vendor for advice about city matters, especially if there have been repeated transactions to the point that the individuals come to be known to one another. Information requested may range from the location of a government office or a doctor, to the best places to buy patent medicines or special items of clothing. Most vendors seem to give such information freely and conscientiously. Good advice is recognized as a way of building confidence in buyers or suppliers. In effect a somewhat impersonal type of friendship relationship may be involved, but it rarely extends much beyond the market situation.

The degree of bargaining in transactions among vendors also appears to involve some personality differences. Some vendors dislike bargaining. If pushed into it by buyers, especially those who push hardest for bottom prices, they may resort to some deception in weights or in quality. Other vendors, however, brag about their skill at bargaining and discuss their strategies at length. They gauge their customers and the best approaches to use. Asking prices may vary with the vendor's estimate of his customer. Generally speaking, the asking price for city people is apt to be lower than for country people. The rationale is that city people generally are less persistent in their bargaining and that their offering prices are generally higher than the offering prices of the peasants. By starting with a higher asking price for the latter, the area of maneuver is greater. Actual selling prices may be about the same in both cases.

Vendors of items bought only rarely, such as rebozos, may be quite aggressive and condescending with country people, especially those from the Sierra, but admit the latter are hard bargainers who usually get the lowest prices. Highest asking prices are usually reserved for tourists by those who have goods appealing to tourists. The tourist often is less apt to bargain or is not familiar with current market prices; hence the chance of concluding a transaction at a high price is good. The tourist, moreover, is less apt to be a repeat customer, and thus may be overcharged with impunity.[8]

Some *mercado* vendors quote special prices for the purchase of larger quantities, usually to small revendors or *ambulantes*. Some *puesteros* in effect act as semijobbers for *ambulantes* or small revendors based in villages. Often the revendor is a fairly steady client and occasionally short-term credit is offered, normally not exceeding four days and often for as little as one day.

Marketplace *puesteros* have varied ideas about the causes of success or failure. The principal influences mentioned are location, variety and quality of goods offered, and manner of dealing with customers. These factors are given varying weights by different vendors. Location determines the number of potential customers who pass a *puesto* or *caseta*. The other factors determine whether buyers will return or not. Price is rarely mentioned as a competitive factor and, in fact, variations in asking prices between dealers are small.

The vendor has little control over location, for this is usually determined by the availability of locations and their assignment by the *Administración de Mercados* and the market unions. Several interesting aspects of location emerged with the rebuilding of the central part of the *mercado* Benito Juárez. This involved standardization of stall sizes, change in numbers of available stalls, and extensive relocation both for types of goods and for individual vendors. The administration first proposed a lottery system. This was in fact carried out, and objections arose only after the lottery was held. Some holders of corner locations protested violently if they had drawn less desirable locations. Other objections, however, were noneconomic. Vendors generally wanted to be among other vendors they knew and trusted. Others objected to being located near vendors they disliked. The final decisions ultimately were left to the unions, which achieved a redistribution after extensive and sometimes acrimonious discussion. In effect, the redistribution of

---

[8] Contempt is frequently voiced of tourists who pay asking prices without bargaining.

stalls was heavily influenced by a desire to restore preexisting social relationships among vendors.

Variety of goods is affected somewhat by available space and by capital. For most stalls, permanent capital investment is small, and fruit and vegetable dealers appear to have rarely more than $1,000 tied up in current stocks. Often this figure is reduced substantially by use of credit from wholesalers. For other dealers, for example, those handling ready-made clothing, dry goods, and groceries, not only is the capital involved in equipping a *caseta* greater but their stocks may be worth as much as $20,000. Clearly, in the latter cases ability to offer a variety of goods is limited by available capital. While some credit is available to them, most of it is in the form of the usual 30-day billing by suppliers.

Despite the relative unimportance of competitive price cutting, most *mercado* vendors recognize that they are engaged in competitive business. The competition is phrased, however, in the factors of variety, quality, skill in buying, and ability to deal with customers.

MAYORISTAS OR WHOLESALERS

Oaxaca City probably has a long history as a wholesale center. Its antecedent Aztec town was a center for the Pochteca, that is, traders to the Isthmus and the southern Chiapas coast (Soconusco). Although documentary evidence is lacking, it probably was also a headquarters for tribute collectors after the Aztec conquest of the region. In Colonial times it was a major way station in the trade between Mexico City and Peru and Central America.

The importance of the wholesale and interregional trade for traditional market system in earlier times probably was small. Before the building of the railroad, all goods entered and left the Valley region by pack mule or, in pre-Spanish times, on the human back. Trade in salt and raw cotton is documented (chap. 3), and with some confidence we may surmise trade in cacao, cochineal, metals, and other luxury items. In the Colonial period and after, machine-loomed cloth, iron and metal implements, and a few other semiindustrial goods presumably were imported into the region and became more important after the completion of the railroad. Moreover, there were undoubtedly some *acaparadores* who sought staple goods during harvest periods of low prices and stored them against times of scarcity and high prices. Hoarding to manipulate prices is said to have been common. The extensive growth of wholesaling, however, came after completion of the Pan American Highway. Wholesaling consequently is primarily a phenomenon of the modern industrializing national economy and its penetration into Oaxaca. Nevertheless it has come to play a significant part in the traditional market system as it functions today. This importance varies with type of goods handled; wholesalers of industrial goods, for example, sell largely to stores outside the traditional system.

One type of wholesaler important to the traditional marketing system deals in some regionally produced staples such as maize, beans, garbanzos, coffee, nuts (walnuts, pecans, and peanuts), salt, dried fish and shrimp, dried chiles, alfalfa seed, and castor beans. Some also at times handle such items as carrots, onions, cabbage, radishes, peas, wheat, broad beans, squash seeds, alfalfa, loquats, mangoes, and avocados. Of major importance and manifest utility are the wholeslaers of fruits and vegetables, a type of wholesaler who appears to have come into being after the opening of the highway. Certainly they are not mentioned by Malinowski and de la Fuente (1957). At the time of our study, four produce wholesalers did the bulk of the business but there were about 20 smaller wholesalers. Most of the wholesalers originally were from Puebla and were independent owner-driver truckers before becoming wholesalers.[9] Waterbury suggests that local people lack sufficient knowledge of the national economy to carry on such a business successfully. In addition, requirements of a high capital investment, including sizable liquid working capital, and establishment of a substantial line of credit with suppliers, are further obstacles to entry into the wholesale business. It is doubtful if even the smallest business can operate with a capital of less than $100,000 to $120,000. Part of this capital may derive from installment buying of equipment, especially the indispensable truck, and from short-term credit from suppliers.

With few seasonal exceptions for such products as watermelons, wholesalers handle few locally grown products. Some products, such as tomatoes, are imported by wholesalers only when local supplies are inadequate to meet demands. The major part of the wholesaler's business is in produce not grown locally at all or grown only in very small quantities. The main sources of goods are primarily the large wholesale markets in Mexico City, and secondarily, large growers in producing centers. One large wholesaler, for example, has a contract with a grower in San Luis Potosi to supply at least 80 tons of oranges from each harvest, and another with a grower in Loma Bonita in northern Oaxaca State to supply a minimum of 57 tons of pineapples. On some occasions purchases are made from regional wholesalers outside Mexico City. Seasonally, trucks also are sent to acquire supplies from growers in locations as far distant as Sinaloa, Chihuahua, Coahuila, and Tamaulipas. Usually advance arrangements are made with such growers by telephone but at times trucks will be despatched to seek out supplies. Purchases from growers ordinarily are on a cash basis. This means that truck drivers must be entrusted with substantial sums and even trusted to make purchases, although usually the latter are first checked by telephone. Because of risks involved, relatives are preferred as truck drivers.

[9] A more extended discussion of wholesalers is given by Waterbury (1969).

On occasion the Oaxaca wholesalers also buy for the Mexico City market. As an example, if a driver reports by telephone that a large supply of limes is available at a good price in the Isthmus, the dealer will telephone the information to Mexico City. If arrangements are satisfactory, he will call back to his driver to buy a load of limes for delivery in Mexico City. More commonly, however, trucks are sent out empty from Oaxaca to return with produce, and smaller wholesalers with only one truck will buy almost all their produce from Mexico City wholesalers.

Bargaining between buyers and sellers accompanies most purchases from Mexico City wholesalers. This usually is conducted over the telephone. The Oaxaca buyer is at a disadvantage in this situation for he must accept the supplier's statements about quality as well as depend on credit offered by the Mexico City wholesalers. Most Mexico City wholesalers require a minimum of 50 percent cash even from regular customers and expect payment of the balance the following week when the Oaxaca dealer's truck makes its next trip to Mexico City. For larger wholesalers in Oaxaca with two or three trucks, this interval may be as little as three or four days. Exceptions to these credit limitations are made in two situations. A valued Oaxaca dealer with a temporary cash shortage may get 100 percent credit for the same short period. Also, the Mexico City wholesaler may make an exception if he has an oversupply of less perishable goods such as apples or melons that he can offer at low prices. In such cases the Mexico City wholesaler may urge the buyer to take an extra truckload on credit. This will be shipped on a hired truck. Purchases from growers outside Mexico City usually are on a cash basis. In the exceptional cases where credit is allowed by a supplier or large producer outside Mexico City, payment is made by postal money order unless the wholesaler's truck is returning to the same area within a few days.

The biggest customers of the larger Oaxaca City fruit and vegetable wholesalers are wholesalers from the Isthmus of Tehuantepec and Chiapas, principally from the towns of Tehuantepec, Juchitán, Tuxtla Gutiérrez, and Tapachula. Often these buy most or all of their goods from a single Oaxaca City wholesaler, partly to save time, partly because concentrating their purchasing power ensures favored treatment as customers. For example, a woman from Tuxtla Gutiérrez makes one trip a week. She buys at least one truckload and more commonly two truckloads of produce. She pays cash and ships her goods by hired truck. Another woman buyer from Tehuantepec makes two trips a week. Second in importance as buyers for larger wholesalers are smaller inter*plaza* traders who sell in the *plazas* of the Isthmus or the Valley of Oaxaca. The third most important class of wholesale buyers are the *puesteros* in the *mercado* Benito Juárez or in the secondary *mercados* in the City. A fourth class of wholesale buyers is from hotels and the larger restaurants in the City. Wholesalers make special efforts with these buyers in the hope of having them as regular customers and becoming their primary suppliers.

Other special customers are operators of refreshment stands on the main Zócalo. Two of these were observed to buy 6,000 and 8,000 oranges, respectively. A final class of purchaser are *ambulantes* within the City or individuals from nearby villages buying for resale in the village. These are treated essentially as retail customers.

All the bulk buyers are quoted wholesale prices. Bargaining is customary, although the spread between asking and selling price is usually small. If small purchasers such as *ambulantes* attempt to bargain too sharply, the wholesaler may break off the transaction if larger buyers are awaiting attention.

Most *puesteros* in Oaxaca buy on credit and most wholesalers pay special attention to this problem. Major purchases by *puesteros* are made on Tuesdays and Fridays. Generally the wholesaler or his wife visits *puesteros* on Thursdays and Sundays to collect amounts due from earlier transactions. If the entire amount due is not paid on these days, the *puesteros* are required to complete payments before additional goods are supplied. Occasionally a *puestero* will seek to buy from another wholesaler without discharging his debt. But wholesalers usually cooperate in such matters, exchanging information by telephone on slow or bad credit risks.

Most wholesalers also have a retail section near the door and on *plaza* days maintain a sidewalk *puesto* outside the warehouse. Wholesalers insist that their retail prices are at the going market rate; to undercut the *puesteros* would be unfair and bad business. Retail sales are always for cash. Customers are householders, not only from Oaxaca City but from surrounding villages. In addition to the normal retail sales, most wholesale establishments do a fairly lively business in fruits for immediate consumption, selling either whole overripe fruits or, for pineapples, melons, or papayas, slices cut from damaged or partially spoiled fruits. Prices for these may be as little as $0.20 a slice. Although total retail sales may be relatively small, they represent sheer gain from fruits that otherwise would be a total loss.

Although most wholesalers attempt to stock a considerable variety of goods, many tend to specialize somewhat, maintaining large stocks of oranges or apples or other fruit, or emphasize vegetables rather than fruits. Two at least specialize in bananas, and the largest banana dealer handles nothing else. For him, special storage rooms are required to control ripening of the fruit. Nevertheless, most wholesalers try to supply most of the wants of their customers, and if they do not have a wanted item for a large cash buyer, they will undertake to buy it from another wholesaler.

Knowledge of market conditions obviously is essential in buying and is equally important in setting the asking prices. Wholesale prices vary from day to day. During any one day they tend to be unstable early in the morning, reach a stable level at about 10 A.M., and remain steady the rest of the day. Two items of information are essential to the individual wholesaler: prices asked by competitors and stocks held by competitors. One source of needed information is the customers themselves. Many of the customers shop around and do not hesitate to point out lower prices asked by other wholesalers. If customers fail to buy, their comments are taken seriously. In addition, wholesalers send their employees out to observe the stocks held by competitors and to overhear prices asked in transactions.[10] The amount and quality of information possessed by vendors is critical to successful pricing.

In general, wholesalers seem to average over 20 percent markup above their basic cost price and seldom go below a 5 percent markup. All are agreed that they never will go below cost of merchandise, preferring instead to allow goods to spoil. This practice appears to stem from fears of mutually destructive competition and belief that buyers would soon expect exceptionally low prices as a regular thing. The most unpredictable factor in marketing is the sudden appearance of an independent trucker with a load of a single item that he offers for sale at a very low price.

Skill in selling clearly is quite as important to success as skill in buying. Generally speaking, the larger the purchase, the lower the selling price. Cash buyers receive special favors, not only in lower prices but also they are permitted to be more selective about the merchandise they accept. The wholesaler seeks to maintain friendly attitudes and long-term regular customers may be addressed by special nicknames. When transactions are concluded they may be offered a beer or, if it is meal time, invited to eat as the guest of the proprietor. The life is not an easy one. On Tuesdays, Thursdays, and Saturdays the market opens at 5 A.M., on other days at 6 A.M. The majority of large sales have been made by 10 A.M. but the *bodegas* are open until at least 6 P.M. and sometimes until 7 or 8 P.M. In the less active times of the workday, stock is rearranged and appraised, buying plans are made, deals are made by telephone, and trucks dispatched. When the *bodega* closes, usually there are books to be kept, plans to be made, and often the proprietor may not leave until 10 P.M. Not without justice, a *puestero* characterized a wholesaler as a man with a telephone at his ear and ulcers in his stomach. Yet some seem to thrive on the hard work, and as a class wholesalers are well nourished, sharply dressed, pleasant, and even jovial in manner.

Case History of a Fruit and Vegetable Wholesaler

This summary case history is of one of the larger fruit and vegetable wholesalers in the market. He was intensively interviewed over several months by a member of the staff who worked as a volunteer in his *bodega,* observing transactions, talking with employees and customers, and even selling and making bookkeeping entries

---

[10] The crowded conditions of the marketplace during busy hours makes private deals difficult.

at busy times. The owner permitted us to borrow his records of purchases and sales covering over six months of the then current year. He did not allow us access to his full set of books on the excuse that they were in the hands of his bookkeeper, and he was reticent on some details that might affect his tax status.

As with all wholesalers, the core of the business is familial, including the husband as head of the enterprise; the wife, who assists in selling and takes charge in the husband's absence; and an unmarried younger brother of the husband who drives one of the trucks, exercises some independence in buying when on trips, and assists about the *bodega* when not on a trip. The husband's mother lives with the family, keeps the house, and exercises some influence in the business. None of these family members draws any salary from the enterprise, but there are paid employees. A female servant helps in the house and is paid $100 a month. Two truck drivers are paid by the trip, the amount varying with time involved. One has been with the enterprise for eight years. Two *mozos* are paid $40 and $30 weekly, respectively. They sleep in the house, act as *macheteros* on the trucks, help in loading, unloading, and in moving stock in the *bodega,* and sometimes help in selling. A part-time bookkeeper is paid $50 a month.

Husband and wife are both from the state of Puebla. The wife's father was a cattle buyer and the husband worked for him for a while, buying and transporting cattle in Oaxaca. Husband and wife eloped to Oaxaca and regularized their union by both civil and church marriages six months later. In Oaxaca the husband first worked as a truck driver. Later he sent for his older brother and the two became cattle buyers for a while. The husband's mother later came to Oaxaca and obtained a fruit *puesto* in the *mercado.* A younger brother, who formerly helped in the *bodega,* is now married and works as a truck driver for a competing firm. A sister, also married, now operates the mother's fruit stand in the *mercado.*

The husband made the down payment on his first truck from part of an inheritance the wife received from her parents, and began to buy bananas in Tabasco. He supplied his mother's *puesto* and sold to other *puesteros* in the *mercado.* Later he established relations with a dealer in oranges in Córdoba, Veracruz, and visited Mexico City, where he established credit with suppliers and entered into his present general fruit and vegetable business. He now operates three trucks representing a capital investment of $255,000. Equipment in his *bodega* cost an additional $10,000, and his liquid capital is at least $50,000. This figure, supplied reluctantly by the wholesaler, undoubtedly is low. Operating expenses for gasoline, rent, taxes, utilities, and wages run well over $9,000 a month (this does not include repairs to trucks, taxes levied on the highway, occasional rental of additional trucks, and other irregular expenses). (For further details see Waterbury 1968:157–158.)

No wholesaler would provide us with an estimate of gross sales, and this dealer was no exception. Possibly, if we had been permitted to keep the ledgers long enough, an estimate might have been made. As do most wholesalers, this dealer keeps two current ledgers. One ledger lists credit sales with name, amount, and date. When a debt is paid, the item is crossed off. The second ledger records dates, amounts, and kinds of goods purchased, the price per unit and, if bought on credit, the amount owed to the supplier. This dealer, as do some others, also keeps a record of prices paid and wholesale and retail prices at which the goods were sold. All other accounts are kept by the bookkeeper; his main function involves handling tax technicalities and the minimization of tax payments. Waterbury (1968:151) estimates an average markup of 25 percent for this wholesaler. A reanalysis of the data gives an average markup of 30 percent of cost prices for wholesale sales and 56 percent for retail sales.[11] Although the dealer says he occasionally sells at the cost or purchase price, this does not appear on the records examined. The lowest markup discovered was 8.8 percent of cost, on papayas. On no other item was this figure less than 20 percent of cost. Operating costs the dealer estimates at about 10 percent of purchase cost. Hence any sales at less than a 10 percent markup apparently are at a loss but nevertheless contribute to meeting total expenses. It seems evident, however, that the dealer has no accurate idea of his profits or the amount drawn from the business to meet household expenses.

Some idea of the volume of business done is afforded by the following analysis of a truck operations. Three trucks normally make two round trips a week, bringing loads of eight or nine metric tons each trip. Additional purchases are sometimes brought by hired trucks. Trucks are scheduled to arrive Mondays and Thursdays or before the beginning of the major sales periods on Tuesdays and Fridays. On these mornings goods are sold directly from the trucks. Unsold goods are moved into the *bodega* in the afternoon or when the truck must leave on another trip. This means that normally nearly fifty tons of produce a week are handled by this wholesaler. The peso value of these goods varies greatly according to the commodity involved and with seasonal price changes.

Although superficially the Oaxaca market wholesaler would seem to resemble closely a modern marketing institution in the size of business and the way it is conducted, in fact only scale differentiates him significantly from the middlemen of the traditional market and *plaza* system. Like theirs, his business essentially is a family enterprise, and business and family budgets are not separated. Transactions, whether in buying or selling, are essentially dyadic affairs involving negotiated prices within the limits set by market conditions. In scope, the wholesaler's business goes far beyond the regional marketing system, but an important function

[11] While markup is usually stated as a percentage of selling price, the wholesaler starts from his cost price in arriving at his minimum asking price for sales.

of his business is to feed goods into the traditional marketing system through his sales to inter*plaza* traders. Although he uses some sophisticated forms of credit in his business, especially in the purchase of trucks, when he needs short-term cash he turns to the traditional moneylender (where he pays 2 percent a month rather than the 5 percent or more that is more common) rather than to the Banco de Pequeño Comercio.

9
Price Making and
Market Results

The preoccupation of Oaxaca peasants with prices has been noted by many observers, and price is a favorite topic of conversation even though no immediate purchase or sale is contemplated. "How much is it?" and "What will you offer?" are among the two most frequently used phrases in the Oaxaca marketing region. Of the village of Mitla, Parsons observed several decades ago:

> Mitla is a business town. Trade permeates its whole life; price is of supreme interest to young and old, men and women, the poor and the well-to-do. . . . The Mitleyeno is price minded. Money cost enters into the evaluation of things and experience to a degree I have never found equaled in any other society, including the most plutocratic circles (1936:12–13).

This comment gains force because Parsons lived for many years in the best known "plutocratic circles" of the late nineteenth and early twentieth centuries.

In Oaxaca villages, strangers often are approached with a question about the price paid for goods carried or of a garment worn. The object may be carefully examined and (with clothing) the fabric felt between the fingers. People returning from the marketplace not only are asked what they paid for their purchases or the price they received for the goods they sold, but are expected to have some idea of current market prices for a variety of other commodities.

Much of the questioning and discussion forms part of an informational system related to anticipated participation in the market as a seller or buyer. If the item is unusual, the questioner often is interested in whether it might be a profitable item of trade. On other occasions, questions may reflect a long-felt want rather than a more immediate intention to buy. In the Mixe area in 1933 the most frequent question I was asked was the price of sewing machines. At that time sewing machines were new in the area and few were available but already they were greatly desired, for most clothing was handsewn at home.

GENERAL CONSIDERATIONS

A few general remarks about price seem in order before discussing the phenomenon in Oaxaca. Price often is considered only in a passive sense, but it may be thought of as being functionally active as well. The more usual view of price emphasizes its passive role as an indication of value at a given time and place.[1] But price also has a more active function in controling the flow of goods and services through distribution channels. In this latter role "price" has great relevance to our study of the Oaxaca market system, and the Oaxaca peasant's preoccupation with the subject reflects his involvement in the market system.

Prices usually are considered primarily in terms of supply, that is, the quantity of goods or services offered at various prices, and demand, that is, the quantity of goods and services taken at particular prices. In the hypothetical situation of a perfect market (to be discussed later), over time an equilibrium situation tends to develop in which the quantity of goods desired and the quantity available will be balanced and the prices in all individual transactions will be the same. Even if this is not so, in a hypothetically stable system, amounts taken should diminish and amounts offered increase as prices rise, or the reverse should occur as prices fall, in response to the impersonal and automatic market mechanism.

Although supply and demand factors are always present in market situations, numerous other factors may act to skew the usual supply and demand curves. Within limits, in some circumstances, the amount of goods taken by buyers may remain fairly stable regardless of price, that is, demand is unelastic. This is especially true when buyers feel they must have a constant minimum quantity of a particular good, for example, in Oaxaca, maize to meet minimum daily household food requirements. Where sellers base their prices on cost only, and where such cost is fixed or unvarying over the short term, stable prices may be maintained in the face of declining demand. Special need situations may lead some, and often many, buyers to purchase more goods despite higher prices. The possibility of

---

[1] "The value, that is the exchange value, of one thing in terms of another at any place and time, is the amount of that second thing which can be got there and then in exchange for the first. Thus the term value is relative, and expresses the relation between two things at a particular place and time" (Marshall 1920:61).

substituting one good for another may result in a greater-than-predictable decline in the demand for one commodity and an increase in the demand for another. Prices in individual transactions may vary because of special needs of seller or buyer or differences in their information, the type of commodity involved, or the situation in which the transaction occurs.[2] Some of these factors are important enough in Oaxaca markets to merit special comment later.

Transactions are usually effected by a buyer's acceptance of a seller's firm price offer (nonnegotiated price situations) or by bargaining from a flexible initial offer (negotiated price situations). Goods are exchanged for money or, occasionally, for other goods (barter situations).

Ethnographers have reported cases of exchange in simple economies in other parts of the world where the quantities demanded or offered for exchange are traditionally established, that is, where both seller and buyer know that exchanges have "always" involved the same quantities. Prices are fixed, bargaining is absent, and all that is necessary to complete an exchange is for both seller and buyer to express an interest in trading and to offer the traditional amounts of the two goods involved. Such situations are often said to represent nonmarket prices. It is suspected that most such prices in fact do change very slowly over a period of years if amounts available come to exceed amounts required or buyers compete for a scanty supply. The data suggest that traditional prices in the usual sense do not exist or are extremely rare in Oaxaca.

Tradition nevertheless may have some effect on the processes of price formation in two very limited senses. In the first, the memory of past prices may affect what the seller will ask or the buyer will offer. In the second sense, traditional, socially dictated needs for goods, for example, for the sponsorship of a traditional ritual, may motivate the buyer to pay a higher price than he otherwise would pay. In addition, because production is a way of life, some producers may continue to produce a traditional commodity even in a situation of oversupply, with a resulting decline in price, while some consumers with traditional desires may continue to demand products in short supply rather than shift to alternative products at lower prices.

PRICING SITUATIONS IN OAXACA

Discovery of prices and the multitude of factors related to them is difficult in a market characterized by innumerable small and unrecorded transactions, especially when many prices are negotiated. Such success as resulted from this phase of the

---

[2] Convenient relevant discussions are to be found in the *International Encyclopedia of the Social Sciences*, 4:96–97, and 12:457ff.; and in Cassady (1962:21–42).

study was very largely because of the unusual cooperativeness of the people of Oaxaca, the great interest they have in prices, and a great expenditure of time and effort on the part of the project staff.[3]

Negotiated prices. In Oaxaca it is usual to negotiate prices for many goods produced by or sold to peasants. This includes most farm products, animals, and handicrafts as well as such industrial products as shawls (rebozos), clothing (*ropa hecha*) and textiles (*telas*). Negotiation or bargaining for these products prevails at both the wholesale and retail levels. An important exception occurs among stallkeepers in the daily *mercado* of Oaxaca City, where a few sellers even post prices on fruits and vegetables, although this may be only a point of departure for bargaining.

In negotiated price situations each transaction is theoretically independent. Procedures may differ markedly according to the commodity involved, the numbers of potential sellers and buyers, and the customary patterns in vogue in a particular marketing system, but throughout the world negotiated price situations have some things in common:

1. Meeting of a seller and a buyer either by the seller's seeking out potential buyers or the reverse.
2. Initiation of negotiations by an opening price offer and counteroffer (both are necessary before negotiations can really begin).
3. Continuation of offers and counteroffers, often interspersed with arguments and discussions aimed at persuading the other party to accept an offer, until the parties reach agreement on a price and the sale is concluded, or one party breaks off the negotiations. The course of negotiations is far from uniform among sales.

In Oaxaca almost all retail transactions are initiated by the buyer's approaching a seller and opening negotiations by asking the price of an item he desires. The principal exception is the door-to-door peddler who approaches the prospective buyer, but even here the initial move in the transaction is made by the buyer asking the price. The situation is reversed in sales to wholesalers or storekeepers; these sellers approach buyers and take the initiative by asking the proprietor how much he will offer, the reversed sequence of offers reflecting bargaining situations of seller and buyer.

[3] Data collected included the following:

(1) Many extended interviews concerning prices and pricing policies with all kinds of buyers and sellers. (2) Observation and recording of the details of hundreds of individual transactions. (3) Records of prices currently paid by many buyers. (4) Examination of the books of a major wholesaler, including his records of cost and sale prices. (5) Inventories of goods offered by all kinds of vendors including producer-vendors, *regatones,* stall and store operators, and wholesalers. Wherever possible, statements about cost and sale prices were obtained. (6) Inventories of goods in village households with remembered prices and dates of purchase. (7) Comparison pricing between vendors in the same and different marketplaces and between village and city stores.

Cassady (1968) has analyzed retail negotiated-price transactions as they are carried on in the Oaxaca marketing system and has developed several models showing the various possible outcomes. In figure 1, the seller has in mind a minimum price he will accept and the buyer has in mind a maximum price he will pay. Unless these coincide or overlap, negotiations will be unsuccessful. The buyer ordinarily asks the price of an item. The seller names a price and frequently adds, "What will you offer?" to make sure the buyer understands that negotiation is expected. The buyer responds with a counteroffer. These first two bids are critical; if either party considers the price quoted by the other to be out of all reason, the transaction may be aborted immediately. If the seller's price is considered too high, the buyer customarily leaves unless called back by a lower price quotation. Alternatively, if the buyer's counteroffer is considered unreasonable, the seller may reject it verbally, or by turning to another customer, turning his back, or starting a conversation with his neighbor. Otherwise a series of offers and counteroffers normally continues until the seller and buyer close the gap between their original price offers, or negotiations are broken off because the gap cannot be closed. When this occurs, the seller may shake his head, say he cannot accept the buyer's best offer and put the merchandise away. Or the buyer may say "No" or "Too expensive" and walk away.

Breaking off negotiations does not necessarily mean that a transaction is permanently aborted. The buyer may go away, bargain elsewhere, and return to resume negotiating. If so, the position of the seller usually is strengthened; he may, in fact, consider it a new transaction by increasing his asking price. If there are few buyers in the marketplace, however, a disruption of negotiations may strengthen the position of the buyer. If too many sales are aborted and the buyers do not return, the seller comes to realize that his prices are too high. But if a transaction is completed very rapidly, the seller may suspect that his minimum price is too low, or the buyer may feel that he has been over-eager and paid too much.

In figure 2 Cassady shows a skewing of the final price toward the seller's initial offer, with the buyer making most of the concessions. Figure 3 shows skewing toward the buyer's initial offer with the seller making most of the concessions. In this case, a reluctant buyer may not respond with a counteroffer. If the seller is eager to make a sale, he makes a series of price concessions despite the absence of counteroffers until he names a price the buyer will accept or to which he responds by bargaining. In some cases the buyer's reluctance may be due less to a desire to wring concessions from the seller than to uncertainty as to whether he really wants the item; or it may be that he has decided to buy it only if he can get it at a very reduced ("bargain") price.

But the most important function of the various bargaining patterns described is

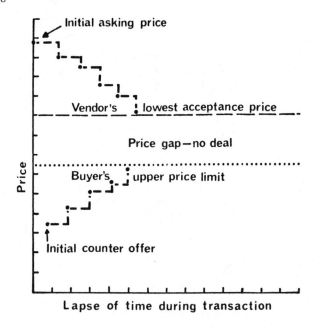

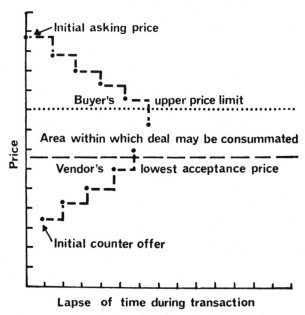

FIG. 1. Effect of contrasting positions of vendor maximum and buyer minimum prices, where they exist, on the potential consummation of a negotiated price deal (Cassady 1968:56, fig. 2)

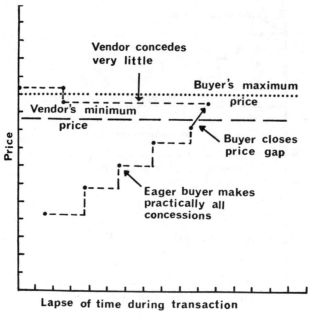

FIG. 2. Skewing of final price toward vendor's initial offer (Cassady 1968:61, fig. 3)

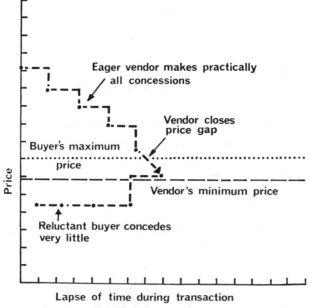

FIG. 3. Skewing of final price toward buyer's counteroffer (Cassady 1968:62, fig. 4)

to discover the true worth of an object. As Tax (1953:137) has said in relation to a similar marketing situation in Guatemala,

> Bargaining has a genuine commercial function with respect to commodities that cannot have fixed and stable values: only by bargaining experiences of the particular market day can the buyers and sellers determine how much they are worth. So values are fixed for a given time and place.

A seller in an advantageous position may make his first offer at about the minimum price he has decided to accept and will not respond to counteroffers. For example, I once observed a man with five large and exceptionally attractive shoats on his way to market. Before he reached the street location set aside for young pigs, he was accosted by prospective buyers and soon had a circle of possible buyers and lookers-on. The seller quoted a price of $60 per shoat. Although there was some halfhearted bargaining, he quickly sold two at his asking price. One buyer then offered him $35 for a shoat, which the seller flatly rejected. The buyer raised his offer slowly to $45, despite the obvious indifference of the seller. At this point the prospective buyer became abusive, saying such things as, "Why did you come to market if not to sell?" To which the seller responded, "Of course I came to sell, but not to give my shoats away." Eventually, after considerable harassment, the seller said, "All right, I'll bargain. I'll sell a shoat for $58." At this the buyer cried, "I thought you were going to bargain." The seller replied, "I am bargaining. I offered the shoat for $58 to get rid of you. Now take it or go away."

In the course of this transaction it became apparent that the buyer's wife, rather than the man conducting the bargaining, was controlling the negotiations. Each time before raising his offer, he consulted his wife. In one of the intervals the seller sold a third shoat for $60. Eventually, after moving away for a while, the buyer agreed to buy at $58 but then had to get the money from his wife. When I left, the seller was still holding out adamantly to other would-be buyers for $60 for his final shoat. Presumably he sold his final animal without ever reaching the pig-selling locale, thus avoiding the *plaza* tax. It seems clear that this seller had set a reasonable price for the animals. Had he wished to bargain, he probably would have set his asking price at $70 or even $80.

Much more goes on in negotiations than the mere exchange of offers and counteroffers, especially if either party at any point shows reluctance to shift his position. The seller may explain how his price really is quite low or point out the superior quality of his merchandise. A seller may claim that the price the buyer is offering is for a different quality or size of merchandise, which the seller may tender to the buyer at the latter's last-quoted price. A frequent ploy with a reluctant buyer is to get him to take the merchandise in his hands and then refuse to take it back, trying to persuade him that he should pay the price asked. The buyer, in contrast, may himself pick up the merchandise and examine it carefully, pointing out defects and claiming that the seller's price is much too high. Nevertheless, in most cases either the seller eventually offers the goods at or below the maximum price the buyer is willing to pay, or the reverse occurs, and the transaction is completed and money and goods change hands.

Quasi-negotiated prices. The term "quasi-negotiated prices" is here applied to sales of goods offered in small piles (*montones*) or bunches. Offered in piles are most of the deciduous fruits from the Sierra, pecans and walnuts, small chile peppers, and sometimes small amounts of other vegetables. Of a similar nature is the offering in small containers of salt, lime for preparing maize, peanuts, and toasted grasshoppers (a local delicacy). Offered in bunches are onions, garlic, and radishes. Piles or bunches tend to be uniform in price, and often some care is taken to make piles equal. I have observed a woman setting up small piles of dried chiles on a cloth spread on the ground carefully weigh each pile, changing weights for each class of pepper. On this occasion no prospective buyers happened to be watching.

The prices of piles or bunches are usually uniform as among vendors, and as prices rarely change, they may be regarded as traditional to some degree. What may vary over time or among vendors of the same class of goods is the size of pile or bunch, a response to cost of goods or supplies available. Some vendors are *propios* who have no clear idea of costs. But if the vendor is a trader, it is likely that he tries to set the size of piles or bunches so that his total sales will return the cost of goods and provide some margin of profit. In either case, however, the minimum size of piles or bunches offered is set primarily by competition.

In quasi-negotiated prices, bargaining occurs with respect to amount and quality, not the monetary price. Sellers of similar goods usually are in the same location, and buyers may easily compare offerings. Sometimes the buyers, especially men or children buying fruit as a snack to eat at once, conclude the transaction without bargaining. More frequently the buyer asks the price, examines the merits of several piles (or containers or bunches) and selects one. Very often the buyer then objects that the quantity is too small or that a particular item is defective. The seller may simply defend his goods, or may add to the pile, or may replace the allegedly defective item. Negotiation thus is common but it concerns quantity and quality rather than monetary values.

While direct price cutting in this class of goods is rare, some semiprice cutting occurs by changing the quantity offered while maintaining the prevailing price per unit of sale and may be accompanied by active promotional effort. Toward the end of the *plaza* day a vendor of onions, for example, may begin to walk the streets waving a bunch of onions in one hand and a couple of additional onions in the other, calling out, "Buy my onions for twenty (*centavos*) and I'll give you two more." Those who sell by the *montón* or pile do not move about but wave an additional item or two as an inducement. Sharp buyers may defer purchases until late in the *plaza* day to take advantage of this, but they run the risk that supplies may be exhausted if the market has been unusually active. In such instances sellers are responding either to a general oversupply situation in the marketplace, to being themselves overstocked, or to a need to increase their cash intake for the day.

Nonnegotiated prices. The term "nonnegotiated prices" is used for situations where prices are set by the seller on the take-it-or-leave-it basis common in most retail trade in the United States. The seller establishes his price on the basis of cost of the goods sold, costs of doing business, desired profit margins, occasionally a highly desired brand name, and, sometimes, the goal of achieving a certain volume of sales. Competition also is important. A seller who sets prices appreciably higher than those of his competitor may lose his customers; if he sets them too low he may not only reduce his profit margins but may stimulate ruinous competitive price cutting. In situations, common in many parts of the world, where all sellers view their businesses as a way of making a living rather than seeking constantly increasing profits, and where all sellers have access to the same sources of supply at similar prices, there is little incentive to increase volume of sales by lowering retail prices. In a given marketplace, prices therefore tend to be uniform among various sellers and most competition occurs in the quality and variety of goods offered, in seeking advantageous locations with exposure to many buyers, and in the extension of credit to buyers.

In Oaxaca nonnegotiated prices prevail for most goods sold in stalls in the daily *mercado* and in retail stores. This is especially true of staple groceries, hardware, notions and sundries, soap and toilet articles, refreshments (whether sold at stands or from mobile carts), and a few items hawked on the streets, especially on *plaza* days, such as plastic sheets for raincapes and bags of detergent. Except for some refreshments, most of these goods are relatively modern industrial products. The dichotomy is clear in furniture. Prices of furniture made in villages or small shops in the city are negotiable while prices of industrially produced furniture in stores ordinarily are not.

The pattern for most transactions in this category is as follows: the buyer indicates the item he wants, the seller names the price, and the buyer either makes the purchase or goes away. There is very little and sometimes no difference in prices asked by various competing sellers; the goods in many cases are standardized; and in most transactions the buyer accepts the price quoted. This does not mean that price shading never occurs. For a regular customer, a storekeeper sometimes will shade prices slightly, especially if he is somewhat overstocked in the goods the buyer desires. This action is not the result of bargaining but is unilateral on the part of the storekeeper.

Nonnegotiated prices respond slowly over time to supply and demand considerations. As supplies of goods from outside the region are relatively unlimited from the viewpoint of the Oaxaca dealer, prices change mainly in response to cost changes and slackening of demand affecting producers who serve the larger national market. Oaxaca prices therefore change slowly over a long time span and in a short-term situation tend to be stable and well known to buyers.

Barter. Barter involves trading one commodity for another. In one form of barter, two parties with goods to exchange reach agreement on the quantities of their respective goods they are willing to give and to accept. In another form, both parties agree on the monetary prices of their goods and exchange quantities of equal monetary value. Unless traditional values exist for the commodities, both kinds of barter involve bargaining either with respect to the quantities to be exchanged or as a means of reaching agreement on monetary prices. Barter may be resorted to in monetary economies because potential traders use unexchangeable currencies (as in international barter deals), or because there is not a sufficient supply of currency in circulation for the volume of exchange, or because potential buyers lack cash and sellers will accept payment in goods rather than lose sales. In special cases a trader may see a possibility for increasing gains through resale in another marketplace of some particular good offered to him in barter.

Interest in barter transactions among both anthropologists and economists seems to stem from two viewpoints. One is that barter represents a "primitive" or premarket type of exchange; the other is that barter is not "tainted" by the competition of the marketplace or of maximization. The data from Oaxaca give little support to the view that barter is a primitive survival, as market considerations enter into most barter transactions.

The most frequently observed cases of barter in Oaxaca were mostly in village stores where such products as maize, beans, or eggs are exchanged for some item carried by the storekeeper. A money value is established for the item offered by the customer. For such divisible goods as maize, beans, noodles, lard, candy, or crackers, the storekeeper offers an equivalent amount. For undivisible items such as candles or canned goods, the goods offered must equal or exceed the value of the item desired. In the latter case, the storekeeper may pay the few *centavos'* difference to the customer.

A more specialized type of barter occurs in Santa María Atzompa and perhaps in other places. Some peddlers not only exchange their goods for pottery but often say they prefer this type of exchange. Here the motivation is that the peddler expects to increase his gains through resale of the pottery at higher prices in some other location.

In market *plazas* occasional cases of direct barter are observed. As an example, a woman may approach a row of bean vendors with a bowl of tomatoes, calling out, "I have tomatoes. Who will give me beans?" Sometimes she gets no response. On other occasions she may be offered what she considers an inadequate quantity of beans and refuses the exchange. If she is unsuccessful among the bean vendors, she may move on to a row of vendors of some other product such as onions and repeat the process. A second kind of barter observed involved deciduous-fruit *propios* from the Sierra. Very often such vendors bring a dozen or so of pomegranates in addition to their principal fruit items (apples, pears, or peaches, for example). The pomegranates are not offered for sale but are used to trade for prepared food. The main deciduous fruits, however, rarely if ever are bartered but are sold for cash.

Despite these examples, in the 1960s barter transactions apparently were relatively infrequent in Oaxaca, and the quantities involved in most transactions were very small—two or three pomegranates for a half dozen tortillas, or a half dozen small tomatoes for a handful or two of beans. In view of the importance attributed to barter in Oaxaca by Malinowski and de la Fuente (1957:124–132) although the amounts involved in the transactions described by them seem miniscule), it appears that since 1940 the frequency of barter transactions may have declined substantially. But it is also possible that Malinowski, with his early experience in nonmonetary exchange systems, made a special effort to find examples of barter, thereby exaggerating their relative frequency, whereas my staff recorded them only as they came across them and did not make any special effort to find them. In any case, the overwhelming number of barter transactions observed involved the establishment of mutually acceptable monetary equivalences rather than pure barter on the basis of traditional exchange equivalencies.

FACTORS AFFECTING PRICE LEVELS

Identifying the various situations in which price is of importance tells us little about how prices are formed in each or what factors operate. Deeper understanding requires examination of how sellers determine their prices and how buyers respond to them in different situations and in relation to various kinds of commodities. In the ensuing discussion it should be understood that the pricing phenomena described are in terms of a single marketplace and that under special circumstances individuals may depart from the more general practice.

Supply and demand. Supply and demand factors underlie price formation in the Oaxaca market as a whole, although their effects may be modified or obscured by other factors to be considered later. Many examples of the influence of supply and demand factors have been given in the discussions of production and the dynamics of the market system. Peasants frequently increase production of some agricultural products or shifts to new crops because they offer better returns. In other instances, producers of handicrafts increase or decrease production seasonally in accordance with the changes in supply and demand. This has been best documented for metate production by Cook (1970). It must be pointed out, however, that the quantity of any regional agricultural product entering the market in a given year is not in direct response to an anticipated level of demand but is dependent upon crop conditions. This does not vitiate the principle that prices will respond to the supply and demand situation.

In the Oaxaca market it is apparent that the operation of supply and demand often is most effective at an individual level. The vendor is less affected by the total supplies of goods in the market system or even within his marketplace than he is by the amount of merchandise available which competes with his own. In addition, both sellers and buyers often see the supply and demand situation, especially in weekly *plazas,* primarily in terms of the numbers of sellers and buyers present on a given day. These determine the individual's estimate of the market as being active or sluggish, and he tailors his selling or buying plans accordingly. Classical models of supply and demand factors seem clearly relevant to price formation in the Oaxaca marketing system as a whole, but a great deal more research is needed to ascertain how they operate at the level of individual transactions.

Cost factors in pricing. Cost plays an important part in the selling prices of most *regatones.* In negotiated price situations the dealer sets the minimum price he will accept, based in part upon the cost of his merchandise plus the amount he thinks he must get to make it worth while to do business. As an example, one Atzompa pottery *regatón* selling in the Oaxaca *plaza* sets his minimum at, say, $24 a dozen for a particular sized jar. His asking price will be $36 a dozen to give himself leeway for bargaining with the expectation of an average sale price of $30 a dozen (individual retail sale prices will be slightly higher but proportional). In the course of a day he may, if his stock does not move well, sell at less than $30, but rather than sell below $24 from his street location, at the end of the day he will sell his remaining stock at a somewhat lower price to a large wholesale dealer. Usually this is a dealer with whom he does business more-or-less regularly. In this case the purchase price of goods plus transportation costs plays an important part in determining the minimum price acceptable, while the higher price goals the dealer has set represent his attempt to achieve the desired margin. Fluctuations in the production of pottery as well as the amount sought by buyers occur only seasonally or over a considerable time span, and therefore the dealer may be able to follow a cost-plus pricing policy successfully. Similar price policies may be followed by sellers of clothing and textiles that are subject to negotiation of prices in retail sales.

Storekeepers handling staple groceries, hardware, and similar industrially-produced goods for which prices usually are not negotiated, follow different policies. Although each dealer has several potential sources of supply, competition normally keeps their asking prices within quite narrow limits. Suppliers or their agents also often suggest retail prices to their customers. But competition prevents individual retailers from asking significantly higher prices than do others. Ideas of increasing volume through lower prices or the use of loss leaders are rare, and most dealers say that significant price cutting simply will cause competitors to lower their prices, to the ultimate disadvantage of all, unless demand is very elastic.

Dealers in perishable goods, whether wholesalers or retailers with stalls in the *mercado*, must be much more flexible in pricing, for the quantity of goods entering the market varies from day to day and even from hour to hour, with corresponding variations in the cost of goods. Competitors who have bought at lower prices may force a rival dealer to lower his asking price. He may resist lowering his price below his merchandise cost as long as he can, but the dealer will usually sell below cost rather than have his goods spoil, consoling himself with the thought that the next time there is a swing in prices it may be advantageous to him. Dealers in some goods may resort to various expedients to avoid soft price situations. Tomato sellers, for example, may cull their stock, cutting out the spoiled parts of the fruits and selling the remainder in bulk to restaurants for making chile sauce, while at the same time improving the quality of their remaining stock.

The most dramatic threats to prices based on costs are truckers who arrive suddenly with a load of some commodity such as papayas or oranges and begin retailing on the street at prices much below those formerly prevailing. Wholesalers of these goods usually keep a cash reserve to buy the trucker's entire load so they can partially control the impact of sudden supply changes. Occasionally, in the case of such a highly perishable fruit as papayas, the wholesaler may even allow part or all of the truckload to spoil, calculating that the losses will be less than what would result from a major price reduction.

In interviews, many dealer-respondents emphasized the importance of the cost of goods in their pricing policies. It would appear that only as a result of competitive pressure, heavy buyer resistance, or some special motivation will a wholesale dealer lower his prices, and he resists to the utmost of his ability lowering prices below the cost of his goods. That is, he foregoes the opportunity to cut short-term losses by selling below cost to avoid initiating a cycle of competitive price cutting.

In contrast to dealers, the peasant producer-vendor selling in the *plaza* has little or no idea of the cost of his goods. If he elects to sell at retail, his asking prices are determined by his ideas about prevailing market prices modified sometimes by the necessity to dispose of his stock within a limited time span, usually one day or at most two days. If he elects to sell his goods wholesale, usually he names no price but may seek out the best offer among several wholesalers. Alternatively, he may accept the first offer if he believes the price to be fair.

"Market" and "fair" prices. While ordinarily "market price" refers to any price at

which a given transaction is completed, Oaxaca peasants and dealers think rather in terms of prevailing or "going" price, and this influences the formation of selling prices, especially in negotiated price situations. Usually a current price figure can be elicited from both sellers and buyers when they are questioned outside actual transactional situations. Ordinarily the figures given will be fairly similar, but they are not identical, for each respondent is making a subjective judgment based on the transactions he knows about. The function of the market in establishing the price for a given commodity is well recognized and is at the bottom of the preference, already noted among villagers, to buy or sell in the marketplace rather than within the village. This is clear not only from the relative scarcity of intravillage transactions but also in various volunteered statements such as: "In the *plaza* the market establishes the price," or, "How do I know in the village what a proper price should be?" The motivations in such cases are not entirely those of maximizing returns, although this motivation is present. In addition to concern about prevailing prices, peasant buyers are concerned that the price in any transaction be reasonable or fair.

Individuals thus distinguish between a current price and a fair price that, depending on individual circumstances may be higher or lower than the current price. This is most apparent in many negotiated transactions as well as from interview material. For many commodities the seller views as a fair price one that will bring him a reasonable return above his cost and which is not seriously out of line with prices being obtained by other sellers. If he believes the current market price to be above this, his asking price will be higher. His minimum selling price also may be higher, and he will be more reluctant to lower his price toward the buyer's bid. If, however, the current market price is lower than the fair price, he will try not to reduce his asking price to a point where he fears prices may become permanently depressed. Similarly, the highly motivated buyer may pay more than what he considers to be a fair price if he believes the current price to be higher. At the opposite extreme is the reluctant buyer or bargain hunter who may have come to the marketplace resolved to buy only if he can do so at or below his idea of a "fair" price.

The differing individual conception of fair or current prices arise in part out of imperfections in the information system and the way information is interpreted. Each individual "knows" the prices paid in only a limited number of separate transactions through observation, casual conversations, and questioning; and individual experience is varied. The interpretation is affected by individual needs and desires; the buyer hopes that prices really are a bit lower or that he can find an eager seller, while the seller hopes that he can sell at a higher-than-prevailing price.

When a *propio* arrives at a marketplace he establishes his selling place in a section of people selling similar goods, and he can observe the transactions of others. He also observes that buyers either reject his goods and buy from others, or leave other sellers to buy from him. Moreover, some buyers may price the goods offered by several vendors, then return to buy from him. In the first instance he realizes that his price is too high; in the other two instances he suspects that his prices are too low. In addition, he may get information in conversations or by walking about the marketplace listening to transactions.

Although it is possible to discuss "prevailing" and "fair" prices in general terms, it is important to remember that basically, in this sense, they are abstractions. Such reality as they have is as conceptions held by individual sellers and buyers; they are effective only in relation to individual transactions. Their influence is most apparent in interviews with sellers and buyers about negotiated pricing situations. Nevertheless, they are also an important factor in nonnegotiated sales. The buyer who accepts the fixed price of a storekeeper does so because he considers it to be fair or reasonable.

Motivations of individual traders. Prices at which individual transactions are completed differ in part because of the respective motivations of the seller and buyer. The seller may have urgent need for cash for a variety of reasons. These may be sickness in the household, shortage of cash to meet current household food expenditures, repayment of a debt, or a desire to accumulate a quantity of cash rapidly to make some advantageous purchase. In such cases, especially in negotiated price transactions, the seller's asking price often is lower than it otherwise might be; he presses harder for a sale and is more apt to conclude a sale at below prevailing or even fair prices. A buyer may have an urgent need for goods to feed the family or may require supplies for a wedding, a saint's day celebration, or some ceremonial obligation. Such a buyer may make purchases at above what he ordinarily would think of as a fair price. A few ceremonial events, especially All Saints Day and the Christmas-New Year period, are observed by everyone. At these times the supply-demand curves are skewed. Although there are more goods on the market, prices rise since there are more buyers and they are willing to pay higher prices, that is, demand is relatively stronger.

Another rather obscure factor affecting prices is the feeling of many people aspiring to higher social status in the city and larger towns that bargaining is demeaning. Such buyers are much less apt to bargain or shop around for lower prices if they feel that the offering price is fair. Frequently they leave the daily shopping to servants on the theory that they will bargain or seek out sellers with the lowest prices. These attitudes may offer a clue to the future of bargaining in developing societies.

PRICE VARIATIONS IN THE MARKET

Price variations in the Oaxaca market system are of several kinds: changes in price levels in the course of the day, most evident in the sale of perishable goods on *plaza* days; seasonal changes either in general price levels or in prices of individual commodities; price differentials occurring between marketplaces; and long-term price trends. Each of these is discussed below.

On *plaza* days, prices for many commodities may change during the course of the day. Prices vary most in the early hours and tend shortly to stabilize for the remainder of the selling day, except perhaps in the closing hours of the *plaza* when either sellers find themselves overstocked or buyers have difficulty finding what they want. How these price norms become established and known in a setting where posted prices are rare, and where there is no published information on prices, has been discussed at the beginning of this chapter.

Seasonal fluctuation occurs in the prices of many commodities. General price levels are highest around the almost universally observed fiesta of All Saints Day and, to a lesser degree, Christmas and the New Year. These are traditionally periods of high consumption for many goods, not only foods but also household equipment and clothing. In addition, these periods are associated with the completion of the main harvests, when peasants have the most money and the most leisure in which to spend it. Prices are lowest during the planting season and the interval between planting and harvest, when peasants have the least money and often are too busy to visit the marketplace. For some agricultural products, prices also vary according to seasonal changes in thir supply.

Within villages significant price variations are rare, just as they are in major marketplaces, but some mild price cutting is reported. One storekeeper at Magdalena Ocotlán claimed that he undersold his nearest competitor since opening his store earlier in the year (1967), for example, by $0.05 on a $0.55 item and $0.20 on a $1.20 item, or by about 10 percent to 15 percent of retail prices. A man planning to set up a store in Santa María Atzompa said that one had only to undersell by a few *centavos* to acquire a clientele, and proved his point to his own satisfaction when he established the store. A new maize mill in the same village set lower prices than those previously existing when it opened in 1969.

Significant price differentials do exist among marketplaces and between the marketplace and the village. The higher prices in secondary marketplaces and villages are possible because of greater convenience for local buyers and the saving of transportation costs to more distant marketplaces. But upper limits are imposed, for if local prices are too high, buyers with cash will make the effort to go to a major marketplace for their purchases. The individual seller is thus constrained in his asking price by the competition of other sellers within the community, while the sellers in a village are constrained as a group by the competition of the other marketplaces.

Perhaps most important to the functioning of the regional marketing system are the intermarket variations. Comparative retail prices for selected items at five marketplaces (app. 30) suggest that items passing through the Oaxaca marketplace increase in price in lesser marketplaces. Exceptions are items that are locally produced, for example, eggs and chayote, and which entail no transportation costs. Such comparisons suggest two or three limitations on this oversimplified analysis of pricing. Common units of sale often differ from one marketplace to another and are not easily equated. Moreover, many items show seasonal fluctuations in price and hence data collected on different dates may be misleading. Finally, qualities and varieties are often different. Prices on tomatoes, for example, are meaningless unless type, size, and quality as well as seasonal variations are taken into account.

The latter consideration is illustrated by chile peppers, which are sold both fresh and dried. The largest street stand specializing in dried chiles on *plaza* days in Oaxaca City offered 36 different kinds of dried chiles. Some of the differences may have reflected only size or quality variations. Nevertheless, the different kinds of pepper are not interchangeable for the most part, and price, especially for dried chiles, is affected by size, condition, and moisture content. Although some buyers may substitute one type for another for particular uses, depending upon price and quality, specific types of chile often are bought for specific purposes. A cook in our employ, for example, would not make a kind of stuffed chile unless she could find a particular variety of chile grown in a particular *municipio,* meeting her own criteria of size and quality. The latter criterion involved the ease of completely removing the central spine, seeds, and skin (after boiling). Clearly, pricing studies that are really meaningful must be carried out with full knowledge of each product class. The problem also suggests that being an intelligent consumer in Oaxaca probably involves as much knowledge and skill as finding one's way through a supermarket in the United States.

As an aside, the seller whose chile stand was described above faces problems not faced by the supermarket manager. At the opening of the *plaza* day in Oaxaca City he must erect his stand, transport to it each variety of goods, separately sacked and in varying quantities depending upon the estimated demand for each type, and arrange his display. He uses no price labeling and hence must know and be able to quote instantly the price for each item. At the close of business he must resack the remaining goods, dismantle his stand, and move goods and stand materials to a storage place or to another *plaza.* Yet his problems are somewhat simpler than those of a dealer in more perishable goods. Dried chiles properly stored usually will keep for many months. Thus, unlike dealers in perishables, he is able to buy in quantity and to take advantage of especially good offers. To do so, of course, he must have a fairly accurate estimate of future prices.

Whether one deals with actual market prices or ideas of prevailing prices, any findings apply only to a single marketplace. Viewing the Oaxaca marketing system as a whole, there is no single system-wide set of prices. Rather, there exists a series of market price ranges that prevail within different segments of the system. These price differentials are the basis for most of the movement of goods between *plazas,* and knowledge of them is essential to the operations of the inter*plaza regatones* of various types. This is made explicit in studies of some of the *regatones* and to some extent in the activities of some *propios* who have alternative marketplaces available to them. Inter*plaza regatones* frequently describe their experiments in visiting "new" *plazas*—new in the sense that they had not previously visited them. A *regatón* specializing in Atzompa pottery, for example, mentioned "discovering" a *plaza* slightly outside the normal Oaxaca marketing system where he could get much higher prices. The disadvantages were that it involved a rather strenuous journey, more time, and higher transportation costs. Ultimately he abandoned the marketplace for these reasons, but there is some suggestion that another reason was that others followed his example, and the price differentials diminished to the point where profits were reduced. In other cases, *regatones* abandoned one of the *plazas* on their former circuit in favor of another, after a few experimental visits.

To some extent, inter*plaza* price differentials are a function of time and transportation costs. Modernization of transportation within the system has reduced inter*plaza* differentials by lowering such costs. Differential supply and demand factors also may play a part, at least on a short-term basis. The entry of additional suppliers into a marketplace in time will result in lower prices. Market price differentials between various marketplaces continue to exist, but they are kept within limits by competition and similar cost and supply factors within the system.

Long-term price changes can be given only for a few items where earlier writers have provided data. At the top of the next page, data for the village of Mitla are reported for around 1930 by Parsons (1936) and for 1968 by Ramírez (1968).

These limited data suggest that in the 35-year period, prices increased from five to forty times, depending upon the item. Incomplete qualitative data from informants support the general changes suggested here. The increase in prices in part undoubtedly reflects inflation. It may also reflect increasing competition among buyers resulting from expanding population and changing consumption patterns, higher living levels, and the effects of new higher-cost supply sources outside the system.

A few price variations are now controlled by external forces. Malinowski and de la Fuente (1957) considered maize supplies and prices to be the key determinant of

	1933 (*Parsons*) Price/unit	1968 (*Ramirez*) Price/unit
	(Prices in Mexican pesos)	
Adobe bricks	$25.00/1000	$400.00/1000
Cartage	$5.00/trip	$30.00/trip
Wage, field labor	$0.50/day	$15.00/day
Maize, white	$0.22/*almud**	$3.85 or more/*almud* ($1.10/kilogram)*
Grinding of *nixtamal* (maize dough)	$0.08/*almud*	$0.40/*almud*
Oranges	$0.06/five	$18.00–$19.00/100 (from Mixería)
Horse	$50.00–$150.00	$400.00–$500.00
Ox	$50.00	$900.00
Wool	$0.25/pound	$13.00/pound

* Parson's data apply to local *criollo* maize, Ramirez's to imported Chiapas maize. Very little if any local maize had entered the market in early 1968; it normally would command a slightly higher price.

all other prices and levels of market activity in Oaxaca. As the principal crop, the amount of maize available and the prices at which it sold determined the amount of money available for the purchase of other goods. Informants generally agree that in the past the price of maize fluctuated, not only from year to year as the result of the abundance of the harvest, but also on a shorter-term basis as the result of activities of *acaparadores* who often bought maize when prices were low and withheld it from the market to force prices higher.

The size of the maize crop still is important but the activities of government agencies (described in chap. 4, above) have changed the character of the maize market. Prices at which government agencies buy and sell are set annually on the basis of the national production and are uniform throughout the country. As government maize is considered inferior, however, there is still some seasonal price fluctuation for preferred local varieties, generally known as *maíz criollo.* These fluctuations depend in part on the amount of *criollo* maize available but they occur within rather narrow limits set by the existence of the government base price. Government maize may produce inferior tortillas, but if *criollo* prices become too high, many consumers will shift to government maize. This results in a ceiling on *criollo* prices and limits the operation of supply and demand factors.

In the Oaxaca City *mercados,* meat prices also are controlled. As a result, meat quality is low and there is some fairly open black marketing at higher prices for superior meat.

Improvements in the transportation system place further restrictions on price fluctuations. As prices rise locally, goods from lower-priced sources begin to flow into the system or, within the system, flow from one marketplace to another. The reverse may also occur, either throughout the system or locally: as prices decline, goods begin to flow outwards.

MARKET RESULTS

Here we examine the effects (or results) of price and pricing on sellers and buyers and on the dynamic flow of goods through the marketing system. Many of these effects are implicit, and sometimes explicit, in several previous chapters that discuss production and consumption systems and the dynamics of the marketing system. What is said in this section makes these results more explicit and provides additional illustrations.

Results on sellers. Sellers in the Oaxaca marketing system, as previously indicated, may be either dealers (*regatones*) who buy goods for resale, or producer-vendors (*propios*) who sell their own products. Their characteristics are described in chapter 7.

Oaxaca dealers may obtain goods in several ways. Suppliers of goods from the modern sector of the economy often seek out the Oaxaca dealer. For most such commodities there are several competitive sources of supply offering similar goods at about the same prices. These prices tend to be stable over substantial time intervals. Such a dealer makes his choice among suppliers, less on the basis of price than on considerations of quality of goods, reliability of supplies, and advantageous credit terms and discounts for quantity purchases. Although there may be relatively few alternative suppliers, from the standpoint of the individual Oaxaca dealer, the quantity of goods available is essentially unlimited.

Dealers in goods originating in the traditional sector also have a large number of potential suppliers, including many farmers or makers of handicrafts, as well as other dealers. Prices of traditional goods are less stable and often are subject to negotiation. Moreover, these products are less uniform in quality, and supplies in the market may fluctuate rapidly. In these circumstances the dealer makes his purchases bearing in mind the state of the market and the effects of competition on potential resale prices.

Regardless of supply sources, dealers must also attract patrons and, if possible, retain them as regular customers. In other market systems dealers often actively seek out customers, but in Oaxaca, except for a few street or door-to-door vendors, the dealer remains in his selling location and waits for customers to come to him. With few exceptions—for example, automobiles and trucks—the only form of advertising is by word of mouth and the display of goods. But few dealers attempt to increase their volume of sales or attract customers through extensive price cutting. A further restraint on price cutting is that various sellers of similar commodities often are located side by side and some reside in the same small community. Consistent price cutting may result in socially disruptive antagonisms. Dealers may not like their competitors but they recognize that they must live with them.

The "dash" or bonus offer so often reported from African marketplaces is almost absent in Oaxaca. Dealers in some products—the most frequent cases observed were vendors of maize and peanuts—sometimes will add a small quantity *after the sale has been completed,* especially for good frequent customers or for those who have not tried to bargain too persistently. The bonus thus does not form part of the bargaining; its purpose is to create customer good will.

In contrast to the dealer, the producer-vendor has only one source of supply, his own household's output (unless he also acts as a dealer, buying from his neighbors for resale). Depending upon the commodity, he has a wide variety of alternatives for disposing of his product. He may elect to sell at the point of production, or he may take his goods to a marketplace. Once arrived at the marketplace, he may sell at retail on the street, on a *plaza* day, or may sell at wholesale to a *regatón,* the type of *regatón* depending to some extent on the commodity. His pricing policy, or more accurately, his price expectations, do not depend on cost, which he knows only vaguely, but on his information concerning the state of the market and, if he sells wholesale, on what he may be offered by various dealers.

An example may illustrate the degree of sophistication about price potentialities required for making effective decisions. A man from the Zimatlán area brings one or two large sacks of peanuts to Oaxaca City on the bus. Already he has decided that he will not sell at the point of production or in the local Zimatlán marketplace. He would have saved time and transportation costs, but he believes he will receive a higher price in Oaxaca City. When he arrives at the bus terminal in the City, he may sell his peanuts immediately to one of several dealers who meet the bus. A sale at this point saves time but may mean a lower price than he could get by retailing or by approaching wholesalers at their places of business. It also means that in the confusion, especially if two or more buses arrive about the same time, he may evade the overworked tax collectors and thus save taxes as well as storage or porterage costs. The decision must be made almost instantaneously, based on whether he thinks the price offered is fair in light of alternative opportunities.

If he has no better use for his time or is for some reason anxious to maximize his returns, he will elect to try to sell at retail or, in larger quantities, to street *regatones.* This means hiring a porter and, if he retails his goods, paying a fee for a location in the *plaza.* Should he not move all his stock at retail, he still may sell the remainder to a wholesaler at the end of the day but probably at a price lower than he would have received earlier. Finally, he may decide that he can get a better price than that offered at the bus terminal by going to each of several wholesalers at their places of business and negotiating the best possible price, bearing in mind that he may have to pay porterage fees and possibly a small storage fee while he negotiates the sale. From our interviews it seems likely that most peanut growers are aware of all these alternatives and make choices among them, based on information about the market and personal motivations to save time or to secure the maximum possible cash returns.

The producer of a nonperishable item such as peanuts has the additional possibility of withholding most of his crop from the market for a time in the hope of higher prices at a later date, assuming he is not forced by household needs to sell. In any case, he is only an occasional vendor in the marketplace. Growers of some seasonal crops such as deciduous fruits also are infrequent vendors in the marketplace, but they cannot withhold their crops from the market. Growers of nonseasonal crops or briefly storable crops such as potatoes or onions, however, may be weekly visitors to the marketplace throughout much of the year. The quality of information about the market will vary to some extent with the frequency of attendance.

Another category of producer-vendors is comprised of those who bring only a small quantity of goods to the marketplace at a particular time to get enough money to meet urgent household needs. Such a vendor also must have some idea of the state of the market. He estimates what will be the cost of the goods he needs and what return he may expect for the goods he brings to the marketplace. In effect, the minimum price such a vendor seeks is one that will produce enough cash for his needs. This does not mean that he will accept the first offer meeting his minimum price, for if he senses that the current market price is higher, he may await a more favorable offer, unless he is pressed for time.

An example of such a producer-vendor is a woman who takes a single chicken to the *plaza* because the family is out of both maize and money. She expects or hopes to get a specific price. This expectation has some justification, for prices of poultry are fairly stable over the short range; but sometimes an unusually large number of birds reaches the market on a *plaza* day with consequent pressure on prices. Moreover, chicken sales always involve negotiation based not only on the going price but also on the size, age, weight, and condition of the bird. The vendor may be overoptimistic either about market prices or about the quality of her chicken, and instead of the $15 she anticipates, she may get only $10 or $12. The situation might be interpreted as a forced sale, but in a sense all the chicken vendors face this, including those with several birds to sell, for they usually have brought them from a distance and do not want to take them back.

Producer-vendors who sell only to meet some urgent need might be viewed not as vendors but as consumers who happen temporarily to be out of cash. Small as their selling activities are, however, they do influence the state of the market.

Results on buyers. Price conditions also have results on the behavior of buyers. As with sellers, several categories of buyers are identifiable. The most common are consumers who purchase to satisfy immediate or long-range household needs, farmers or artisans buying goods to carry on or to enhance their production activities, and various kinds of *regatones* buying goods for resale either locally or elsewhere. With few exceptions, each of these categories of buyers has several possible sources of supply. Each also seeks to buy at the lowest possible price but also may be influenced by convenience and the immediacy of his needs.

As one example, a villager may purchase small quantities of goods from a local store although he knows its prices are higher than those in town or City marketplaces. He does so either because the need is urgent or because the amount involved does not justify the time and cost of visiting a marketplace. In a sense he uses the local store as a convenient storehouse for occasionally needed items. But if the quantity desired is large, perhaps for a fiesta, or if a trip to the marketplace is planned for other purposes, the villager will go to a marketplace town to make his purchase. Often, especially for goods not sold through stores, he more commonly tries to borrow the item temporarily rather than buy from a fellow villager. Like the village producer-vendor, he prefers to deal in the marketplace because he has confidence in its price-forming functions.

For some commodities, consumers may habitually travel some distance to make purchases. For example, although there are butchers in Santa María Atzompa, they do not supply all local needs and their prices are higher than those in Oaxaca. Many consumers in Atzompa consequently make the bus trip to Oaxaca to buy meat. But at the time of the study, meat prices in Zaachila were lower than in Oaxaca and some buyers took a second bus trip to that town to purchase meat.[4]

Price results and the flow of goods. An important result of the Oaxaca price structure is the part it plays in activating the flow of goods within the marketing system and in supporting or making possible the role of intermediaries or *regatones*. Hypothetically, it is possible for the producer and the consumer to bypass intermediaries, and many marketplace transactions are direct from grower-maker to consumer-purchaser. Since in all transactions sellers seek the highest possible price and buyers seek the lowest price, how does the intermediary survive, and why do

[4] The lower prices at Zaachila in 1967–1968 possibly resulted from the butchering of many animals because of an epidemic disease threatening cattle in that district. As a result, the supply of meat was outrunning the local demand. Even at other times, however, Zaachila appears to have had a considerable quantity and variety of meat for the size of that marketplace, as indicated by our 1964 and 1965 marketplace counts: meat sellers at Zaachila comprised approximately 11 percent of the total number of vendors—a greater percentage than in any other secondary marketplace in the Valley except Tlacolula. Perhaps relevant is the fact that after 1580, cattle raising in the Valley was restricted to the Tlacolula and Zimatlán arms of the Valley (Taylor 1972:120), Zaachila being in the latter.

commodities that theoretically are always available directly from producers often pass through not only one, but several intermediaries before reaching the ultimate consumer? One reason for the survival of the intermediary is the generally accepted view that prices should be lower for bulk sales than for retail sales. This differential provides a margin for the middleman. Moreover, the minimum price the *propio* selling directly to consumers has in mind is influenced by his knowledge of what the intermediaries are asking for the same goods. The consumer may gain some price advantage from dealing directly with a *propio* rather than an intermediary, but ordinarily this advantage is very limited. But the basic reason for the existence of the intermediary is the efficiency of his specialized effort in assembling and transporting goods from more distant places.

Looking at the efficiency aspect of the matter, the fact that time is not of zero utility, as most perfect-market models usually assume, contributes to the need for intermediaries. So, too, do transportation and other out-of-pocket costs. To ignore time input may seem reasonable in that time (or labor) rarely is included by Oaxaca producers in their replies to questions concerning production costs. Yet both producers and consumers are well aware that time spent in selling or buying is time not available for productive or socially valued activities. Such considerations often are paramount for the producer in choosing between the alternatives of maximizing returns by selling retail directly to consumers or of accepting a lower per-unit return by selling in bulk to an intermediary. Often there are limits to the amount of time he is willing to spend seeking the highest price.

On the buyer's part, traditional consumption patterns are important. Throughout Mesoamerica many householders tend to buy some foods on the basis of daily needs or, at best, to buy supplies for only two or three days. In part this is a function of the precarious economy of many households that lack enough money at any one time to buy foodstuffs for future consumption, although absence of refrigeration or safe food storage facilities also is important. For such purchases the role of the intermediary in the *plaza,* store, or *mercado* is essential.

The need for intermediaries is reinforced by both the patterns of village specialization in production in Oaxaca and the extent of the marketing areas, which limit opportunities for buyers and sellers to meet face to face. A given *plaza* offers such opportunities for the buyers and sellers from the villages within a marketplace area; it provides no such opportunities for those living at greater distances. Theoretically it is possible for the individual producer to travel to all those localities where there is a market for his product, and for the buyer to travel to those places where goods he wants are produced. In fact, this is simply impracticable, if not impossible, even within the confines of a single marketplace area. The *plaza* hence is an essential institution at the local level, and the inter*plaza* intermediary is indispensable for the wider region of the marketing system.

This becomes evident if we try to chart the flow of products in the system. Figure 4 presents a generalized flow chart from the standpoint of the producer. This is somewhat simplified and no doubt can be refined with further research and analysis. Not all peasant-produced commodities follow all the paths outlined in the chart. Despite its imperfections, the chart makes clear the various alternatives open to peasant producers and shows that commodities may be involved in as many as four transactions before reaching the consumer. Actually, the path may be more complicated. Before some peasant-produced goods reach peasant consumers, they may have passed from local *plaza* to central *plaza* to another local *plaza,* in a corresponding number of transactions.

Figure 5 shows the flow of goods from the standpoint of a peasant consumer in similar generalized fashion. The consumer still has a choice of supply sources for various goods, but before reaching him the goods may have passed through a series of transactions after leaving the producer's hands.

Figure 6, prepared by Scott Cook, presents a flow chart from the producer to the consumer for a specific commodity, metates. This chart is far more precise than is figure 4 because it deals with a single item produced in a very limited number of villages. It suggests that a fruitful area for further research on the Oaxaca market system would be additional studies of specific commodities.

The flow of goods through the Oaxaca marketing system occurs in very large part because the systems of specialized production result in a market spatial separation between producers and ultimate consumers. The intermediary performs an important function in this distribution of goods by assembling them at or near their sources and transporting them nearer to the consumer. His specialized knowledge of commodities often contributes to the effectiveness of this distribution process. He is thus able to buy more effectively on the basis of price and quality and use the most efficient means of transportation. The "lubricant" of this process is the price structure with its price differentials between marketplaces and between bulk and retail transactions, which not only make it possible for intermediaries to function but also make goods conveniently available to ultimate consumers, usually at a lower cost than would be possible if the consumer went directly to the production sources.[5]

IMPERFECTIONS IN THE OAXACA MARKET

Tax (1953:13) suggests that markets in the Mesoamerican area tend to be perfectly competitive, and this opinion has been accepted by most other writers.

[5] In case this is still not evident, the consumer otherwise would have a much greater expenditure in time, would have higher transportation costs, and would not be able to secure bulk prices.

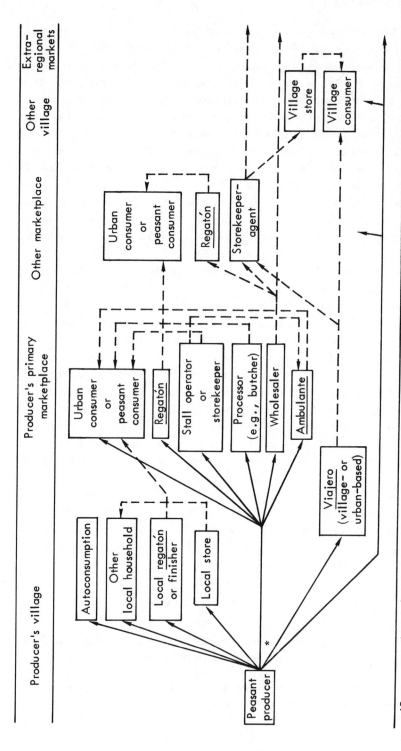

| Producer's village | Producer's primary marketplace | Other marketplace | Other village | Extra-regional markets |

Producer's village:
- Autoconsumption
- Other local household
- Local regatón or finisher
- Local store
- Peasant producer
- Viajero (village- or urban-based)

Producer's primary marketplace:
- Urban consumer or peasant consumer
- Regatón
- Stall operator or storekeeper
- Processor (e.g., butcher)
- Wholesaler
- Ambulante

Other marketplace:
- Urban consumer or peasant consumer
- Regatón
- Storekeeper-agent

Other village:
- Village store
- Village consumer

*Peasant producers have eleven alternatives for disposing of their products, although not every alternative is available for every product. The chain of disposal may include up to four links, more for export to extraregional markets.

Fig. 4. Flow of peasant-produced commodities

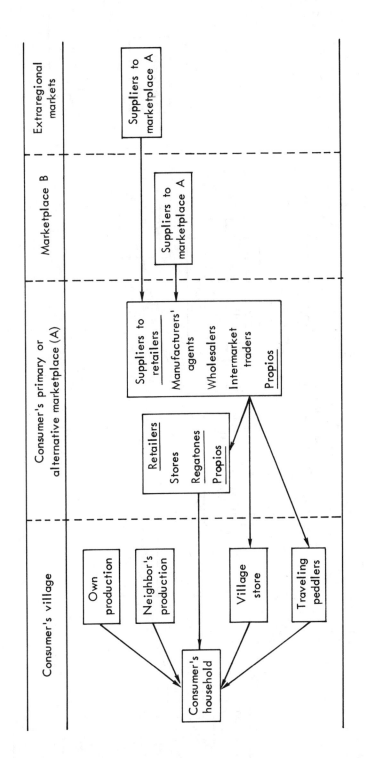

FIG. 5. Circulation of goods to consumer

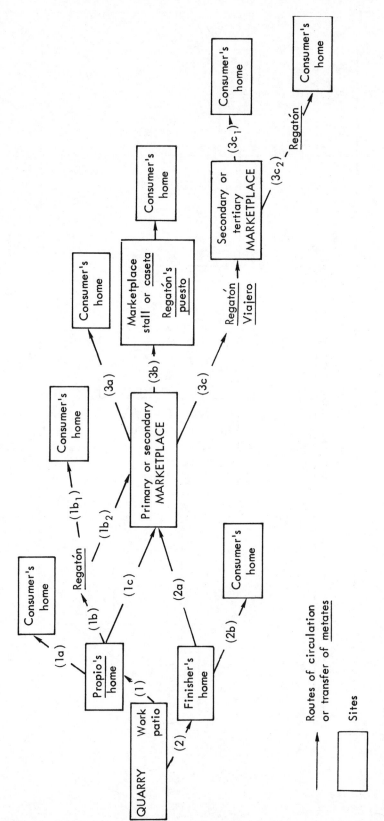

Fig. 6. Spatial patterns in metate marketing (adapted from Cook 1971)

Although not strictly relevant to our discussion of prices, this seems an appropriate place to examine the validity of this view with respect to the Oaxaca marketing system.

Waite and Cassady (1949:78–79, 274) among others have pointed out that the hypothetical model of "perfect" competition cannot exist in a real market situation. This model requires that entry of sellers and buyers into the market be completely open, with a large number of sellers and buyers in order that no single transaction influence total market results; that sellers and buyers are equally knowledgeable and share complete information about market conditions; that commodities be homogeneous in quality and location; and that the factors of production be readily divisible and mobile in response to fluctuations in supply and demand (an impossible condition in the real world). Under such conditions prices theoretically would become the same in all transactions. In addition to these usual conditions for "perfect" competition, the Oaxaca situation suggests that all sellers and buyers would have to be equally motivated to sell or buy at any particular time, and that all sellers and buyers should be equally able to delay trading to await the most advantageous moment.

Waite and Cassady feel that no market could possibly meet all of these conditions at any one time, although some markets may approach meeting one or more of the first three conditions. Some markets thus may be more "perfect" than others. The model hence is useful only for hypothetical purposes and should never be employed as a standard toward which an economy should be directed. In Oaxaca none of these conditions is met, although some may be approached. Testing the various conditions for the "perfect" market in the Oaxaca situation, we find with regard to the second criterion listed above that local peasants and dealers place great stress on the need for information. It might seem that the nearest approach to "perfectly" shared information in Oaxaca should occur in transactions that take place directly between peasant producer and peasant consumer, especially when these are within the same village or between individuals from nearby villages. But as has been shown, such transactions are in fact few because, in the village, both sellers and buyers feel that their information about market conditions and the range of market prices is inadequate. They prefer to forego the convenience of selling or buying locally in favor of trading within a marketplace or *plaza* where, as they frequently comment, "the market makes the price." Thus, in even the simplest market situation, information is not equal as among sellers and buyers. The same is true in the marketplace, whether dealing with the *mercado* or the *plaza*. Although sellers and buyers clearly see that an important function of the marketplace is to provide more information, sellers and buyers are not equally knowledgeable either about general market conditions or the conditions obtaining for any particular commodity.

The condition of homogeneity is also absent in Oaxaca. In the more modern sector of the market system, packaging and the use of brand names differentiates the market. In the traditional sector goods vary almost infinitely in size and quality, and only the most naïve or superficial observer could consider goods in the peasant market to be homogeneous.

Superficially, the marketplace in Oaxaca gives the appearance of meeting the criterion of openness, that is, being completely accessible to all sellers and buyers, with large numbers of sellers and buyers for any commodity. In fact, numerous restrictions exist for entry into the marketplace. Except in some village situations, sellers must be able to pay market taxes. The minimum tax is the charge for space in a street *plaza*. Only small *ambulantes* are exempt from this. Sellers may also have to pay transit or entry taxes on their goods. Under a variety of circumstances either sellers or buyers may be restricted in their market activities by transportation costs.

The importance of some taxes is indicated by the efforts to avoid them. Peasants on foot or with burro loads of goods, as well as some truckers, attempt to avoid entry or transit taxes by following devious routes or by traveling at night. In Oaxaca City, burro loads of goods arrive at the back doors of certain houses on the edge of town. Later, trucks load goods from the front doors for transport to the central market district. The participants are not communicative, but from observation from the second floor of a nearby house the volume of goods so transshipped is appreciable, although this observation gave no information concerning the kinds of goods or the nature of the transactions.[6]

Transportation costs also are often unavoidable. In larger marketplaces at the time of our study, most sellers and buyers arrived by truck or bus, rather than with animal transport or on foot, evidently considering that the saving in time outweighed the cost of transportation. In the diminishing number of cases where goods are brought on burros, the seller has an investment in the animals if he owns them or pays rent for their use; and he must feed them. In addition, since burros are now prohibited in the central districts of most towns, he must pay a fee either to a *mesón* (an inn with a central courtyard for animals), or to a householder with a patio or, in Oaxaca City, to the operator of one of the two "burro parks." If he has a large supply of goods to carry, he must pay a porter to help take them to the marketplace district.

---

[6] This example may be viewed as a form of smuggling, a common activity. Illicit, that is, untaxed mescal in considerable quantities is said to be transported on burros over back trails. Smuggling of some manufactured goods from Guatemala may be inferred. Japanese-made transistors are almost certainly smuggled into Oaxaca in quantity. Some cacao from Chiapas is smuggled, according to informants. Other examples could be given.

A further "imperfection" in the competitive market situation arises because prices for some of the most important commodities traded in Oaxaca are subject to regulation or are determined by market forces outside the region. For example, the basic prices of maize from outside the Oaxaca system, which to some degree affect the price of local maize, in turn are affected by more than simple and direct supply and demand factors even at the national level. The prices set by CONASUPO (see chap. 4, above) certainly reflect the estimates of supply and demand for human consumption in addition to purchase and distribution costs. In periods of high national supply, prices are lowered to a point where the feeding of maize to animals will be encouraged (a desirable goal for a country with a significant animal protein deficit) and export facilitated, with profit to the national economy. Once the latter consideration is allowed, world market prices come into the picture.

There are similar considerations for other commodities, especially those produced outside the region, and local products for shipment outside the system. For example the price for castor oil, and hence the volume of production of castor beans, is almost wholly dependent upon world prices. As the plants normally have a profitable bearing period of three years, the amount of production can change relatively quickly. It should be noted, however, that a further constraint is introduced by state controls that require the beans to be processed within the state so that only the oil is exported.

As another example, coffee production is less responsive to price, for coffee plants take longer to come into bearing and have a longer productive life. But local consumption accounts for only a small part of the production, and prices again are almost wholly dependent upon the international market. Some Oaxaca avocado producers may sell through the traditional *plaza* system, but large-scale growers ship most of their production directly to Mexico City, bypassing the *plaza* system. Those products passing out of the system are more subject to taxing policies, particularly the taxes levied on goods in transit and, with export goods, to international agreements and the quotas and import systems of foreign governments. Yet it is precisely these goods that provide the main flow of money into the region and which indirectly influence levels of demand for all but the most basic commodities.

Whatever may occur in other Mesoamerican market systems, the Oaxaca system does not present an example of "perfect" competition. Neither does it fit well with the model of quasi-perfect competition suggested by Waite and Cassady (1949) in which complete fluidity or mobility of production factors is eliminated as a condition. I suggest that under equally close scrutiny, other Mesoamerican systems would not approach the perfect competition model either. Certainly the price structure of the Oaxaca marketing system, although basically related to competition and supply and demand factors, also is modified by the constraints of cost factors, including transportation, by taxation and government regulation, and in individual transactions, by a variety of situational and motivational factors.

10
Growth and Change

The initial assumptions of this study included the hypothesis that the impact of the modern national economy would modify the traditional market system in significant ways. Many of these changes have been mentioned in preceding discussions. In this and the next chapter, the various points mentioned are pulled together, some generalizations are attempted, and additional evidence is presented.

THE COLONIAL ERA

The assumption that the impact of the modern economy has influenced the traditional marketing system does not imply that change did not occur earlier. The extent of these historical changes has not been explored in detail because they lie outside the scope of this study. In general terms, in the transitional period from the aboriginal marketing system to the colonial system, there were undoubtedly many changes in production with the introduction of new plants, animals, and technology, as well as some reorganization of the land tenure system and the introduction of coinage for exchange. The main plants introduced were wheat, cowpeas (*habas*), chick-peas (*garbanzos*), vegetables, and fruits. The most important of the last two were cabbage, onions, garlic, herbs, quinces, apples, peaches, and citrus fruits. Although many others were introduced, they were of lesser importance. Chickens, pigs, draft oxen, sheep, and burros were the more important animal introductions. Ownership of horses by Indians was restricted in Colonial times, and these never became numerous. Technological innovations included the plow, iron tools such as the ax, machete, and the *coa,* a hoelike instrument based on an aboriginal model, wool and the broad loom for textiles, new forms of clothing, and fired brick and tile for building. Even changes in land tenure probably were not of major significance in the traditional system, either in the early colonial period or subsequently. *Haciendas* were not large compared with landholdings in other parts of Mexico and their residential labor forces were relatively small, while most villages retained control of at least part of their lands. Sharecropping, I suspect, was the predominant way in which the village labor force was utilized by the Spanish *haciendas*. The relative importance of the *hacienda* is perhaps indicated in modern times by the limited numbers of *ejidos* formed following the disestablishment of the *haciendas* in post-Revolution times.

One reason for the failure of *haciendas* to become numerous or large is that few Oaxaca products were exportable to distant regions. Most were too bulky and low in value to be profitably transported any distance by existing means of transport. Silk, a Spanish introduction, was important for a century or so, although the major production was in the Mixteca, not in the Valley region. Cochineal appears to have increased in importance; Miahuatlán was its major center. Until the midnineteenth century, cochineal was the main cash-producing crop exported from the region. Some of the production may have been rationalized on *haciendas,* and the external trade was largely in the hands of Spaniards or mestizos. When coffee was introduced in the late nineteenth century as the major cash crop to replace cochineal, its initial production was on *fincas* established by the mestizos of Miahuatlán. Most of these *fincas* appear to have been established in *terrenos baldíos* or vacant Federal lands, or on lands obtained by negotiation from villages (Rojas 1962, 1964). Production soon spread to the villages that today produce much of the crop. Mineral production also has provided a continuing regional export. In the earlier Colonial period gold exportation apparently increased briefly with the same disruptive effects on local populations noted elsewhere in Mexico, but the best placer deposits were quickly exhausted and few workable ore deposits were found. By and large, in much of the Colonial period Oaxaca exports may have been less varied than in aboriginal times. Demand for feather work, stone, bone, and shell ornaments declined.

The lack of significant exports other than cochineal and later coffee meant that the flow of money into the region was limited. Coinage rather easily replaced the earlier exchange media of cacao beans and copper hoe blades, but it remained in short supply, especially in the smaller denominations. The shortage of coinage affected exchange methods in the traditional market. How extensively paper currency was used in the Republican period is unknown, but for a time after the Revolution it had limited use. In 1933, for example, paper money was not accepted in most villages, especially in the mountains. One of the early effects of increased outside influence was the restoration of paper currency and the greater flow of fractional coinage, giving considerably more flexibility of transactions in the traditional marketing system.

Two endogenous sources of change in the traditional marketing area are population increase and the growth of the City and the towns. In the earlier Colonial period Oaxaca population declined, then began a slow increase continuing to the present. Only in the 1930s did this increase accelerate and begin seriously to affect the economy, transforming the region from one of self-sufficiency in the basic maize staple to one of maize deficit. It is doubtful if the recent population increases could have been sustained by the traditional economy alone. Both the region and the state as a whole today import maize.

Unlike many peasant marketing systems, the provisioning of the City and the towns always was a minor aspect of the traditional Oaxaca marketing system. The Spanish certainly modified the preexisting *plaza* system to serve their new settlements, but it is doubtful if this function was more important during the Colonial and early Republican periods than it was in aboriginal times. At no time during this period did the Oaxaca region play a significant role in supplying goods to the more distant extraregional cities and towns (silk and cochineal excepted). Certainly provisioning Oaxaca City was not important either during much of the period. The period of urban growth followed the impact of the modern economy and was accompanied by expansion of what I have called a transitional form, the daily *mercado,* distinct from the *plaza.* (See chap. 3, above for population figures.)

THE MODERN NATIONAL ECONOMY AND ITS LOCAL EFFECTS

The impact of the modern national economy stimulated important changes in the traditional village-based economy and the marketing system. In summary these included:

1. Changes in the production system
    a. New technologies, principally fertilizers and tractors. These have had a noticeable but still minor impact.
    b. New farm products for export, principally avocados, alfalfa seed, and cheese; increased coffee and castor bean production. In the Isthmus, commercial pineapple growing has developed and cattle export has increased.
    c. Increasing production and diversification of many handicrafts, principally for the tourist trade.
    d. Decline of wheat production and local flour milling.
    e. Decline in local production of some textiles and possibly other goods.
2. Changes in the consumption system
    a. Availability for purchase of better and more varied industrial products, including production tools and household equipment. The sewing machine, and more recently the lantern (or electricity) and the transistor radio, approach

the level of necessities. Processed foods and industrially bottled drinks are more widely used.

b. Replacement of certain local products by manufactured imports such as wheat flour, candles, cloth, and clothing.

c. Availability of many food products the year around rather than seasonally, or in greater abundance or better quality, for example, fruits, tomatoes, onions, and to a lesser extent other produce items. Especially important is the import of maize, mainly but not exclusively through government warehouses, to support the burgeoning population.

3. Changes in the marketing system

a. Expansion of the daily *mercado* in the city and larger towns and, to a limited extent, in larger villages; increasing institutionalization and politicalization of the *mercado* in larger places.

b. Increased variety of goods distributed through the traditional *plaza* system.

c. Improved accessibility to the marketplace for producers, through use of buses and trucks.

d. Increased mobility of inter*plaza* traders.

e. Partial replacement of the *arriero*-trader by the independent trucker-trader.

f. Increased numbers of *regatones,* some from outside the region, possibly with a relative decrease in the number of *propios.*

g. Expansion of distribution through modern stores, especially for industrial goods and processed foods, and extension of stores into most villages. It should be noted that the village store is commonly owned and operated by village residents who either are still partly peasant producers or formerly were such producers.

h. Appearance of modern specialized wholesalers, resulting in increased efficiency in relation to regional export and import of goods.

i. Increased buying by traders at the point of production. Formerly confined almost wholly to coffee, such buying is now common for avocados, cattle, pigs, and some handicrafts. In some instances this buying is through local resident agents, usually storekeepers. The village-based traders of Mitla and San Antonino also buy a variety of goods at the point of production, as do the village-based dealers in maritime products in Tehuantepec. Some of these goods bypass the regional marketplaces, especially avocados, cattle, the modern pineapple production in the Isthmus, and onions exported to the Isthmus and Chiapas by San Antonino dealers. Some cheese producers in the Etla region export directly to Mexico City; some textile and pottery producers ship directly to customers as far away as the United States.

A key factor in many of these changes is the modernization of transportation and functional specialization. Much of the increased flow of industrial and other goods from outside the region, the increase in wholesale activities, and the expansion of stores into the village is related to the truck. It also has contributed to the expansion of markets for regional products. The most striking aspect of modern transportation, however, is its role in increasing the efficiency of the traditional marketing system. The intervillage and inter*plaza* trader can carry more goods and visit more places in a shorter time than he could before. The producer-vendor can get to the marketplace with much less expenditure of time, carry more goods on a trip, and often at less cost than in the past. Or he can sell to marketing specialists and use his time more advantageously in his own production tasks.

Except in a few sectors, modern transportation has not radically modified the traditional marketing system and its operations; rather, the system has adapted to use the new transportation to achieve greater efficiency. At the same time, modern transportation has permitted an expansion of the modern economic marketing system through wholesalers and stores, but in large measure this expansion has not been directly competitive because it deals mainly in different kinds of goods, although some of the new goods have entered the traditional distribution channels.

An important function of modern transportation also has been to facilitate the outward flow of population from the Oaxaca area. Figures from the 1960 census are given in appendix 31. They show a total of 209,362 persons born in the state of Oaxaca who at that time lived in other states. (Figures for the additional number migrating to the United States are not shown.) At the time of the census, nearly half lived in the federal district and approximately a quarter lived in Veracruz. Probably about half this outmigration was from the area of the Oaxaca marketing system. It is significant that more women than men had emigrated. Emigration from the state was offset in part by immigration: in *exdistritos* wholly or mainly within the area of the marketing system, 24,661 persons had been born outside the *exdistritos* where they resided (*Cuadro* 9, 1960 census), but probably the majority of these were from other *exdistritos* in the region.

To attribute all the outflow of population to the mere presence of transportation is an oversimplification. The spread of the federal rural school system into the villages has also played a part, not only in giving more people facility in Spanish and other skills for successful city living, but in supplying knowledge of some of the alternative ways of life. Before 1940 few villagers had ever been to Mexico City; in the Sierra many people had never been to Oaxaca City. Knowledge of the United States was most vague: in Mitla, in 1933, the U.S.A. commonly was thought to adjoin a few other vague entities such as Germany and England, and a common question was, how many days' ocean voyaging it had taken me to get to Mexico. Today most villagers either know someone who has been there or they have been in the United States themselves.

Not only does the outflow of population relieve some of the rising demographic pressures in the region, but also migrants contribute directly to the regional economy through remittances to family and to villages or by returning home with savings. Of 80 households sampled in Atzompa, 33 reported one or more relatives living elsewhere, the number living outside the community totaling more than 59 (where informants said "cousins" or "nephews" without stipulating the number, these are counted as one relative). Of those living "abroad," 12 were reported to send money home. Generally these were unmarried children who sent money to parents, although some parents sent money to support dependent children left behind with relatives.

Emigrants also contribute to community activities such as fiestas and public improvements. Berg refers to a former resident of Zoogocho in the Sierra now living in Los Angeles, California, who regularly contributes the cost of an additional bull to slaughter for the fiesta of the patron saint. Some villagers send appeals by mail to former residents for contributions when some major improvement is undertaken, with some success. Carlos Orellana (1972) reports that emigrants to Mexico City from a village in the Mixteca Alta not only maintain an organization in Mexico City duplicating the village hierarchy of political offices, but also largely control the selection of officials within the village and determine and finance most village improvements. No similar study has been undertaken of emigrants from the villages within the Oaxaca marketing system, but it seems likely that Orellana has described an atypical case.

Nevertheless, most emigrants do maintain close ties with their villages. Many return home for visits at the time of the fiesta of the patron saint and for the Day of the Dead. For two days following the Day of the Dead, lines of people returning to Mexico City extend four abreast for two blocks or more outside Oaxaca's main long-distance bus terminal. Many emigrants return to the village to seek spouses; others return permanently after they have accumulated a reserve of money. Orellana reports that emigrants from the Mixtec village he studied, even those who had resided many years in Mexico City, expected to return home eventually.

Emigration clearly operates to support some kinds of stability. The relief of demographic pressures lessens the need for endogenous changes in the economic system. The remittances sent home by emigrants likewise serve to maintain the system. But the contacts of emigrants with the home community, and particularly the return of emigrants after experience with the outside world, are important channels for the transmission of new ideas and technologies.

MEASUREMENT OF GROWTH AND CHANGE IN OAXACA CITY

The measurement of growth and change in quantitative terms over even relatively short time periods is difficult in a society where microstatistics are lacking and macrostatistics are unreliable. Structurally, the greatest change seems to be the developing modern economy in the region. Although attended by modifications in the traditional marketing system, already described, the more

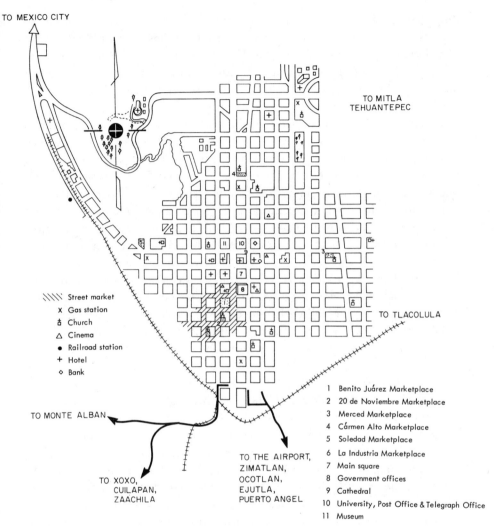

TO MEXICO CITY

TO MITLA
TEHUANTEPEC

\\\\\ Street market
X Gas station
⚲ Church
△ Cinema
● Railroad station
+ Hotel
◇ Bank

TO MONTE ALBAN

TO TLACOLULA

TO THE AIRPORT,
ZIMATLAN,
OCOTLAN,
EJUTLA,
PUERTO ANGEL

TO XOXO,
CUILAPAN,
ZAACHILA

1   Benito Juárez Marketplace
2   20 de Noviembre Marketplace
3   Merced Marketplace
4   Cármen Alto Marketplace
5   Soledad Marketplace
6   La Industria Marketplace
7   Main square
8   Government offices
9   Cathedral
10 University, Post Office & Telegraph Office
11 Museum

MAP 8. The main sector of Oaxaca City, showing covered marketplaces and location of street vendors

obvious changes perhaps have been the development of a modern sector characterized by modern commercial establishments and the increased importance of full-time traders in the *mercado*.

The growth of the modern sector of the economy has meant that the total economy has become less peasant in its character. Berg (1968) has suggested a way of measuring the "peasantness" of a local economy by analyzing household involvement in the market, and has attempted to apply it for the *plaza* of

Zoogocho in the Sierra. System-wide application of the technique, however, requires far more detailed data than are available. Means do exist, however, for some measurement of the relative growth of the traditional and modern sectors in the city of Oaxaca (map 8), although the data still do not permit any estimate of the growth either in volume or value of goods passing through either system.

Three types of data were found to be available from the city's *Administración de Mercados:* (1) income from *tarjetas* (rental cards issued by the month and punched daily as rents are collected; see fig. 7), representing fees paid by *locatarios*, occupants of permanent open stalls or *casetas* in the market building, supplemented by some special censuses of the *mercados;* (2) income from *boletos* (daily fee receipts; see fig. 8), representing fees paid by vendors in the street market and other market vendors without permanent locations, supplemented for some dates by total numbers of *boletos* sold and by some street censuses; and (3) income from the public toilets (*inodoros*) in the marketplace district, and totals of tickets sold, reflecting the attendance of both vendors and buyers in the marketplace.

Tarjetas. Rents are assessed on the primary basis of the square meters of space occupied, but there are some deviations, especially in the earlier years. Theoretically, rents are collected from the assignee for each day regardless of whether the stall is in use, and the total collections are entered in the records. In the earlier years collection was less systematic and evidently some stall holders paid for several days at a time, usually on Saturday, the day business was best. Even in later years *locatarios* who were poor or had suffered business reverses might get considerably in arrears; but even if they lost their rights to their stalls, the new occupants had to pay the back rents.

Income from *tarjetas* is taken as reflecting in a general way the number of stalls and *casetas* in service at various times. There are several indications, however, that this is not completely a one-to-one relationship. In general, rents collected were commensurate with the size of the space occupied, but there is evidence that not all assessments were based on area. A review of a census of the Benito Juárez marketplace carried out in 1958, and data for this and other marketplaces of the City in 1960 and 1961, show variability of charges even for vendors selling the same product, in stalls of the same construction with the same space and frontage. Although, generally, the minimum rate was $0.40 daily at that time, a few occupants were paying only $0.20 or $0.30 daily. Few paid more than $2.00 per day in the Benito Juárez marketplace in 1958 even with 16 square meters of space.

Moreover, for earlier time periods, minimum rates were lower. Price increases in rental fees were relatively small, however, and growth in income from *tarjetas* reflects mainly an increase in the number of permanent vendors. Certainly increased prices appear to account for only a fraction of the rise in *tarjeta* income of more than 8600 percent for the sample month of February, between 1938 and 1966

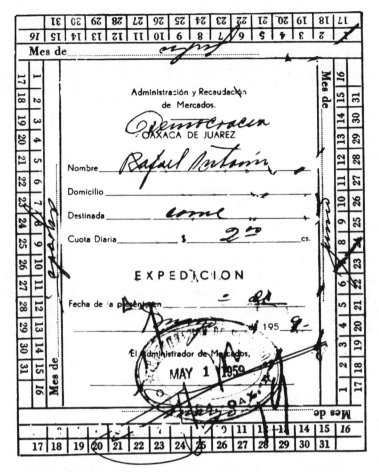

FIG. 7. Example of *tarjeta*

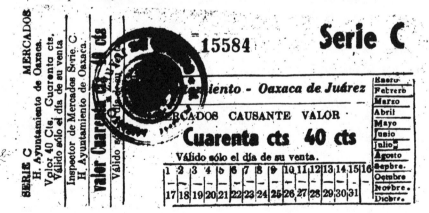

FIG. 8. Example of *boleto*

(app. 32). Detailed marketplace censuses suggest that probably the greatest change in the number of stalls occurred in the major market building, Benito Juárez, in the earlier years, and later in the expanding secondary marketplaces of the City.

Boletos. The *boleto* is a numbered fee receipt good for one day only. *Boletos* have a range of prices that depend on the amount of space occupied and to some extent on the kind of merchandise sold. The determination of fees in specific instances involves some judgment on the part of the collector and may be the source of vigorous dispute. The collector's views, however, usually prevail: in case of refusal to pay, merchandise is confiscated. Although in theory the *boletos* give no legal right to a particular location, market custom and sometimes official action support the prior right of many regular vendors or groups of vendors to the same locations every Saturday.

In earlier years many permanent *locatarios* paid their fees by *boleto* rather than by *tarjeta.* The numbers sold (see app. 32), however, especially in later years, reflect in the main the number of transient vendors on a particular day. The graph figures (12–14, 19, 22), utilizing the total income from *boletos,* hence are a fair indicator of attendance for short-range comparisons. (Income in pesos is used for most comparisons because it is the only figure available for some years and is quite adequate to show short-term fluctuations.) Aside from possible statistical errors, the main inaccuracies occur because *boleto* prices have increased over time and also the numbers sold at different price levels have varied. For example, in 1959 the largest number of sales was in the $0.40 category, but in 1966 the largest number was at the $1.00 level. The graphs in figures 12, 13, 14, 19 and 22 show some daily and weekly fluctuations and the relative importance of the Oaxaca Saturday *plaza.*

Admissions to public pay toilets (inodoros). Daily reports of the numbers of admissions tickets sold correlate closely with the number of vendors in the market, especially with the numbers of *boletos* sold. The increase in numbers of admissions sold on *plaza* days as compared with other days is taken to reflect, in part, the large number of vendors and buyers from outside the city.

Scope of the Data

Probably the number of admissions to the public toilets is the most accurate indicator of the daily fluctuations in the number of persons present in the market. Although the price of admission tickets rose from one *centavo* in 1938 to $0.025 in 1947 and reached $0.20 in 1966, data for 1966 covering a major price change from $0.10 to $0.20 show no discoverable effect of price on the number of admissions sold.

The three types of data available do not, of course, give any quantitative information on the number of transactions or the kinds or quantities of goods changing hands. The principal value of the data and the analysis is the indication

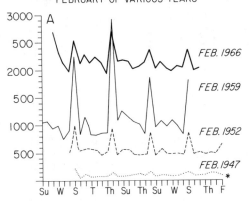

REVENUE FROM <u>TARJETAS</u> IN PESOS
FEBRUARY OF VARIOUS YEARS

FIG. 9.

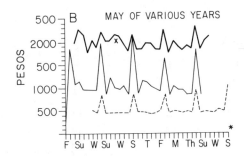

MAY OF VARIOUS YEARS

FIG. 10.

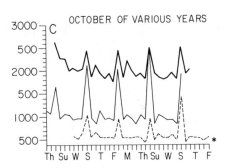

OCTOBER OF VARIOUS YEARS

FIG. 11.

* 1938 REVENUE VARIES BETWEEN 17 AND 38 PESOS
x DATA MISSING

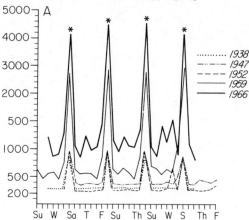

FIG. 12.

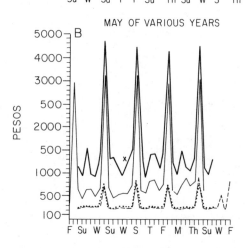

FIG. 13.

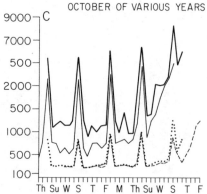

FIG. 14.

* SATURDAYS

x DATA MISSING

NUMBER OF <u>INODORO</u> ADMISSIONS SOLD,
FEBRUARY OF VARIOUS YEARS

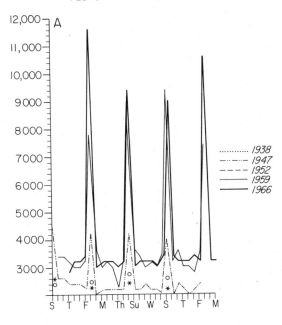

FIG. 15.

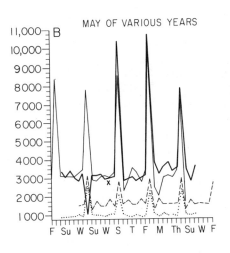

FIG. 16.

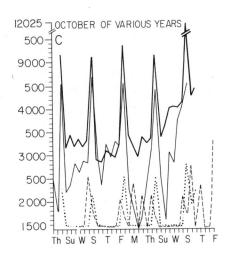

FIG. 17.

* SATURDAYS 1938   x DATA MISSING
o   "   "   1952

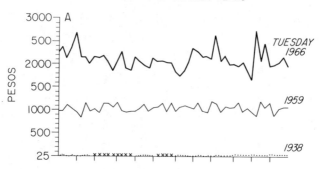

REVENUE FROM <u>TARJETAS</u> IN PESOS,
TUESDAYS OF VARIOUS YEARS

FIG. 18.

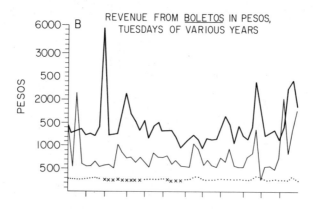

REVENUE FROM <u>BOLETOS</u> IN PESOS,
TUESDAYS OF VARIOUS YEARS

FIG. 19.

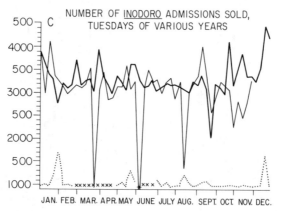

NUMBER OF <u>INODORO</u> ADMISSIONS SOLD,
TUESDAYS OF VARIOUS YEARS

FIG. 20.

JAN. FEB. MAR. APR. MAY JUNE JULY AUG. SEPT. OCT. NOV. DEC.

x - DATA MISSING
* CLOSED FOR REPAIRS

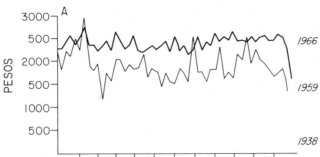

FIG. 21. In 1938 *tarjeta* revenue varied between 24 and 27.

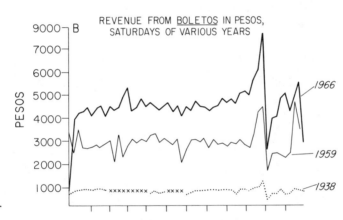

FIG. 22.

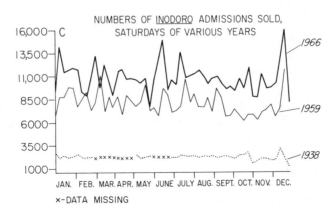

FIG. 23.

x-DATA MISSING

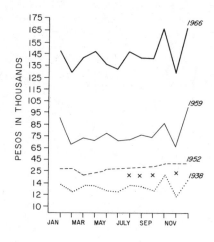

x – DATA MISSING (1952)

FIG. 24. Revenue from all sources, monthly, for various years

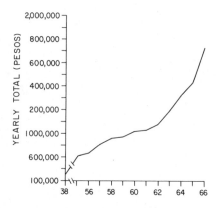

FIG. 25. Revenue from all sources, yearly, 1938, 1955–1966

of changes in the number of participants in market and *plaza* activities over time. I believe it may legitimately be assumed that these changes in the number of participants correlate, at least in a rough manner, with the number of transactions and with the volume of sales. Government statistics do exist for the gross movement of some bulk products and industrial goods into and out of the area, although the possible margin of error is considerable because of the way data are collected. No statistics exist on the movement of goods in the *mercado* or the *plaza*. Such statistics perhaps could be collected for current movement, although at a prohibitive cost. They would not, of course, permit any time comparison.[1]

[1] As the primary concern here was with the peasant market, no effort was made to collect data on such aspects of the marketplace as the number of stores, wholesale establishments, or marketing

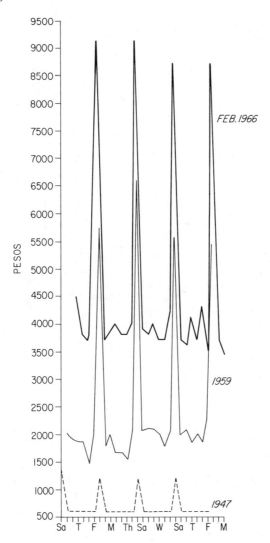

FIG. 26. Revenue from all sources, daily for February of various years

Data were extracted from these records for the years 1938, 1942, 1947, 1952, and 1955 to 1966. The records for 1955 to 1966 were found in the storeroom of the Market Administration offices, nearly complete and in good condition. Those for

organizations such as the government maize warehouse or the coffee-marketing organization, which are not under the Administration of Markets. Neither do the data collected cover the *ambulantes,* small vendors who move about without a fixed location, carrying their merchandise with them, and who are not licensed or taxed.

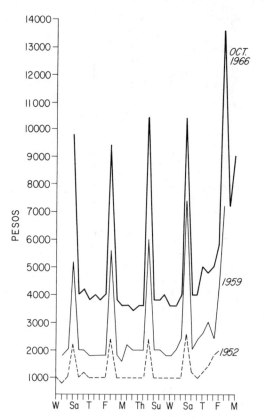

FIG. 27. Revenue from all sources, daily for October of various years

earlier years were encountered in the Municipal Archives and were very incomplete and in poor condition. The 1952 records seem especially badly kept and of dubious value.

Not all the records available were copied, and not all of those copied are used here. Daily records of numbers of *boletos* sold at each price level, total income from *boletos,* income from *tarjetas,* number of admissions to public toilets (*inodoros*) and income from *inodoros,* were recorded completely for the years 1959, 1960, and 1966. Because of time limitations, for 1961 through 1965 my staff copied complete daily records only for the months of February, May, and October. For 1955 through 1966, monthly and annual grand totals of revenue were copied. For the earlier years records were incomplete. For the year 1938 the carbon copies of original daily reports were obtained for all months except March, April, and June (monthly totals of income were available even for the latter months, however). For 1947 a complete record was recovered for February only, but for 1952, daily records were found for the months of January, February, March, May, June, October, and December.

Interpretation of the Records

To demonstrate growth in detail over a series of time intervals covering the greatest possible time span, the years 1959 and 1966 were selected, as there were complete daily records for those years, and the available data from 1938, 1947, and 1952 were used. In appendix 32 the year 1963 has also been included.

The first series of graphs, figures 9 through 17, shows daily records of income from *boletos* and *tarjetas,* and numbers of *inodoro* admissions sold, for the months of February, May, and October of the years selected. The subsequent series shows the record for Tuesdays and Saturdays throughout various years. (As indicated, records for the earlier years are incomplete; therefore not all of these years appear in all of the illustrations.) Tuesday was selected because it is normally the day of lowest market activity, while Saturday is normally the day of peak activity. The months of February, May, and October were chosen as being representative of varying market conditions, both in the collection of the data and in much of the analysis. From inspection of the records and the unanimous opinion of informants, October is the month of greatest economic activity and highest seasonal prices. This is because the most generally observed ceremonial period, All Saints Day and the Day of the Dead, fall at the beginning of November. Much of the harvest is in, and money is most plentiful. At this time everyone who can makes special purchases of foods, often including luxuries and ceremonial foods. It is also a high point in the year for buying household equipment and new clothing and for other deferred expenditures.

Although informants generally believe October to be the month of greatest activity, it is usually exceeded by December, a month marked by important celebrations for Christmas and the New Year, the Virgin of Guadalupe, and the Oaxaca City fiesta of the Virgin of the Soledad. February was selected as one of the months of lowest—if not the lowest—level of economic activity (in some years November was lower) and because it is the month for which we found a complete record for 1947. Except for a few hardy vegetables, there is practically no farm production or income in February. Preparations for early planting occupy some farmers. May was selected on the opinion of informants that it is a more-or-less average month, an opinion supported by the records. Some early maize has been harvested and the fate of the rest of the early crop is determined; preparations are under way for the main planting of maize; and some vegetable crops in specializing villages are beginning to produce, providing more money in the peasant sector.

The data were analyzed for daily and monthly variations. In figures 9 through

17, comparison of the selected months gives a reasonable picture of seasonal fluctuations in activity, while comparisons of different years suggest longer-range changes in activity. Within each month, the greater importance of Saturady activity is clearly shown. The contrast between the high and low points of the week is emphasized in figures 18 through 23.

Figure 24, showing total Market Administration income from all sources for each month of the years 1938, 1952, 1959, and 1966, again reflects February lows and October highs as well as the increase in total income over time. Figure 25 shows the increase in income from all sources for all years between 1938 and 1966 for which annual totals were available. Fluctuations in total daily income for the month of February in various years are reflected in figure 26, and for October in figure 27. (The figures for 1938 were too low to be meaningful in the latter comparisons, and October data for 1947 were unavailable.)

The graphs are supplemented by data in tabular form (appendixes 32 through 35), which include records of the numbers of *boletos* sold.

Daily rhythms. Both observation in the marketplace and the simplest inspection of the records attest to the enormous increase in sellers and buyers in the central marketplace on Saturday, the day of the *plaza*. Daily comparisons for the months of February, May, and October (figures 9 through 17) give a more precise observation. The most sensitive indicators are the figures for *boletos* and admissions to *inodoros*. On Saturdays these increase to three or four times more than the figures for other days of the week. From the Saturday high they drop sharply on Sunday, although a few peasant vendors may remain, often visiting some of the satellite marketplaces in the city. Monday is usually the lowest day of the week. Friday usually shows a significant increase; many trucks arrive that day, as do a few peasant vendors.

The weekday figures for toilet admissions reflect the attendance of sellers and buyers at the daily *mercado*. They are approximately 1.6 to 1.9 times the number of *boletos* sold (app. 32). The *boletos* sold during the week represent such groups as tortilla sellers, who are more-or-less regular attendants, mostly from three nearby villages, and a few vendors of produce, for the most part resellers, who find a place in the aisles and entrances of the *mercados* and on the adjoining sidewalks.

Daily fluctuations in the income from *tarjetas* cannot be explained in terms of daily attendance in the *mercado* except very indirectly. Theoretically, in any one month or even in any one year, the income from *tarjetas* should be approximately the same each day. Nevertheless, not only are there variations from day to day but also there is a Saturday peak as there is in the other types of data. The variations may reflect to some extent the absence of some holders of permanent stalls and *casetas* on weekdays when collectors make their rounds. On Saturdays, however, almost everyone is present, and the peak on these days represents almost entirely the collection of rentals in arrears for other days of the week.

Monthly variations. In addition to the weekly cycle of activity emphasizing the importance of the *plaza* on Saturdays, there is variation in activity from month to month, as has been noted. In general the first month of the year, January, is a period of declining activity. February is one of the lowest months of the year, while succeeding months (except perhaps November) show a varying but somewhat higher level of activity. October shows a marked increase in activity followed by a sharp drop in November. December again is high and in some years may be the month of greatest activity. These variations are reflected in figure 24, which shows total monthly income for the Market Administration for the years 1938, 1952, 1959, and 1966. The monthly fluctuations in the various years are very similar. They reflect the seasonal variations in income among the peasant population and variations in the agricultural cycle, as well as months when ceremonial observances call for high expenditures simultaneously in all villages and in the City. (For a detailed comparison, see Waterbury 1969:77.)

Annual variations. The data in figures 9 through 23 show the seasonal fluctuations in market activity through the year and the much higher level of activity connected with the Saturday traditional markets or *plazas*. The comparison of the various years also indicates a rising level of activity for the time covered. This increase is given more precisely in figures 24 and 25, showing the growth in Market Administration income from about $160,000 in 1938 to $1,734,000 in 1966. The greatest rise in total income occurred in the years 1959 to 1966. The size of the increase between 1963 and 1966 is somewhat misleading, for it appears to include income from a special temporary assessment on permanent stall holders inside the Benito Juárez market to help pay costs of remodeling.

Some variations in the rate of increase in total income also may result from external factors. The low rate of increase in 1959, for example, may reflect an extended strike by permanent vendors in the market during that year. The small rate of increase in 1961, in contrast, may reflect the fact that this was a very bad crop year, reducing the buying power of the peasant sector of market patrons.

Even making allowance for these extrinsic factors, the data show a substantial and continuous increase in Market Administration income throughout the years for which data are available, although the rate of increase fluctuates considerably from year to year. The gross figures, however, do not give any clear indication of the extent to which the increases reflect greater economic activity or are the result of increased fees collected by the Market Administration. Neither do they show the relative contributions of the permanent market and the Saturday *plaza*. For this, more detailed analysis is necessary.

The contribution to gross Market Administration income from the permanent market, as has been indicated, is represented by collections from the permanent stall and *caseta* occupants in market buildings and on the streets, who hold *tarjetas*. In 1938 income from *tarjetas* was negligible, amounting to between $17 and $38 daily, or less than $1,000 a month, for the months examined. Between that year and 1952 there was a startling increase, varying, for the months analyzed, between 2064.4 and 2501.6 percent. Part of this increase undoubtedly was because of changes in classification of vendors and increased fees charged. For example, in both 1938 and 1952 the classification *arrendamientos* (rents) appears in the records. No one today is quite sure what this represented, but it probably reflects rental charges for some class of fixed sales locations. After 1952 this classification appears to be merged with *tarjetas*. If *arrendamientos* are included in the calculations for *tarjetas* in the early years also, the percent of increase for the months compared in 1938 and 1952 drops to between 816 and 1178 percent—still a substantial increase. Another important source of the apparent increase may have been that many permanent vendors in the early period were allowed to buy *boletos* instead of *tarjetas*. Fragments of market censuses indicate that the line between *boleto* and *tarjeta* holders was rather vague. If many *boleto* purchasers were required to shift to *tarjetas,* this would account for part of the increase in *tarjeta* income and also for a decline in the number of *boleto* purchasers in the same period.

In addition to these factors, basic charges to *tarjeta* holders undoubtedly increased. Early census data indicate considerable fluctuation in the amounts charged vendors selling similar merchandise and occupying similar space. In later years *tarjeta* charges became more standardized, based on the square meters occupied.

With all these qualifications, however, it seems probable that a substantial part of the increase in income from *tarjetas* between 1938 and 1952 represents an increase in numbers of permanent vendors, reflecting greater economic activity. Part of this increase resulted from the opening of new secondary marketplaces in the city during the period. In addition there is evidence for a considerable growth in other commercial activity. Tamayo Lopez Portilla (1960:72) reports that the number of commercial establishments licensed by the state of Oaxaca in 1955 represents an increase of about 15 times over 1939. This time span covers the opening of the Pan American Highway, which unquestionably resulted in a great increase in commercial activity in the City. New external markets became accessible to Oaxaca products, most of the wholesale trade in imported fruits and vegetables began, and many new products appeared on the market. It seems likely that this increase in economic activity was reflected in the permanent marketplaces as well.

This conclusion is reinforced by the data for the period since 1959. By that year the classification of *tarjeta* holders and the charges assessed were well standardized, although some variations still appear in the census for 1961, and a minority of stall holders still paid by *boleto* rather than *tarjeta*. Moreover, the basic fees per square meter of space occupied did not change from 1959 to 1966. The figures for gross income to the market administration in 1966 may be slightly distorted because of a special assessment on some stall holders in the Benito Juárez marketplace to pay for remodeling of the central floor space, but the assessment did not seriously affect the upward trend for the months compared between 1959 and 1966, which was on the order of 1.7 or 1.8 times (app. 32). The evidence seems conclusive that, except for the limited special assessment confined to the holders of open stalls in the Benito Juárez market building, the increase in Market Administration income for this period is primarily owing to a rise in the number of permanent vendors. This supports the view that a significant part of the earlier increase, between 1938 and 1955, was owing to the same causes. These increases may be presumed to reflect increased economic activity, although part of the increase in Market Administration income may reflect more vendors rather than increased volume of sales.

The situation with *boletos* is somewhat more complex. Because comparative data on total income from the sale of *boletos* are much more extensive than data on the number of boletos sold, income data were used for the graphs. For short-term comparisons such as daily and monthly variations the use of income figures is reasonably accurate, but for reasons already given this is not true for long-term comparisons over a number of years. Appendix 32 shows clearly a generally steady rise in *boleto* income from 1938 through 1966. The numbers of *boletos* sold between 1938 and 1952 declined sharply, however, with the greatest decline between 1938 and 1947. Since 1952 there has been a significant increase in the number of *boletos* sold (although there was a minor decline between 1959 and 1963), but in none of the months compared does the number sold in 1966 approach the number sold in 1938. Clearly, a substantial part of the long-term increase in the income from sale of *boletos* has been owing to higher prices, and occurred despite a decline in numbers sold.

As the major sales of *boletos* are to peasant vendors in the Saturday street market or *plaza,* does the decline in numbers of *boletos* sold represent a decline in the peasant sector of the market vendors? Data to answer this question are very fragmentary but suggest that most of the decrease was because of transfer of daily vendors in the marketplaces from the *boleto* category to the *tarjeta* category. Prior to 1947 relevant data are entirely lacking. For the period 1947 to 1959 total sales for Tuesdays (a day with few transient vendors) in the month of February declined from 8,300 to 5,600, while Saturday sales for this month increased from 17,100 to 18,600 (app. 33). Between 1959 and 1966, numbers of *boletos* sold on both Tuesdays and Saturdays generally increased; but the increase on Saturdays was substantially greater than that on Tuesdays for two of the three months compared. Comparisons of weekday lows and Saturday highs in sales between 1959 and 1966 (app. 34) also indicate a relatively stable level of sales on weekdays, both between the months compared in each year and between the two years, but show Saturday sales that are very substantially higher in 1966 for the months compared. It is very possible that the large decline in the number of *boletos* sold between 1938 and 1952 represents in part a decrease in peasant vendors as well as shifts of permanent vendors to the *tarjeta* classification. Since 1959, however, the fragmentary evidence strongly suggests a substantial increase in the number of peasant vendors in the Saturday *plaza*. The data support opinions of village informants that there has been an increase in the number of peasant vendors.

The third component of market income is the admissions to public toilets. Part of the growth in income to the Administration clearly results from increased admissions charges; but we have data on actual numbers of admissions sold, and it is obvious that the numbers of persons utilizing the services increased moderately between 1938 and 1952 and very substantially since then. Users of the public toilets are primarily the permanent and transient peasant vendors in the marketplace plus buyers, especially those from out of town, a conclusion supported by the high Saturday figure for admissions. The growth in numbers of toilet admissions on weekdays is a measure of increasing activity in the daily market. The rise in attendance on Saturdays is a measure of the growth of the *plaza*, reflecting primarily an increase in the number of peasant sellers and buyers.

A factor not considered in the above discussion is the possible effects of population increase upon the market activity (see chap. 3, above). Undoubtedly they are considerable. Nevertheless, a part of the increase in market activity still must be attributed to a higher general level of economic activity. This conforms to the evidence for an increased number of commercial enterprises, growing "exports" and "imports" in the regional market, and the consensus of most observers that the level of living of Oaxaca peasants as well as city folk has risen during the time period.

To sum up, between 1938 and 1966 the annual total income of the Oaxaca City Market Administration increased 10.8 times or 980 percent. The daily variations indicate the relative importance of the traditional street market or *plaza* held on Saturdays as compared with the daily *mercado*. The monthly variations show the influence of seasonal factors associated with periods of important festivals and seasonal agricultural activity on the market. Part of the increase in total Market Administration income may be attributed to increased charges to vendors and patrons in the marketplace and the *plaza*, and part to growing population, but a significant although not measurable part of the increase seems attributable to an increased rate or level of economic activity.

An examination of the data for the various components of the Market Administration income suggests that they have not grown equally. The income from *tarjetas,* representing collections from holders of permanent locations or stalls, was negligible in 1938 but in 1966 furnished close to half the total income. Part of this increase may be because of an increase in the number of permanent vendors in the *mercado,* part may be because of different methods of classification and higher base fees, and perhaps part because of increased efficiency in collections. Between 1959 and 1966, however, there was no increase in basic fees; income growth in these years may be attributed to a greater number of *mercado* vendors, reflecting increased economic activity. The very large rise in *mercado* activity after 1938 probably results from the economic stimulation furnished by the opening of the Pan American Highway and the growing industrial production in the national economy.

Growth in income from the sale of *boletos* to vendors in the *plaza* clearly is in part the result of higher charges. The number of vendors, as represented by the number of *boletos* sold, shows a sharp decrease after 1938, followed by an irregular increase in subsequent years. By 1966, however, the total number of *boletos* sold was still less than the number in 1938. The opening of the Pan American Highway thus may have had a depressing effect upon that portion of the traditional market system represented by the Oaxaca *plaza.* Yet part—perhaps most—of this apparent decline is because of changes in the classification of vendors and standardization of collections. Fragmentary data indicate that at least since 1947 the number of peasant vendors in the Saturday *plaza* has increased substantially, following the decline after 1938. As many wholesale establishments postdate the opening of the highway, it is also possible that many peasant vendors began to sell to wholesalers rather than to retail their goods in the *plaza.*

The principal patrons of the public toilets are peasants from out of town. The great increase in numbers of admissions sold on Saturday supports this conclusion. The steady increase in admissions over the years suggests that the number of peasant buyers steadily increased. Between 1938 and 1966 the number of admissions sold rose about 3.5 times.

The growth of municipal income from all sources in the *mercado* and *plaza* has some further consequences. Today the *Administración de Mercados* produces better than 50 percent of gross municipal revenues. Concurrently, the vendors in the *mercado* exercise increased political power: through unions they now have a voice in the administration of the marketplace and in the allocation of new or vacated stalls or *puestos.* (See chap. 12, below.)

The interests of the vendors in the *mercado* and in the *plaza* have diverged over time. The earliest main market buildings were constructed to move the *plaza* vendors from the central square where they were located in the nineteenth century.[2] Over the years the *plaza* vendors have been forced into the streets owing to the construction of more and more permanent stalls in the buildings; today almost all of them operate in the streets about the market buildings. On Saturdays, too, vendors from the *mercado* set up temporary stands on the street, paying for *boletos* as well as for their day's stall rental. From time to time the vendors in the *mercado* propose that the *plaza* vendors be moved from the streets around the market buildings toward the outskirts of town or even suppressed entirely. Many recognize that without the *plaza*, however, most out-of-town buyers would not come to Oaxaca but would go instead to other *plaza* towns. For this reason, and because the *plaza* serves a number of economic and social functions that are not considered here, it seems likely that for some time to come the *plaza* will continue to be an important component of the total marketing system.

[2] When I first visited the mercado Benito Juárez in 1933 there were almost no permanent stalls. Most vendors offered their goods on mats on the ground as street vendors do today.

11
Growth and Change in Mitla

Growth and change of the marketing system have been documented for Oaxaca City in the preceding chapter. Since the Oaxaca marketplace is the focal point of the system, changes there may be assumed to have affected the system as a whole. This chapter examines change and economic adaptations at the level of the villages, where most Oaxaca people live.

While we have current data for other communities, Mitla is chosen as a case example because we have better data on premodern conditions than for any other Oaxaca village. Elsie Clews Parsons's (1936) study,[1] conducted between 1929 and 1933, until recently was the only relatively thorough ethnographic study of a Zapotec community. The village has long been deeply involved in the traditional marketing system and has undergone major changes under the impact of modern conditions. In neither its traditional nor its modern aspect, perhaps, is it as representative as would be a smaller farming or farming-artisan community, but

[1] Elsie Clews Parsons lived in Mitla for several prolonged periods between 1929 and 1933. Her book, *Mitla: Town of the Souls* (1936), is used as the base line for the discussion of change here. Beals spent about four weeks in Mitla in 1933 in Dr. Parsons's company and paid brief visits to the village between then and 1968. Modern data are from a survey conducted in 1968 by Miguel Ramirez Ochoa. Ramirez, although not trained in anthropology, hopes to be a writer and has schooled himself to be an accurate and perceptive observer of people. He lived in Mitla for about a year. For several months he worked for the project in Oaxaca City, abstracting data from the records of the Market Administration and municipality. Subsequently he returned to Mitla for about two months, during which time he collected most of the 1968 data under Beals's direction.

the relative richness of the data affords more profitable comparisons than would alternative communities.

Mitla is located at the end of the eastern or Tlacolula arm of the Valley of Oaxaca at the juncture of three natural routes into the northern and eastern mountains. In prehispanic times it exercised political control over a part of this mountain area, extending 58 miles from north to south in its greatest dimension and including eleven subordinate towns. Nevertheless, it is probable that Mitla in turn often was politically subjugated by larger and more powerful neighbors. Its prehispanic importance as a religious center probably was greater than its political power: Mitla is the site of the largest and most elaborate group of ruins in the Valley of Oaxaca after Monte Albán. (Its Zapotec name, "Lyoba," means Place of Tombs; its Aztec name, "Mictlan," refers to the underworld home of the dead [1–2][2].) In view of the rather limited arable lands, subject to inadequate and unreliable rainfall, it seems likely that even in the distant past the population of Mitla could be supported only by external trade. The close relationship known to have existed between ceremonial and trading centers in much of prehispanic Mesoamerica reinforces the assumption of a long history of the trading specialization.

In 1933 Mitla could be described as a community of farmers and traders. In a region remarkable for a high degree of village specialization, this village had no other economically significant specialties; the few specialties that existed served primarily the internal needs of the community. The traders, however, comprising about half the adult male population, played a major part in an extensive trading network that included the Isthmus of Tehuantepec, the Valley of Oaxaca and the northern mountains. Travel was on foot, and goods were transported on pack animals, principally burros. This was the predominant mode of transport throughout the Valley also except for a narrow-gauge railway and a slightly improved road from Oaxaca City to Tlacolula, seven miles west of Mitla. Trucks and cars only occasionally reached Mitla over an unimproved cart track.

The importance of Mitla traders is a little unexpected, if only because the village did not have a daily or periodic market of any importance. In contrast, Tlacolula has long had a large and very active Sunday *plaza* that provides a market and supply point for a large area. Yet very few, if any, of Tlacolula's residents were traveling traders except as they bought and sold in the Oaxaca City *plaza*.

Although the 1968 survey was concerned primarily with trade and handicraft production, it pointed up a few other obvious physical and social changes since Parsons's day. The percentage of houses with tile roofs has grown from 58 to 90

---

[2] Roman numbers in parentheses refer to page numbers in Parsons 1936. Italicized numbers in parentheses refer to page numbers in the Ramirez field notes 1968.

percent.[3] Householders are still required to sweep the streets in front of their houses, now on Thursdays and Sundays, and the fine for noncompliance has increased from $0.25 for the first offense to $2.00. A potable water system has been installed, with pipelines on five streets with six public faucets. Fifty-five families have faucets in their house yards for which they each pay $20 a month. Others feel that this is too expensive, but some of those who have not installed faucets pay a water carrier $1.00 a day. The *temazcal* or aboriginal sweat bath has disappeared, although after childbirth women take an improvised sweat bath under a sheet. There are two public bath houses, one recently established. Whereas in 1933 there were only two barbers with "shops," there are now five barber shops with chairs and mirrors, served by ten barbers who charge $2.50 to $3.00 for a haircut (as compared with $6.00 in Oaxaca City). In the early 1930s there was one *nixtamal* mill charging $0.04 to grind a half *almud* of maize; now there are seven, and the charge is $0.40 per *almud*.

Women have abandoned the wraparound skirt, formerly worn with the *huipil*, an aboriginal untailored blouse. All now wear dresses or skirt-and-blouse combinations. Only a few elderly men still wear the loose cotton trousers (*pantalones* or *cotones*) held by a woven belt. In Parsons's time only a few storekeepers dressed *"catrín,"* that is, in city clothes. Nevertheless, some customs have changed little. Even today only the wealthier Mitleños use beds; the majority still sleep on floor mats. Farmers still use the same agricultural techniques. Traditional ceremonies have even increased in number and elaboration.

The principal streets in Mitla are maintained in passable condition for trucks and cars. The paved Pan American Highway passes within a few hundred yards of the town, and a paved spur traverses the center of town and continues to the principal ruins. There are a great many more two-story houses than there were earlier. In the central area most houses are built directly on the street with an interior patio, not inside fenced yards as before. Shops catering to tourists line the entrance road while various other stores occupy much of the central area.

Mitla also is much larger than it was. Parsons (10) estimated its population as about 2,500, based on a survey showing 446 households. The 1960 census gives a population of 3,651 for the town or *Villa* and 5,122 for the *municipio*. (Cecil Welte writes me that the as yet unpublished 1970 census will show a population of 4665 for the *villa*.) Parsons estimated an average of five persons per household but allowed in her total for married children's households that had not been reported separately. Assuming no significant change in household size since then, 730 households may be inferred from the population figures for 1960.

[3] The "ethnographic present" is used, here referring to the 1968 survey.

TRADE AND MARKET ACTIVITIES

One reason for the restudy of Mitla was interest in the activity of the traders who were so numerous in 1933. A second was the great increase in handicraft production since that date and its relation to changes in trading activity.

Internal trade. In 1933 (and also in 1968) most internal trade arose from the differentiated occupational and productive patterns within the village (app. 36). In 1933, 202 of the 446 households owned land. This did not represent all the farmers, for anyone who wished to farm could cultivate communally owned lands, usually of poor quality, or could obtain lands from large landholders on a sharecropping basis. Production of maize, beans, and squash was sufficient to supply local consumption. Other crops mentioned were wheat (locally milled and consumed), castor beans, alfalfa (a recent introduction), a nopal (a cactus, sometimes classed with the *Opuntia;* fruits and tender young leaves eaten), and the maguey or *Agave* sp., used for fiber or to make pulque or mescal (51, 54). Most of these were consumed locally, and only a small amount was sold outside the community. Some farmers had supplementary occupations as well. Of 371 men interviewed concerning their occupations, 98 listed themselves as laborers and 140 listed themselves as merchants or travelers. Some of the merchants also farmed, while 70 of the farmers were also engaged in trading (63). Appendix 36 lists the other occupations reported by Parsons but it is unlikely that these were all full-time occupations.

Even though Mitla as a community was self-sufficient in some basic foodstuffs, this clearly was not true for many of its households. Thus there was an internal market for any surplus goods and services produced. Most of this trade apparently went on informally between households, but a few goods were offered for sale in the town square on an irregular basis or were bought and sold by storekeepers. Moreover, many essential foodstuffs and other goods were imported. The money needed for these imports was acquired primarily through the activities of Mitla men acting as external traders and middlemen.

By 1968 internal trade diminished in relative terms, and more reliance is placed on imports. Although the large land holdings have been converted to *ejidos* (there are about 200 *ejido* holders), many people do not farm or do not produce enough for their own needs. Ninety-two ox teams are owned by 83 families. All the ox team owners are landowners. Some also plow for others, charging $20 a day. Sharecroppers are few, as sharecropping is regarded as more risky and less rewarding than handicrafts (20–21). The only new crop mentioned in 1968 is chick-peas. There is also some increase in dairying. Although specific data are lacking, it is likely that Mitla is self-sufficient today only in such items as cactus and maguey production. Production of maguey has increased greatly, and mescal is a significant export of the community.

External trade. In 1933 and also in 1968 various nonindustrial consumer's goods were brought into Mitla from other villages in the Oaxaca marketing system. Appendix 37 lists those "imports" reported in 1933, most of which were brought in and sold by the producers. Some, notably coffee, were brought for sale in Oaxaca City, either by producers or by Mitla traders. Mitla today depends on imports for a large part of its farm produce, which it pays for by exporting handicrafts. Approximately 20 metric tons of maize are imported from the Isthmus every month by truck (32). Some probably is also bought by Mitleños in the marketplaces of Tlacolula and Oaxaca City. In 1933 small quantities of maize apparently reached Mitla from the Sierra. Today the trade is reversed, and an unknown amount of Mitla maize imports is resold to Sierra communities (see below). And despite the great increase in handicrafts, most clothing or the cloth to make it is imported. Other important new import items are chile and avocados from the Sierra.

In 1933 consumer's goods were brought into Mitla by several types of traders: (1) people from nearby villages, both *propios* and middlemen; (2) people from more remote Sierra villages who sold all or part of their products in Mitla on Saturday and went on to Tlacolula to buy goods at the Sunday market there; (3) Mitla traders who went to nearby villages to buy goods for resale in Mitla; and (4) Mitla traders who went to distant villages primarily for such goods as coffee for resale, but sometimes brought back consumption goods such as oranges. The Ramirez data are less detailed for these categories than are Parsons's, but they suggest that the number of vendors from the Sierra has increased over the years. Most of the vendors and products identified by Parsons (app. 37) are from villages in the Valley of Oaxaca or the nearby Sierra. The main products from the more distant Sierra that Parsons mentions are coffee, cedar bark for dyeing, maize, and beans. The 1968 data (app. 38) suggest that the main products from the Sierra now are avocados, coffee, and chile peppers.

External trade based on Mitla production was very limited in 1933 if we may judge by Parsons's data and my own observations. Probably some maize and other farm produce may have been sold in Tlacolula to meet cash needs, and some household production of mescal may have been marketed. Mitla traders to Ayutla regularly carried considerable quantities of bread baked in Mitla. But the main cash income of the village for purchase of "imports" appears to have been the profits of the traveling traders acting as middlemen. In 1968 income from trading activities was augmented by extensive handicraft and industrialized mescal production.

Storekeeping and the plaza. In 1933 storekeeping was the peak of personal ambition. There were eight stores in the village, tended mostly by women and children (13). All carried soap, candles, cigarettes, matches, needles, thread, cotton goods, colored tissue paper, salt, sugar, rice, chocolate, candy, dried shrimps, and crackers. Two carried a larger stock of dry goods and "fancy articles." Some storekeepers advanced goods to traveling traders, to be paid for when the traders returned from their trips, thus serving as jobbers. Parsons attributed the decline of the Mitla marketplace or *plaza* to the presence of the stores; there is no evidence, however, that the Mitla *plaza* was important in recent times.[4] In 1933, almost any day one could see at most a dozen or so local women offering goods, mostly produce from other towns. On Saturdays a somewhat larger number of outsiders on their way to Tlacolula offered food products for sale. By the 1960s a small permanent *mercado* building existed on a corner of the town square. On a typical week day in 1967 it sheltered five food stalls (*fondas*), five meat sellers, eight fruit and vegetable sellers, and one display of cloth from a nearby truck.

Now there are nine large stores and 30 fair-sized stores—five times as many as before. In addition there are possibly as many as 70 *changarros,* stands in doorways or front yards selling soft drinks, maize, sweets, candles, bread, and fruit. Ramirez counted only 40 of the *changarros* but estimated that there were some 30 more hidden in back streets, many of them selling only now and then. These figures do not include the shops and stands selling handicraft goods to tourists or the mescal depots or restaurants.

The larger stores deal extensively in the buying and reselling of coffee and avocados, thus acting as wholesalers. They finance some of the traveling traders, but details concerning such operations are lacking. Each also owns one or more trucks. The trucks may be used to haul goods for the store or to take coffee and avocados to market in Oaxaca City, but in the main they appear to function in general hauling and long-distance trading. Therefore the trucking activities of storekeepers will be dealt with later, in discussing truckers generally. Several of the 30 smaller stores deal in coffee and avocados to some extent but only five are seriously engaged in this trade (72–78).

Without taking into account the stores and stands catering primarily to the tourist trade, it seems clear that well over 100 households, or perhaps one in six Mitla households, are involved to some degree in selling, or buying and selling, from a fixed place of business. If the small *changarros* are eliminated, around 40 households, or one in 16, gain their primary income from storekeeping. Case histories of ten storekeepers are summarized in appendix 39.

Traveling traders. In 1933, as indicated above, about half of the able-bodied adult

---

[4] Taylor (1972:103) says Mitla had a weekly market on Thursdays in the eighteenth century. Today, Thursday is of no significance.

males in Mitla engaged in long-distance external trade.[5] Traveling on foot and carrying goods on burros, or occasionally on their own backs, they ranged from Oaxaca City and Ocotlán in the west to Tehuantepec, Juchitán, and Salina Cruz in the Isthmus of Tehuantepec to the east. They were commonly visitors in many of the Mixe towns and most of the Zapotec Sierra towns between the Isthmus and Mitla, and also reached many villages in the Cajonos basin as far as Yalalag and Betaza. In the Mixe area and in the western Sierra, traders from Yalalag were almost their only competitors. Otherwise they carried on most of the intervillage and intermarket trade in this part of the Oaxaca marketing system.

Four major patterns of trade existed. Between the Valley of Oaxaca and the Isthmus, Mitla traders had a virtual monopoly of trade. A second group also went to the Isthmus first, but then returned to Mitla through the Mixe Sierra. Goods bought in Oaxaca City or elsewhere in the Valley were sold in the Isthmus, where traders bought dried fish, shrimp, salt, coconuts, and sometimes other Isthmian products that they peddled through the Sierra in the Zapotec and Mixe towns, at the same time buying coffee there which they then sold either in Mitla, Tlacolula, or Oaxaca. The timing of these trips often was regulated by the occurrence of periodic markets held in connection with major fiestas in the villages. A third group of some 20 traders made regular weekly trips between Mitla and the sole regular *plaza* in the Mixe country at Ayutla, carrying bread, matches, cigarettes, candles, dry goods, and notions. At Ayutla they bought coffee from producers who came from farther north and east in the Mixería. A fourth group traveled from village to village over various routes into the Mixe and Zapotec mountain area. All these routes are shown in map 9 from Parsons (10–11; 568–569).

By 1968 trucks and buses had altered many of these patterns. The paved Pan American Highway had connected the Valley of Oaxaca with the Isthmus for about 25 years; truck roads now reach many of the nearer Sierra towns and extend to Ayutla and Yalalag. All goods exchanged between the Isthmus and the Valley, and most goods exchanged between the Valley and Ayutla and Yalalag, are carried by bus or truck. Burros have virtually disappeared, completely so on the Isthmus-Valley section. Nevertheless the traditional *viajeros* still function, especially in the Sierra region. Some now travel by bus or rent space on trucks, but many still travel with pack animals in the Sierra beyond the road heads. In the Mixería they have extended their range to more distant villages, especially from Yalalag to Choapan and Santa María, an area formerly visited solely by traders from Yalalag (see map 10). Because of their greater carrying capacity, mules have

---

[5] In a partial occupational census including 371 men, Parsons (63) lists 140 merchants and traveling men. This presumably refers to primary occupations. Then as now, trading was a part-time occupation of several men.

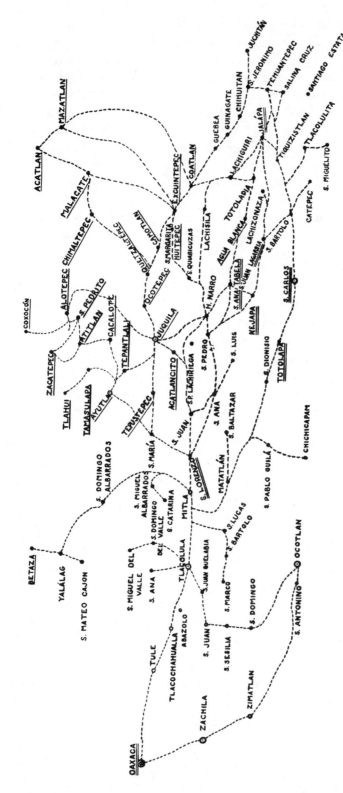

MAP 9. Trade routes of Mitla traders, 1930s. Drawn by Eligio Santiago. Zapoteca towns are not underscored; Castellano towns are underscored ———; Mixe towns, ——— (Parsons 1936: map 3). Reprinted from Elsie Clews Parsons' *Mitla: Town of the Souls*, by permission of the University of Chicago Press. Copyright 1936 by the University of Chicago. All rights reserved.

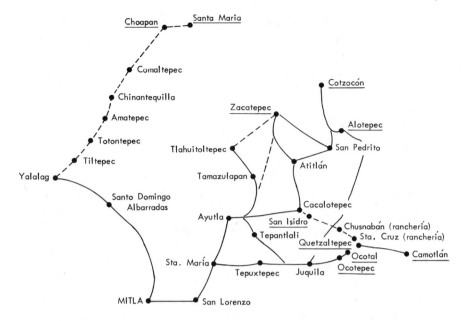

Coffee-producing towns are underscored.
Routes in the Mixe region not indicated by Parsons: — — — —
(from Ramirez 1968)

MAP 10. Present routes of Mitla traders (1968)

replaced the burros to a large extent. These animals are left at the road head while
viajeros or traders take their purchase by truck or bus to Mitla, returning with a
fresh stock of goods from the Valley to make a new trip into the back country.
Many places in the Sierra today have regular *plazas* (Beals 1967).

Some of the Sierra routes shown on the 1968 map (map 10), but not given on
Parsons's map, represent adaptations to improved conditions. The route from
Ayutla to Juquila through Tepantlali, for example, is more easily traveled than the
route through Tepuxtepec, and goods can be brought to Ayutla by truck. Trails for
the two new routes shown to Zacatepec presumably have been improved; in 1933
they were in dangerous condition. The one from Tlahuitoltepec, for example,
passes almost over the summit of Zempoalteptl, the highest mountain in the state.

The Ayutla marketplace or *plaza* continues to be an important center in the
Mixe region. Nearly every week, except in the season of heavy rains, some thirty
Mitla traders visit the *plaza,* arriving on Saturday and leaving usually on Monday.
This represents not only an increase in the number of regular traders but also an
innovation in the mode of travel: eight of the traders operate their own trucks
(seven of these truck owners are former *arrieros*) while the others travel by bus.
Some of these trucks make as many as three round trips a week to Ayutla. Eight
other truckers visit Ayutla on a less regular basis (See app. 40). In addition, a
variable number of truckers from Oaxaca travel to Ayutla.

In both 1933 and 1968 numerous buyers in the Ayutla *plaza,* and many of those who sold avocados, coffee, and other Mixe goods at Ayutla, were from more distant Sierra towns. (The Ayutla *plaza* in 1933 is described briefly in Beals 1945.) Usually vendors carried their goods on their backs. Ramirez feels that the Mitla traders still dominate the Ayutla *plaza;* he contends that, although there are relatively few, they supply all the maize and control the maize depots, bring the largest quantities of goods of all types, and buy most of the Mixe exports offered for sale. Nevertheless, because of the number of traders the situation is highly competitive, and at least one or two of the Mitla traders go only to buy, taking no goods with them to Ayutla. The Mitla traders now have increasing competition from various Mixe sellers and traders, some of whom buy goods in the Valley for resale (see app. 41). Ayutla traders have also broadened the scope of their activities considerably and still control the trade in meat as they did in 1933. Another change is the obvious decline in the number of vendors from Yalalag. Impressionistically, the Ayutla *plaza* has expanded in all respects, in the variety and amount of goods bought and sold as well as in the number and variety of the vendors and traders.

Not all Mixe traders are competitors. Some have come to be regular suppliers of Mitla traders to Ayutla. The data are summarized in appendix 42.

Most Mitla traders sell their Ayutla coffee purchases to one of three buyers in Mitla who send it to Mexico City in their own trucks. Avocados are sold to one of five buyers in Mitla; four ship the goods to Mexico City in their own trucks and the fifth ships by public transportation. Beans go into the local market for sale at retail, as do oranges. Castor beans all go to one wholesale buyer in Mitla. Traders to Ayutla by bus spend about $40 a trip each, including meals, and ordinarily make a profit of $250. When conditions are good they may make as much as $350. During the main season between September and May, such traders appear to clear at least $9,000 each. Details concerning truck owners' commercial activities are given later.

A second group of traditional Mitla traders that are still active consists of those going beyond Ayutla and Yalalag to more distant villages in the Sierra. The routes followed in 1933 are shown in the map by Parsons (map 9), but she gives no data on numbers of traders. In 1968 the total number of regular traders recorded as going beyond Ayutla was 29, as follows (48–49):

To Zacatepec	3
To Alotepec-Cotzocón	7
To Cacalotepec-Ocotepec-Quetzaltepec-Camotlán	11
To Yalalag-Choapan	8

Of those following the same route, several tend to be related to one another as brothers, uncles and nephews, and fathers and sons. Usually such relatives travel together but trade independently. Many have traded along these routes for years, one for at least 40 years. Procedures have changed, however. Now trucks or buses are used to the road heads in Ayutla or Yalalag. Burros or mules then carry the goods to the ultimate destination. Sometimes traders remain with their animals in the mountains, using truckers as agents to carry goods into Mitla and to bring back other goods. In some cases, one member of a group stays with the animals while the others make the trip to Mitla; on the next trip a different member stays.

Coffee is the principal item "exported" from the Sierra, but goods "imported" into the Sierra vary. One trader with twelve burros carries only beer to Zacatepec. Another carries no cargo in, except for occasional commissions given him by Sierra residents. Costs reported by a trader with eight mules who goes to Quetzaltepec are $100 per trip, and profits, $400 per trip. Another who follows the same route with ten mules reports costs of $300 per trip and profits of $1,000 per trip. Each seems to sell his coffee to the same buyer in Mitla, who indeed may have advanced the capital needed to buy the coffee. In the Sierra most of the traders have informal agreements with producers who sell only to them. Case histories of several of these traders are given in appendix 43.

It cannot be established whether or not the number of Mitla traders to the Sierra has changed significantly over the years, but it is clear that the scope of trading activities has expanded and that the quantity of goods they carry into and out of the Sierra has significantly increased.

The character of economic activity has also changed noticeably. Production of coffee, in 1933 the principal export from the Mixe country, has apparently increased. In 1933 wild avocado trees were preserved in any clearing operation and their stringy and often slightly bitter fruit was sometimes used, but now avocados supplement coffee as a significant export. The present production clearly is from extensive planting of commercially desirable, domesticated varieties. A third change is the increasing export of chile peppers and beans from the Sierra. In contrast, the small flow of maize out of the Sierra in 1933 has been markedly reversed, and the Sierra now imports maize.

Most Mitla traders make a good living out of the Sierra commerce, but Ramirez feels that they also have greatly stimulated new production and increased trade, with beneficial effects to the Sierra, especially the Mixe, economy. The coffee trade especially has been responsible for the growth of new population centers. San Isidro and Ocotal, for example, once *rancherías,* are now *agencias municipales* (36).

Truckers. A striking change in Mitla trading patterns is the appearance of truckers (*camioneros*) wherever roads or truck trails have been opened. Truckers mentioned in connection with storekeepers and traders specializing in the Ayutla *plaza* trade are included in the following discussion. (See also app. 44.)

Many Mitla trucks are owned by storekeepers, who usually are also wholesale dealers, mainly in coffee or avocados. These probably are used primarily in connection with the owners' businesses. Some truck owners, however, are essentially traditional *viajeros* who have switched from animal transport to trucks. Only two mention that they carry freight for others on occasion, but it is probable that all do so when their trucks are not loaded to capacity and freight is available. Often they also carry passengers, although this is illegal and they are subject to fine if caught. In all there are 29 trucks owned by 27 truckers (two owners each have two trucks), covering a total of 34 truck routes. Sixteen routes are driven by the truck owners, five by family members or relatives, 13 by hired chauffeurs. Ordinarily each driver is accompanied by an assistant (*machetero*). A total of about 58 persons in Mitla are directly engaged in trucking.

Truck drivers are paid according to the length of the trip. The trucks to Ayutla make two or three round trips a week, for which the driver is said to receive $60 per trip and the *machetero* $20. As driving time is only one day, this suggests that considerable time is spent assembling and disposing of cargo for each trip. Trips to the Isthmus vary from two to three days depending upon ultimate destination (some go as far as Tapachula on the Guatemalan frontier or to Tuxtla Guitierrez, capital of Chiapas), drivers receiving from $100 to $150 per round trip. Trips to Mexico City take about three days, and drivers receive $200 per round trip. These figures seem high, but if they are taken at face value, and if we assume that owner-drivers earn at least as much as chauffeurs, the income of Mitla drivers and *macheteros* solely from trucking activities could easily amount to $8,000 per week. Thus trucking may generate personal incomes through wages or equivalents in the community of over $400,000 a year, quite aside from profits in trading activities.

One or more trucks arrives or departs daily on the Ayutla route. Trucks also arrive and depart daily for the Isthmus. Each truck on this route makes approximately two round trips a week. The main imports from the Isthmus are easily gathered at the shipping point: about 20 metric tons of maize and an equal quantity of salt are brought to Mitla monthly. Trucks going to Mexico City make about one round trip a week. Of the two trucks covering Oaxaca, one operates daily, the other according to local demands and the availability of freight.

Taxi business. Roads and modernization have created a new occupation and service, the taxi. In 1968 there were seven driver-owned taxis in Mitla. Much of their business consists of transporting Mitla residents to Tlacolula or Oaxaca City. The most common arrangement is for five passengers to join, paying $2.00 a head for the trip to Tlacolula or $5.00 a head to Oaxaca. Special business trips also can be arranged. For example, the buyer for the relatively well-known restaurant in Mitla's main inn often makes trips to the Oaxaca market by taxi.

Drivers gross about $100 each on weekdays and $200 on Sunday, the day of the Tlacolula *plaza*. From this they must meet operating expenses and installment payments on their vehicles (all are bought "on time"). The success of the taxi business must be considered against the existence of frequent bus service to both Tlacolula and Oaxaca. Some of the buses are owned by Mitleños, as are the two buses that make daily trips to Ayutla. To complete the transportation picture, buses between the Isthmus and Oaxaca pass nearby. Most of the travel, whether by bus or taxi, is connected with buying and selling activities.

If the *changarros* and daily vendors in the *mercado* are included, it would appear that at least 245 households now derive part of their income from trading activities or providing transport for goods. This does not include assistants (*mozos*) hired by some storekeepers and traders to the Sierra. Of the 245 households, about 165 or over 65 percent probably derive their principal income from commercial and trading activities. Although all stated income figures are suspect, especially those given by storekeepers, the available information suggests that most of these, except the *macheteros,* earn at least $9,000 a year or $24.66 a day, that is, more than the $20 a day often mentioned by peasants as the amount necessary for an average household to maintain a satisfactory level of living.

The number of Mitla residents directly engaged in trade outside Mitla—traveling traders and truckers—is about 116, a reduction from the 140 or more full-time and additional part-time traveling traders reported in 1933. Rather conservative estimates of carrying capacities and transportation activities, however, suggest that the volume of goods transported may be at least two to three times greater today. The number of storekeepers has grown from 8 to 39; many of these derive much of their incomes from external trade—providing goods to local traders and to travelers from the Sierra, and buying and selling coffee, avocados, and other items. The number of households currently deriving support from external trade hence may be 135 or more. These speculative figures do not take into account the number engaged in production or sale of handicraft items for the export trade.

HOUSEHOLD INDUSTRY

Household industries or handicrafts (*artesanía*) in 1933 were quite limited. Most of the production was for local consumption, with the exception of some production of "idols" and onyx or marble beads for exterior trade. Weaving, today the most important handicraft, was done almost entirely on the backstrap loom. Ten weavers, nine men and one woman, made materials for women's wraparound skirts. The one broadloom had been recently introduced by a man who learned the craft in Teotitlán and had begun weaving woolen blankets and copying designs from the ruins, mainly the Mitla key design. Weavers bought the little wool produced locally but also purchased wool in Tlacolula (45).

The principal dyes they used were vegetable and the traditional cochineal (a cactus-plant parasite), but some German aniline dyes were used also. The wool usually was prepared entirely by the weaver's family: it was picked over, washed, spread to dry, carded, spun, dyed, and wound at home. Sometimes cleansed or carded wool could be bought from another weaver, and some Mitleños specialized in spinning. Spinning was accomplished by whirling a stick-and-whorl in a bowl. Cloth was woven for traditional woolen belts and woolen or cotton skirts, and these articles were sold in Mitla and traded to Tlacolula (36, 43–45).

In 1953 Ervin R. Frissell, founder of the small archeological museum at Mitla, had five large Oaxaca-made looms set up for the weaving of shawls and tablecloths and brought in a professional weaver from another village to supervise the project. Eight Mitleños were employed as apprentices there until 1955, when the project was abandoned. Two of the apprentices—brothers—afterward set up their own looms and continued to weave in the new manner. In time others began to emulate them, although most could afford only small, improvised looms (colloquially, *machetes*). Ramirez points out that increasing population pressure in a land-poor village gave impetus to the industry, especially as the old-time traveling traders found that they could not compete with modern bulk transport and cast about for other employment. The entrance of new money with *braceros* returning from the United States, and the developing tourist market, provided additional means and opportunity (61–62).

The aforementioned brothers who began as apprentices in Frissell's shop are the principal loom owners of Mitla; each owns several looms (see app. 45) and maintains a spacious shop with a show area. Owners of large looms number about 100 and those with *machetes* about 200, but most own from two to four looms. The most important loom owners employ at least one salaried weaver and a young apprentice (65). Professional looms are bought in Tlacolula or Oaxaca for about $1,100 new or $650 used; *machetes* can be set up for about $30 (68).

Apart from the loom, a weaver's investment in materials comes to about $300 a week in thread or yarn and $50 in dyes. Cotton thread costs $75 to $85 the package in Oaxaca, the higher price being for warp thread. One can buy wool yarn in Chichicapan (in the hills between Mitla and Ocotlán) for $5 per half pound, or if yarn is not available, raw wool is obtained for $13 per pound in Mitla, where there are four or five sheep raisers who sell it.[6] If the weaver buys raw wool, it is usually spun in the household. The work of unraveling skeins of yarn and winding them on loom spools is performed also by the family or friends of the weaver—a chore that may require two days of the week. Commonly weavers cooperate in helping one another with such tasks if one needs assistance but cannot pay for it. The wool is washed and dyed with modern dyes bought in Oaxaca. Only for special orders is the traditional cochineal dye used (68–70).

[6] These prices are suspect; raw wool should not cost more than yarn.

Shawls, blouses, and dresses are finished by the symmetrical knotting of yarn ends, which may be done in the weaver's household or, if finances permit, may be contracted out to individuals at a usual rate of $1.50 for a shawl, $2.00 for a blouse, or $5.00 for a dress (*18*). Ramirez estimates that approximately 45 percent of the population is engaged (usually part time) in the new occupation of knotting. Even marketplace vendors busy themselves with it between sales (*20*).

One weaver can produce 50 shawls or 60 blouses (which are basically folded shawls) in a week on the professional loom (*69*). For each hour of work that can be performed on a professional loom, the improvised loom requires five to nine hours. Sale prices of finished garments depend on the quality of the weaving and the type of buyer. Cotton articles command as little as $3 each but typically sell for $4 to $6 each. Woolen goods generally sell for $10 to $15 the piece except for shawls, which bring as little as $7 or $8 (*70*). Part of the output is said to go to distributors, storekeepers, and other quantity buyers in Oaxaca, some of whom resell in Mexico City and towns on the United States border. A few weavers are themselves buyers and resellers (*regatones*), and some travel to Mexico City to sell (*63*); substantial amounts, however, are sold locally to visiting tourists. Not only are there several shops of varying sizes along the road entering Mitla, there are also perhaps thirty or forty stands between the parking area and the ruins. In addition, women and children with a few items for sale cluster hopefully about the entrance to the Frissell Museum or track tourists through the streets.

A sample of seven major loom owners was interviewed. Data concerning the backgrounds and business operations of respondents are presented in appendix 45.

Silversmithing had much the same start in Mitla as the modern weaving industry, but this craft has not flourished as weaving has. In 1953 a silversmith was brought in from Taxco for two years to teach his craft under a project initiated by Howard Leigh called *Junta Cultural Zapoteca*. Only one of his students went on to establish a silverworking shop in Mitla, while two became general jewelers, producing chains, medallions, necklaces, rings, and the like. The other apprentices went to work in Oaxaca (*63*).

The silversmith works alone. He says he invests $1,600 in a two-kilogram bar of silver every three months and nets about $600 from jewelry sales over a four-month period. Of the two jewelers, only one is presently active; he works with five employees who each are paid $10 a day or $60 a week (*71*). (These figures seem improbably low.)

The manufacture of stone figurines resembling pre-Columbian idols also contributes to the tourist trade and supports fifteen to twenty families (*64*).

On the basis of the figures given, it is doubtful if more than half of the estimated total of 652 Mitla households today gain their principal income from farming, and most of the farmers have other part-time occupations. At least 116 gain their principal livelihood as external traders or truckers, not including *mozos* or *macheteros*. The latter are mostly young men who are part of a household with other sources of income. Storekeeping is the main source of livelihood for 39 households. Approximately 100 households operate broadlooms; some own two or three looms and employ weavers. (Another 200 households weave on *machetes* (backstrap looms), but this is probably not their main source of income.) If we add to these other types of specialists, at least 325 households gain their principal livelihood from nonfarm activities. This does not include persons employed in various activities such as mescal production, bus driving, silversmithing, and so on. Many of these also have supplementary occupations. For example, if we include those engaged part time in knotting and other weaving-related activities with those actually operating looms, more than half the households in Mitla must gain some income from weaving.

On the surface, Mitla has changed radically since 1933, but it is still, as Parsons noted earlier, a business town that has capitalized on its earlier trading and handicraft traditions. As indicated in appendix 36, only taxi driving and jewelry making are listed by Ramirez as wholly new occupations, while some of the old occupations apparently have disappeared. The mixture, however, has changed to take advantage of new opportunities provided by modern conditions. But even weaving, the occupation showing greatest change, was a traditional occupation.

Mitla undoubtedly presents an extreme case of change. More isolated communities with more flexible land bases and less exposure to the tourist trade, have changed much less. But this is because of lack of opportunity, not to any blind clinging to tradition. At the same time it is important to note that change in Mitla has not resulted in a breakdown of the traditional marketing system but rather in its augmentation under the influence of the modern national economy. As a result of these changes, Mitla appears to be more prosperous. This prosperity, however, is precarious because it depends so heavily on the continuance of the tourist market for handicrafts.

12
Concluding Observations

The inquiry into the scope, structure, and functioning of the Oaxaca marketing system shows that within the region involved, market factors pervade the entire economic system. This does not imply that all production is for the market or that all consumption needs of all the participants are satisfied through the marketing system. Many Oaxaca peasant farmers satisfy most of their food consumption needs through their own production. Nevertheless, all to some degree must obtain part of what the culture defines as basic commodities through the marketing system. As a producer, the peasant is involved in the market through the hiring of labor, the purchase of tools and other capital goods, or the purchase of raw materials for handicrafts.

What is more important is that the marketing system provides many options and alternatives and that peasants make their economic decisions in the light of their knowledge of them. In selecting his occupational role combinations and in choosing the crops he will plant, including his decision concerning the ratio of subsistence to cash crops, the Oaxaca peasant has made rational judgments based on market considerations. People who elect to maximize the subsistence aspects of their economic activities do so, not because they are unaware of alternatives, but because they either cannot find ways to take advantage of them or are fearful of the consequences of failure if they change their economic strategies. Even those peasants who elect for minimum involvement in the market are still market oriented.

Although much more information is needed about how and why individual Oaxaca peasants make the decisions they do, it is apparent that their economic decisions and choices conform to many of the same economic principles to be found in larger and more complex capitalistic economies. Within the limits of their information, they seek to avoid risks, minimize costs, and maximize returns. They operate in part in a very open market with extensive competition for production factors and for customers. Recognition of supply, demand, and competitive forces constantly plays a part in their economic decisions, and sellers and buyers are intensely interested in prices and the "movement" or activity in the marketplace. These characteristics are not always immediately apparent to observers immersed in more complex Western economies because traditional economic activities in Oaxaca are influenced by different social ends and cultural values and a different institutional setting.

One such difference is the absence of the corporate economic institutions that so dominate Western economies. This absence is almost complete in the traditional system and nearly so in the modern aspects of the Oaxaca economy. Only a few partnerships or cooperatives have a vaguely corporative character. Observers often are so bemused by the manifold social functions of many peasant economic institutions that they fail to see the nature and importance of economic processes. The literature is replete with anecdotes to suggest that Mexican peasants go to marketplaces to socialize rather than to trade. Although Oaxaca peasants do socialize at marketplaces and engage in other noneconomic activities in connection with them, trade is the primary purpose for their presence there.

SOCIAL ENDS OF ECONOMIC ACTIVITY

For most Oaxaca peasants, economic activity is shaped by social ends. In this they are not unique. Whatever is unusual about the Oaxaca situation is in the nature of the social ends, the specific forms they take, and the ways in which they modify economic activities whether in production or in the marketplace. Certainly the economic activities of Oaxaca peasants are rarely limited to meeting the biological necessities for subsistence and reproduction. Even in these matters the definition of "necessities" and the food and other items to satisfy them are culturally determined. This is even more true of wants and needs beyond the survival minimum. Not only is much economic activity dedicated to the accomplishment of social ends, but economic means are frequently subordinated to those ends.

A vivid example of the latter point is provided by the *mayordomía*, a religiously oriented institution utilizing economic means and involving a social type of consumption. In one aspect it involves redistribution, in that the *mayordomía* may be undertaken only by those with adequate economic resources, who are expected to feed and entertain their guests on special religiosocial occasions. Most of the expenditures are for food and drink ingested by the participants and guests, but some are for satisfying the senses (music) or the soul (masses), and some goods are even destroyed (fireworks). Values widely held in the society, in this case a community, require the undertaking of the *mayordomía*, and pressures may be exerted on individuals to accumulate and use economic resources to carry it out on at least a minimal level. But not all members of the community share equally in the redistribution process. Not all individuals are fed, and relatively few are fed at every meal. Moreover, most of those who are fed make some material contribution. Sometimes the latter is cash, which may be required of all households for major fiestas; but sometimes only cigarettes, mescal, soft drinks, or beer, or labor assistance in food preparation are called for.

The *mayordomo,* especially if he volunteers for the undertaking, makes an economic decision to divert his labor from productive or commercial activities and to consume his material resources for spiritual satisfactions and enhanced prestige. Further, within his conduct of the *mayordomía* he makes additional economic decisions. Although he must meet the minimal requirements of the particular *mayordomía,* he still can decide how lavishly he will feed the guests, how sumptuous the fireworks display will be, and how long he will pay the musicians to perform. In making these decisions, he is balancing economic considerations against the amount of social prestige he can expect to achieve.

MAXIMIZATION BY OAXACA PEASANTS

The peasant maximizes satisfactions in the light of his values. By participating in the maintenance of village welfare and social cohesion through office holding, contributions of money and labor, and sharing the burdens of the *mayordomía* system, he conforms to the traditional ideal of the "good citizen" and enhances his status. As a result, the peasant household's productive behavior may seem uneconomic in the conventional view. To meet the temporary cash needs for a civic obligation, it may be forced to expand its farming activities into marginal lands yielding minimal returns, increase handicraft production to the point where it may have to accept lower prices, sell some of its lands or other capital goods (thus reducing future productive potential), or, if office holding is involved, reduce its production because of time expenditures required by the office. Economic goals are thus subordinated to sociocultural ends. This phenomenon, exemplified in conspicuous consumption to enhance status, is present in Western societies also. As Waterbury has pointed out in conversation however, for the majority of Western societies increased consumption and rising scales of living have become goals in themselves. In comparative economics, this leads to an essentially ethnocentric evaluation of the efficiency of economic systems solely in terms of the degree to which they contribute to higher levels of consumption. If proper account be taken of absence of this coincidence of social and economic goals in Western societies, the operation of maximization principles and rationality in peasant economics becomes more evident.

In his efforts to maximize in the more purely economic sphere, the Oaxaca peasant likewise does not respond solely to immediate considerations but responds to longer-range goals. The peasant producer frequently feels that maintenance of friendly relationships with his buyers and suppliers will have economic advantages. In the same fashion, traders often moderate their behavior in the hope that customers will return. In many situations sellers do not undercut their competitors because they must continue to associate with them over time. Both maximization and competition, then, are influenced by long-range market considerations and by the restraints of continuing social relationships.

The market behaviors of Oaxaca peasants are further modified by the quality of the information available. Some details of this problem have been presented in chapter 9. In general, decisions are rational or economic within the framework of available information. The major exceptions are susceptibility to impulse buying and to the seductions of the relatively new installment-buying opportunities. These seem most common in connection with clothing and with new industrial items. Such buying is related in part to the frequently admitted difficulty of saving cash. For clothing, significantly higher prices often are paid for items purchased on installments. As installment sellers of clothing make house-to-house visits in the villages, however, often the buyer lacks the normal information sources such as comparison shopping in the *plaza*. Impulse buying at times is related to the coincidence of a large sale of one's own goods for cash and an opportunity to buy. But what may appear to be an irrational impulse purchase often can be put to good use for economic gain, as in the purchase of a phonograh described in chapter 5, above.

Another characteristic of the Oaxaca peasant economy which gives difficulty to economists is the attitude toward labor. In attempting to assess the relative utility of various economic factors in this labor-intensive economy, labor must be considered somewhat differently than it would be in most studies of Western economies. But there is evidence that the peasant sees labor as a commodity even though he does not normally calculate it as part of his costs. He is well aware that in choosing some options he is using potential productive labor-time for nonproductive purposes. This includes such values as leisure as well as the prestige-producing activities of the *mayordomía* or public office holding. Awareness of the value of his time is also apparent in the use of buses and trucks to save time in visiting marketplaces and in some selling decisions including, indeed, the choice of marketplaces. The producer-vendor moreover, frequently chooses to sell wholesale although by the investment of time he could increase his return by selling retail. The deciding factor in his choice between the latter two alternatives is the amount of time he can save for other activities. This is most clear for the farmer who is more apt to sell wholesale if he is in the midst of important planting or harvesting activities that require his full attention.

The quality of economic judgments in Oaxaca also may be obscured by the inadequate ideas of cost. Some behavior that appears to be uneconomic, however, may be justified by the problems of marketing. Malinowski and de la Fuente (1957:147–150) recount a case in which it was demonstrated to a group of village-based traders that they made practically no margin on three of four items they customarily carried back to the village. When it was suggested to them that they would make more profits if they used all their capital and transport capacity to carry back only the most profitable item, they were prompt to reply that all the items were needed in their village. The implication is that if they brought only the one item their customers would desert them for traders offering a complete line. At a more sophisticated level, I have already cited the case of Oaxaca wholesalers (chap. 8, above) who will buy items not in stock from other wholesalers to accommodate steady customers, even though there is no profit in these transactions. Marketing considerations may override purely profit-maximization goals in particular transactions. In any case, it is incorrect to impugn the economic judgment of buyers or sellers because they lack information or are poor cost accountants, or indeed have different ideas about maximization than do the critics.

The society and its goals and values in which the Oaxaca marketing system is embedded are different from those of industrialized Western economies. The system functions with a less sophisticated information system and very limited accounting practices. Nevertheless, the underlying principles governing its functioning appear to be very similar to those of its "more advanced" counterparts and seem to be amenable to many if not all of the same types of technical economic analysis.

THE ANTIQUITY OF MARKET CONSIDERATIONS IN OAXACA

It might be argued that the importance of market factors in the Oaxaca regional economy is merely an indication that the local peasant economy has been fully drawn into the Western type of market economy. It is clear, however, that the main features of the Oaxaca market economy were well established when it was relatively isolated from the Western industrial economy. In the Colonial period, cochineal played an important role in the export trade of Oaxaca. But this probably was true of the pre-Spanish economy as well. The prices of imported cacao, salt, and cotton undoubtedly affected the regional economy, as did the demand for exports such as gold and other minerals, cochineal, feather work, possibly textiles, and some other handicrafts of which the most widely distributed may have been the iron pyrite mirrors found from Arizona to Guatemala.

The unequal distribution of critical resources and resulting trends toward local specializations also antedated the Colonial era. Ignacio Bernal (personal communication) feels that pottery from the Santa María Atzompa area was widely distributed throughout the Valley and adjacent areas in quite early times. There is thus considerable reason to believe that marketing activity has existed in the Oaxaca region for a very long time. Certainly the contrary cannot be assumed until extensive historical evidence has been produced for such an assumption. (In this connection, Millon [1970] estimates that perhaps 25 percent or more of the population of Teotihuacan in the Valley of Mexico was engaged in craft activities and many more in marketplace and long-distance trade.) It is a likely conclusion that, except in some details, the traditional market economy of Oaxaca was not exclusively the product of involvement with Western economies even in the preindustrial period.

The traditional market system evidently came into existence as a means of moving goods from producer to consumer in a region marked by great variation in the distribution of resources and in farm production and with a strong tendency toward village-based craft specialization. In this situation, coupled with the large number of individual or household consumers and producers in the region, the marketplace and the professional trader have provided marked efficiencies in the distribution of goods. Without them, the consumer would spend an inordinate amount of time in locating suppliers for the goods he desires. The marketplace provides the consumer with the opportunity to meet face to face with several producers of a particular commodity and to find in one place all the variety of goods he desires, while the producer is able at one time and place to meet several buyers, none of whom individually would buy his entire production. The trader serves a similar function by assembling products from many sources and transporting them to a location in which several buyers are concentrated. His function is particularly important where the suppliers of each of the various marketplaces offer goods not available in others.

THE MARKET AS AN EXPLOITATIVE DEVICE

Characteristically, the substantivist economists and many anthropologists see the market as an exploitative device. This is especially true of those with Marxist or neo-Marxist orientations. Marroquin (1957), in discussing the Tlaxiaco market system in the Mixtec area of Oaxaca, emphasizes its exploitative character and suggests that it is without any other useful economic function. Eric Wolf, although he recognizes the function of the "Indian" market in providing a wide exchange of goods among specialized producing villagers, stresses the actual or potential exploitative character of the modern market and underestimates the importance of the intermediary in traditional marketing systems (1953:54–55, 1955: 459–460, 1956:1073). In much other literature the concept of power is used to explain why the peasant produces for the market. The possibility that the peasant enters the market to satisfy his own needs is frequently ignored. Often the characterization of the market as an exploitative mechanism is based not upon observations but upon ideological views that class any intermediaries in the exchange and distribution process as exploiters rather than as persons rendering a service (a notable exception is Mintz 1955, 1957).

Objectively, exploitation may be claimed whenever an exchange is unequal or is so perceived by one of the parties to the transaction. Most commonly inequalities exist (1) when one party is able to coerce the other, (2) when there are no alternative buyers or sellers, or (3) when intermediaries serve no useful social or economic function. In general, these conditions do not exist in the traditional Oaxaca marketing system. Producers usually have alternative buyers, including the consumer; buyers usually have alternative sources of supply. The *regatón* and the storekeeper are seen by the majority of Oaxaca peasants as performing a useful function in facilitating the distribution of goods, and it is expected that a profit will be made by the intermediary. "The *regatón* must live too," as one peasant put it. Even in those areas of negotiated prices where haggling is most prevalent and vigorous, it is recognized that differences in the buyer's desire to buy and the seller's desire to sell enter legitimately into the final price agreed upon. Because of the presence of alternative suppliers and buyers, haggling takes place within limits set by supply and demand functions which are modified by the quality of the information available to the participants. Only rarely does the Oaxaca peasant feel he is exploited. He may complain about prices but he does not necessarily blame them on the individual with whom he deals.

This is not to deny that exploitation occurs or has existed in the past. The clearest example is the *acaparador* who buys basic necessities cheaply and may withhold goods from the market to force an increase in prices. For the most important staple, maize, CONASUPO now regulates prices (see chap. 4, above). The hoarder essentially has been eliminated, but the government agency is now in a potential position to be the exploiter. To the extent that the regulating agency is overstaffed with high-paid and often unneeded executives and administrators from influential families, the peasant still is exploited.

Some other cases of exploitation can be identified objectively. Some of these are in the area of handicrafts, primarily those for which there is a high tourist demand.[1] In an important weaving village one family has gained control of a significant part of the production through making interest-free loans to producers, in return acquiring the product at a lower price than the artisans would get from alternative purchasers. Externally stimulated efforts to break this near monopoly by establishing a marketing cooperative have been relatively unsuccessful because of lack of understanding on the part of the producers. To succeed, the cooperative also must make advances to the producers. In one unsuccessful government-sponsored cooperative, however, these loans carried interest. Although the interest rate was very low and prices obtained were significantly higher, final settlements were slow and most producers were unable to perceive the advantage in comparison to the "interest-free" advances by the private entrepreneur. In addition, the costs of the cooperative were unnecessarily high because of the employment of a relatively high-salaried manager from the Oaxaca upper class.

Occasional examples of coercion also exist. Mestizo vendors, especially of manufactured goods, sometimes attempt to bully buyers into purchasing from them, especially if the buyers are obviously from more remote villages. In none of the cases observed were they successful. In contrast, buyers of such goods as coffee sometimes attempt to bully producers into selling at low prices. In an observed instance a Mixe coffee producer complained to his municipal authorities, and the traveling Zapotec buyer was haled into the municipal building. After a shouting match with the mayor and members of the council, he was released with the admonition that if another complaint was made he would be thrown in jail.

With industrial goods, where the buyer's information is inadequate some exploitation must exist, especially in relation to interregional exchanges. Berg's (1968) data on the developing avocado trade in the Sierra, for example, strongly suggest that a disproportionate amount of money flowing into the Sierra from the shipment of avocados to Mexico City goes to the truckers and storekeepers who act as agents for Mexico City buyers. Even so, the peasant sometimes succeeds in bypassing ordinary commercial channels.

Important actual or potential sources of exploitation today in part are external to the marketing system as such. Among these might be mentioned uses of credit, either to gain control over a peasant's land, when he is forced to borrow to meet a major emergency, by insisting that land be pawned as security under conditions where the borrower will have difficulty redeeming it, or through liens on future production at lower-than-market prices. Possibly high interest rates sometimes demanded by moneylenders also represent exploitation. The major source of exploitation today, however, is perhaps the manipulation of government controls

---

[1] The readiness of Oaxaca peasants to exploit the lack of market information among tourists to obtain high prices suggests widespread willingness to engage in exploitation if opportunity offers.

and taxation to the disadvantage of the peasant. This includes taxes on the transport of some goods on the highways or when they are introduced into the city by public transportation. In Oaxaca City there also has been some question as to whether the *plaza* and *mercado* are not made to bear a disproportionate share of the costs of municipal government. As a result, market organizations have developed considerable political influence. Now there is usually a market stall holder on the city council, and often one has been named as alternate deputy to the state legislature. Also, because so large a portion of the City's budget is derived from the *mercado* and the *plaza,* the strike has proved an effective weapon, not only depriving the urban population of food supplies but also seriously reducing revenues to the City government.

Perhaps the more serious threat to the open character of the Oaxaca market is the formation by external agencies of marketing cooperatives whose function often is creating well-paying jobs for favored members of the bureaucracy or their relatives rather than serving the needs of producers. One effort in the weaving trade has been mentioned. Although it has not been studied in any detail, a more flagrant case is that of the so-called fisheries cooperative, which has attempted, with only partial success, to establish a monopoly over the supply of fresh fish to the City. While the cooperative has introduced modern—and costly—methods of transporting and handling fresh fish, it has driven many small-scale fish dealers out of the market and has created a situation that on superficial observation appears to benefit primarily a top-heavy and unnecessarily costly administrative bureaucracy rather than the consumers of fish or the fishermen.

Thus it is not the market that is exploitative. Rather, there are individual exploiters who are able to use the market system to their ends and to take advantage of ignorance on the part of buyer or seller. This potentiality is far outweighed by the function of the market—particularly in its traditional aspect—in the distribution of goods, which serves important economic and social ends.

CAPITALISTIC CHARACTER OF THE MARKETING SYSTEM

The modern sector of the contemporary Oaxaca economy is clearly a local adaptation of the national economy of Mexico. The latter is essentially a capitalistic market economy modified by state regulatory controls and ownership of key industries. For this study the principal interest in the modern economy is the degree to which local modifications and adaptations have been affected by the traditional economy and, far more important, the degree to which the influence of the modern economy is responsible for the characteristics of the traditional sector.

The data presented suggest that the traditional peasant economy not only is capitalistic but that its marketing system offers perhaps a much closer approximation to a "perfect" market situation than does the modern economy. This view is supported by the importance of maximizing behavior, the predominance of negotiated prices, responsiveness to supply and demand considerations, the importance of market knowledge, the numerous alternatives in production, marketing of products, and supplying consumer wants, and the importance of profit-motivated traders in the distribution process. The impact of the modern national economy has modified some features of the traditional marketing system, but the system's essential characteristics as reported by Malinowski and de la Fuente, and to some extent by other writers, were well established before there was any significant impact from the modern economy. How far back in time capitalistic features existed cannot be determined at present, but almost certainly such professional trading classes as the Pochteca among the Aztecs had a profit motivation.

Peasant economies rarely have been characterized as capitalistic, although many of them exhibit processes similar to those found in Oaxaca. Tax (1953) called the economy of Panajachel in Guatemala an example of "penny capitalism," allegedly operating in what approaches a perfectly competitive market situation. This characteristic Nash (1967) extended to Mesoamerican peasant markets in general, and with qualifications it applies to the Oaxaca system. The Oaxaca traditional market has imperfections (see chap. 9, above), but it has fewer restrictions than does any modern market. Tax saw the main restriction on the development of Panajachel capitalism (beyond the small scale of operations) to lie not in the imperfections of the market but rather in the absence of mechanisms to promote the accumulation and use of capital in the expansion of economic enterprises.

As has been shown, virtually all economic activities in the peasant sector of the Oaxaca economy require capital or access to it through the credit system. Even landless laborers and certain service specialists usually own some capital goods such as a house and lot, furnishings, and perhaps some equipment that may be converted into productive forms. The real issue, however, is how and to what extent capital may be accumulated.

The major potential sources of capital—inheritance, savings, and credit—have been described above (see chaps. 4 and 5). The first, inheritance, is especially important in land acquisition. In a society in which all offspring theoretically inherit equally, one might expect that in a few generations land would be fragmented into uneconomic parcels. But Theodore Downing has shown (1971) that, in fact, extreme fragmentation rarely occurs and is counterbalanced by various mechanisms: combining inheritance of husband and wife, expanding holdings through purchase, and selling land parcels and dividing cash receipts among the heirs. Individuals also may own land in several locations. In such cases, the estate may be divided among heirs without any fragmentation of land parcels.

Accumulation of capital through saving cash, though difficult, is not impossible.

Many peasants avoid the temptation to use cash in nonproductive ways by investing in animals or trade goods. Animal investment is especially favored. A small investment in young poultry may be pyramided by selling mature birds, using the proceeds to buy piglets, and selling the mature hogs for enough money to buy an ox or even (usually with the use of some credit) an ox team. Such a procedure, again with the possible use of credit, may permit purchase of a small piece of land. Another favored method of saving, among farmers, is the reinvestment of cash from bulk sale of their products in land or productive activities, while relying on wage labor, sales of animals, or even credit to meet household expenses until the next harvest.

Credit, although perhaps more often used to meet emergencies, may also be employed in various ways to supplement savings and to make productive investments. In some rather infrequent cases, land is mortgaged to buy additional land. That not many peasants use these means of increasing capital is beside the point. What is more important is that they are available, and some peasants do use them. Men starting life as landless laborers have become prosperous farmers. Farmers have increased landholdings, established stores, or bought trucks or tractors. Although many do not take advantage of the opportunities, most Oaxaca peasants are aware of the potentialities of manipulating capital to agument production or to engage in trade. They also are aware of the possibilities of savings and the use of credit to obtain capital.

It is true that there is a considerable quantum jump in the capital required to become an urban or town storekeeper. It is perhaps even more difficult to become a contemporary trucker-vendor; the down payment on a truck may be as much as $40,000, and successful operations in addition require substantial operating capital and established credit. Nevertheless, some peasants do surmount these hurdles.

The continuing small scale of most peasant economic activities in Oaxaca cannot be attributed solely to the difficulty of accumulating capital. The explanation for it lies in other characteristics of the marketing system. Of these, perhaps the most important is the relative stability of the amount of the more important peasant-produced goods absorbed in the market, the relatively small amounts of capital required for most productive and trading activities, and the existence of a large number of peasant or peasantlike competitors satisfied with a relatively low standard of living. This is especially apparent in trading activities where most entrepreneurs view trading simply as a way of making a traditional living or augmenting income. The relatively small amount of capital required means that as markets expand, so does the number of traders. Informants with many years of experience as traders repeatedly asserted that in the past there were fewer traders doing a larger volume of business and making more money than is true at present.

hypertrophy of the tertiary sector

Another obstacle occurs because most economic skills are learned from relatives or from close observation of fellow villagers. Here the specialized nature of the village economies limits opportunities to learn. A successful maize farmer on piedmont lands cannot easily learn to farm humid bottomlands or to shift readily to new crops or to establish a dairy. Traders in vegetables do not necessarily know how to trade in fruits, let alone in cheese or dry goods. Being a trader may look easy, but the rate of failure appears to be high.

A third barrier to expansion is added costs and supervision required for hired labor once an enterprise or landholding requires more labor than can be provided by the household. Many larger landowners hence prefer employing sharecroppers instead of expanding their own farming activities. Indeed, some landholders prefer to give all their lands to sharecroppers so they can engage in storekeeping or in operating a truck for hire. Such individuals, according to Waterbury's evidence from San Antonino as well as other data, tend to be conservative in farming: they prefer a crop such as maize, produced by traditional methods, which is less subject to vagaries of price or of supply and demand fluctuations. Some weavers and potters employ labor. The most successful artisans having shops with employees are those with special skills in design or in marketing. Storekeepers, when their enterprises reach a certain size, must also hire salespeople. Larger enterprises require not only more capital but considerable skills in managing stocks and in accounting.

The small scale of trading enterprises in the traditional market and in some types of enterprises in the transitional *mercado* appears to be owing not so much to the lack of capital, or access to it, as to the other factors described, especially the easy entry of new competitors into the market and the greater skills required in the management of larger-scale enterprises. In a sense it is the relative perfectness of the market which impedes the development of larger enterprises. The situation is different with some aspects of the modern sector such as wholesale enterprises, large stores or supermarkets, or industrial enterprises, which require very substantial capital. Few peasants have made the transition into the modern sector of the economy. Nevertheless it is worth noting that a man who at age 36 was one of the most successful businessmen in Oaxaca City was born in a village and began his business life as a *mozo* in a stall in the Mercado Benito Juárez.

SPATIAL ASPECTS OF THE OAXACA MARKETING SYSTEM

Mesoamerican marketing systems have sometimes been called solar systems (for example, Nash 1966, 1967). In the sense that Oaxaca marketplaces are surrounded by a varying number of "satellite" villages whose inhabitants carry on their primary selling and buying activities in the marketplace, and that the various marketplaces are in turn related to the central or primary marketplace of Oaxaca City, the term may seem apposite, but it is at best a superficially descriptive term.

Central place theory at first sight offers a more promising way of analyzing the Oaxaca system, but it too has limitations. Some shortcomings and problems in the application of central place theory in Africa were recently discussed at a conference on African urbanization (Deshler 1971). At the conference, Skinner, who has done impressive studies of the development of marketing and market towns in China (Skinner 1964), questioned the comparability of the Chinese situation with Africa. It appears that neither the several African situations described nor the Chinese situation are wholly comparable with Oaxaca. In central place theory, periodic markets are associated with demand that is too low to support full-time traders. Robert H. T. Smith at the African conference felt that although the evidence is not conclusive, it favors the view that periodic markets in Africa serve primarily to maximize the customer's access to want-satisfying goods through space and time. Alternative hypotheses are (1) that periodicity and location of markets are primarily ways to minimize the costs to traders, and (2) that the time interval of markets arises out of local social and economic conditions.

In Oaxaca the prevalence of village specialization in production reinforces the importance of the periodic market for consumer convenience. The periodic market provides a time and place for the customer to satisfy all his wants. The situation is complicated, however, because many customers are also *propios* or sellers for whom the periodic market provides assurance of the greatest number of potential customers. A good deal of the exchange is horizontal trade, between residents of the villages within the local marketplace trading area. Most of these trading areas, however, also have wants that must be supplied from outside, primarily by full-time intermediate or long-distance traders. In the main, the argument that the periodic character of the marketplaces results from too few customers to justify daily trading is inadequate. The problem is not that there are too few customers but that there are too many traders in relation to local demand. If the number of customers were equally distributed through time, a smaller number of traders could operate economically on a daily basis.

At the conference on Africa it was noted that many contemporary marketplaces developed around political and administrative centers. This may be true of Oaxaca City and to some extent of one or two other marketplaces of the Oaxaca region. In the main, however, it appears that in Oaxaca the converse is true: administrative and political centers have grown up about marketplaces. Certainly this is evident in the great proliferation of modern administrative activities—tax offices, health centers, educational centers, *ejidal* offices—in long-established market towns. It seems unlikely, on a basis of the foregoing, that any single hypothesis will serve to account for the periodic market phenomenon.

In areas with periodic markets, the various marketplaces give the appearance of forming a hierarchy in their importance. This is most evident in the size of market towns and the numbers of consumers and vendors attending the periodic markets. This hierarchy, however, does not apply to all commodities. The primacy of Ocotlán and Tlacolula as cattle markets has already been noted. Moreover, if the trading areas of particular market towns are examined in relation to particular commodities, a much more complex picture emerges. Cook (1972) has shown that metates are made in four locations—Magdalena Ocotlán, San Juan Teitipac, San Sebastian Teitipac, and Tlacolula—and has mapped out the alternative pathways by which they may move from the producer to the ultimate consumer (see chap. 9, above, and fig. 6). Not all of these routes, however, are used by all producers, nor do metates from all of the production points pass through all marketing areas. Ninety-five percent of the metates produced at Magdalena are sold by the producer or finisher at retail in the Ocotlán marketplace to buyers who come overwhelmingly from the local trading area. Similarly, Tlacolula producers sell at retail in the Tlacolula marketplace to buyers who are predominantly from that town's trading area. Although a few Teitipac metates are sold by producers at retail to buyers from the local Oaxaca City marketing area, the majority are sold to wholesale buyers who either resell them at retail in Oaxaca or distribute them to such distant regions as the Isthmus, the Miahuatlán or Pochutla districts to the south, small outlying marketplaces especially to the west and southwest, or parts of the Sierra de Juárez outside the Tlacolula trading area. With respect to metates, at least, the market towns of Ocotlán, Tlacolula, and Oaxaca do not stand in a hierarchical relationship to one another. Rather, they constitute three relatively independent marketplaces, handling merchandise that shows the consistent differences in quality, kind of finish, and price which characterize the different sources of supply, and serving three distinct marketing areas. For the Oaxaca marketplace, the marketing area is discontinuous. Similar detailed studies of particular commodities almost certainly would reveal many other marketplaces that fail to conform to the hierarchical model.

Another weakness of central place theory, as it often is used, is its emphasis on vertical aspects of marketing systems. This is apparent in Skinner's (1964) study of Chinese marketplaces, which gives the impression that most trade consists of peasant products ascending a vertical structure to townspeople and town products descending to peasants. Again Oaxaca does not conform. The "central place" city of Oaxaca has never been a major supplier of goods to the peasantry, although it has been a center for the assembly of goods leaving the marketing system and for the distribution of goods entering it from outside. This is perhaps more true today than it has been in the past, but some goods leaving the system bypass the central marketplace entirely, for example, avocados and some handicrafts. This has been true in the past also; at times the cochineal traders of Miahuatlán bypassed not only Oaxaca City but Mexico City, selling directly to the exporters of Veracruz.

Within the system, most vertical trade consists of peasant products ascending through the marketplace to resellers, only to descend to consumers in other parts of the system. The principal occasion for such a flow of goods is where secondary or smaller marketplaces are widely separated in space. If communications and distance make it feasible, goods may pass directly between secondary marketplaces, or the producers themselves may elect to sell in a marketplace serving a distant market area.

Central place theory offers some interesting suggestions for ways of looking at the Oaxaca marketing system but does not provide a satisfactory model for it. As Skinner suggested for Africa, the Oaxaca system involves so many variables that comparison with other systems such as that in China is very difficult.

UNIQUE ASPECTS OF THE TRADITIONAL SYSTEM

The preceding discussion of the Oaxaca marketing system has suggested many ways in which it differs from other peasant systems that have been described. In chapter 1 I discussed briefly the difficulties of fitting Oaxaca peasants into some of the general discussions and typologies of peasantry. This problem is not, however, a central one for this study and need not be pursued further. There is still the question of how far the Oaxaca system conforms to generalizations about peasant marketing systems, when compared with peasant markets on a worldwide basis or with other systems in Mesoamerica. A résumé of some of the special characteristics of the Oaxaca marketing system and the peasant economy of which it is a part seems a fitting close.

1. The Oaxaca system seems unique in the number of economic roles occupied by the participants or open to them. Whether we look at particular villages or at the system as a whole, most Oaxaca peasants occupy several economic roles. This is perhaps another way of saying that we are dealing with an economy with many specialized roles. The most striking fact, however, is that the distribution of roles does not permit creation of a useful typology of classes of participants, except in a few instances such as the landless village laborer and some types of full-time traders. Although many roles or role classes require special skills, there are an impressive number of economic options open to the Oaxaca peasant, and characteristically he makes use of several of these either concurrently or sequentially in the course of a year or during his lifetime. I suspect that this also may be true of some other peasant economies if they were to be studied from this point of view.

2. The Oaxaca system is characterized by an unusually high degree of economic

interdependence among villages, a function of environmental differences and of a tradition of village specialization. This point has been dealt with at some length. In this respect the Oaxaca system is similar to other Mesoamerican market systems and perhaps the Peruvian highlands, but similarities are not so evident in the descriptions of marketing systems in Africa and southeast Asia. This characteristic does not seem to apply even to Caribbean markets, for which it appears that both the producer and the "higgler" attempt to spread risk by producing or handling a wide variety of products; in Oaxaca the tendency is to specialize.

3. Provisioning of the urban center or of a more distant region is not the primary function of the Oaxaca marketing system. Rather, its primary function is the interchange of goods between villages and subregions. The urban supply function is perhaps growing through the intermediate form of the *mercado,* but the *plaza* still is primarily a mechanism of intervillage exchange and is likely to continue to be so for some time to come.

4. Related to the foregoing, even most intravillage exchange occurs through the *plaza.* The small producer sells principally through the *plaza* rather than to residents in the same village, in part, at least, because he must patronize the *plaza* to buy goods he wants or needs, and in part because he depends upon the price-fixing functions of the *plaza* to ensure a proper return for his product.

5. The Oaxaca marketing system appears to handle an unusually large variety of both farm and handicraft products. This impression is not verifiable at present as complete lists are not published for many of the marketing systems described in the literature.

6. The *plaza* system serves both consumption and distribution functions. Apparently this is not uncommon, but it does differ from the situation in northeast Brazil described by Forman and Riegelhaupt (1970), where *feiras* (marketplaces) of distribution (producer to trader) and *feiras* of consumption (trader to consumer) are held separately. In this Brazilian instance, peasant-type production and the associated marketing system developed to supply a burgeoning export-oriented plantation system and its administrative and commercial cities. Hence the origins and functions of Brazilian and Oaxaca peasants and their respective marketing systems are entirely different.

7. In contrast to some other systems described, producers do not normally sell on credit.

8. On the production side, except for a few items with government price controls (government-warehoused maize, and in urban areas, meat), the producer's control of the prices at which he sells is impaired only by market considerations, unless he has accepted an advance price for a loan. The sharecropper normally controls the sale of his portion of the crop; if he pools his share for sale with the

landowner, this is an arrangement of convenience for one or both parties and not a condition imposed by the landowners.

9. The Oaxaca peasant appears to be much more preoccupied with economic factors and processes, especially price and market potentialities, than are buyers and sellers in most societies.

10. On the basis of present evidence, the principle of Limited Good advanced by Foster (1965, 1967) as a common characteristic of peasants in Middle America and elsewhere seems absent or of little importance. The Oaxaca peasant is well aware of the manifold opportunities for greater economic gain through expanding landholdings, expanding handicraft production, or entering trade on a part- or full-time basis. Although he sometimes attributes his own setbacks or the successes of others to "luck" or "fortune," he also is aware of the importance of frugality and savings, and skill, especially in trading activities.

11. Accumulation of wealth is accepted as a legitimate goal, and differences in wealth even within the village are accepted without *envidia* in economic matters (Foster 1967). This is not to say that envy, jealousy, or criticism of fellow villagers are not present (cf. Foster 1972), but that it is rarely expressed overtly and it is not economically motivated. Those accumulating wealth are criticized only if it is believed that they do not bear their proportionate responsibility in the ritual and civic concerns of the community. A man is criticized not for being well off but for lack of proper concern for the welfare of the village. This and the preceding statement need further investigation and may be modified in some of the village studies; but it would appear that in Oaxaca *envidia* is not a significant factor inhibiting individual enterprise.

These various unique features of the Oaxaca marketing system raise the question of the validity of some generalizations about peasant marketing systems. This might suggest that comparative studies of peasant marketing systems are not fruitful. Such a conclusion would be unjustified, as many of the special characteristics listed are attributable to unique regional situations and specific structural arrangements. Rather, these findings suggest that comparison should be based on the examination of processes. The Oaxaca case indicates that there are widespread economic processes and behaviors that may be examined usefully within the framework of formal economic analysis. The important criteria for comparison between peasant economies are the extent to which they exhibit similar economic processes and how these processes are modified by historical tradition and cultural variables. Such an approach will facilitate disentangling economic factors from the varied structural and institutional frameworks in which they operate, to deal with the discrete cultural and social matrices in which they are embedded. The result should permit sounder generalizations about peasant economies and exchange systems. The study of the Oaxaca marketing system also suggests that at the processual and behavioral level these generalizations will also be relevant to the development of a more comprehensive body of economic theory.

ADAPTATION AND THE FUTURE

A striking characteristic of the traditional Oaxaca marketing system is its vitality and adaptability in the face of the fairly massive impact of the modern industrializing and commercial national economy. In a sense, the modern economy has introduced a parallel and competitive distribution system with an expansion in the numbers and kinds of middlemen or full-time traders. The modern distribution system, however, does not compete directly, for primarily it brings to the town and to the village new kinds of goods that supplement rather than replace many of the goods handled in the traditional system. The competition is for a share of the peasant's *peso* rather than for all the custom served by the traditional marketing system. That this kind of competition can exist occurs in part because the modern economy has in a sense increased the quantity of *pesos* or buying power through the introduction of new techniques, encouragement of new kinds of peasant production, and expanded markets for peasant products. One aspect of the impact of the modern economy appears to be an improved standard of living.

Such an assertion is difficult to document adequately. By many criteria most people in the Oaxaca region are desperately poor, and there are many who by local standards live in misery, perhaps more in the City than in the villages. Many have to seek temporary work outside the region, for example, in the cane fields of Veracruz, to maintain their meager living levels. Yet over a long period of observation, it seems clear that many people in villages are better housed, better clothed, and perhaps even better fed than was so thirty or forty years ago. This is more true of the Valley than of the more remote villages of the Sierra, although there, too, change for the better is apparent. More objectively, these impressions are supported by the rise in wage levels in villages as well as in the City, and in seasonal shortages of farm labor in some villages.

The traditional marketing system of Oaxaca operates both as a unifying and a stabilizing force and as an agent for change. To paraphrase Chiñas, in Oaxaca heterogeneity is taken for granted. The ways of other villages are viewed as good for them, just as the ways of one's own village are good for its members. This is particularly true of economic activities; not only those of other villages but also members of one's own village may follow different paths to earning a living. Participation in the marketing system brings familiarity with alternative life styles and imposes a certain toleration for them, despite the occasional expressions of contempt, derision, or condescension by the Valley dweller for the *serrano,* or the town dweller for the *campesino.* The marketing system also makes possible continuance of economic diversity at the village level and the village's persistence as a small, close-knit social and cultural entity.

At the same time, the marketing system imposes its own conformities. Participants must learn to behave in ways appropriate to the marketing situation—ways often different from those appropriate to the village of residence. In a significant sense, the Oaxaca peasant lives in two cultures. At home he functions in a small, relatively homogeneous, and distinctive social unit. In the marketplace he must learn to interact without conflict with people from diverse backgrounds and to meet them in a variety of places. The regional character of the marketplace culture does not encourage innovations or change which might make movement of people between marketplaces more difficult.

Alternatively, the marketplace brings the village peasant into contact with new ways of life and exposes him to new cultural phenomena. Villagers in the marketplace exhibit a lively curiosity not only about prices, a basic part of the information network of the marketing system, but also about new products and technologies observable therein, and make preliminary evaluations of their possible utility in the village. For a minority, the marketing system affords an avenue for leaving the village and entering into the traditional intermarket trading activities or even, through the intermediate form of the *mercado,* entering into the modern economic system. Villagers enter commerce, become wage earners in factories, clerks, bookkeepers, or civil servants. The role of the marketplace as an agent of change, however, is partially limited by the aforementioned tolerance of diversity: curiosity about new things or new ways of behaving may not be accompanied by a desire to emulate.

The marketing system itself has shown considerable adaptability in the face of the modern economy. Not only have many new products come to be distributed through the traditional channels of trade, but also modern transportation has been fully accepted. Trucks and buses are almost universally used for the transport of goods and the movement of people, and many of these are owned by villagers. Few *viajeros* still drive burros; most use modern transportation. As a result, peasants find they can do several hours of work in the fields the same day that they attend the *plaza.* Traders and even producers of some handicrafts have used trucks or buses to seek out new marketplaces. Traders from San Antonino Ocotlán buy in Guanajuato and sell at the Guatemalan border.

The greatest immediate threat faced by the traditional marketing system seems to lie not in commercial competition from the modern economy but in the latter's growing political influence. Full-time traders in the Oaxaca City *mercado* seek to move the Saturday *plaza* to the outskirts of town or even to abolish it. More recently, the larger stores and commercial interests have agitated to move the central *mercado* itself away from the center of town to the outskirts. Either of these efforts, if successful, may be self-defeating, for the market is the main reason why many villagers and tourists come to the city. Abolition of the Oaxaca City *plaza,* I suggest, may result in moving much of the trading activity to other *plazas* in the Valley, especially Ocotlán and Tlacolula. Until the modern commercial distribution system provides as efficient a means for the essentially horizontal trade between villages, the traditional system probably will persist. In the Oaxaca area it still has considerable vitality and probably will survive indefinitely as an important factor in distribution. It will do so because marketplace vending requires a low capital investment and offers opportunities to a large number of people who are willing to accept a low standard of living or for whom no more attractive alternatives are available.

The impact of the modern economy has resulted in higher living standards and, for much of the population, higher living levels. It has stimulated higher living standards in part through newly created wants that can be satisfied through the modern distribution system. It also has furnished new alternatives in employment and migration. It has improved living levels by providing more reliable and larger markets for Oaxaca peasant products. Nevertheless, the steadily rising demographic pressures in recent times have prevented full realization of these possibilities, and the fact that the living levels of much of the population are still fairly low means that any economies of scale effected by the modern distribution methods are inadequate to compete with the traditional market system, at least for many products. The possibilities of improving one's economic position through emigration and education are more and more widely recognized, but any major decline in the peasant marketing system is unlikely so long as mounting population pressure on local resources acts to maintain its personnel.

Further evidence of the viability of the traditional peasant marketing system lies in the relative dependence of various sectors of the Oaxaca economy upon it. In the unlikely but still conceivable event that the modern sector of the economy, based largely outside the region, should suddenly revert to its pre-1940 level, the effects would be far more drastic for the towns and the City than for the village. Villagers would have to shift away from much of their market-oriented production. Coffee would bring a lower price and be more difficult to market, and the avocado export market would disappear. The burro would make a triumphant comeback. Tools would be scarcer and more expensive, and ready-made clothing, shoes, transistor radios, and a host of other industrial products would vanish. Outlets for surplus population would largely disappear and—perhaps the most drastic change of all—maize imports would cease. With all this, however, village specialization and the *plaza* system would survive, as an essential mechanism for intervillage exchange. The effect upon towns and the City would be far more drastic. Not only would they suffer the same losses as the villages, but also a very substantial part of their population would lose their means of livelihood. The *mercado* system would decline and most of the commercial distribution system of wholesalers and retail stores would lose its reason for being.

In contrast, instant abolition of the *plaza* system and its associated trading mechanisms would be catastrophic at all levels. Not only would continued village specialization be impossible but in most villages even many traditional items would be obtainable only by great individual effort as each consumer sought out distant sellers in many locations. In towns and in the City, food would be almost unobtainable, and a large part of the population would be unable to continue its present occupations. It would appear that at present, at least, the modern economy needs the *plaza* system more than peasant village economy needs the modern industrial-commercial world.

One possible threat to the *plaza* system may rest in the development of local industrial enterprise which could draw personnel away from small-scale production and sale. Santa María Atzompa, for example, now has a wool sweater factory employing some 60 local girls. This may have drastic effects upon the future production of Atzompa pottery and the market for woven men's jackets (*gabanes*) made in Diaz Ordaz and Santa Ana del Valle. Coupled with more commercially oriented farm production, such industrialization might undermine much of the village specialization that underlies the *plaza* system.[2]

A much more real threat to the *plaza* system lies in the continued "modernization" of the distribution system through increasing manipulation of demand through brand packaging and consumer-exploitative advertising such as is common in the United States. The trend in this direction is well developed in the national economy of Mexico and is visible in Oaxaca in such classes of goods as canned and packaged foods, cigarettes, beer and bottled soft drinks, and some pharmaceuticals.

Peasant markets are a frequent target of criticism and even outright attack by activists in the development field who point out that the low capitalization results in failure to develop economies of scale and involves a heavy use of manpower, with resulting high distribution costs. Such arguments do not take into account the absence of alternative opportunities available for manpower which might be released by modernization of the distribution system, and ignore the demand-manipulative and consumer-exploitative aspects of many modern distribution systems. It is far from certain that this is a good direction for the market to take from the standpoint of the Oaxaca peasant or even of the urban consumer. Certainly the question deserves more attention than it has thus far received, and

---

[2] According to a 1973 letter from Atzompa, this enterprise already has failed.

any light thrown upon it might tell us much about how well and how long the *plaza* system in Oaxaca may survive.

There is little doubt that the Oaxaca *plaza* system as well as peasant market systems elsewhere will continue to change under the impact of continuing industrialization. But it is at least an open question whether planners and "developers" should concentrate their efforts on promoting and accelerating changes in this sector of the distribution system. It may well be that in the long run they should devote their efforts to curbing or eliminating undesirable features in modern distribution systems.

Appendixes

P = Present; ? = Presence uncertain; D = Present, importance declining; I = Present, importance increasing; M = Present, minor importance; — = Absent.

I. PRODUCTIVE ROLES

A. Independent or semiindependent producers.

Mostly village dwellers or *campesinos,* usually thought of by city dwellers as farmers, but often earning their living by other means. Many of the rural nonfarming occupations also occur among city dwellers.

	Traditional	*Modern*
1. Farmer *(labrador* or *agricultor).* The classification here is based on access to land. Subsidiary roles also can be classified by crops (maize, beans, fruit, vegetables, flowers, coffee, agave, alfalfa, etc.); or by technology used (slash-burn, humid-land or dry farming, pot or well irrigation, ditch irrigation, flood plain irrigation, or pump irrigation). The various crops and techniques may require significant differences in production and marketing methods.		
a) Small landowner (*propietario*)		
(1) *Propietario*-cultivator who works his own land.	P	P
(2) *Propietario*-cultivator who hires labor to work his land.	P	I[1]
(3) *Propietario* noncultivator. Rents land on shares or occasionally for cash.	P	P
b) Cultivator with temporary use rights on public (usually village) land. Most common in the mountains.	P	P

APPENDIX 1 *(continued)*

    c) Cultivator of government-grant land *(ejidatario)*, with inheritable but not salable use rights on public lands belonging to a corporate body, the *ejido;* a post-Revolutionary phenomenon.   M   I

    d) Sharecropper *(mediero)*. Cultivates private lands or lands belonging to a village, on shares. The term is also applied to one who raises animals on shares.   P   P

    e) Cash renter *(arrendatario)*. This type of cultivator is rare because the landowner does not share crop risks.   ?   M

  2. Stock farmer. (Fowl and pigs may be raised by anyone, even in the city.)

    a) Raiser of cattle *(vaquero)* for meat or draft purposes.   P   P

    b) Sheep or goat raiser *(borreguero, chivero)*.   P   P

    c) Dairyman *(lechero)*. Sells milk or processed milk product, mainly cheese.   P   I

  3. Producer or gatherer of nonagricultural products (lumber, firewood, charcoal, lime, clay, soap root, wild fibers, fish and seafood; formerly, dyestuffs, e.g., cochineal and sea snails).   P   P

  4. Artisan *(artesano)*. Full-time or part-time specialist transforming raw materials for sale. Examples: producers of textiles, pottery, clothing, fiber products, wooden articles (e.g., spoons, bowls, benches, chests, chairs, tables, house beams, lumber, plows, carts, yokes, looms), iron work, metates, fireworks, adobe or fired brick, tile, basketry, and mats. Production of textiles, pottery, and similar goods includes a number of subspecialties. Such occupations as baker *(panadero)*, tortilla maker *(tortillera)*, or pot-still producer of mescal *(mezcalero)* are usually referred to by the occupation title.   P   P[2]

B. Service roles.

  1. Sellers of traditional specialized services: carpenter *(carpintero)*; mason *(albañil)*; stonecutter *(cantero)*; plow assembler *(aradrero)*; cart assembler *(carrocero)*; curer, wizard, witch *(curandero, hechicero, brujo)*; marriage arranger *(chigule* or *huehuete)*; midwife *(partera)*; butcher *(carniecero)*; barber *(peluquero)*; blacksmith *(herrero)*; musician *(músico)*; seamstress *(costurera)*; ox-team renter.   P P(D)

  2. Purveyors of modern specialized services: mechanic, teacher, medical and paramedical personnel, machinery salesman, fertilizer salesman, agricultural adviser.   —   I

C. Auxiliary roles.

  1. Laborer *(jornalero* or *mozo)*.[3] Unskilled or slightly skilled wage worker in agriculture or "industries." Some are iden-

tified by their work, such as *destejero* (worker who cuts and binds corn stalks for fodder, usually by contract); herdsman for cattle, sheep, or goats; or an apprentice or helper working with a mason, carpenter, baker, etc. — P P

2. Employee *(empleado)*.

    a) Employee of rural credit service, e.g., Banco Ejidal. — — I

    b) Employee of electrification, water supply, or similar program. — — I

    c) Non-manual employee in industrial enterprise, e.g., telephone operator, secretary, accountant, etc. — — I

C. Hacienda-based production roles.

  1. Hacienda owner *(hacendado)*. — P —[4]

  2. Hacienda supervisor *(mayordomo)*. — P —

  3. Worker attached permanently to hacienda *(peón)*. Usually received cultivation rights to a plot of land, and often small wages. — P —

  4. Sharecropper *(terrazguerro)*. Usually permanently bound to the hacienda. — P —

  5. Laborer *(mozo* or *jornalero;* terms interchangeable, the first commonly used by employer, the second by the worker). Often resided in village separate from the hacienda. — P —

  6. Specialized personnel. Artisans and skilled workers permanently employed by the hacienda. — P —

D. Roles in industrial activities or semi-industrialized ("rationalized") craft production. Found mostly in the city, also in towns and even villages. Each industry may include the following roles:

  1. Owner and/or manager *(empresario)*. — M I

  2. Worker *(jornalero* or *obrero)*. — M I

  3. Helper, apprentice *(mozo, aprendiz)*. — M I

Similar roles may be found among the self-employed or in family enterprises. Industrial activities and semi-industrialized craft production include:

Ceramic production	P	I[5]
Cotton textile manufacturing	P	I[2]
Woolen textile manufacturing	P?	I[2]
Production of ready-made clothing	P	P
Tanning	P?	M
Ixtle fiber extraction and processing	P?	I
Sandalmaking and shoemaking	P	P
Iron working	P	P
Industrial lime production	P	P
Operation of bakeries	P	I
Coffee processing	P	I

(handwritten note spanning cotton and woolen textile lines: *tourist mkt.*)

APPENDIX 1 *(continued)*

Cheese making	P	I
Maize, coffee, and chocolate milling	P	P
Flour production (mainly wheat; some production of bean, garbanzo, and maize flour, by individuals)	P	D
Brown sugar production *(trapiche* methods)	P	D⁵
Bottling of soft drinks	—?	I
Ices and ice cream production	P	I
Mescal production (industrialized)	P	I
Castor oil extration	P	P
Furniture making	P?	P
Soap manufacture	P	P

II. EXCHANGE ROLES

    A. Vendor of own goods *(propio)*. The term *"propio"* is usually applied to a producer who sells small and specialized stock away from the point of production, either in other villages as an itinerant or in a marketplace.   P   D⁷

    B. Reseller *(revendedor)*. In the broadest sense, anyone who buys and sells goods for a profit; often identified more specifically by the kind of goods sold or location of activities.

        1. Trader *(regatón)*, buying and reselling in the same village (rare); buying in one village and reselling in another; or buying anywhere and reselling in a *plaza,* usually following a regular cyclical route of *plazas.*   P   I

        2. Traveling trader *(viajero)*, a *revendedor* who travels long distances or to remote areas to buy and/or sell, transporting goods on his own back, or by pack animals, or on modern vehicles.   P   I

        3. Peddler *(ambulante)*. Small-scale retail vendor selling on streets or from door to door; stock small enough to carry with him; exempt from taxes unless he operates in a *mercado* building. *Ambulantes* are often difficult to distinguish from *propios* by observation.   P   I¹

        4. Vendor with fixed location, usually in a daily market *(locatario)*.   P   I

            a) Puestero. Daily vendor with fixed, unenclosed stall in a daily market structure or on the street.

            b) Casetero. Small retailer with enclosable permanent selling place *(caseta)* in a market structure or on a street.

        5. Storekeeper *(tendero)*. May own and operate a *tendejón,* a very small store in village, town or city; or a *tienda,* a fair-sized store, in village, town or city; or a large urban store called *almacén* or *bodega.* The owner of the latter may be denominated *"comerciante"* (literally, a merchant) and may be involved in wholesale operations.   P   I⁵

6. Wholesaler *(mayorista)*. One who buys or sells in large quantities, specializing in a limited variety of goods.

    a) Assembler or bulker *(acaparador)*, buying small quantities and selling in bulk. The term *"acaparador"* also is used pejoratively to identify a person who buys nonperishable goods, usually seasonal farm products, in quantity and stores them to force the price up; a hoarder. Government actions make hoarding increasingly rare.   P   P

    b) Bulk breaker. Wholesaler who buys in bulk and resells in smaller quantities. In Oaxaca, most bulk breakers deal only in goods from a distance and buy either from manufacturers or Mexico City wholesalers.   M   I

7. Field buyer. Entrepreneur or agent of a firm who buys directly from the producer at the point of production. For agricultural products, the field buyer may buy the standing crop and conduct the harvest. In villages, the storekeeper sometimes is agent for a *comerciante* or bulker in the city.   —   I

8. Agent *(agente)*. Traveling salesman for large enterprise who takes orders for regular customers. In smaller communities *agentes* usually travel about by car seeking buyers, using samples to take orders, and delivering merchandise personally.   P   I

9. Truck owner, usually driving own truck *(camionero-comerciante)*. Travels to buy goods for resale on full-time basis, or to secure a return load after making a delivery for a client. Differs from other truckers in that he takes risks and must have adequate liquid capital.   —   I

C. Exchange-facilitating roles.

  1. Transportation roles.

    a) Muleteer *(arriero)*. Drives burros or mules belonging to himself or to others to transport goods for others.   P   D

    b) Truck and bus transport roles.

      (1) Driver *(chofer)* of truck or bus owned by corporation, individual, or business. May be salaried or may be paid by trip. A *Chofer* may become an owner-driver in time.   —   I

      (2) Helper *(machetero)*. Assists truck or bus driver, and time may become a *chofer*.   —   I

      (3) Truck owner, who either drives his own truck or has a hired driver. Uses the truck in his own business, or carries freight, or combines the two.   —   I

      (4) Bus owner. Often belongs to a cooperative; if he owns more than one bus, he employs drivers.   —   I

      (5) Employee (dispatcher, bookkeeper, ticket seller,

APPENDIX 1 *(continued)*

mechanic) for corporate or cooperative freight or bus
line.   —   I

  c) Porter *(cargador)*. Carries goods locally for sellers or
  buyers.   P   P

2. Service roles.

  a) Commission agent *(comisionista)*. Businessman who
  handles buying and selling transactions for a flat fee,
  usually representing extraregional producers or buyers.
  Small-scale *comisionistas* operate betwen villages and
  plazas, but this activity is increasingly handled by bus   P
  drivers who are paid essentially in tips or gifts.   P   (D)

  b) Moneylender *(prestamista)*. Private lender of money at
  high interest rate; transactions rapid and with minimum
  red tape.   P   P

  c) Employee of a specialized credit agency such as a bank.   —   I

3. Auxiliary roles.

  a) Assistant *(jornalero* or *mozo)*. Helper to a *regatón* or others,
  usually for a daily wage.   P   I

  b) Storekeeper's staff.   M   I

  c) White-collar worker *(empleado)*. Includes bookkeepers,
  accountants, secretaries, etc.   M   I

  d) Public servant. Includes market administrator, collector, police, inspector of scales, sanitation inspector,
  meat inspector, street sweeper, garbage collector, etc.
  (mostly salaried or on regular wage).   M   I

III. OUTMIGRANTS *(EMIGRANTES)*.

Seasonal or contract workers in the sugarcane fields of Veracruz, the
cotton fields of southern Chiapas, or with the *bracero* program in the
United States, etc.; or, on a longer-term basis, domestic personnel,
blue- and white-collar employees in cities. Outmigrants are included here as a group because of their collective role in remitting
monies from other regions to family members in the home village,
and because migration is thought of as a distinct way of making or
supplementing a livelihood.   M   I

---

[1] Increase may reflect only population growth.

[2] Expansion of tourist or systematic export demand.

[3] Employers automatically use the term *mozo;* workers prefer the term *jornalero.*

[4] Absence may not be total. The 1969 Census shows 14 *"haciendas* or *fincas"* still present in the state of Oaxaca, but this form of landholding is essentially insignificant or absent so far as the Oaxaca market is concerned.

[5] Increases reflect expanded markets.

[6] Production formerly on haciendas growing own cane. Today most of the cane is bought by mills, often owned by *exhacendados.*

[7] Declining only because the number and percentage of producers selling at the point of production are increasing. The *total* number of *propios* is increasing through population increase.

APPENDIX 2

OCCUPATIONAL STATUSES AND THEIR DISTRIBUTION AMONG 327 MALE AND 29 FEMALE HEADS OF HOUSEHOLDS IN SAN SEBASTIAN TEITIPAC

(Adapted from Cook 1968:101)

Primary		Secondary		Tertiary or service	
Agric.					
1. Peasant (*campesino*) or tiller (*labrador*)	327	1. Butcher of cattle and goats (*carnicero*)	3	1. Shepherd (*pastor*)	7
2. Sheep raiser (*borreguero*)	2	2. Hog butcher (*tocinero*)	7	2. Castrator (*capador*)	
3. Cattle raiser (*vaquero*)	1	3. Wool shearer (*trasquilador de borrego*)	1	a. of bulls	3
4. Goat raiser (*chivero*)	8			b. of hogs	2
5. Beekeeper (*enjambrero*)	2			c. of goats	3
Total	**340**		**11**		**15**
Non-Agric.					
1. Metate maker (*metatero*)	42	1. Finisher of *manos* and metates (*labrador de mano y metate*)	13	1. Metate trader (*regatón de metates*)	10
2. Firewood cutter (*leñero*)	13	2. Tortilla maker and seller (*tortillera*)	58	2. Barber (*peluquero*)	4
3. Broom maker (*escobero*)	13	3. Miller (*molinero*)	1	3. Scribe (*escribano*)	2
4. Basket maker (*canastero*)	9	4. Blacksmith (*herrero*)	2	4. Storekeeper (*tendero*)	8
5. Charcoal maker (*carbonero*)*	8	5. Tailor (*sastre*)	3	5. Musician (*músico*)	24
6. Hut maker (*jacalero*)	8	6. Seamstress (*costurera*)	2	6. Drummer (*tamborillero*)	1
7. Adobe maker (*adobero*)	7	7. Baker (*panadero*)	3	7. Flutist (*chirimitero*)	2
8. Stonecutter (*cantero*)	7	8. Fireworks maker (*cohetero*)		8. Marriage broker (*huehuete*)	3
9. Well digger (*pocero*)	5	9. Adobe house builder (*albañil*)	6	9. Grave digger (*sepulturero*)	3
10. Maker of grinding stones for *nixtamal* mills (*labrador de piedra*)	4			10. Midwife (*partera*)	4
				11. Curer (*curandero*)	2

APPENDIX 2 (*continued*)

11. Tile maker (*ladrillero*)	1	10. Carpenter (*carpintero*)	1	12. Bone setter (*huesero*)	2
		11. Plow maker (*aradrero*)	8	13. Masseur (*sobador*)	5
		12. Wagon maker (*carrocero*)	3	14. Maseuse (*sobadora*)	3
		13. Harness maker			
		(*aparejero*)	2		
		14. Candle maker (*velero*)	4		

Total 117   107   73

* Prohibited by governmental decree and discontinued.

APPENDIX 3
Occupations in Tlacolula
(Adapted from Diskin 1967:144)

Agriculture

Farmer *(agricultor, campesino, labrador)*
Vegetable grower *(hortelano)*
Wage worker *(jornalero)*

Crafts and Services

Adobe maker *(adobero)*
Baker *(panadero, marquesotero))*
Basket maker *(cestero, canastero)*
Beef butcher *(tablajero)*
Brick maker *(ladrillero)*
Butcher *(carnicero)*
Candle maker *(velero)*
Carpenter *(carpintero)*
Fireworks maker *(cohetero)*
Gold worker *(orfebrero)*
Hatter *(sombrerero)*
Iron worker *(herrero)*
Mason *(albañil)*
Metate maker *(metatero)*
Pork butcher *(tocinero)*

Rope maker, cordage, and fiber pro-
    ducer *(mecatero, jarciero)*
Sandal maker *(huarachero)*
Shawl and napkin maker *(mantelero)*
Silver worker *(platero)*
Shoemaker *(zapatero)*
Solderer *(soldador)*
Tanner *(curtidor)*
Tin worker *(hojalatero)*

Trade

Businessman *(comerciante, negociante)*
Cattle dealer *(comprador-vendedor
    de ganado)*
Clerk *(empleado)*
Mescal dealer *(comprador-vendedor
    de mescal)*
Notions vendor *(mercero)*
Stallkeeper in plaza *(comerciante en
    pequeño)*
Storekeeper *(tendero)*
Trader in market *(regatón)*

APPENDIX 4
SUPPLEMENTARY SOURCES OF INCOME FOR POTTERS' FAMILIES
IN SANTA MARÍA ATZOMPA*

Corn mill ownership
Storekeeping
Butchering
White-collar work in Oaxaca
Farming
Pottery dealing
Employment with bus company in Oaxaca
Blue-collar work in Oaxaca and other towns
House construction
Moneylending
Truck driving (Atzompa trucks)
Periodic trading of older ox teams for younger ones
Animal raising for profit
Truck loading (Atzompa trucks)
Corn mill hand
Dressmaking
Mining clay and temper for resale
Vending in Atzompa marketplace
Ox team rental
Barbering
Buying wood for resale
Buying glaze in Oaxaca for resale in Atzompa
Seasonal contract work in other regions
Odd jobs in Oaxaca
Phonograph rental
Tortilla vending
Laundering

Purchasing unfired pots for finishing and sale
Milk and/or cheese vending
Egg vending
Herding
Burro rental
Odd jobs in Atzompa (making adobe bricks, helping mason, building fences, grinding glaze, carrying water, fetching kindling, fetching clay or temper, firing pots for others, substituting for citizen assigned to communal work projects)
Porter for Atzompa pottery dealers or local marketplace vendors
Tamale vending (occasional)
Chocolate vending
Oxcart rental
Buying soft drinks for resale
Glaze mill rental
Musician
Singing or praying for religious occasions
Slaughtering pigs for fiestas
Midwifery
Selling red dye (slip for washtubs)
Kiln building
Irregular work as field hand
Beekeeping; sale of honey and wax
Curing, traditional
Plow assembling
Marriage bokerage, traditional

* Roughly in order of profitability.

APPENDIX 5
EXTENT OF OAXACA MARKET SYSTEM
(Statistics from VIII *Censo General de Población*, 1960)

Exdistrito	Total population	Total number of municipios	INCLUDED IN THE OAXACA MARKET SYSTEM Number of municipios	Number of towns, villages and hamlets	Number of towns and villages with 500 or more inhabitants	Population
Centro	112,455	21	21	68	25	112,455
Choapan	20,318	6	1.5	10	2	2,969
Ejutla	32,594	13	13	55	24	32,594
Etla	56,414	23	19	84	29	48,403
Ixtlán	39,704	26	23	65	24	34,147
Juchitán	146,631	22	13	130	44	112,185
Miahuatlán	71,072	32	32	119	53	71,072
Mixe	49,260	17	17	76	34	49,260
Ocotlán	41,873	20	20	45	23	41,873
Tehuantepec	77,112	19	16.5	76	22	68,217
Tlacolula	62,373	25	25	129	24	62,373
Villa Alta	34,867	25	25	48	26	34,867
Yautepec	24,758	12	11	63	16	21,304
Zaachila	17,047	6	5	35	6	12,994
Zimatlan	36,768	13	13	41	18	36,768
			255	1,044	370	741,481

APPENDIX 6
INCOME SOURCES, OAXACA VILLAGES

I. PRODUCED IN ALL VILLAGES. Surplus above consumption needs is sold in market.

    A.   Maize: Individuals in any village may sell surplus to fellow villagers or in market. Only some villages regularly produce a net surplus for the market; other villages have a net deficit.

    B.   Maize fodder

    C.   Beans: Individuals in any village may have a surplus, but normally only villages (or individuals) that grow specifically for market have a surplus; many villages have a net deficit.

    D.   Squash (various varieties): Same as beans.

    E.   Animals   Burros   Chickens   Oxen   Pigs

II. FOODS AND RAW MATERIALS PRODUCED IN SOME VILLAGES ONLY. While some villages may produce the items listed only for internal consumption, each of the items listed is produced by one or more villages specifically for the market.

    A.   Special Crops

Agave (for fiber or mescal production)

Alfalfa

Alfalfa seed

Bananas (several types)

Barley

Beans (including several species of *Phaseolus,* especially varieties of the species *vulgaris*)

Beets

Broadbeans (Horsebeans, *Viscia faba*)

Cabbage

Cane (for house construction, fences, baskets)

Carrots

Castor beans

Cauliflower

Chard

Chayote

Cherimoya (a fruit)

Chick-peas (*garbanzos*)

Chile peppers

Citrus (limes, oranges, and grapefruit)

Coconuts

Custard apples

Figs

Flowers

Garlic

Gourds (*Lagenaria*)

Guaje (acacia beans, only semicultivated)

Guavas

Herbs

Jícama

Lentils

Lettuce

Loquats

Maguey (for fiber, mescal, pulque)

Maize, green

Mamey

Mangoes

Manioc

Melons

Nopal (a cactus), fruit

Nopal, leaves

Onions, green and dry

Palm nuts

Papaya

Passion fruit

Peanuts

Peas, dry

Peas, green

Pecan nuts

Pineapples

Pomegranate

Potatoes, regular (most only technically from Valley. Main source is around 3000 meter elevation)

Potatoes, sweet

Radishes

Sesame seed

Star apple

Sugarcane

Tobacco

Tomatoes, regular

Tomatoes, husk

Watermelon

Wheat

Zapote (plumlike fruits, four species)

Exclusive to some Sierra villages: chiles (some varieties), avocados, walnuts, deciduous fruits, coffee.

B. Animals

        Asses
        Bees
        Cattle (draft, dairy, and beef animals)
        Goats
        Horses
        Mules
        Sheep
        Turkeys

C. Animal Products

        Barbacoa (mutton or goat meat cooked in earth oven)
        Beef (dried and fresh)
        Beeswax
        Eggs
        Hides
        Honey
        Milk and milk products, mainly cheese (both cow and goat milk)
        Mohair
        Pork and pork products (cracklings, sausage, lard)
        Silk
        Wool

D. Processed Foods for Sale

        Bread
        Brown sugar *(panela)*
        Cakes and cookies
        Candies
        Flour (of wheat, maize, beans, and chick-peas)
        Maize products (tamales, tortillas, totopos)
        Mescal
        Squash seeds

E. Extractive Products

        Beeswax
        Broom and brush material
        Clay (for molding pottery and for slipping pottery)
        Copal
        Fish and shrimp (Isthmus and coast regions only)
        Game
        Grasshoppers (for food)
        Greens, wild
        Guajilote—legume pods
        Guayeniquil—legume pods
        Honey, wild
        Maguey worms
        Nanché (fruit)
        Onyx
        Salt (mainly Isthmian region)

APPENDIX 6 (*continued*)

Sand, stone, gravel

Tejocote (wild, crab applelike fruit)

Temper (for making pottery)

Tree gourds

Tree products (timber, firewood, pitch pine, copal, thatching materials)

F.   Processed Raw Materials (Nonfood Items) and Handicrafts

Baskets (many types—of cane or palm leaf)

Bottle gourd, dippers

Brick (fired or unfired adobe)

Brooms and brushes (mostly Sierra region)

Candles (handmade, often of beeswax, including decorated *mayordomía* candles)

Fireworks

Hats (felt or palm leaf)

Hide and leather products

Ironwork (forged items, e.g., plow points)

Jarciería (maguey fiber products such as rope, cord, nets, bags, harnesses)

Lime (for maize preparation)

Mats (tule or palm leaf)

Metates and manos

Pottery (many sizes, shapes, and qualities; four communities only in Valley, plus Oaxaca City)

Textiles, handloomed (serapes, *gabanes,* pelusa [wool and mohair], belts and sashes, rebozos, cotton cloth)

Tile (for roofing)

Wood products

   Carts and cart parts

   Charcoal

   Containers (spoons, bowls, troughs, trunks)

   Furniture (stools, benches, chairs, tables, beds)

   House parts (timbers, posts rafters, beams, planks)

   Ox yokes

   Plows and plow parts

III. SERVICES.

A.   Transportation (porterage, trucking, buses)

B.   Selling special skills (masonry, carpentry, cart building, plow making, loom making, stone working, blacksmithing, witchcraft, curing, marriage arrangement, barbering, music)

C.   Selling unskilled labor (to neighbors in other villages, in Oaxaca, in Veracruz, in Mexico City, in the United States [when possible], and in mining and industrialized lumbering operations).

Note: Some villagers derive much of their income from commercial activities. These are discussed in connection with the functioning of the market.

APPENDIX 7
Village Specializations
(Information from various sources)

Ca = Cañada (north of valley); Co = Coastal region; I = Isthmus; M = Mixteca; S = Eastern Sierra; SW = Western Sierra.

Village or town	Products for market
Abasolo	Baskets, large *piscador* baskets, brooms, cattle, cheese, chile de agua, cumin, flowers, garlic, herbs, milk, onions, oregano, peanuts, peas, string beans, tomatoes
Alotepec (S)	Coffee
Amatengo	Mescal
Amatlán	Walnuts
Analco, San Juan (S)	Huaraches, peaches, quince, walnuts
Animas Trujano	Alfalfa, castor beans, maize, milk
Atempa, San Blas (I)	Bananas, coconuts, mangoes, sesame, tortillas, totopos
Atepec (S)	Apples, avocados, quince, walnuts
Atzompa	Beans, castor beans, chick-peas, maize, peas, pottery
Banda, La	Castor beans, maize
Betaza (S)	Avocados, beans, chile onza, clothing, coffee, ollas, silk products *East of Zoogocho in Villa Alta*
Cacalotepec (S)	Avocados, bananas, beans, coffee
Calpulalpán (S)	Bread
Castillo Velasco: see San Antonino Ocotlán	
Chichicapan	Wool thread
Chilar (Ca)	Mangoes
Chimaltepec (S)	Chile
Cienega, La: Zimatlán	Brown sugar, dairy products
Clavellinas	Apples, chilacayote (squash), granadilla, pears, pomegranates
Coixtlahuaca (M)	Potatoes
Coyotepec, San Bartolo	Pottery
Cuajimoloyas	Broad beans, gladiolas, peas, pitch pine, potatoes
Cuatro Venados, San Pablo (SW)	Apples, peaches, pitch pine, tejocote fruit
Cuicatlán (Ca)	Chicozapote, chile, gourds, lemons, mangoes, papaya, tomatoes
Cuilapan de Guerrero	Chile, husk tomatoes, jícama, peanuts, peas, pecans, squash, tomatoes
Diaz Ordaz	Jackets, sapodilla fruit, wheat, wood beams
Donaji	Tomatoes
Ejutla de Crespo	Black beans, castor beans, castor oil, chick-peas, eggs, maize, palm-leaf mats, tanned hides, tomatoes
Emiliano Zapata	Alfalfa, beans, maize

APPENDIX 7 *(continued)*

Etla, San Pablo	Baskets, bread, castor beans, cheese, chick-peas, gourds, milk, peas, maize, tomatoes, wheat, white beans, wood beams
Guadalupe Etla	Dairy products
Guelaviá, San Juan	Baskets, cattle, goats, hogs, maize, sheep, wheat
Guelavia, San Baltazar	Ixtle, rope, woven palm products
Guelaxe, Santa María	Cheese, chile de agua, cumin, flowers, garlic, milk, onions, oregano, string beans, tomatoes
Guendulain	Peas, wool
Guilá, San Pablo (S)	Beans, castor beans, chilacayote, gourds, mats, mescal, rope, tomatoes
Guiloxi (S)	Avocados, flowers, oregano, peaches, pears, pomegranates
Huave-speaking villages (I)	Fish and shrimp, salt
Huila: see Guilá	
Huitzo, San Pablo	Cattle, diversified economy
Ixtepeji (S)	Walnuts
Ixtlán de Juárez (S)	Bread, meat, quince
Jalapa del Valle	Chile, house poles and beams, tomatoes
Jalpan, San Raymundo	Peanuts, pecans, tejate (maize drink), tortillas
Jaltianguis (S)	Apples, cuajiniquiles, mamey, mangoes, peaches, quince, squash
Julapilla (?)	Tomatoes
Juquila, Santa Catarina (M)	Gourd cups
Juquila Vijanos (S)	Avocados, coffee, maize
Lachichina (S)	Bananas, clothing, *piscador* baskets, sugarcane
Lachigolo, San Francisco	Alfalfa, baskets, beans, cattle, chick-peas, dairy products, flowers, greens, maize, tomatoes
Lachiroag (S)	Aguardiente, brown sugar, carrots, chilimoleras, coffee, garlic, herbs, onions, parsley, wood products, zapotes
Laxopa (S)	Avocados, chayote, flowers, ixtle, maize, oregano, peaches, peas, pitch pine, potatoes, wood products
Macuiltianguis (S)	Clothing, maize, peaches, pottery *In sierra north*
Macuilxochitl, San Mateo	Castor beans *of Oaxaca; no road*
Magdalena Apasco	Dairy products, lumber
Magdalena Ocotlán	Goat cheese, metates
Magdalena Teitipac	Beans, castor beans, mescal, palm-leaf mats, peas, metates, wheat
Matatlán, Santiago	Cattle, maguey, mescal
Matias Romero (I)	Pixtle (mamey nut used in maize drinks)
Miahuatlán	Bananas, baskets, beans, castor beans, coffee, coquitos, palm-leaf mats and rain capes, pineapples, plums, tomatoes, wooden tubs

Mitla	Bread, clothing, mescal, rebozos, serapes
Mixe region (S)	Apples, avocados, beans, chile, coffee, peaches, pitch pine, pixtle, potatoes, tejocote fruit
Mixistlán (S)	Pottery
Mixteca region (SW)	Baskets, canary grass, chile, palm-leaf hats, wool
Mogoñé (I)	Pineapples
Natividad (S)	Maize, pottery
Nazareno Etla	Baskets, cheese, milk
Nejapa (near Isthmus)	Watermelon
Nochixtlán (M)	Canary grass, palm-leaf mats and fans, tomatoes, wool
Oaxaca de Juárez	Baskets, blankets, chickens, cheese, chocolate beaters, ceramics and china, bread and cake, furniture, ironware, engraved knives, husk tomatoes, lumber, mullers, mineral lime, meat, mirrors, soft drinks, sacks, net bags, shovels, plowshares, tinware, turkeys, textiles, clothing, tortillas
Ocotepec (S)	Coffee
Ocotlán de Morelos	Baskets, beans, castor beans, cattle, chickens, chile seco, chocolate beaters, eggs, husk tomatoes, maize, pottery, sugarcane, wool
Otatitlan (S)	Avocados, beans, chile, clothing, coffee, maize *can't find*
Panzacola (Santa Rosa)	Alfalfa
Peñoles (SW)	Apples, charcoal, peaches, wooden doors and other wood products
Porvenir, El (S)	Avocados, chile, coffee, firewood, salt, squash, sugarcane
Praxedis Guerrero	Chile, gourd cups, husk tomatoes
Quetzaltepec (S)	Chile
Quialana, San Bartolo	Beans, castor beans, charcoal, firewood, flowers, herbs, husk tomatoes, ixtle, maize, tomatoes, wool
Raya del Cármen, La (?)	Pears, wool
Rio Hondo (Yautepec)	Hides, pigs
Roalo	Castor beans, chile, goat cheese and milk, peanuts, tomatoes
Rojas de Cuauhtemoc	Alfalfa, dairy products, garlic, tomatoes
Salina Cruz (I)	Fish, coquitos, lobster
San Agustín de las Juntas	Tortillas
San Andrés Yaá (S)	Avocados, chile onza, coffee, peaches, tomatoes
San Andrés Zautla	Milk
San Andrés Peras (SW?)	Apples
San Antonino Ocotlán (Castillo Velasco)	Cabbage, carrots, flowers, garlic, husk tomatoes, milk, onions, tomatoes
San Antonio de la Cal	Mineral lime
San Baltazan Buelavila: see Guelavila	
San Bartolo Coyotepec: see Coyotepec	

APPENDIX 7 (*continued*)

San Bartolo Quialana: see Quialana	
San Dionisio Ocotlán	Beans, mescal
San Felip Tejalapan	Charcoal, clay for pottery, eggs, firewood, tomatoes, wheat
San Francisco Cajonos (S)	Avocados, castor beans, chick-peas, chile, lemons, maguey, mangoes, oranges, peas, potatoes
San Francisco Lachigolo: see Lachigolo	
San Francisco Telixtla-huaca	Tomatoes
San Francisco Yaté: see Yaté	
San Isidro (S)	Coffee
San Isidro Ocotlán	Goat cheese
San Jacinto Amilpas	Grapefruit, guavas, husk tomatoes, lemons, limes, milk
San Jacinto Ocotlán	Milk
San Juan Analco: see Analco	
San Juan de Diós	Alfalfa
San Juan del Estado	Lumber, oxcarts
San Juan Guelavia: see Guelavia	
San Juan Tabaa (S)	Avocados, bananas, beans, chile onza, coffee, loquats, maize, mangoes, oranges, pineapples, squash, tomatoes
San Juan Teitipac	Broad beans, castor beans, kidney beans, chick-peas, chile, metates, peas, cattle
San Juan Yaee (S)	Avocados, beans, chayote, coffee, squash, sugarcane
San Juan Yatzona (S)	Coffee
San Lázaro Etla	Dairy products, flowers
San Lorenzo Albarradas (S)	Charcoal, goatskins, wood, woven palm products
San Lorenzo Cacaotepec	Alfalfa, clay for pottery, grapefruit, limes, milk, *piscador* baskets
San Lucas Quiavini	Beans, charcoal, firewood, husk tomatoes, mescal
San Marcos Tlapazola	Apples, beans, castor beans, cheese, chick-peas, jerked beef, onions, oranges, peaches, pottery
San Martín (?)	Husk tomatoes
San Miguel Albarradas (S)	Beans, charcoal, cheese, house beams, pitch pine
San Miguel Cajonos (S)	Chile, coffee, ixtle, lemons, oranges, potatoes
San Miguel del Valle	Beans, chilacayote, house poles and beams, peaches, pitch pine, wheat, wooden tables
San Pablo Cuatro Vena-dos: see Cuatro Venados	

San Pablo Etla: see Etla

San Pablo Huixtepec   Alfalfa, chick-peas, chile verde, maize, tomatoes

San Pablo Tijaltepec (M)   Eggs, hens, palm-leaf mats

San Pedro Apostol   Anvils, baskets

San Pedro Cajonos (S)   Apples, castor beans, chile, coffee, fruit, potatoes, tomatoes, woven palm products

San Pedro Tidaá (M)   Wooden spoons

San Raymundo Jalpan: see Jalpan

San Sebastian Ocotlán   Cabbage, carrots, flowers, garlic, husk tomatoes, milk, onions, tomatoes

San Sebastian Teitipac   Baskets, brooms, castor beans, chickens, chilimoleras, gourds, metates, peanuts, pottery

Santa Ana del Valle   Black beans, jackets, peaches, serapes

Santa Ana Zegache   Black beans,

Santa Catarina Albarradas (S)   Beans, cheese, hammocks, maize, pitch pine, rope products

Santa Cecilia Jalieza   Wooden spoons

Santa Cruz Mixtepec   Milk

Santa Cruz Papalutla   Castor beans, hogs, maize, onions, tortillas, yokes for oxen, wheat

Santa Inés del Monte   Apples

Santa Lucía Ocotlán   Laborers

Santa María Atzompa: see Atzompa

Santa María del Tule: see Tule

Santa María Guelaxe: see Guelaxe

Santiago Apostol   Cabbage, carrots, flowers, garlic, husk tomatoes, milk, onions, tomatoes

Santiago Etla   Custard apples, dairy products, guavas

Santiago Ixquintepec (S)   Brooms and other stiff grass products

Santiago Ixtaltepec   Castor beans

Santiago Lalopa (S)   Beans, brown sugar, coffee, maize, sugarcane

Santiago Suchilquitongo: see Suchilquitongo

Santiago Tenango (SW)   Baskets

Santiago Tlazoyaltepec (SW)   Apples metate-cleaning brushes, peaches, pears, pine cones, sweet potatoes

Santo Domingo Albarradas (S)   Beans, cheese, fowl, maize, pitch pine, wheat

Santo Domingo Yojoui: see Yojoui

Santo Tomás Jalieza   Wide belts (*fajas*) Cooperative

Santo Tomás Lachitaá (S)	Avocados, bananas, beans, griddles, maguey, maize, mangoes, tomatoes
Santo Tomás Mazaltepec	Eggs, firewood, livestock, yokes for oxen
Sierra Juárez region (S)	Apples, avocados, peaches, plums, tejocote fruit, walnuts, white potatoes
Solaga (S)	Avocados, castor beans, chile, coffee, gourds, mangoes, ollas, oranges, peaches, squash, sugarcane, wood
Soledad, La: Atzompa	Milk
Soledad Etla	Dairy products
Suchilquitongo, Santiago	Black beans, gourds, tomatoes
Tabehua (S)	Beans, chile onza, maize, ixtle, mangoes, guavas, oranges
Talea (S)	Huaraches, maize, pottery, salt
Tamasulapan (S)	Avocados, chile, coffee
Tanivé	Milk
Tehuantepec (I)	Baskets, chicozapote, coconut, coquitos, dried fish and shrimp, lemons, mangoes, palm leaf
Tejas de Morelos	Goat cheese, sugarcane
Temaxcalapa (S)	Coffee, maize
Teotitlán del Valle	Chayote, chilacayote, clothing, custard apples, flowers, pataste, pixtle, plow tongues, serapes
Tepantlali (S)	Avocados, oranges
Tepustepec (S)	Avocados, beans, castor beans, goats
Tlacochahuaya	Alfalfa, brooms, chile, cumin, flowers, garlic, onions, oregano, string beans, tomatoes
Tlacolula	Alfalfa, baskets, bread, cheese, chickens, chicle, clothing, herbs, huaraches, meat products, palm products pottery, metates, raw wool, roof tiles, rope and other ixtle items, tinware, tomatoes
Tlahuitoltepec (S)	Avocados
Tlalixtac de Cabrera	Alfalfa, milk
Tlanichix	Husk tomatoes
Tomaltepec, Santo Domingo	Bread
Tomellín (Ca)	Tomatoes
Totolapam	Chicozapote, lemons, watermelon
Trinidad, La (S)	Peanuts, beans, charcoal, chick-peas, chile de onza, squash, walnuts
Tule	Alfalfa
Union Zapata (Loma Larga)	Milk
Villa Alta (S)	Avocados, brown sugar, chile, clothing, coffee, huaraches, maize, onions, tomatoes
Villa Hidalgo: see	

Yalálag	
Xaagá	Firewood
Xagacía (S)	Rope
Xiacui (S)	Charcoal, fruit, lumber
Xochixtepec (S)	Avocados, mescal, pulque
Xoxocotlán	Husk tomatoes, peanuts, squash, tomatoes, turkeys, walnuts
Yabicilla (S?)	Walnuts
Yagallo (S)	Mangoes, onions, oranges, peas
Yahuiche	Alfalfa, tomatoes
Yahuio (S)	Chayote, cherries, cordage, maize, oregano, peaches
Yalalag (Villa Hidalgo) (S) *Silk*	Bread, chile seco and chile de onza, eggs, firecrackers, hats, huaraches, leather for shoe soles, cordage, meat, onions, pottery, rebozos, tanned hides, roof tiles *in Villa Alta*
Yalina (S)	Adobe, avocados, beans, castor beans, chickens, coffee, huaraches, maize, peaches, potatoes, sugarcane, wood products
Yatateni, San Agustín	Tomatoes
Yaté (S)	Avocados, bananas, beans, coffee, maize, mescal, onions, peas, sugarcane, tomatoes, brown sugar
Yatoni (S)	Avocados, coffee
Yatuni (S)	Potatoes
Yatzachi el Alto (S)	Avocados, chilacayote, chile onza, fowl, maguey, mescal, tomatoes
Yatzachi el Bajo (S)	Avocados, chile onza, fowl, ixtle, maguey, mangoes, mescal, squash, tomatoes
Yautepec district (near Isthmus. See also Rio Hondo.)	Cattle, watermelons
Yavesia (S)	Apples, peaches, pears, wooden chairs and tables
Yohuechi (S)	Bananas, beans, chile onza, ixtle, maguey, maize, mangoes, mescal, pulque, tomatoes
Yojoui	Baskets, tomatoes
Zaachila	Apples, bananas, beans, castor beans, chickens, chile, flowers, husk tomatoes, maize, melons, jícama, peanuts, pecans, soap, sugarcane, tomatoes, walnuts, meat products
Zacatepec (S)	Coffee
Zimatlán	Apples, bananas, beans, brown sugar, castor beans, chickens, chile, flowers, husk tomatoes, milk, peaches, peanuts, sugarcane, tomatoes
Zoochila (S)	Beans, bread, chayote, ixtle
Zoochina (S)	Beans, chile onza, ixtle, maize
Zoogocho (S)	Avocados, chile onza, firecrackers, ixtle pack straps, sugarcane

APPENDIX 8
ALTERNATIVES IN MAIZE FARMING
(Examples from Santa María Atzompa)

Minimizing cash input:

Request government grant land *(ejido)* rather than purchase or rent land.

Give private lands for sharecropping, eliminating cost of ox team and releasing corn stalks and husks (fodder) for sale.

Perform labor oneself, with household members, or reciprocate labor with other households.

Cart the harvest with own oxcart or, lacking an oxcart, with hired oxcart, rather than with hired truck. (Small harvest may be carted on burro back.)

Minimizing time input:

Prepare land with hired tractor, reducing substantially the time required for plowing.

Give private lands for sharecropping, or hire ox team with driver for land preparation and hilling, rather than perform these tasks oneself.

Use hired labor rather than household labor for farm work.

Sell harvest in bulk to wholesalers.

Contract out the gathering of corn stalks for fodder, or sell stalks from the field (buyer cuts them).

Maximizing yield:

Sow subsidiary crop(s) in field with maize; usually, beans and squash, or castor beans are sown between maize plants.

Sow maize twice annually, or rotate maize with another crop, weather and soil quality permitting.

Haul manure to fields for fertilizer.

Purchase chemical fertilizer.

Ditch for irrigation, if streams are running.

Dig well and buy or rent pump for irrigation.

Maximizing returns:

Sell harvest to individuals locally for highest return, or from a stand in the city marketplace

Some cash costs, 1968:

Maize seed: $5 per *almud* - need 4 per hectare

Ox team: $2000 to $3000

Wooden plow: $75

Steel plow: $375

Oxcart: $2500 new

Tractor hire: $150 per hectare

Ox team hire: $20 to $25 per half day

Oxcart hire: $10 per trip
Truck hire: $30 to $50 per trip
Chemical fertilizer: $45 per hectare
Irrigation pump: $5,000
Laborer's wage: $10 per day plus meals

Some time costs
(per hectare):

Land preparation and furrowing: 15 to 25 man-days*
(only 5 to 6 man-days if tractor is used)
Sowing: approximately 12 man-days for humid *(humedad)*
lands, approximately 6 man-days for seasonal *(temporal)*
lands.
First hilling and weeding: 6 to 9 man-days
Second hilling: 2 to 4 man-days
Harvesting: 5 to 6 man-days

Expected yield per hectare, one sowing:

	Shelled Maize	*Stalks*	*Husks*
First-class land	15 to 24 fanegas,** at approximately $96 the fanega when sold in bulk	200 bunches minimum, 750 bunches maximum, at $1 the bunch	1/2 cart to 4 carts at $120 to $200 the cart
Second-class land, good year	20 fanegas	Same	Same
Second-class land, average year	10 to 12 fanegas	Same	Same
Third-class land, good year	5 fanegas	Same	Same
Third-class land, poor year	3 fanegas	Same	Same

* Work day of 5 to 6 hours, often referred to as "a half day."
** A fanega is about 2.7 bushels here.

APPENDIX 9

ALTERNATIVES FOR FARMERS IN SANTA MARÍA ATZOMPA
(Prepared by Charlotte Stolmaker)

Sample of 80 families includes 69 potters: 33 holding lands under cultivation, 3 holding lands not under cultivation, and 2 landless sharecroppers (the remainder being landless noncultivators); 7 full-time farmers; one landholding family combining blue-collar work with farming; one landless schoolteacher; one landless day laborer; and one landless storekeeper-truck driver. Thus, 43 were entitled to crops, as cultivators or landholders or both. Of these 41 were landholders and 30 were active cultivators.[1]

Cultivation	Pot-ters	Non-potters	Total
Active cultivators using plow and oxen for annual land clearing	16	3	19
Active cultivators using hired tractor for annual land clearing	7	4	11
			30
Landholders using own ox team for cultivating	14	5	19
Landholders using hired ox team for cultivating	4	1	5
Landholders using own ox team and hired driver	1		1
Landholders using sharecroppers	14	1[2]	15
Landholders using own ox team with hired driver, plus sharecroppers		1	1
			41
Cultivators and/or landholders bringing in crop by oxcart or for small crops, by burro	26	6.5[3]	32.5
Cultivators and/or landholders bringing in crop by hired truck	9	1.5[3]	10.5
			43.0
Disposal of produce			
Sell in the village	10	2	12[4]
Sell in the city	5	4	9
Sell both in the village and in the city	1	1	2
Claim they do not sell	19	1	20
			43[5]

[1] "Landholding" includes holding of both fields and *ejido*.
[2] Landholder uses sons as sharecroppers.
[3] One landholder brings in winter crop by hired truck, summer crop by hired oxcart.
[4] One, a storekeeper, sells from his store. The others sell from their homes.
[5] Differences in totals reflect incomplete answers.

no surplus?

potters tend to let land on shares — compare with Novelo on Capula

APPENDIX 10
INPUT ALTERNATIVES IN POTTERY PRODUCTION
(Examples from Santa María Atzompa)

Minimizing cash input:	Mine clay oneself
	Mine temper material oneself
	Sell pots crude to avoid cost of glaze and wood (for firing), or work as employee, eliminating all cash input
	Buy glaze in city for minimal price
	Fetch firewood oneself (least cost), or buy from itinerant vendor
Minimizing time input:	Buy clay from resellers, or send laborer (*mozo*) to dig it
	Buy temper material from resellers, or send laborer to dig it
	Buy glaze from local resellers
	Buy firewood from itinerant vendor or local reseller, rather than fetch it
	Store up Mexican sunflower (*acahual*) for kindling, when it is plentiful, thereby reducing time spent fetching kindling when it is scarce, or
	Use large firewood for both bisque and glaze firings*
	If glaze is to be milled in the village for thicker mixture, hire labor for milling
	Contract with dealer for bulk delivery of finished pots
Maximizing profit:	Mine clay and temper material oneself
	Use large quantity of glaze, or extra-thick glaze, which may require milling it oneself
	Include both men and women in pot-shaping stage of production, to maximize household's time use
	Buy crude ware for finishing and resale
	Sell at stand for maximum prices
Some cash costs, 1967–1968:	Clay, at mines: $3 and $5 the burro load
	Clay, from reseller: $12 to $15 the burro load**
	Tempering material: 0
	Temper material from reseller: $2 to $5 the burro load

APPENDIX 10 *(continued)*

   Laborer for mining: $2 to $7 plus meals

   Glaze, liquid, mixed with coloring agent: $6.00 per kilogram in the city, $6.50 per kilogram in the village

   Glaze, pulverized: $5.00 the kilogram in the city, $5.50 per kilogram in the village

   Laborer for milling glaze: $1 per kilogram (about $6 per firing) plus meals

   Glaze mill rental fee: $1 to $2 per task

   Firewood, from itinerant vendors: $7.50 to $8.00 the burro load

   Firewood, from local resellers: $10 the burro load

Representative time costs:

   Mining clay: 1/2 to 1 day per week

   Mining temper material: 1 or 2 half days per week

   Fetching glaze from city: 4 hours per firing

   Fetching firewood from Valley foothills: 10 to 12 hours per firing

   Fetching kindling: approximately 2 half days per firing

   Firing bisque, glazing, refiring: 1 day

   Milling glaze: 3 to 6 hours per firing

---

* It is customary to use light wood for bisque firing and large wood for glaze firing, the latter requiring a higher temperature.

** Reseller's price independent of mine fee.

POTTERY PRODUCTION IN SANTA MARÍA ATZOMPA:
ALTERNATIVES IN PROCUREMENT OF MATERIALS

(69 Potters)

CLAY

	Seek own clay		Purchase from reseller		Send hired band		Obtain clay from buyer of crude ware
	Always	Sometimes	Always	Sometimes	Always	Sometimes	
S. Lorenzo Cacaotepec mines	9	3	9	1	-	-	1
S. Felipe Tejalapan mine	11	6	18	8	3	1	
Communal lands	5	4	-	-	1	1	

Price at the San Lorenzo Cacaotepec mines is 3 pesos the burro load; at the San Felipe Tejalapan mine, 5 pesos the burro load; in the communal lands, nil. Resellers receive 10 to 15 pesos. Hired hands received 2 to 5 pesos (with meals in two cases), and one takes his pay in half the load and use of the "buyer's" burro to transport it.

TEMPERING MATERIAL

	Seek own temper		Purchase from reseller		Send hired band		Use no temper	Obtain temper from buyer of crude ware
	Always	Sometimes	Always	Sometimes	Always	Sometimes		
S. Lorentepec mines	6	-	2	-	-	-	1	2
S. Catarina Montaño mines	37	-	10	-	5	-		
Communal lands	5	-	1	-	-	-		

Santa Catarina Montaño mines are also in the common lands, but within a hamlet of the *municipio*. Price at the San Lorenzo Cacaotepec mines is 2 pesos the burro load; at the Santa Catarina Montaño mines and in the common lands generally, nil. Resellers charge 2 to 5 pesos the burro load; hired hands receive 2 to 5 pesos (with meals in two cases). Two take half the load in payment and use the "buyer's" burro.

GLAZE

	Buy liquid glaze from Oaxaca dealer	Buy liquid glaze from Atzompa dealer	Buy powdered or solid glaze from Oaxaca dealer	Buy powdered or solid glaze from Atzompa dealer	Use no glaze
Always	20	29	3	5	9
Sometimes	1	1	1	3	

WOOD

	Buy from S. Felipe Tejalapan vendors	Buy from Atzompa dealers	Buy from S. Tomás Mazaltepec vendors	Buy from S. Pedro Ixtlahuaca vendors	Travel to S. Pablo Cuatro venados	Do not use wood
Always	38	15	1	1	2	8
Sometimes	4	3	-	1		

All "vendors" are itinerant, sell in the village. Potters selling crude ware and some griddle makers (who use kindling only) need no wood.

APPENDIX 12
ANNUAL MAIZE PRODUCTION INPUTS
(Selected Examples from Atzompa, 1968)

Case 1. Full-time farmer

Investments in major equipment:	Steel plow for preparing land	$	250
	Wooden plow for furrowing and cultivating		75
	Ox team		3000
	Oxcart		800
		(bought in 1950)	

Inputs per hectare, 1968 costs:

	Humid lands		*Seasonal lands*	
	Time	*Expense*	*Time*	*Expense*
Seed: Kernels remaining from previous harvest, worth $20 (4 almuds).				
Preparing land:	25 days, landowner only	0	25 days, landowner only	0
Sowing:	2 days, landowner and 4 hands	$80	3 half days, landowner and 1 hand	$15
First hilling and weeding:	4 half days, sometimes less, landowner and 1 hand	$20	3 half days, landowner and 1 hand	$15
Second hilling:	4 half days, landowner only	0	3 half days, landowner only	0
Harvesting:	1 day, landowner and 4 hands	$40	1 day, landowner and 4 hands	$40
Cutting stalks:	6 days in the early mornings only, landowner and sons	0	6 days in the early mornings only, landowner and sons	0
Tying stalks:	2 mornings, landowner and sons	0	2 mornings, landowner and sons	0
Hauling:	1 part day, landowner and sons	0	1 part day, landowner and sons	0

Case 2. Full-time farmer

Investments in major equipment:	Steel plow	$	375
	Wooden plow		75
	Ox team		3500
	Ox cart (loaned by father)		0

Inputs per hectare, 1968 costs (all lands are humid lands):

APPENDIX 12 (*continued*)

	Time	*Expense*
Seed: Kernels remaining from previous harvest, worth $20 (4 almuds)		
Preparing land:		
Tractor hire	1 day, tractor driver only	$150
Plowing, furrowing	6 days, landowner only	0
Sowing:	1 day, landowner and 8 hands	$ 96
First hilling and weeding:	2 half days, landowner and 3 hands	$ 30
Second hilling:	3 half days, landowner and family	0
Harvesting:	1 day, landowner and 6 hands	$ 72
Cutting and tying stalks:	Time input unknown; job awarded on contract basis	$40 to 50
Hauling:	1 part day, landowner and family	0

Case 3. Potter-farmer

No equipment investment

Inputs per half hectare, 1968 costs (all land is humid land):*

	Time	*Expense*
Seed:		$10
Preparing land:		
Tractor hire	1 day, tractor only	$110 (tractor hire)
Plowing	5 half days, ox team driver	$75 (ox team hire)**
Furrowing and sowing:	1 part day, landholder, ox team driver, 2 hands	$35
First hilling and weeding:	1 half day, landholder, ox team driver, 2 hands	$35
Second hilling:	1 half day, ox team driver	$15
Harvesting:	1 day, landholder and 2 hands	Approximately $40 in maize
Cutting stalks:	1 half day, landholder and 2 hands	$20
Tying stalks:	1 half day, landholder and family	0
Hauling:	1 part day, landholder and truck driver	$30 (truck hire)

* Tractor cost was $35 more than is normal for a half hectare. Labor for weeding was remunerated at a high rate of $10 per man-day; $5 was a more common wage at the time. Cash wages for harvesting would have been only $20 for two hands; pay in kind, in this case, was worth twice that amount. Thus, normal cultivation costs for the half hectare could have been $65 less, and if the lands were seasonal instead of humid, sowing costs would have been less also. The cost of ox team hire, however, was minimized by paying for it in advance.

** Landholder need not be present when team driver is working alone, but meals must be prepared for the driver.

APPENDIX 13

DAIRYING COSTS AND RETURNS

(Examples from San Lázaro Etla, 1968)

Number of cows milked	Daily milk production	Milk purchases	Fodder	Cheese sales	Milk sales	Whey sales
Case 1. One (home bred, worth $400 at 15 months)	4-5 liters	4/10-5/9: $1812.70 5/10-6/9: $2142.65 6/10-7/9: $2177.15	$15/day alfalfa for cow, calf and two young bulls*	4/10-5/9: $2250 5/10-6/9: $2280 6/10-7/9: $2665**		$ 1.90 $11.70
Case 2. Two cows, one worth $2300 at 9 years, other worth $1900 at 7 years	(1) 15 liters; (2) 11 liters		4 baskets of alfalfa worth $5/basket for three cows, 2 calves, young bull, and burro*	4/3-5/2: $366 5/3-6/2: $210 6/3-7/2: $140		
Case 3. Two cows, one worth $1200, one worth $1500	(1) 8 liters (2) 8 liters, increased to 12		6 bunches maize leaves daily, worth $6, for three cows, two bulls, four calves; and 5 tercios alfalfa worth $15*		5/22-6/21: $274.40 6/22-7/21: $419.40 7/22-8/18: $400.00	
Case 4. Two cows, one worth $2000 at 12 years, one worth $1900 at 7 years	(1) 7.5 liters (2) 6 liters		Alfalfa worth $5 to $7 daily, 5 to 6 bunches maize leaves daily worth $5 to $6, 2 baskets of grass and 1 basket maize husks,	April: $480 May: $422.45	May: $140 June: $617	

APPENDIX 13 (continued)

Case 5. Two cows, one worth $1800 at 6 years, one worth $2000 at 4 years

(1) 12 liters
(2) 15 liters

5/22-6/21: $169.75
6/22-7/21: $348.00
7/22-8/21: $541.00

for three cows, young bull, and burro*

Alfalfa worth $15 to $25 daily, and maize stalks, for two cows, calf, sow, and two burros (Occasionally gets fodder free from father.)

5/22-6/21: $685
6/22-7/21: $607.50
7/22-8/13: $740.50

REPRESENTATIVE TIME COSTS

Case 1. Morning: Husband cuts alfalfa, 2 hours; husband and wife pick up purchased milk (they must milk the cows), 2 hours; husband delivers cheese to vendor in city, 2 to 3 hours.

Afternoon: Husband and wife work cheese, 2 to 3 hours; husband cuts alfalfa, 1 hour.

Evening: Husband and wife pick up purchased milk and make cheese again at night.

Case 2. Morning: Husband cleans "stable", 1 hour, cuts alfalfa, 1.5 to 2 hours; husband and wife water cattle, .5 hour.

Evening: Husband cuts and irrigates alfalfa, 1.5 hours; wife milks cows, 1 hour, and makes cheese last thing at night.

(This household also produces baskets.)

* Fodder from own lands.

** Figures include returns from milk produced by informant's own cow and from purchased milk.

APPENDIX 14

Average Monthly Expenses and Income in Pottery Production

(Examples from Santa María Atzompa, 1968)

Type of pottery	Number of pot formers	Time input, estimated	Cash input	Receipts	Net profit
Case 1[a] Casseroles	1	Fetch clay: 8 half days[b] Fetch temper: 8 half days Fetch wood: 0 Fetch kindling: 12 hours Fetch glaze: 0 Pulverize temper: 12 hours Form pots: 192 hours Fire bisque, glaze, refire: 1 day	$159 for clay, wood, glaze, glaze grinding, freight, fee for selling in Oaxaca *plaza*	$549	$390
Case 2. Decorative ash trays	2	Fetch clay: 0 Fetch temper: 0 Fetch wood: 0 (No kindling used) Fetch glaze: 8 hours Pulverize temper: 3.5 hours Form pots: 440 hours Firebisque,glaze,refire:4days	$464 for clay, temper, wood, glaze, freight, fee for selling in Oaxaca *plaza*	$1,600	$1,136
Case 3. Griddles of two sizes	1	Fetch clay: 6 hours Fetch temper: 3 half days Fetch wood: 0	$30 for wood and kindling	$450	$420

Fetch kindling: 3 half days
Pulverize temper: 12 hours
Form pots: 120 hours
Fire: 6 hours

Case 4. Ollas of medium size	1	Fetch clay: 4 days Fetch temper: 6 half days Fetch wood: 24 hours Fetch kindling: 6 half days Fetch glaze: 0 Pulverize temper: 12 hours Form pots: 144 hours Fire bisque, glaze, refire: 2 days	$81.50 for clay, wood (fetched by potter at minimal cost), glaze, freight	$500 to $520 for glazed ware; approximately $78 for unfired ware	$506.50 on the average
Case 5. Small tubs of two sizes	1	Fetch clay: 0 Fetch temper: 4 half days Fetch wood: 0 Fetch kindling: 8 half days Fetch glaze: 0 Form pots: 240 hours Fire bisque, glaze, refire: 8 half days	$222 for clay, wood, glaze (all purchased from resellers at maximum prices)	$600	$378

Case 6. Casseroles	2	Fetch clay: 4 days Fetch temper: 4 half days Fetch wood: 0 Fetch kindling: 4 half days Fetch glaze: 12 hours Pulverize temper: 40 hours Mold pots: 320 hours Firebisque, glaze, refire: 4 days	$488 for clay, temper, wood (purchased from resellers), glaze, freight	$1,125	$637
Case 7. Large ollas, several sizes	3	Fetch clay: 0 Fetch temper: 8 half days Fetch wood: 0 Fetch kindling: 12 half days Fetch glaze: 0 Pulverize temper: 30 hours Mold pots: 540 hours Firebisque, glaze, refire: 6 days	$360 for clay (sometimes purchased from resellers), wood, glaze, freight, fee for selling in Oaxaca *plaza*	$1,100 on the average	$740 on the average

a In the first example records of expenses and income were kept over an 8-month period; "cash input" and "receipts" are monthly averages of the data from these records. In the remaining examples "cash input" and "receipts" were estimated by the informants.

b All day and hour inputs are man-days and man-hours. Where two persons work at the same task (as in case 2), their have been totaled. For conversion to monthly figures, weekly expenses and income were multiplied by 4 and biweekly data by 2, for simplicity. Multiplying by 4.3 (ratio of weeks to month) and 2.15 would yield slightly higher figures for both inputs and outputs. Frequency of pottery firing in households ranges from twice a week to once a month; the usual interval is biweekly, but weekly firing is not uncommon.

c Glazed ware sold to an urban dealer, approximately 29 dozen pieces per month; unfired ware sold to fellow villagers, approximately 13 dozen pieces per month.

APPENDIX 15
Household Consumption Records

The need for more detailed and precise information on consumption appeared only late in the period of field study and even then was followed up only as an adjunct to the study of production and trading activities at the village level. Some information was collected as opinions and estimates by various informants, but the most important data are the detailed records of daily expenditures compiled by 19 families in three villages. Some examples are given in appendix 15A, and data for 14 families whose reporting was of sufficient duration to permit meaningful analysis are summarized in appendixes 15B and 15C.

The method of collecting data required persuading families to keep detailed daily records of expenditures. This usually involved a small payment or gift each week or month. Field investigators visited the families at varying intervals and discussed the records with them.

Some of the deficiencies in the records should be borne in mind:

1. The families are not representative. They are all functionally literate and are self-selected in the sense that they were willing to cooperate in the record keeping. Some families in each peasant village are not literate while others in the three villages simply were not interested in cooperating. Differences also existed in their interest and involvement in the project. Some families participated only as a favor to the investigator or for the small payments they received. Other families were interested or became quite interested in finding out how they spent their money.

2. There was some variation in the interest of the investigators and the consistency and thoroughness with which they discussed the records with the cooperating families.

3. The cooperating families tended to overlook certain types of expenditures. These included some regular expenditures such as the cost of milling maize as well as repayment of debts and some gifts and ceremonial expenditures.

4. In general there was failure to distinguish between household budgets and production budgets. This is especially true of expenditures for maize for feeding animals. The one large average weekly expenditure for milk is by a cheese-making family and certainly does not represent milk for family consumption.

5. Family size varied from three (increased to four during the period of record keeping) to ten. Any effort, however, to correct for variations in size of family is impossible because of the varying ages of family members.

6. The records covered differing periods of time. Only those that covered more than a two-month period have been included in the summary in appendixes 15B and 15C; these range from 77 to 313 days. None covers a full year.

7. The item "House" in appendix 15B comprises various kinds of essentially capital expenditures, including purchase of animals. Amounts spent by each of the 14 families are quite variable, and the variability may appear to distort the figures in appendix 15C. The category is included, however, because over a longer time period several of the families would probably show some large expenditures of this nature.

8. Few of the families kept records of items consumed which were produced by the household. The listed expenditures for maize are particularly vexing. Six of the 14 families bought tortillas made by others most of the time instead of using their own maize or buying maize and making their own tortillas. Families using their own maize entered only the costs of milling. Families buying maize, in contrast, tended not to enter the costs of milling. Finally, as mentioned above, most families showing expenditures for maize or for milling costs were feeding an undetermined amount to pigs or fowl.

Despite these limitations of the data, several interesting points emerge. Although the average weekly expenditures varied markedly, all households reported some outlay in the "House" category (rent, house improvements, and purchases of animals), which amounted to 29.4 percent of all average weekly expenditures. (Because of the possible sources of error, percentages were not extended beyond one decimal place.) All households reported purchases of luxury items such as sweets, refreshments, and cigarettes, and all but one household reported expenditures in the "Personal" category. If these two categories are added to the "House" expenditures, the average weekly outlay was 39.5 percent of the household budget. As all items in these three categories are deferable, except for the few cases where rent was paid, it appears that all the households reporting felt that their food budgets were at least minimally adequate. This conclusion is reinforced by other data (see chap. 4, above).

Turning to food expenditures, an average of 15.8 percent of the household budgets was spent for maize, part of which was for animal consumption. Somewhat surprisingly, in view of the usual stereotypes concerning the reliance on maize in the diets of Indian and peasant populations in Mexico, all of these households reported expenditures for bread; the average weekly expenditure for bread was 10.4 percent of the total average weekly expenditures. Combining expenditures for bread and maize, 26.2 percent of the average weekly expenditures went for these two items. In addition, all families reported purchases of sugar comprising, on the average, 2.2 percent of average weekly expenditures. (This refers to refined sugar and does not include limited amounts of *panela*, unrefined brown sugar, included in the "Miscellaneous foods" category). Including sugar expenditures; foods high in carbohydrates averaged 28.4 percent of average weekly budgets. All families reported purchases of meat averaging 7.2 percent of average weekly expenditures, beans averaged 4.6 percent. All families reported expenditures for eggs and cheese, mostly the latter, averaging 2.5 percent of average weekly expenditures. The total for foods high in protein, then, is 14.3 percent of average weekly expenditures.

Turning to other food categories, all families report some expenditures for chocolate, fruits, vegetables and herbs; all except household 1, which consolidates spices in reporting, lists expenditures for salt, chile peppers, lard, and miscellaneous foods (mainly items obtained from stores), and all but two report purchases of onions. In nonfoodcategories, only two families do not report purchases of medicines (including veterinarian supplies). All but two families report expenditures for transportation.

The averages discussed tend to conceal variations from family to family. These can be identified in appendix 15A, and ranges are given in appendix 15B.

APPENDIX 15A

SUMMARY OF AVERAGE WEEKLY EXPENDITURES (IN PESOS) OF 14 HOUSEHOLDS BY ITEMS OR CLASSES OF ITEMS PURCHASED

(Items or classes of items purchased)

Village	Household	Number in household	Number of days recorded	Maize	Meat	Eggs and cheese	Beans	Lard	Choco-late	Bread	Tomatoes (jitomate and miltomate)	Chile
Atzompa	1	4	241	17.99[c]	14.80	4.03	1.38	2.58	.67	8.08	1.57	1.42
"	2	5	180	16.07[d]	16.36	1.68	6.61	.77	1.16	10.30	2.03	2.18
"	3	6	303	41.85[d]	25.41	3.21	4.66	1.26	3.18	19.06	5.30	2.43
San Lázaro	4	7	132	23.86[c]	6.02	1.57	3.93	.97	3.17	11.11	1.64	.69
"	5	7	208	24.72[d]	10.46	2.93	7.86	1.99	2.50	14.29	2.74	.75
"	6	5	90	18.92[c]	7.73	8.92	7.58	4.81	6.58	17.68	3.58	.73
"	7	5	109	28.46[c]	5.91	5.91	8.15	2.54	1.14	11.12	2.84	1.33
"	8	6	112	37.94[c]	17.12	3.03	6.94	.66	.38	25.56	3.53	1.18
"	9	3[f]	202	7.89[d]	8.32	5.64	5.06	2.85	1.67	7.63	1.80	.42
"	10	7	77	16.48[c]	5.61	1.64	5.80	1.23	2.47	12.26	1.37	.43
"	11	8	88	6.06[h]	10.35	2.97	6.45	4.20	7.37	19.31	.55	.26
"	12	11	84	40.23[d]	12.33	5.67	22.90	1.98	2.04	48.92	2.33	1.71
"	13	9	90	49.73[h]	10.62	7.25	12.76	4.30	3.75	19.28	6.53	1.52
Magdalena	14	6	313	17.53[h]	7.58	.34	2.47	.60	.48	4.60	1.05	1.26
Average Expenditure, all households:				24.84	11.33	3.91	7.33	2.20	2.61	16.37	2.63	1.17

Rice	Onion	Fruits, vegetables, herbs	Salt	Sugar	Milk	Misc. foods[a]	Sweets, refreshments, cigarettes	Other personal	Medicine	Trans- portation	House[b]	Weekly household total
.18	.02	3.36	—	.36	.62	2.98	2.79	6.03	1.18	2.70	11.47	84.21
.15	.23	3.83	.19	1.78	—	.11	1.08	6.11	—	1.78	2.23	74.65
1.75	.12	7.91	.08	6.99	.06	1.00	.41	6.89	4.39	1.76	13.76	151.48
.74	.04	7.78	2.00	1.57	—[e]	7.13	15.46	11.84	6.43[g]	1.28	60.60	167.83
.93	.31	13.26	.27	3.49	—	1.12	12.51	16.38	6.84[g]	3.44	53.89	180.68
.85	—	7.80	.20	.89	—[e]	18.38	16.12	4.57	20.46[g]	.77	234.98	381.55
1.95	.20	3.23	.25	2.96	1.37	4.96	4.54	—	—	.77	24.51	112.14
.41	.14	10.50	.68	2.34	—[e]	24.25	20.73	7.65	1.88	.75	50.83	216.50
.84	.10	3.88	.64	2.84	—	1.67	7.81	.11	13.65	3.75	67.97	144.54
2.25	—	3.67	.75	3.40	—[e]	2.48	6.24	9.54	1.18	.35	16.28	93.43
1.09	.10	5.25	.16	3.51	—[e]	1.49	2.88	9.50	5.69[g]	—	61.23	148.42
1.96	.12	1.70	3.75	10.06	—[e]	5.29	6.75	13.56	.71	1.00	11.33	194.34
.31	.64	6.65	.45	4.98	.25	.38	8.98	4.95	.19	—	14.47	157.99
.08	.16	2.54	.14	2.32	—	2.19	5.33	13.48	1.91	8.47	25.17	97.70
.96	.16	5.81	.68	3.39	.16	5.24	7.97	7.90	4.61	1.92	46.34	157.53

a Includes consolidated "*tienda*" items such as noodles, coffee, crackers, canned goods.
b Includes animal supplies, rent, house improvements.
c Household purchases ready-made tortillas.
d Tortilla purchases and milling costs for maize included.
e Cheese-making household; home consumption of milk unspecified.
f Household increased to four members during period of study.
g Includes veterinary medicines.
h Milling costs for own maize.

APPENDIX 15B
RANGES OF WEEKLY EXPENDITURES FOR ITEMS OR CLASSES OF ITEMS BY HOUSEHOLD (IN PESOS)

Item or class of item	Minimum weekly expenditure	Maximum weekly expenditure	Household with minimum expenditure	Household with maximum expenditure
Maize	6.06	49.73	11	13
Meat	5.61	25.41	10	3
Eggs and Cheese	.34	8.92	14	6
Beans	1.38	22.90	1	12
Lard	.60	4.81	14	6
Chocolate	.38	7.37	8	11
Bread	4.60	48.92	14	12
Tomatoes	.55	6.53	11	13
Chile	.26	2.43	11	3
Rice	.08	2.25	14	10
Onion	.04*	.64	4	13
Fruits, vegetables, herbs	1.70	13.26	12	5
Salt	.08*	3.75	3	12
Sugar	.36	10.06	1	12
Milk	0.00	1.37	2, 5, 9, 14	7
Miscellaneous foods	.11	24.25	2	8
Sweets refreshments, cigarettes	.41	20.73	3	8
Other personal	0.00	16.38	7	5
Medicine	0.00	20.46	2,7	6
Transportation	0.00	8.47	11,13	14
House	2.23	234.98	2	6

* Very low or nil reporting of important spices usually results from such items being included in a general category of *recaudos* or *sabores*. For this reason the nil reports for onions and salt, as well as the low report for onions by household 1 (which usually consolidated this item with *recaudos*, are not considered as minimum expenditures here.

APPENDIX 15C
Representative Examples of Daily Food Purchases

HOUSEHOLD 1[1]

Locality: Santa María Atzompa
Family members: Parents and children aged 11 and 8
Occupations: Potter, musician.

Bread (6 buns)	$1.00
Tortillas, 10	1.00
Half a round cheese[2]	1.50
Sugar	.20
Coffee	.20
Broad beans, half kilogram	1.75
Tortillas, 15	1.50
Lard, 1 ounce	.30

$7.45

HOUSEHOLD 3

Locality: Santa María Atzompa
Family members: Parents and children aged 23, 17, 13, 10
Occupations: Potter, landowner (land is sharecropped)

Coffee and sugar	$ .70
Tortillas, 20	2.00
Half a round cheese[2]	1.50
Tortillas, 40	4.00
Jerked beef	3.50
Fried potatoes, 1 kilogram	1.40
Lard, 2 ounces	.60
Tomatoes, 5	1.00
Oregano	.20
Coffee and sugar	.50

$15.40

HOUSEHOLD 7[3]

Locality: San Lázaro Etla
Family members: Parents and children aged 27, 22, 18
Occupation: Basketmaker

Eggs, 3	$1.80
Tomatoes and chili	1.50
Lard	1.00
Beans, 1 kilogram	3.20
Tortillas	4.00

$11.50

APPENDIX 15C *(continued)*

Maize	$3.30
Cheese	3.00
Bread	1.50
Peas	2.00
Lard	1.00
Tomatoes	.50

$11.30

HOUSEHOLD 10

Locality: San Lázaro Etla
Family members: Parents and children aged 17, 16, 13, 9, 6
Occupations: Farmer, wage worker, dairyman

Tortillas	$2.00
Bread	2.00
Sugar	1.00
Coffee	.40
Cacao	.80
Jerked beef	1.00
Bananas	1.00
Rice	1.00
Broad beans	3.00

$12.20

HOUSEHOLD 12

Locality: San Lázaro Etla
Family members: Parents and children aged 18, 16, 14, 12, 9, 6, 4, 3, 6 months

Bread	$7.00
Maize	4.80
Milling of maize	1.00
Tomatoes	1.00
Potatoes	1.00
Jerked beef	2.00
Broad beans, 1 kilogram	3.50

$20.30

HOUSEHOLD 14

Locality: Magdalena Ocotlán
Family members: Parents and children aged 14, 12, 10, 3
Occupations: Metatero, blacksmith, farmer

Maize, 3 *almuds*	$12.00

Lime	.20
Milling of maize	.50
Coffee	1.00
Sugar	1.70
Meat[4]	3.00
Onion	.20
Garlic	.20
Chile	.60

$19.40

[1] Household numbers refer to identifications in appendix 15B, where average weekly expenditures for specific items are given.

[2] One whole cheese weighs approximately one-quarter kilogram.

[3] This family buys tortillas and maize alternately; hence two budgets are included.

[4] Probably one-quarter kilogram.

APPENDIX 16
Types of Family Economies

To show more concretely the degree to which the Oaxaca peasant is involved in the market by his consumption and expenditure patterns, and how income production to support his consumption needs may also involve him in the market, I have generated four annual budget estimates that represent levels of living ranging from what most Oaxaqueños would regard as a bare survival budget (Type A), to one that is "satisfactory" (Type D). No operational budgets are included except for agriculture and animal husbandry; most families, except Type A, would have some trade or engage in handicraft production.

Ideally these should be the actual budgets of a carefully selected sample of households. In the absence of more comprehensive data, I have drawn on the actual budgets analyzed in appendix 15 but in addition have brought together other relevant material, including less systematic observations of households, general statements by a large number of informants, household inventories, price data, and occupational patterns. The expenditure and income schedules that follow hence are in some measure subjective, but they have been cross-checked for consistency with many sources and are offered with some confidence that they constitute a reasonably close approximation of reality.

For these hypothetical household budgets, the community is assumed to be an "ideal" one in which the predominant resources are agricultural. The postulated family consists of a man and wife, a son of 8 years and a daughter of 6. Prices are based on 1966–1968 data. In actual cases some of the assets of a permanent nature, including all of the fixed assets, would have been acquired more cheaply in preceding years. Types of families considered are as follows:

Type A. Family with no land or house lot, no artisan skills or trade (*oficio*) and no investment in animals. It must live off the wage labor of its members. The hypothetical budget for this type of family approximates the minimum that would permit survival; most Oaxaqueños would consider such a standard of living to represent poverty (*pobreza*) but not misery (*miseria*).

Type B. Family with house lot and access to enough land to produce maize for 9 months' consumption in an average year. Such a family is poor but enjoys a few amenities.

Type C. Family with house lot and access to enough land to produce, in an average year, all the maize it consumes.

Type D. Family with house lot and access to enough land to produce all needed maize and to market 500 kilograms in an average year. Such a family lives on the margin of comfort but is not rich.

FAMILY TYPE A
Assets or capital goods with long life and low liquidity:

I. *Shelter*

(It is assumed that the family squats or has permission to live on a piece of land or portion of a house lot owned by others. Alternatively, it might rent shelter.) One *jacal* (cane structure) of moderate size, dirt-floored, serving as both kitchen and sleeping quarters.

Materials

*	6 *horcones* (wall supports) ....$	30.00
**	2 *pies de caballo* (ridge pole supports)	14.00
**	1 *caballete* (ridge pole)	24.00
**	4 *soleras* (plates)	70.00
*	32 *latas* or *latillas* (rafters)	160.00
**	1 *cincho* (cross beam between soleras).	15.00
**	200 lashings of maguey fiber or wire ..	40.00
*	200 *carrizones* (canes) for roof	30.00
*	400 *carrizos* for walls and bracing	60.00
**	2 kilograms *riatas* (maguey ropes or cords for lashing poles)	5.00
**	1 kilogram nails	3.00
**	32 sheets laminated tar paper	72.00[a]
	4 kilograms bottle tops for use in nailing tar paper	8.00

Total cost of materials $531.00

Balance forward: $531.00

Labor, approximately 21 days at $10.00 .. 210.00

Total investment value: $741.00

Estimated life of the structure: 15 to 20 years. No depreciation or repair costs included in the budget. A somewhat smaller structure is possible, which in 1954 would have involved a materials cost of about $150, or in 1963 about $300.

II. *Household Equipment With Long Life*

**	Metate ....$	50.00[b]
**	*Mano* (grinding implement for metate) .	8.00
**	*Baúl* (trunk)	100.00[c]
**	Kitchen knife	10.00
**	2 flatirons	7.00

Total investment value: $175.00

III. *Tools and Equipment*

**	Machete ....$	20.00[d]
**	Scissors	15.00

Total investment value: $ 35.00

Total long-lived assets: $951.00

APPENDIX 16 *(continued)*

Short-lived assets:

I. *Kitchen and House Furnishings*

**	1 pottery *molcajete* (chile grinder)	$ 1.00
**	1 pestle for *molcajete*	2.00
**	1 *comal* (baking dish for tortillas)	3.50
**	1 *escobeta* (brush for cleaning metate)	.40
**	1 *batea* (wooden trough for maize when grinding)	4.00
**	1 *pichancha* (pierced olla for draining cooked maize)	5.00
**	1 olla for water storage	13.00
**	2 cooking ollas	7.50
**	3 cooking pots, $5.00 each	15.00
**	1 *lavadero* (large pottery washbasin)	18.00
**	1 *apaxtle* (small basin)	3.00
**	1 jar	4.00
**	2 jars, $1.00 each	2.00
**	2 twenty-liter cans for carrying water	10.00
**	1 gourd for dipping water	1.00
**	4 eating bowls	4.00
**	1 wooden spoon	1.50
**	1 *tenate* (tortilla basket)	2.00
**	1 broom	1.00
**	1 small handled basket for storing sugar, etc. (suspended on rope from ceiling beam)	2.00
**	2 storage baskets, $5.00 each	10.00
**	1 can for storing lard	1.00
**	1 jar or bucket for storing ashes	4.00
**	1 small galvanized bucket for mixing lime and water	5.00
**	1 brazier	5.00
**	1 *morral* (man's carrying bag)	3.50
**	1 *mecapal* (tumpline)	6.00
**	1 carrying net	7.00
**	2 blankets, $15.00 each	30.00
**	2 sleeping mats, $10.00 each	20.00

Total short lived assets $191.40

The above inventory represents a selection from a family in somewhat better circumstances, with 1966–1967 prices. The prices may be a little high, but in this type of village many household possessions are bought in a secondary market.

Current expenditure requirements:

I. *Replacement of kitchen and household furnishings*
   (assume 40 percent replacement) . . . .$ 76.55

II. *Clothing and related expenses*

   A. Men's clothing:

           ** 2 pairs trousers, $20.00 each $40.00
           ** 2 shirts, $15.00 each 30.00
           ** 2 undershorts, $7.00 each 14.00
           ** 2 undershirts, $6.00 each 12.00
           ** 1 hat . . . . 6.00[e]
           ** 1 belt 3.50
           ** 1 pair huaraches . . . . 20.00[f]

   B. Woman's clothing (assuming that she makes her clothing with purchased
   materials)

           2 dresses . . . .$30.00[g]
           2 undergarments . . . . 42.00[h]
           1 apron 10.00
           ** 1 *rebozo* 20.00

   C. Boy's clothing

           ** 2 pairs trousers, $15.00 each 30.00
           ** 2 shirts, $10.00 each 20.00
           ** 2 undershirts, $5.00 each 10.00
           ** 2 undershorts, $4.00 each 8.00
           ** 1 pair huaraches 14.00

   D. Girl's clothing (homemade)

           4 dresses . . . . 28.00[i]
           1 undergarment 7.00

                                                   $344.50

        Total of clothing, assuming annual replacement:

Related expenses, assuming annual replacement:

           ** 2 wooden combs, $1.00 each 2.00
           ** Needles, thread, etc. 5.00
           ** 2 plastic sheets for rain capes
               $1.00 each 2.00
             Total of related expenses: 9.00

III. *Food and related expenses*

        * Maize: 730 kilograms, at $1.05 . . . . . .$766.50
        * Beans *(frijol):* 78 kilograms at $3.00 . . 234.00
        * Meat, fish, cheese, eggs 520.00
        ** Sugar, $3.60 the kilogram 125.00
        ** Coffee 36.50
        ** Lime for tortillas 29.20
        * Lard 36.40
        ** Salt, $0.05 the kilogram (second grade)   7.50

APPENDIX 16 *(continued)*

** Tomatoes, regular and husk 88.40
** Garlic 5.20
** Chile 40.00
** Onions 6.25
* Fruits, vegetables, greens .... 130.00[k]
** Lighting (pitch pine, candles,
     kerosene) .... 40.00[l]
** Matches 10.40
** Soap and detergents 26.00

$2,122.35

This budget allows for no treats such as soft drinks, assumes that all maize is hand milled and that firewood can be gleaned along roads or on public lands. At a pinch the expenditures for meat, beans, and sugar could be reduced, but not regularly.

Total annual budget $2,552.40

Summary—Capital goods or properties previously acquired: $1,142.40
            Current annual expenditures: 2,552.40

Over time, this should be close to a minimal survival budget. Some expenditures might be deferred and those for food and clothing reduced somewhat, but it is difficult to see how they could be much less over any significant time period. The budget allows nothing for emergencies such as illness, leisure, assessments *(cuotas)* for school and municipal affairs, or for any ritual obligations such as baptisms, confirmations, etc.

Income possibilities:

     Employment as a laborer *mozo*) full time at an average of $10.00 daily for 300 days (excluding Sundays and an estimated 13 holy days)[m] . $3,000.00 This is an optimistic assumption both for the number of days worked and the average wage. If these assumptions are not met, the following are some alternatives:

       Work as mozo in Oaxaca City for maximum wage of $15.00 daily without food.[m]
       Work 90 days cutting sugarcane in Veracruz State for $20.00 daily with food and lodging.[m]
       Odd jobs as porter *(cargador)* in marketplace.
       Sale of tortillas or laundering services by the wife.
         With four customers she might pick up a $1,330 net profit from tortilla sales; but unless she has this maize as well as the family's supply ground in a corn mill, adding approximately $365 to the budget, she would have little time for household chores.

If all optimistic assumptions are fulfilled, the family might have a budget surplus of almost $500 a year. If we further assume no emergency expenses, it might meet some social obligations and still have surplus cash. With this surplus the family might:

Buy two pigs for $100 and fatten them, netting as much as $230 (an optimistic figure in the light of most data on production;) or

Raise and fatten a half dozen chickens, netting from eggs and fowl perhaps $200 while increasing the stock in the second generation. (Without a fenced house lot, however, this might involve substantial labor costs that are not calculated in the net gains.)

With these extra income sources and perhaps a windfall with earnings from a good season of cane cutting, the family might apply for government-land (*ejido*) or enter into a sharecropping (*mediero*) arrangement, acquiring an ox team for cultivation by purchase or by hiring one for cash or for a share of maize. As can be seen from the budget for Family Type B, this might permit a slight improvement in living standards and reduce dependence on wage labor but would not materially increase the family's economic position. A family member might also become a small-scale trader. The life-history documents suggest all these as realistic possibilities.

FAMILY TYPE B

Controls land yielding enough maize to feed the family nine months of the year at a rate of 950 kilograms annually (slightly more than the amount consumed by Family Type A); owns house lot but no ox team or farming equipment.

Assets or capital goods with long life and low liquidity:

  I. *Arable land* (bought or inherited)

   3 *almuds* yielding 700 kilograms of maize in an average year. This would be second-class land described as *delgado* (thin). Value of land at $700 per *almud* of seed or half day of plowing $2,100.00

 II. *House lot* (bought or inherited):

   Land value $1,000.00

   Improvements (outside fencing of organ cactus, interior fencing of cane [*carrizo*]: 8 bunches of cane at $2.50, plus labor costs)... 200.00   1,200.00

   (No estimated value for trees or shrubs)

III. *Shelter and storage structures*

   Two cane houses (*jacales*), one for sleeping, one for cooking and maize storage (see cost analysis for Family Type A), one smaller than the other $1,200.00

 IV. Miscellaneous goods on house lot:

   Wooden or stone water containers for animals, estimated value $20.00

   Shades or improvised shelters for animals........ 20.00   40.00

APPENDIX 16 *(continued)*

V. *Household equipment with long life*

Items held by Family Type A $175.00

Additional items:

  ** 3 chairs (1 small) 15.50

  ** 1 mirror 1.00

  ** Flower pots and planters, ceramic and metal   20.00   211.50

VI. *Tools and equipment*

  ** Machete $22.00

  ** Hand sickle.......................... 10.00

  ** Shovel 9.00

  ** Crowbar 27.00

  ** Hunting-type knife and scabbard 12.00

  ** *Coa* or hoelike instrument 11.00

  ** Scissors 15.00   106.00

Total long-lived assets: $4,857.50

Short-lived assets:

I. *Kitchen and House Furnishings*

Items held by Family Type A .... $ 191.40

Additional items:

  ** 1 gourd water bottle.................. 3.00

  ** Pottery cups and bowls................ 4.50

  ** Pottery cooking vessels 31.00

  ** Pottery containers to take meals to the field   6.00

  ** *Atole* jar to take to the field 6.00

  ** 2 galvanized iron buckets 10.00

  ** *Reata* and rope 10.00

  ** 1 heavy colander for sorting grains *(harnero)*   12.00

  ** 7 gourd bowls *(jícaras)* 6.40

  ** 2 petroleum lamps (made from beer cans) .. 3.00

  ** 1 metal cooking spoon 3.50

Total short-lived assets: $286.80

Current expenditure requirements:

I. *Replacement of kitchen and household furnishings*

(assume 40 percent replacement) .... $ 114.72

II. *Clothing and related expenses*

Items held by Family Type A .... $ 353.50

Additional items:

  ** Man's *gaban* or serape 36.00

  ** Women's plastic shoes 18.00

  ** Boy's huaraches 14.00

  ** Boy's hat........................... 3.50

  ** Children's clothes for special school events..   29.00 $ 454.00

III. *Food and related expenses*[n]
*   Maize: 250 kilograms, at $1.05 . . . . $ 262.50
*   Beans *(frijol):* 60 kilograms, at $3.00 . . . .   180.00
*   Meat, fish, cheese, eggs 624.00
**   Sugar, $3.60 the kilogram 125.00
**   Coffee 36.50
**   Lime for tortillas 38.00
*   Lard 104.00
*   Tomatoes, regular and husk 93.60
**   Salt, $0.05 the kilogram 10.40
**   Garlic 7.80
**   Onions 10.40
**   Chile 62.40
*   Fruits, vegetables, greens 150.00
**   Lighting 52.00
**   Matches 15.60
**   Soap and detergents 52.00
*   Chocolate, once a week 26.00
*   Bread, once a week 52.00
*   Soft drinks and sweets, very few 52.00
*   Firewood (to supplement gleaning) 40.00
*   Maize milling 180.00 $2,174.20

IV. *Animal expenses*
*   10 chicks, at $1.00 . . . . $ 10.00
*   10 turkey chicks, at $5.00 . . . .   50.00
*   1 piglet 50.00
*   215 *almuds* insect-damaged maize *(maíz picado),*
      at $3.00, for feed. 645.00   755.00

V. *Agricultural expenses*
Hiring ox teams for plowing, cultivating,
            18 days at $1.50 . . . . $ 270.00 [o]
Hiring ox team and cart for hauling harvest 36.00
(Labor aid by friends and relatives.) 306.00

VI. *Taxes and assessments for school, community, etc.*   150.00
Total annual budget $3,953.90

Summary—Capital goods or properties previously acquired: $5,144.30
              Current annual expenditures: 3,953.90
This budget still does not allow for recreation, medical expenses, or increase in capital expenditures. It only slightly improves living standards over what is allowed by the budget for Family Type A. There is allowance for a little more food and clothing with a bit more variety, an occasional treat such as a soft drink *(refresco),* and meeting some social obligations. Yet, despite the fact that three-quarters of the maize consumed by the family is produced on family lands (the value of this autoconsumption is not calculated in the

APPENDIX 16 (*continued*)

budget figures), the cash requirements for Family Type B are $1,401.50 more than the annual cash requirements in the Type A budget.[P] Expenses for farming and animal raising account for most of this.

Income possibilities

Sale of 500 eggs at $0.50	$ 250.00
Sale of 10 chickens at $16.00	160.00 [q]
Sale of 10 turkeys at $50.00	.500.00 [q]
Sale of one pig	400.00
Total income from animals:	$1,310.00
Sale of corn stalks and husks	420.00
Work as laborer, 203 days, at average wage of	
$10.00 daily plus food......................	2,030.00 [r]
	$3,760.00

Other alternatives, to achieve a surplus: trade (carpenter, mason, barber); craft (weaving, pottery, metate making, lime production, etc.); cultivation of supplementary crop such as castor beans, fruit, coffee (depending on location); cultgivation of winter crop such as peas, chickpeas, wheat, for cash sale; storekeeping or trading.

As an alternative, Family Type B may own an ox team, saving the expense of hiring one but forfeiting the annual sale of corn stalks and husks, which must be used for feed. Capital equipment would be increased by:

* Ox team	$2,500.00
* Plow.......................................	60.00
* Yoke.......................................	50.00
* Yoke straps (2)..............................	20.00
	$2,630.00

In the current expenditure budget, agricultural expenses would be modified to exclude ox team hire, and income possibilities would be modified to exclude sale of maize feed:

Expenditure requirements reduced by $270.00 to.....	$3,488.90
Income reduced by $420.00 to	−3,340.00
Deficit:	$ 148.90

The ox team can be rented out, but this would reduce the number of days available for wage labor commensurately.

Income increased by ox team rental, 100 days at $15.00	$1,500.00
Income reduced by wage labor, 100 days at $10.00 ...	−1,000.00
Net increase in income:	$ 500.00
Less deficit:	−148.90
Surplus:	$ 251.10

If we assume that the additional feed for the ox team can be made up by grazing, collection of weeds in the fields, etc. (a somewhat hazardous assumption), Family Type B would be much better off with an ox team. Considerably more time would be taken in chores (the 8-year-old boy could help with these) but chances of chances of developing some surplus are much better.

FAMILY TYPE C

The family owns land, or has access to land, which produces in a good year 950 kilograms of maize, enough to satisfy its maize needs the year round. It also owns an ox team.

Assets or capital goods with long life and low liquidity:

I. *Land:*

2 *almuds* of 1st-class (humid) land, yielding 720 kilograms of maize in an average crop year	$2,000.00	
1 *almud* of 2nd-class land, yielding 240 kilograms of maize in an average crop year	700.00	$2,700.00

II. *House lot:*

Land value	$1,000.00	
Improvements	200.00	1,200.00

III. *Shelter and storage structures:*

2 *cane huts (jacales),* one for sleeping, one for cooking	$1,200.00	
1 storage shed of corn stalks and leaves	400.00	1,600.00

IV. *Miscellaneous goods on house lot:*

Wooden or stone water containers for animals	$ 20.00	
Shelters for animals	20.00	40.00

V. *Household equipment with long life:*

Items held by Family Type B	$ 211.50	
Additional items:		
** Altar goods (pictures or images of saints, candlesticks, etc.)	65.00	$ 276.50

VI. *Tools and equipment:*

Items held by Family Type B	106.00	
Additional items:		
* Ox team	2,500.00	
* Plow	60.00	
* Yoke	50.00	
* Yoke straps (2)	20.00	
* Burro (pack animal)	150.00	$2,886.00

Total long-lived assets: $8,702.50

Short-lived assets:

I. *Kitchen and House Furnishing*

Items held by Family Type B	$ 286.80	
Additional items:		
** 2 large baskets for harvesting and storage . .	18.00	
** 1 additional handled basket, for shopping . .	4.00	
** 1 chocolate beater *(molinillo)*	1.50	
** 1 wooden shelf, for altar	7.00	

Total short-lived assets: $ 317.30

APPENDIX 16 (*continued*)

Current expenditure requirements:

I. *Replacement of kitchen and household furnishings*
   (assume 40 percent replacement) .... $ 126.90

II. *Clothing and related expenses*
   Items held by Family Type B .... $ 454.00
   Additional items:
        ** Woman's dress for special occasions 50.00
        ** Girl's plastic shoes 5.00
        ** Man's hat, good quality palm leaf ....   12.00 $ 521.00

III. *Food and related expenses*[s]
      *   Beans (*frijol*): 39 kilograms, at $3.00 .... $ 117.00
      *   Meat, fish, cheese, eggs 624.00
     **   Sugar, $3.60 the kilogram 125.00
     **   Coffee 36.50
     **   Lime for tortillas......................   38.00
      *   Lard 104.00
      *   Tomatoes, regular and husk 93.60
     **   Salt, $0.05 the kilogram 10.40
     **   Garlic 7.80
     **   Onions 10.40
     **   Chile.................................   62.40
      *   Fruits, vegetables, greens 150.00
     **   Lighting 52.00
     **   Matches...............................   15.60
     **   Soap and detergents 52.00
      *   Chocolate 33.50
      *   Bread 240.50
      *   Soft drinks, sweets, ice cream 100.00
      *   Firewood..............................   40.00
      *   Maize milling 180.00 $2,092.70

IV. *Animal expenses*
      *   10 chicks, at $1.00 .... $ 10.00
      *   10 turkey chicks, at $5.00 ....   50.00
      *   3 piglets, at $50.00 ....   150.00
      *   370 *almuds* of insect-damaged maize (*maiz
        picado*), at $3.00 ....   1,110.00   1,320.00

V. *Agricultural expenses*
   Labor for sowing, weeding, harvesting .... $ 110.00
   Oxcart hire for hauling 2 cartloads of maize and 2
   cartloads of stalks 36.00   146.00

VI. *Taxes, assessments, social obligations*   350.00[t]

Total annual budget $4,556.60

Summary—Capital goods or properties previously acquired: $9,019.80

Current annual expenditures: 4,556.60

This budget allows for a significant increase in living level and greater expenses for animals.

Income possibilities are enhanced:

Sale of eggs, 500 at $0.50	$ 250.00
Sale of 10 chickens, at $16.00	160.00
Sale of 10 turkeys at $50.00	500.00
Sale of 3 pigs (one inferior)	1,200.00
Sale of litter of 6 shoats, at $50.00	300.00
Rental of ox team, 100 days at $15.00	1,500.00
Total income from animals:	$3,500.00

Probably additional feed will be needed for the ox team, especially alfalfa if they cannot be pastured the year round. In a good crop year, however, there might be enough maize to sell, possibly 3.5 *fanegas* at $100.00 the *fanega*.

Alternative income sources to make up deficit of $1,056.60 and possibly achieve a surplus: winter cash crop of peas, beans or chick-peas; castor bean crop planted in the fields or in the house lot; additional rental of ox team; wage work; sale of tortillas; storekeeping or trading.

In a bad crop year, Family Type C may be almost as hard pressed as Family Type A, but in an average crop year it can count on some surplus if it exploits additional income sources; and in a good year it could be very much better off than Family Type A. Barring serious illness or obligations for costly religious *cargos,* Family Type C has a good chance of bettering itself both in capital goods and in living standards.

FAMILY TYPE D

The family produces a surplus of at least 500 kilograms of maize annually in average crop years.

Assets or capital goods with long life and low liquidity:

I. *Land*:

1 hectare of first-class land		$4,000.00

II. *House lot*

Land value	$1,000.00	
Improvements	200.00	1,200.00

III. *Shelter and storage structures:*

Adobe house with porch[u]

Materials:

*	24 roof poles at $325 per dozen	$ 650.00
*	5 beams at $50	250.00
**	2000 roof tiles	900.00
*	2000 adobe bricks	450.00
	2 loads dung for adobes	80.00

APPENDIX 16 *(continued)*

** 500 bricks at $30 per hundred	150.00	
** 130 bricks	30.00	
** 18 cartloads of foundation stone, at $5 per cartload	90.00	
* 800 canes *(carrizo),* $25 per hundred	200.00	
** Lime, 16 sacks	80.00	
** Nails, 1/2 kilogram	7.50	
** Cord, 12 kilograms	72.00	

Total materials cost: $2,959.50
Labor:

Mason's fee for 24 days' work . . . . $ 500.00
4 laborers for 24 days at $6.00 per day 576.00
Total labor cost: $1,076.00
Small hut for kitchen and storage area, of maize stalks
and leaves . . . . $ 300.00 $4,335.50

IV. *Miscellaneous goods on house lot:*
Wooden or stone water containers for animals . . . . $ 20.00
Shelters for animals 20.00 $40.00
V. *Household equipment with long life:*
Items held by Family Type C . . . . $ 276.50
Additional items:
  ** Radio 250.00
  ** Flashlight 20.00   546.50

VI. *Tools and equipment:*
Items held by Family Type C $2,886.00
Total long-lived assets: $13,007.50

Short-lived assets:
I. *Kitchen and house furnishings*
Items held by Family Type C . . . . $ 317.30
Additional items:
  ** 1 heavy blanket 40.00
Total short-lived assets $ 357.30

Current expenditure requirements:
I. *Replacement of kitchen and householf furnishings*
(assume 40 percent replacement) . . . . $ 142.90
II. *Clothing and related expenses*
Items held by Family Type C . . . . $ 531.00
Additional item:
  ** Woman's *rebozo* for special occasions 35.00   566.00

III. *Food and related expenses*
Identical to the food budget for Family Type C except
that refreshments are increased to $150 ....   2,142.70
IV. *Animal expenses*
Identical to the animal purchase and maintenance
budget for Family Type C 1,320.00
V. *Agricultural expenses*
Agricultural expenses for Family Type C .... $ 146.00
Cart rental for one additional load of maize and one
additional load of maize stalks 18.00
Additional labor, 2 *mozos* for 2 days at $10 each per
day 40.00ᵛ   204.00
VI. *Taxes, assessments, social obligations*
Expenditures of Family Type C .... $ 350.00
Additional small party, or additional expenditures for
more elaborate saint's-day party 200.00   550.00

Total annual budget $4,835.60

Summary—Capital goods or properties previously acquired: $13,364.80
Current annual expenditures: 4,835.60
Income possibilities:
Gains from animals, including ox team rental, identical
to those for Family Type C $3,910.00
Sale of 500 kilograms of maize at $0.95/kilogram 475.00

         $4,385.00

Additional possibilities to make up deficit of $450.60 and achieve a surplus: winter cash crops, additional ox team rental, tortilla sales, breeding of pigs and sale of shoats, trade, craft, commercial enterprise. In a very good crop year the maize surplus would be greater, perhaps 1,000 kilograms above subsistence needs. The ox team can be sold in three or four years' time and a younger one bought, for a net gain of perhaps $1,000.

Uses for surplus cash: increase living standards (food and material goods), increase investments in land or animals, take land in pawn and sell the crop, send child to secondary or technical school.

This family has the possibility of achieving a comfortable level of living by village standards and a degree of security. It would, however, still face the catastrophic effects of serious illness and almost certainly would be expected to discharge some costly religious obligation (*cargo*). Since *cargo* expenses are cushioned by the custom of reciprocation in gifting and invitations, however, the family would be fed at fiestas many times in return for its participation in the community's festive life.

* Item may be available in home village, at least in part.
** Item usually originates in another village.
a 1961 price. Sugar-cane thatch would have cost $25.00 in 1961.
b Usually a wedding gift. Price assumes that metate is of medium size, bought on a favorable market.
c Usually a wedding gift, and the last possession a family would relinquish.

APPENDIX 16 *(continued)*

d May be acquired from one's father.

e This quality might not last a year.

f As an alternative, huaraches could be home made with purchased materials.

g 10 meters of cloth at minimal price of $3.00 per meter.

h 6 meters of cloth at $7.00 per meter.

i 2 meters of cloth at $3.50 per meter, for each dress.

j Estimated consumption as follows: for maize, .5 kilogram per person per day; for beans, 1.5 kilogram per week for the household; for meat-fish-cheese-eggs, the equivalent of 1 kilogram of pork and 1 cheese per week; for lime, $0.20 per 5 kilograms of maize (actual expenditure); for regular tomatoes, 10 per week for the household; for garlic, one head per week, and for onions, one to two per week (at village-store prices).

k The highest expenditure in this category would be for string beans, broad beans, garbanzos, and peas, which in season are welcome alternatives to *frijol*.

l Berg's estimated use of pitch pine by households in Zoogocho, in the Sierra de Juárez, for 1967 would require expenditures of $0.75 per week (1968: 41–42). In the Valley, pitch pine is seldom usd for lighting. Small candles may be purchases daily for $0.20 each; or alternatively, $0.20 of kerosene (village-store prices) could last a household for two days or more.

m Note that wages (as well as prices) are substantially higher than they would have been ten or even five years ago. Usually the *mozo* also is fed, thus reducing his family's food requirements.

n Estimated consumption: for maize, .63 kilograms per person per day, 700 kilograms of it from the family's lands; for beans, 1.5 kilograms per week, 18 kilograms of it from the family's lands; meat, etc., the equivalent of one kilogram of boneless pork per week; some fruits from family's house lot; garlic, 2 heads per week; chile, $1.20 per week; onions, 2 per week; lighting, 1/4 liter of kerosene daily at $0.40 per liter (village-store price).

o Food given to ox team owner-driver not included in calculation.

q Assumes that all fowl survive.

r Food received in addition to wages not included in calculation.

p In a bad year, Family Type B might be worse off than Family Type A because it would have to buy more maize without reduction in agricultural expenditures. But Family Type B has a litle more leeway for retrenchment and deferral of expenditures.

s The food budget is essentially the same as that for Family Type B except that there is no cost for maize and half cost for the 78 kilograms of *frijol*, both of these foods grown on the family's lands; bread consumption is increased to allow for sweet bread on Sundays and plain bread on other days; chocolate consumption is increased to allow for 14 holy or festive days as well as Sundays; and the allowance for "treats" is almost doubled.

t Allowance is made for a small saint's-day party costing $200.00.

u The majority of village families would have at least one adobe structure.

v Food given in addition to wages not included in calculation.

APPENDIX 17

Food and Food-Related Items Consumed in Valley Villages

Key: *Frequency of consumption*

* = Items regarded as basic and indispensable by all; # = Items consumed frequently by families in middle brackets; % = Items considered essential for special occasions by families in middle brackets; Unmarked items are of casual, occasional or luxury consumption.

Sources

1. Produced in all villages, but in some villages not in sufficient quantity for local consumption.
2. Produced in only some Valley villages but consumed in most, if not all; some quantities may also be imported to Valley.
3. Produced in system but not in Valley, or Valley supply is supplemented from elsewhere within the system on occasion.
4. Supplemented from outside system.
5. Imported wholly from outside system.

		1	2	3	4	5
#	Acacia beans (*huajes*)	x				
#	Alfalfa fodder		x			
%	Almonds (*almendras*)					x
#	Apples, criollo (*manzana*)			x		
	Apples, "modern" (*manzana*)					x
	Apricots (*chabacano*)			x		
#	Avocados (*aguacate*)			x		
#	Bananas (*plátano*)			x	x	
*	Beans (*frijol*)	x			x	
	Beans, broad (*haba*)		x			
#	Beans, green (*ejote*)	x				
*	Beef (*carne de res*), dried beef (*tasajo*)	x		x		
#	Beer (*cerveza*)					x
#	Beverages, carbonated				x	
#	Bread (*pan*)		x			
#	Cabbage (*col*)		x			
	Carrots (*zanahoria*)		x		x	
	Cauliflower (*coliflor*)		x			
#	Chayote (*chayote*)		x		x	
*	Cheese (*queso*)		x			
	Cherimoyas (*chirimoya*)		x			
	Cherries (*cereza*)			x		
	Chewing gum (*chicle*)					x
%#	Chickens (*pollo*)		x		x	

APPENDIX 17 *(continued)*

	Item						
#	Chick-peas *(garbanzo)*		x				
*	Chile, various fresh and dried varieties *(chile)*		x		x	x	
%#	Chocolate *(chocolate, cacao)*						x
#	Cigarettes *(cigarros)*						x
#	Cinnamon *(canela)*						x
%	Cloves *(clavo)*						x
	Coconut varieties *(coco, coquito)*			x			
#	Coffee *(cafe)*			x			
#	Coriander *(cilantro)*		x				
	Crab apple *(tejocote)*			x			
%	Cumin *(comino)*		x				
	Custard apples *(anona)*			x			
#	Eggs *(huevos, "blanquillos")*	x		x	x		
	Figs *(higo)*			x			
%#	Fish and shrimp, fresh and dried *(pescado y camarón)*			x			
#	Flour, wheat *(harina)*		x		x		
*	Garlic *(ajo)*		x				
	Grapefruit *(toronja)*		x		x		
	Grapes *(uvas)*						x
#	Grasshoppers *(chapulines)*		x				
*	Greens *(chepiles, chepiches, verdolaga, guías de calabaza,* etc.)	x					
#	Groceries (commercially packaged foods) *(abarrotes)*						x
	Guajilote (a pulpy vegetable)		x				
#	Guavas *(guayaba)*		x				
*	Herbs *(hierba)*	x					
#	Ices, ice cream *(nieve, paletas)*		x				
#	*Jícama* (a turnip-like root)		x				
*	Lard *(manteca)*		x		x		
	Lemons *(límon)*		x				
	Lemons, sweet *(lima limón, limón dulce)*		x				
#	Lentils *(lenteja)*		x				
	Lettuce *(lechuga)*		x				
*	Lime *(cal)*		x				
#	Limes *(lima)*		x				
#	Loquats *(níspero)*		x				
*	Maize *(maiz),* maize fodder *(zacate)*	x			x		
	Mamey *(mamey),* mamey nut *(pixtle)*			x			
#	Mangoes *(mango)*		x		x		
	Melons *(melón)*		x				
#	Mescal *(mezcal)*		x				

		C1	C2	C3	C4	C5
#	Milk (*leche*)	x				
	Nanches (a berry-like fruit)	x				
#	Noodles (*pasta, fideo*)					x
	Nopal (a cactus, leaves and fruit eaten)	x				
	Nuts, pecans (*nuez*)	x				
	nuts, walnuts (*nuez de castilla*)			x		
*	Onions (*cebolla*)	x			x	
#	Oranges (*naranja*)			x	x	
#	Oregano (*orégano*)	x				
	Papaya (*papaya*)			x	x	
	Passion fruit (*granadilla*)			x		
#	Peaches, criollo (*durazno, prisco, melocotón*)			x		
	Peaches, "modern" (*durazno, melocotón*)					x
#	Peanuts (*cacahuate*)	x				
	Pears (*pera*)			x	x	
#	Peas, green, fresh and dried (*chícharo, "alverja"*)	x				
	Pepper (*pimiento*)					x
	Pineapple (*piña*)					x
#	Pitahaya (cactus fruit), (*"pitaya"*)	x				
	Plums (*ciruela*)			x	x	
	Pomegranate (*granada*)			x		
*	Pork (*carne de puerco*), pork cracklings (*chicharrón*), pork sausage (*chorizo, salchicha*)	x	x			
#	Potato, white (*papa*)	x			x	
	Potato, sweet (*camote*)	x				
#	Prepared foods, e.g., *tortilla* (maize cake), *molote* (potato dish), *nicuatole* (maize custard), *barbacoa* (cooked goat meat)	x				
	Quince (*membrillo*)			x		
#	Radishes (*rábano*)	x				
#	Rice (*arroz*)					x
	Sage (*salvia*)			x		
*	Salt (*sal*)			x		
#	Sesame (*ajonjolí*)					x
#	Soft drinks	x				
*	Squash, various types (*calabaza*); squash seeds (*semilla de calabaza*)		x			
	Sugarcane (*caña*)	x				
*	Sugar, white (*azúcar*)					x
#	Sugar, brown (*panela*)	x				
	Sweets (e.g., candy, cookies) (*dulces*)	x			x	
	Tamarinds (*tamarindo*)					x
	Tangerines (*mandarina*)			x		
*	Tomatoes, regular (*jítomate*)	x			x	
*	Tomatoes, husk (*miltomate*)	x			x	

APPENDIX 17 *(continued)*

%# Turkeys *(guajolote)*	x			
# Vanilla *(vainilla)*				x
Watermelon *(sandía)*		x	x	
Worms, maguey *(gusano)*		x		
Zapote *(zapote, chicozapote)*			x	

SUMMARY

A. Items regarded as indispensable by all ... 17
   1. Produced in all Valley villages (supplies inadequate in many villages) ... 7
   2. Produced in some Valley villages; part or all of supplies obtained from elsewhere in the Valley ... 9
   3. Part or all of supplies obtained from outside the Valley but within the Oaxaca market system ... 3
   4. Valley supplies supplemented from outside the Oaxaca market system ... 7
   5. All supplies imported from outside the system ... 1

B. Items frequently consumed in Valley villages; some produced in Valley villages as specializations ... 8
   1. Produced in all Valley villages ... 5
   2. Produced in some Valley villages; part or all of supplies obtained from elsewhere in the Valley ... 26
   3. Part or all of supplies obtained from outside the Valley but within the Oaxaca market system ... 9
   4. Valley supplies supplemented from outside the Oaxaca market system ... 7
   5. All supplies imported from outside the system ... 10

C. Items considered essential for special occasions ... 7
   1. Produced in all Valley villages ... 2
   2. Produced in some Valley villages; part or all of supplies obtained from elsewhere in the Valley ... 1
   3. Part or all of supplies obtained from outside the Valley but within the Oaxaca market system ... 2
   4. Valley supplies supplemented from outside the Oaxaca market system ... 0
   5. All supplies imported from outside the system ... 3

D. Items of occasional or luxury use ... 42
   1. Produced in all Valley villages ... 0
   2. Produced in some Valley villages; part or all of supplies obtained from elsewhere in the Valley ... 18
   3. Part or all of supplies obtained from outside the Valley but within the Oaxaca market system ... 17
   4. Valley supplies supplemented from outside the Oaxaca market system ... 6
   5. All supplies imported from outside the system ... 7

APPENDIX 18
Nonfood Items Often Used in Valley Villages

Produced in Some But Not All Valley Villages

Adobe brick
* Animals (beasts of burden, draft animals)
Baskets
Brick, fired
* Brooms, brushes
Candles, ceremonial
Cane (for house construction, fencing, basketry)
Carts, complete
Ceramic ware
* Charcoal
Cheese molds and presses
Clay for ceramics
* Firewood
Forged hardware
Lime for house construction
Looms and loom parts (not produced in villages where used)
Maguey fiber products (*jarcieria*): rope, cord, nets, bags, harness goods
* Mats
Metates
Palm products (some)
* Pitch pine
Plows, complete
Plow points, iron
Rawhide straps, *riatas*
Rock
Sand
Sandals (*huaraches*)
Sieves, strainers
Thatching materials
Tiles for roofing
Wood for fuel

* Wooden cart parts
* Wooden house parts: posts, beams, rafters, stringers (*latillas*), planks
* Wooden household equipment: rough shelves, stools, chairs, tables. stepladders, troughs, bowls, spoons, chocolate beaters
* Wooden plow parts
Wool, raw (little)
Wool carders
Wool products: serapes, gabanes, rebozos
Woven belts and sashes
* Yokes

Originating in the City of Oaxaca

Calendars
Candles
Ceramics, polychrome
Clothing, ready-made (little)
Cotton textiles (little)
Finished furniture: wardrobes, chairs, tables, chests, beds
Forged iron ware
Ice (preservative)
Laundry soap (some)
Leather goods
Newspapers, local
Sandals (*huaraches*)
Tin ware

Originating Outside the System

Automotive equipment
Tractors; modern farm implements
Insecticides and chemical fertilizers
Corn mills and motors
Sewing machines
Radios
Loudspeaker systems
Store equipment: scales, show cases, ice boxes
Trunks
Flashlights
Irons
Most tools and hardware (except hand forged)
Nails and wire
Cement
Galvanized iron products
Corrugated roofing paper and sheets
Petroleum products
Kerosene and gasoline lanterns
Glaze for ceramics
Plastics: bags, sheets for rain capes
Most machine-woven textiles
Blankets
Cotton: most cotton cloth
Most ready-made clothing
Most raw wool
Palm fiber products (most): baskets, bags, fans, rain capes
Palm straw hats
Felt hats
Shoes
Jewelry
Notions: needles, thread, scissors

* Supplemented from elsewhere in the system.

APPENDIX 18 *(continued)*

Mirrors	Stationery supplies;	Matches
Puebla ceramics	notebooks	Soap and detergents;
Religious objects	All groceries and canned	starch
Newspapers	goods	Patent medicines

APPENDIX 19
SOURCES OF SOME IMPORTED PRODUCTS CONSUMED BY OAXACA PEASANTS

Product	Sources
Almonds	Veracruz State
Apples	California, USA; Puebla State (San Andres Calpan); Mexico City (transshipped only)
Apricots	Cuicatlán in the Cañada, Oaxaca (north of the Valley of Oaxaca)
Aprons	Mexico City
Bananas	Coastal Mixteca (Pochutla); Tabasco State; Veracruz State (Poza Rica)
Baskets	Puebla State (Tehuacan); Tlaxcala State
Beans *(frijol)*	Mixteca; Chiapas State
Beer	Baja California; Mexico City; Monterey
Belts, factory made	Mexico City
Blankets	Puebla State; Tlaxcala State
Bolt cloth	Mexico City; Puebla State (especially Atlixco)
Burros	Coastal Mixteca (Candelaria Loxicha)
Cacao	Chiapas State; Tabasco State (especially Villahermosa); Veracruz State
Carrots	Puebla State
Cattle	Chiapas State
Chayote	Mexico City (transshipped only); Puebla State
Chickens	Puebla State
Chick-peas	Puebla State
Chilacayote	Coastal Mixteca (Puerto Escondido)
Chile (gordo, poblano, serrano, ancho)	Puebla State
Chile amarillo	Cuicatlan, Oaxaca
Chile mora	Loma Bonita, Oaxaca (near Veracruz State line)
Chilpoche	Veracruz State
Cigarettes	Baja California
Cinnamon	Tabasco State; Veracruz State
Clothing	Mexico City; Morelos State (Cuernavaca); Puebla State (especially Atlixco); Nuevo Leon State (Monterrey)
Cloves	Veracruz State
Coconuts	Chiapas State
Coffee	Coastal Mixteca (Pochutla); Veracruz State
Cotton, raw	Chinanteca (northern Oaxaca State)
Drugs	Central Mexico
Eggs	Coastal Mixteca (Pochutla); Puebla State (Tehuacan)
Fish	Coastal region (Puerto Angel); Veracruz State
Flashlights	Mexico City

APPENDIX 19 *(continued)*

Flour	Puebla State
Flowers	Morelos State (Cuautla); Veracruz State (Orizaba); Hidalgo State
Garlic	Puebla State
Glaze for pottery	Nuevo Leon State (Monterrey)
Gourds	Puebla State; Coastal Mixteca
Grapefruit	Puebla State; Veracruz State (Córdoba)
Grapes	Baja California; Aguascaliente State; Coahuila State
Industrial products, wholesale	Mexico City
Japanese goods (ceramics, fabrics, radios [smuggled])	Sinaloa State (Mazatlan); Guatemala
Knives	Puebla State; Veracruz State; Guatemala
Lemons	Veracruz State
Maize	Tuxtepec and Valle Nacional, northern Oaxaca State; Puebla State; Chiapas
Mangoes	Cuicatlán, Chilar and Tomellín, in the Cañada (north of the Valley of Oaxaca)
Melons	Morelos State; Michoacán State; Puebla State
Metates and Manos	Puebla State
Mirrors	Puebla State; Guatemala
Mortars and pestles, stone	Puebla State
Mules	Coastal Mixteca (Candelaria Loxicha)
Onions	Guanajuato State; Michoacán State; Nuevo Leon State Puebla State (especially Atlixco); Tamaulipas State
Oranges	Veracruz State (Córdoba, Minatitlán and Tlapacoyan); Michoacán State; PueblaState; TabascoState; MorelosState; Tamaulipas State
Palm leaf products	Mixteca Alta (Yutanduchi and Tlaxiaco); Puebla State (especially Tehuacán)
Papaya	Veracruz State (especially Soledad); Cuicatlan in the Cañada
Peaches	Puebla State (San Andres Calpan)
Pears	Puebla State (especially San Andres Calpan)
Pepper	Veracruz State
Perishable goods generally, wholesale	Mexico City
Pineapples	Coastal Mixteca (Pochutla); Loma Bonita and Tuxtepec, Oaxaca (near Veracruz State line)
Plums	Coastal Mixteca (Cozaltepec, Cuixtla, Paso Ancho, Pochutla); Chiapas State; Puebla State; Mexico City; Cuicatlan, Oaxaca
Potatoes	Puebla State

Pottery	Hidalgo State (Actopan); Morelos State (Cuautla); Puebla State; Guatemala
Quince	Puebla State (San Andres Calpan)
Rebozos	Guanajuato State (especially Moroleon); Jalisco State (Guadalajara); Puebla State; Mexico City
Rice	Morelos State
Serapes and sleeveless jackets	Tlaxcala State (Santa Ana Chiautempan)
Sesame	Chiapas State
Shirts, poplin and gabardine	Puebla State; Mexico City.
Shoes	Puebla State; San Luis Potosi State; Yucatan State (Merida); Mexico City
Soft drinks	Puebla State
Squash	Coastal Mixteca (Puerto Escondido)
Sugar, white	Veracruz State
Tangerines	Veracruz State
Tinware	Mexico City
Tomatoes	Guanajuato State; Morelos State (Cuautla); Puebla Cuicatlan, Oaxaca; Chiapas State; Mexico City
Towels	Mexico City
Trousers, khaki and gabardine	Puebla State; Mexico City
Trousers, Italian fabric	Nuevo Leon State (Monterrey)
Vanilla	Veracruz State (especially Papantla)
Watermelons	Camarón and Tuxtepec, Oaxaca State (near Veracruz State line); Michoacán State (especially Ápatzingán); Puebla State Teahuacán); Sinaloa State; Mexico City (transshipped only)
Wheat	Mixteca Alta

APPENDIX 20
Composite Inventory of Household Items[1]

		Purchase Price (in Pesos)	
	Number of Households	Range	Average
KITCHEN ITEMS[2] (36 households reporting)			
Apaxtle (tub)	6	$1.00-$3.00	$2.60
Baskets:			
Altillo (tall, stiff)	10	—[3]	—
Chiquihuite (small, rounded, stiff)	3	$3.00-$12.00	$4.30
Media medida (fairly large, flaring, stiff)	5	$3.00-$6.00	$5.00
Piscador (very large, flaring, stiff)	23	$3.00-$10.00	$7.20
Tenate (very small, soft)	27	$0.75-$5.50	$2.60
No designation	29	$2.00-$50.00	$18.60
Beater for chocolate	28	$1.00-$2.50	$1.40
Bowl	4	$1.50-$8.00	$3.40
Broom	29	$1.00-$1.50	$1.40
Bule (gourd for carrying water)	6	—	—
Chilimolera (mortar for grinding chile)	5	$2.00-$5.00	$3.10
Colander	4	$2.00	$2.00
Cooking pan	4	—	—
Cups	7	$0.10-$2.50	$1.50
Griddle	19	$1.50-$3.00	$2.03
Jar	18	$1.00-$9.00	$2.80
Jícara (gourd cup)	15	$1.25	$1.25
Metate	32	$8.00-$87.50	$48.60
Olla	24	$0.30-$50.00	$9.80
Pail	24	$3.75-$22.00	$10.50
Plates	16	$0.80-$7.00	$3.30
Sieve	14	$7.50-$25.00	$14.50
Spoon, wooden	16	$1.00-$3.00	$1.65
Tins for carrying water, pair	14	$8.00-$16.00	$12.30
Total of average unit costs			$159.80[4]
OTHER HOUSEHOLD ITEMS (128 households reporting)			
Bed, of boards	15	—	—
Bed, of cane (*carrizo*)	6	—	—
Bed, with mattress	23	$500.00-$850.00	$707.00
Bedclothes[2]	11	$40.00-$50.00	$45.00
Bench[2]	4	$3.00-$5.00	$4.00
Blanket[2]	17	$14.00-$150.00	$44.40
Brazier[2]	11	$5.00-$10.00	$8.00
Camera[2]	4	$45.00-$600.00	$461.00

Chair	45	$3.50-$10.00	$7.50
Chest of drawers	7	—	—
Clock	6	—	—
Cradle[2] (usually homemade)	6	$20.00	$20.00
Fire tongs[2]	13	$3.00	$3.00
Flashlight[2]	14	$9.00-$27.50	$19.60
Flower pot[2]	11	$1.50-$7.00	$4.60
Lamp, kerosene or petroleum	59	—	—
Lamp, gas	3	—	—
Mat[2]	22	$1.00-$16.00	$7.00
Mirror[2]	17	$1.00-$30.00	$11.50
Phonograph	4	$900.00	$900.00
Picture of saint[2]	17	$15.00-$40.00	$22.70
Radio	57	$60-$4500	$521.00
Scissors[2]	20	$8.00-$50.00	$18.00
Sewing machine	18	$80-$2000	$1076.00
Shelf[2]	11	$7.00-$20.00	$14.00
Stepladder	19	$15.00-$50.00	$32.50
Stool[2]	23	$1.50-$4.00	$2.40
Table	42	$10.00-$300.00	$53.00
Trunk	45	$50.00-$150.00	$83.00
Tub	32	$6.00-$32.00	$15.00
Valise	35	$87.50-$100.00	$93.75
Vase[2]	13	$1.25-$15.00	$5.00
Wardrobe closet	28	$200-$600	$433.00
Total of average unit costs			$4611.95[4]

OTHER IMPLEMENTS (128 households reporting

Ax[2]	13	$10.00-$16.00	$13.00
Burro pack	46	$15.00	$15.00
Hoe or digging stick[2]	6	$1.00-$19.00	$10.00
Irons[2]	21	$6.25-$10.00	$8.30
Kiln[2]	12	$25.00-$150.00	$54.40
Machete[2]	32	$10.00-$50.00	$23.25
Pick[2]	9	—	—
Plow	32	—	—
Riata (rope for animal pack)	12	$10.00	$10.00
Rope[2]	3	—	—
Scythe[2]	4	$10.00-$12.00	$10.00
Shovel[2]	11	$5.00-$18.00	$10.50
Sickle[2]	22	$3.25-$12.50	$8.80
Yoke	12	$70-$300	$135.00

VEHICLES (128 households reporting)

Bicycle	12	—	—

APPENDIX 20 *(continued)*

Oxcart	21	$1000-$1300	$1150.00
Tractor	3	—	—

Total of average unit costs		$1448.25[4]

			Current Value *(in Pesos)*
	Number of house-holds	Range	Average
ANIMALS (128 households reporting)			
Burro	60	$50-$250	$155.50
Cattle:			
Calf, heifer	114	$100-$750	$344.10
Cow	62[5]	$1000-$2500	$1700
Ox teams	40	$1500-$4000	$3125.00
Chickens	49	$12-$30	$13.30
Goat	9	$50-$85	$73.40
Horse	9	$3000	$3000.00
Pig	61	$70-$450	$214.00
Turkey	19	$20-$50	$35.00
Total of average unit values			$8660.30

[1] The listed items were reported by three or more households in the villages studied. Reporting by informants was seldom complete or exhaustive; for example, ollas, metates, baskets, and machetes are probably owned by all households but were omitted from some inventories. Nevertheless, the lists are indicative of investments made by Oaxaca Valley peasants to furnish and equip their household. Differences in purchase prices may reflect differences in quality, size, or year of purchase.

[2] Not included in the inventories from San Lázaro Etla.

[3] Price was not reported in every instance. In some cases items do not bear prices because they were homemade or were gifts.

[4] These figures are conservative in terms of current prices. Also, it is usual for a household to have more than one of some items such as baskets and ollas.

[5] The figure representing cow ownership is distorted by the inclusion of 92 household inventories from San Lázaro Etla, a dairying village, where the cow population is considerably greater than in nondairying villages.

APPENDIX 21
OAXACA STREET MARKET: NUMBERS OF VENDORS BY PRODUCT[1]

Product	Date[2]				
	August–October 1964[3]	October 2, 1965	October 9, 1965	October 16, 1965	October 30, 1965[4]
Fruit, all[5]	315	248	249	323	678
Beans	44	12	18	13	10
Potatoes, white	31	18	19	18	2
Garlic	145	23	6	13	20
Onions	142	5	3	9	16
Tomatoes, Miltomate	181	111	146	181	215
Chile	156	130	70	83	77
Herbs, seasonings	80	23	21	25	51
Greens	94	100	33	208	118
Vegetables, other	79	163	185	17	163
Meat products	5	36	40	5	42
Fish and shrimp	22	44	38	20	41
Poultry	35	37	60	73	147
Eggs	8	3	0	0	0
Cheese	6	1	0	1	3
Chocolate	19	14	14	14	6
Cacao and/or coffee	20	20	16	10	17
Sweets	8	8	7	5	10
Nuts and/or peanuts	116	102	109	119	253
Bread	33	29	30	48	88
Maize	42	37	35	33	40
Lime	25	25	32	39	30
Tortillas	36	8	15	11	8
Prepared food, other	64	38	36	51	46
Liquid refreshments, ices	49	39	53	62	51
Patent medicines	1	0	0	1	0
Ocote (pitch pine)	8	0	0	0	1
Dishes	2	0	1	2	0
Pottery	118	107	114	125	167
Chocolate beaters and/or wooden spoons	16	5	5	11	10
Fiber products	29	26	20	21	26
Baskets and/or mats	19	19	21	8	35
Plastics	14	30	28	30	34
Ironware	4	10	15	5	3
Tinware	9	13	11	4	7

APPENDIX 21 (*continued*)

Wood products........	1	11	7	9	13
Dry goods, notions....	67	65	74	48	79
Ready-made clothing .	119	95	105	13	119
Cloth....................	29	50	26	3	19
Rebozos, serapes.......	1	11	6	10	14
Shoes...................	5	5	4	1	3
Hats....................	1	3	0	0	0
Sandals, sandal parts..	0	13	12	13	1
Comic books...........	9	4	6	8	4
Flowers (cut)...........	66	50	41	60	113
Sugarcane..............	5	4	8	10	21
Total, all vendors[6]	1,684	1,814	1,865	2,130	2,906

[1] Project count by R. G. Waterbury and E. B. Waterbury. Vendors selling more than one of the above-listed products are counted more than once. Products most frequently combined by one vendor are: garlic and onions; vegetables and greens; tinware, ironware, and bottles.

[2] All dates are Saturdays, but survey hours vary.

[3] Composite of four lists.

[4] Eve of the All Saints holiday, a very active time for the market, particularly for foodstuffs such as fruit, nuts, and *jícama*. (The figure for vegetables on October 30, 1965 includes 132 vendors of *jícama*.)

[5] Includes citrus fruits and avocados.

[6] Totals include all vendors whether or not their products are listed above. Multiple-product vendors are counted only once.

APPENDIX 22

Permanent Marketplaces of Oaxaca City: Numbers of Vendors

(adapted from Waterbury 1968:90 ff.)

	CENTRAL MARKETPLACES			SECONDARY MARKETPLACES				
	Mercado Benito Juárez	Mercado 20 de Noviembre	Mercado La Industria	Mercado La Merced	Mercado Carmen Alto	Mercado El Marquesado	Mercado Hidalgo	Mercado Venustiano Carranza
Project census,	Sept. 1964	Oct. 1964	April 1965	July 1965	June-July 1964	July 1965	August 1965	—
Puestos	546							
Casetas	248							
Total vendors	794	416	46	201a	174b	105c	61d	—
Census of the Banco de Pequeño Comercio, 12/31/65	815	410	44	220	188	130	80	43

a In addition there were a maximum of 178 vendors outside the covered marketplace.
b In addition there were 120 vendors outside the covered marketplace.
c In addition there were 67 vendors outside the covered marketplace.
d In addition there were 23 vendors outside the covered marketplace.

APPENDIX 23
NUMBERS OF VENDORS IN BENITO JUÁREZ MARKETPLACE, 1958, 1960, 1961, 1964; AND IN 20 DE NOVIEMBRE MARKETPLACE, 1964

Product	Benito Juárez Marketplace				20 de Noviembre Marketplace
	Official Lists[1]			Project Census[2]	Project Census[2]
	1958	1960	1961	1964	1964
Avocados	2	0	10	3	1
Beans (frijol)	16	21	22	31 (16)	
Baskets	1	0	0	8	
Belts, traditional	14	14	18	-	
Cacao	2	0	1	2 (2)	32
Bread	0	0	0	-	83
Cheese	18	18	29	22 (19)	
Chickens	8	10	10	12 (12)	
Chile	62	4	21	55 (12)	16
Chocolate	4	1	4	1	20
Clothing	55	122	91	93 (83)	
Coffee	1	1	0	2 (1)	
Eggs	17	0	12	13 (3)	3
Fish	10	5	11	13 (13)	
Flowers, artificial	3	3	0	4	
Flowers, cut	55	9	55	28 (25)	
Fondas (prepared food)	0	0	0	-	147
Footwear	39	43	41	34	
Fruit[3]	120	89	160	103 (94)	13
Greens[4]	33	12	81	38	
Groceries	40	38	36	30	4
Hats	16	15	13	14 (14)	
Herbs[4]	57	0	14	21 (7)	2
Ironware	20	4	14	18 (16)	
Ixtle products	7	9	6	[5]	
Jewelry	7	5	5	7 (6)	
Lemons and limes	3	0	3	8	10
Meat products	74	65	73	70 (70)	17
Milk	19	10	15	5 (5)	1
Notions	44	33	42	33	
Oil	2	2	3	-	
Onions	47	10	20	44	7
Perfume	3	4	5	2 (1)	
Potatoes white	27	21	29	25	

Pottery	2	0	1	2(2)	31
Rebozos	18	20	20	23(20)	
Refreshments	30	23	25	30	4
Rice, prepared	2	3	2	2	
Rubber	8	9	8	7(5)	
Shellfish	1	1	3	6	
Soap	5	4	3	1	
Sugar, brown	2	1	2	3(3)	1
Tinware	4	3	6	10	
Tomatoes	85	54	92	61	19
Underwear[6]	61	3	26		
Total, all vendors[7]	986	790	1,081	794	416

[1] The official lists of the *Administración de Mercados* include all vendors paying rents. The lists for 1958 and 1961 included some vendors who paid their fees by *boletos* (street vendors' receipts; see chap. 10), mainly vendors of notions, fruits and vegetables. Vendors selling more than one of the products listed are counted more than once, that is, for each product they sell.

[2] Project census compiled by R. G. Waterbury and E. B. Waterbury. The census listed vendors found to be present during the survey (between September 2 and October 1, 1964 for the Benito Juárez marketplace, and between October 6 and October 16, 1964 for the 20 de Noviembre marketplace), regardless of the manner of payment. As with the official lists, multiple-item vendors are counted for each product they sell; where project data indicate that a particular item was the principal one offered by the vendor, however the total number of stands at which the item was the major one (or only one) offered appears in parentheses.

[3] Includes dried fruit. Avocados, lemons, and limes are listed separately.

[4] The overlapping nature of the "greens" and "herbs" categories may account for some of the increase in the former and decrease in the latter in the offical list of 1961. Exclusion of *boleto* holders from the 1960 list may account for the extremely low figures for both products for that year.

[5] Included under "baskets."

[6] The overlapping nature of the "clothing" and "underwear" categories may account to some extent for the simultaneous increase in the former and decrease in the latter, in the official lists.

[7] Totals include all vendors whether or not their products are listed above. Multiple-product vendors are counted only once. If vendors paying by *boleto* are excluded, the official lists show a regular increase in total number of vendors: for 1958, 757 vendors; for 1960, 790 vendors; and for 1961, 898 vendors.

SECONDARY MARKETPLACES OF THE VALLEY: NUMBERS OF VENDORS OFFERING SPECIFIC PRODUCTS ON SPECIFIC PLAZA DAYS[1]

Town and survey date	Time of day	Total vendors[2]	Fruit	Beans (frijol)[3]	Jicama	Garlic, onions	Chile	Greens	Tomatoes, miltomate	Other vegetables	Meat Products	Fish, shrimp	Brown sugar	Cacao and/or coffee	Nuts, peanuts	Bread	Maize	Pottery	Baskets	Dry goods, notions	Clothing	Flowers
Ayoquezco																						
9/21/65, Tues.	?	161	40	0	0	13	13	0	7	0	8	1	2	2	0	5	0	2	8	3	5	16
9/28/65, Tues.	?	218	42	5	0	13	12	0	32	0	11	4	2	1	1	10	23	3	9	4	7	19
10/26/65, Tues.	?	288	48	0	5	24	21	0	24	1	16	4	0	5	9	15	0	7	27	8	13	15
Ejutla																						
9/23/65, Thurs.	A.M.	603	55	12	0	31	55	5	56	21	22	2	15	1	1	29	33	11	17	25	23	8
9/30/65, Thurs.	P.M.[4]	495	35	13	0	15	31	14	38	28	16	5	13	1	1	27	36	12	3	18	24	6
10/28/65, Thurs.	P.M.	829	120	0	17	28	63	6	29	26	21	5	14	2	35	27	62	21	51	29	36	14
Etla[5]																						
9/23/64, Wed.	12–3 P.M.	356	90	0	0	7	31	1	21	20	17	1	1	0	2	10	5	13	6	18	20	0
9/22/65, Wed.	10:50 A.M.	286	43	5	0	7	22	12	21	8	16	0	1	0	0	15	5	6	8	10	12	0
9/22/65, Wed.	3:30 P.M.	383	73	2	0	10	30	4	34	6	18	1	1	2	2	26	7	6	7	13	15	0
9/29/65, Wed.	2–3:30 P.M.	449	89	10	0	18	26	8	51	18	18	1	1	2	0	21	4	7	6	14	18	0
10/27/65, Wed.	1:40–2:50 P.M.	636	138	8	11	22	14	12	41	31	19	0	2	3	64	33	8	20	21	19	18	0
Miahuatlan																						
9/20/65, Mon.	10:15 A.M.	470	4	0	0	41	41	15	63	9	12	9	14	0	1	26	3	25	17	19	30	13
9/27/65, Mon.	?	630	96	0	0	38	52	9	61	54[6]	14	8	13	0	4	23	10	13	9	19	30	79
10/25/65, Mon.	?	943	134	0	3	50	91	1	62	51	16	11	14	1	43	37	9	24	79	31	28	29

Location / Date	Time	Total																				
Ocotlan																						
10/23/64, Fri.	1:30–3 P.M.	834	77	13	0	28	44	47	16	13	45	8	13	10	21	37	13	28	10	25	54	38
9/24/65, Fri.	10–1:35	1346	222	42	1	50	60	31	88	31	31	12	10	18	11	38	156	27	15	32	35	13
10/1/65, Fri.	11–2:00	1061	142	18	0	23	49	55	66	84	56	7	11	18	9	36	80	28	11	26	54	31
7/15/66, Fri.	?	1076	138	20	0	23	94	31	84	58	59	9	7	12	8	31	98	24	37	25	48	16
Tlacolula																						
2/26/65, Sun.	?	676	51	13	0	23	30	6	33	7	72	9	1	25	3	54	17	29	16	24	51	14
Zaachila																						
10/29/64, Thurs.	?	679	87	20	45	15	10	4	21	25	73	0	7	23	8	42	28	20	3	14	21	6
9/23/65, Thurs.	2:30 P.M.	473	44	18	1	3	52	7	44	7	59	3	3	7	26	18	18	8	7	11	19	5
9/30/65, Thurs.	A.M.	720	105	27	8	11	32	2	59	17	81	3	6	11	64	35	46	9	13	11	24	9
10/28/65, Thurs.	3 P.M.	429	21	13	26	26	43	0	34	1	83	2	4	18	14	41	10	11	4	14	18	0
Zimatlan																						
9/22/65, Wed.	A.M.	279	59	1	0	18	55	22	44	3	12	3	1	3	7	15	0	5	6	10	19	21
9/22/65, Wed.	P.M.	403	97	10	0	33	26	18	51	18	15	2	1	3	7	19	7	12	4	13	27	5
9/29/65, Wed.	11:30–1:00	413	62	11	0	38	55	11	44	3	15	7	1	4	15	25	10	12	9	12	16	5
10/27/66, Wed.	11:00 A.M.	708	92	7	20	33	57	10	41	10	26	5	5	6	12	26	8	20	31	15	22	4

[1] Project counts by Martin Diskin, Ronald G. Waterbury, and Ellen B. Waterbury.
[2] Includes all vendors whether or not their products are listed here.
[3] Beans, when not specified, may be included with "vegetables."
[4] Reduced number of vendors because of threat of rain.
[5] Includes indoor and outdoor markets.
[6] Includes large number of vendors of *guaje* beans.

APPENDIX 25

Principal Sales Outlets for Typical Weekly Production of a Sample of 69 Potters,[1] Santa Maria Atzompa, 1968

Pot form[2]	Atzompa finishers of crude Ware[3] Dozens	Atzompa resellers Dozens	Value[6]	Oaxaca resellers[4] Dozens	Value	S. Lorenzo Cacaotepec resellers Dozens	Value	Oaxaca tourist stores[5] Dozens	Value	Oaxaca plaza, street stand Dozens	Value	Oaxaca, peddling in plaza Dozens	Value
Casseroles, small[7]	2.5	32.5	329.50	6.0	72.00					5.0	50.00	2.5	25.00
Casseroles, medium	13.25	33.7	678.00	11.0	210.00	1.0	25.00			49.0	924.50	6.25	42.75
Casseroles, large				1.0	224.00					2.3	150.00		
Decorative ware[8]				—	425.00			—	180.00	—	475.00		
Flowerpots, medium										0.5	12.50	1.5	44.00
Flowerpots, large										0.25	15.00	0.7	80.00
Griddles, small				3.0	15.00								
Griddles, medium				7.0	100.00							2.5	50.00
Griddles, large													
Jars, small	7.0	6.0	72.00	5.0	35.00	5.0	50.00			26.5	311.50		
Jars, medium		6.0	162.00	11.5	292.00	5.0	75.00			1.5	24.50		
Jars, large		3.0	150.00										
Ollas, small	1.75	5.25	55.00										
Ollas, medium	42.75	27.25	524.50	11.0	196.00	1.75	52.50			19.5	382.50		
Ollas, large				4.0	172.50					4.0	250.00		
Plates, all types				3.0	48.00			0.5	11.75	3.0	48.00		
Tubs, small		6.0	72.00										
Tubs, medium	7.5	17.0	326.00							9.5	175.00	3.0	54.00
Tubs, large				0.8	100.00					1.25	180.00		

	Tlacolula plaza		Ocotlán plaza		Etla plaza		Zaachila plaza		Value of ware sold in plazas	Value of ware contracted to resellers
	Dozens	*Value*	*Dozens*	*Value*	*Dozens*	*Value*	*Dozens*	*Value*		
Casseroles, small[7]										
Casseroles, medium			2.25	54.00					1,318.25	1,538.50
Casseroles, large					5.0	72.00			475.00	605.00[5]
Decorative ware[8]									151.50	—
Flowerpots, medium										
Flowerpots, large										
Griddles, small										
Griddles, medium							2.0	50.00	160.00	115.00
Griddles, large							1.0	60.00		
Jars, small										
Jars, medium			15.3	246.00	5.0	77.00			659.00	836.00
Jars, large										
Ollas, small										
Ollas, medium			2.25	54.00					836.50	1,000.50
Ollas, large	0.4	150.00								
Plates, all types									48.00[5]	59.75
Tubs, small	9.0	108.00								
Tubs, medium							2.0	55.00	572.00	498.00
Tubs, large										
									4,220.75	4,652.75

[1] Slightly less than one-fifth of the village's pottery-producing households.

[2] In instances where the household produces more than one form or more than one size of the same form and the proportional production for each was not specified, the total household production is here divided equally among the various forms and/or sizes.

[3] Crude ware is sold for one-third to one-half the price of glazed and fired ware; on a half-shares arrangement, however, half of the finished pots are left with the potter who performs the glazing and firing, in payment for his materials and work.

[4] Includes shops (*casetas*) in Oaxaca market district.

[5] Sporadically, the types of ware sold to tourist stores are also sold directly to tourists who visit the village.

[6] Values are in Mexican pesos.

[7] Sizes have been assigned, somewhat arbitrarily, by value: "small" pots are worth less than $15.00 the dozen, "medium" pots from $15.00 to $40.00, and "large" pots more than $40.00. There are minor price differences between forms, between fully glazed and partially glazed ware, and also due to locus of sale and seasonal fluctuations, but these factors have not affected the above general categories in the cases covered.

[8] Decorative ware is variable in size and value.

APPENDIX 26

DISTRIBUTION OF METATES

(Adapted from Cook, 1971)

Marketplace	Supply source	Total transactions observed	Percent sold at retail	Percent sold to resellers	Destination	Percent	Notes
Oaxaca	San Sebastian Teitipac	624 (1300 metates)	16	84	Southern Highlands and Pacific coast	53	This was for the period 1966–1968. In 1967–1968, 82% of the total sales were to re-sellers, 69% involving more than one intermediary.
					Isthmus	24	
					Sierra Juárez, Sierra Mixteca, and part of Valley	23	
Ocotlán	Magdalena Ocotlán	589	95	5	Ocotlán district	64	Although 68 communities were represented by the buyers, 71% of the product went to buyers from 17 communities.
					Zimatlán district	20	
					Ejutla district	4	
					Various	12	
Tlacolula	Tlacolula, Teitipac villages	80	95	5	Tlacolula district	89	
					Various	11	

APPENDIX 27
HOUSEHOLD AND PERSONAL BUDGET OF MR,
RETAIL VENDOR IN THE OAXACA CITY MERCADO
(Totals are rounded figures and in part are estimates.)

FOOD:

Except for supper, which consists of bread and a beverage, meals are eaten in *fondas* (marketplace stalls offering prepared food). The estimated daily food budget is $30.00, including $2.00 for treats for the children. (An itemized daily budget totaled $29.50.) In addition, MR and his wife consume beer valued at a maximum of $10.00 weekly. For holidays such as All Saints, Christmas, and the New Year, a festive meal costing about $45.00 is prepared at home.

Annual total $11,500.00

OTHER BASIC HOUSEHOLD EXPENSES:

Baths, at public bath house, twice weekly for the family: $40.00 per week.
Man's haircuts, at $5.00, three per month.
Laundress (who provides the soap), $15.00 per week.
Cigarettes, one pack daily, $8.40 per week.
Oil for saints' lamps, $4.00 per week.
Kerosene for lamps and cooking, $1.25 per week.

Annual total 3,750.00

CLOTHING:

Fabric for dresses ....$200.00 annually
Dressmaker expenses, 6 dresses at $18.00 .... 108.00 annually
Shoes, average of .... 350.00 annually
Stockings or socks, approximately...................... 156.00 annually
Hats .... 72.00 annually
(Expenses for underwear and ready-made clothing could not be recalled and are not included here.)

Annual total ....$ 886.00

EDUCATION AND READING MATTER:

School supplies ....$ 30.00 annually
Daily newspapers..................................... 109.50 annually

Annual total ....$ 139.50

HEALTH:

Doctors' visits, 10 at $10.00 . . . .$100.00
Tests (X-ray) . . . . 180.00 annually
Medicine, average of . . . . 250.00 annually
(Expense for doctors varies with health of the family. Actual expenditures
for doctors' visits and tests are given for the year preceding the study. Expenditure shown for medicine is estimated by informant at $200 to $300
per year and includes eye drops and a calcium preparation for the children.)

    Annual total . . . .$ 530.00

RELIGION:

Church contributions, $0.20 to $1.00 weekly,
    averaging . . . .$31.20 annually
Copal (incense) for two holy days, ... 0.40 annually

    Annual total . . . .$ 31.60

ENTERTAINMENT:

Cinema, 10 to 12 times a year, estimate . . . .$165.00 annually
Fairs, minimum . . . . 4.00 annually

    Annual total . . . .$ 169.00

MISCELLANEOUS:

Dog food, ...$2.50 daily
Informant and wife were not able to give estimate of expenses for kitchen
ware (plates, griddles, and ollas are replaced about every two years), or
for children's toys.

    Annual total . . . .$ 912.50

Total annual expenditures, excluding payments for house and land, stock purchases
and other business expenses, and items for which estimates could not be given:
                         $17,918.60

APPENDIX 28
BUYING AND SELLING PRICE COMPARISONS FOR
ATZOMPA STOREKEEPER'S STOCK
1968

Item	Purchase price	Selling price
Paraffin candles	$2.00 per kilogram (11 candles)	$0.20 per candle
Salted crackers, package	$4.50	$7.00
Sweets, package of 104	$3.80	$0.05 per piece
Animal crackers, package	$3.00	$4.00
Sweet cookies, package	$7.00	$9.00
Pork sausage, large	$1.00 for six	$1.00 for five
Pork sausage, small	$1.00 for twelve	$1.00 for eight
Salt, kilogram	$0.40	$0.50
Soap, Perla brand	$0.80	$0.90
Soap, Camay brand	$0.60	$0.70
Sardines, large tin . . . . :	$4.00	$4.50
Sardines, small tin	$2.00	$2.50
Chili guajillo, kilogram	$10.00	$12.00
Soft drinks, small	$0.50, recently up from $0.40	$0.60
Mescal, liter	$5.00	$6.00
Beer, Corona brand, carton	$22.00, recently up from $19.50	$25.00
Beer, Superin brand, carton	$25.00	$30.00
Sugar, second-grade, kilogram . .	$1.60	$2.00
Candles in glass container, 100 .	$10.00	$20.00 ($0.20 each)
Bread	$1.00 for six	$1.00 for five
Cheese (produced locally)	$2.50 each	$3.00 each, or $4.00 if cut up
Liquid glaze, kilogram	$6.00	$6.50
Firewood, "burro load"	$8.00 (sometimes $7.50)	$10.00

APPENDIX 29

BUYING AND SELLING PRICE COMPARISONS
FOR STOREKEEPER'S STOCK AT MAGDALENA OCOTLÁN,
1967

Item	Purchase price	Selling price
Soft drinks (three brands, case	$9.60	$12.00
Beer (two brands), case	$17.00	$24.00
Mescal, liter	$3.40	$5.00
Cigarettes, Faros brand	$5.50 per carton (25 packs)	$0.50 per pack
Tinned sardines, one tin	$1.90	$2.00
Tinned chile, one tin	$0.65	$0.75
Sweets (hard candies)	$7.50 for 200	$0.10 each
Matches	$8.75 for 50 boxes	$0.20 per box
Candles in glass containers	$3.00 per dozen	$0.30 each
Alka-Seltzer tablets	$14.00 for fifty	$0.40 each
Writing tablets	$2.40 per dozen	$0.20 each
Balls of string	$1.00 per dozen	$0.15 each
Spools of thread	$1.00 per dozen	$0.10 each
Sal de Uvas (powder for indigestion), package	$14.00 for fifty	$0.40 each
Mejoral (cold remedy)	$1.00 for fourteen	$0.10 each
Desenfriol (cold remedy)	$1.00 for three	$0.40 each
Pencils	$0.20 each	$0.25 each
Camphor balls	$1.00 for fifteen	$0.10 each
Fab detergent, package	$0.45	$0.50
Cinnamon	$0.20 per ounce	$0.25 per ounce

COMPARATIVE RETAIL PRICES FOR SELECTED ITEMS IN FOUR MARKET TOWNS

Item	Unit	Price				
		Oaxaca (1966)	Tlacolula (1965)	Etla (1968)	Zoogocho (1967)	Tehuantepec (1967)
Apples	Each	$0.04-$0.12	—	—	$0.15-$0.20	—
	Kilogram	—	—	—	—	$9.00
Bananas	3	—	—	—	—	$0.20-$0.50
	Kilogram	$0.10-$1.40	—	$1.40	—	—
Beans (*frijol*)	Kilogram	$2.00-$4.80	$3.50	$3.00	—	$12.80*
	Almud	$9.50-$12.80	$10.00-$15.00	—	$5.00-$12.00	—
Bread, size not specified	Each	$0.10-$0.20	—	—	$0.33-$0.60	—
Brooms, various sizes	Each	—	$1.00-$1.40	—	$1.00-$10.00	—
Cacao	Kilogram	—	$5.50-$8.50	—	$9.00-$10.00	$20.00*
Chayote	Each	$0.50-$0.80	—	—	$0.05-$0.15	$0.60 (large)
Cheese	Pound	—	—	—	$8.00	—
	Kilogram	$20.00	—	—	—	—
Chile, various types	100	$9.00-$12.00	$5.00	—	—	—
	Each	—	—	—	—	—
	¼ Kilogram	—	—	$2.50	—	$0.10-$0.20
	Kilogram	$1.00-$30.00	—	$5.00	—	—

Chilimolera (pottery chile grinder)	Each	$0.90-$1.60	—	—	$1.00	—
Coffee	¼ Kilogram	—	—	—	$2.25	—
	Kilogram	$8.00-$12.00	—	—	—	$6.00-$7.00
	11.5 kilograms (arroba)	—	—	—	$45.00-$56.00	—
Cups, size not specified	Dozen	$8.00-$11.00	—	—	$8.00-$14.00	—
Eggs	Each	$0.60-$0.75	—	$0.60	$0.40-$0.60	—
Garlic	Each	—	—	—	—	$0.20
	10	—	—	$1.00	—	—
	100	$12.00-$30.00	—	—	—	—
Lard	½ kilogram	—	—	$4.50	—	—
	Kilogram	$10.00	—	—	—	—
Lemons	Each	—	—	—	—	$0.20
	2	—	—	—	$0.05	—
	100	$2.50-$20.00	—	—	—	—
Maize	Liter	$0.90-$1.10	$1.10	—	—	$0.85
	Kilogram	—	—	$4.50	—	—
	Almud	$3.50-$5.00	$3.00-$4.75	$4.50	$5.50-$6.00 (heavy maize)	—
Mangoes	Each	$0.10-$0.70	—	$0.20	$0.20	—

APPENDIX 30 (continued)

Item	Unit					
Meat						
Dried beef	Pound	—	—	—	$5.50	—
	¼ Kilogram	—	—	—	—	—
Pork	Pound	—	—	$3.00	$4.00	—
	¼ Kilogram	—	—	—	$3.00	—
Mescal	Liter	—	—	$7.00	$5.00	—
Onions	Each	—	—	—	—	—
	10	—	—	$1.00	—	$0.20-$0.30
	100	$12.00-$30.00	—	—	$10.00-$35.00	—
Oranges	Each	—	—	—	—	—
	2	—	—	—	$0.05-$0.20	$0.20
	5	—	—	$1.00	—	—
	100	$11.00-$38.00	—	—	—	—
Pears	Each	$0.20-$0.50	—	—	—	—
	3	—	—	—	$0.20	—
Pineapples	Each	$0.80-$4.00	$0.80	—	$2.00-$3.00	$2.00
Potatoes	Kilogram	$0.70-$2.00	—	$3.00	$3.00	$1.80-$2.30
Rice	Kilogram	$3.00-$3.20	—	$2.00	$2.00	—
Shrimp, dried	Pound	—	—	—	—	—
	¼ Kilogram	—	—	$2.50	$2.50	—
Sugar, white	Kilogram	$1.50-$1.00	8	$1.80	—	—
Tomatoes	Pound	—	—	—	$0.25-$2.00	—
	Kilogram	$0.75-$9.00	—	$2.50	$2.50	$1.50-$2.00

*Price appears to be suspiciously high.

APPENDIX 31

RESIDENTS OF OTHER STATES BORN IN OAXACA STATE
(From *Cuadro* 10 of the various state censuses for 1960.)

	Men	*Women*	*Total*
Aguascalientes	75	91	166
Baja California........	1,016	808	1,824
Baja California T. Sur	20	5	25
Campeche	156	78	234
Chiapas	3,499	2,943	6,442
Chihuahua............	651	399	1,050
Coahuila..............	361	251	612
Colima................	201	109	310
Distrito Federal.......	44,740	53,768	98,508
Durango..............	412	387	799
Guanajuato...........	299	305	604
Guerrero..............	2,182	2,074	4,256
Hidalgo...............	452	432	884
Jalisco................	6	0	6
Mexico................	3,308	3,088	6,396
Michoacan............	345	282	627
Morelos	1,600	1,478	3,078
Nayarit	148	59	207
Nuevo Leon	592	503	1,095
Puebla	8,506	9,046	17,552
Queretaro............	169	166	335
Quintana Roo.........	130	42	172
San Luis Potosi	742	744	1,486
Sinaloa...............	727	591	1,318
Sonora	1,242	922	2,164
Tabasco..............	701	583	1,284
Tamaulipas...........	1,757	1,629	3,386
Tlaxcala..............	476	479	955
Veracruz..............	26,650	26,277	52,927
Yucatan..............	193	132	325
Zacatecas	191	144	335
	101,547	107,815	209,362

APPENDIX 32

TOTALS OF BOLETOS, TARJETAS, AND INODORO ADMISSIONS FOR SELECTED YEARS, 1938–1966

FEBRUARY

Year	Boletos $	% change	Boletos #	% change	Tarjetas $	% change	Inodoro admissions #	% change
1938	10,381	—	87,850	—	696	—	34,225	—
1947	12,493[a]	+20.3	65,070[a]	−25.9	2,841[a]	+308.2	68,500[a]	+100.1
1952	10,173[b]	−18.6	49,531[b]	−23.8	16,327[b]	+474.7	46,440[b]	−32.2
1959	26,093	+156.5	52,914	+6.8	32,195	+97.2	108,890	+134.5
1963	26,978	+3.4	50,345	−4.8	44,875	+39.4	140,700	+29.2
1966	43,599	+61.6	60,400	+20.0	60,676	+35.2	115,920	−17.6

MAY

Year	Boletos $	% change	Boletos #	% change	Tarjetas $	% change	Inodoro admissions #	% change
1938	10,467	—	87,747	—	779	—	36,903	—
1952	11,007	+5.2	49,335	−43.8	16,861	2064.4	56,440	+52.9
1959	32,600	+196.2	61,057	+23.7	34,776	+106.3	105,689	+87.3
1963	31,107	−4.6	57,469	−5.9	47,027	+35.2	128,887	+22.0
1966	46,739[a]	+50.3	64,644[a]	+12.5	59,510[a]	+26.5	123,490[a]	−4.2

OCTOBER

Year	Boletos	% change	Boletos	% change	Tarjetas	% change	Inodoro admissions	% change
	$		#		$		#	
1938	13,188	–	108,872	–	939	–	41,750	–
1952	14,375	+9.0	c	–32.0	24,429	+2501.6	44,212	+5.9
1959	42,122	+193.0	74,086	–7.6	35,824	+46.6	101,440	+129.4
1963	44,129	+4.8	68,488	+32.4	47,526	+32.7	119,876	+18.2
1966	74,443	+68.7	90,664		63,546	+33.7	145,040	+21.0

a One day's receipts missing
b Month of 29 days
c Data unavailable

APPENDIX 33
Numbers of Boletos Sold[a]

Monthly sales	1938	1947	1959	1966
February	87,800	65,100[b]	52,900	60,400
May	87,700	c	61,000	64,600[b]
October	108,900	c	74,100	90,700
Tuesday sales				
February	c	8,300	5,600	7,400
May	c	c	6,100	10,000
October	c	c	7,300	8,600
Saturday sales				
February	c	17,100	18,600	22,200
May	c	c	23,700	22,100
October	c	c	27,500	34,600

[a] Figures rounded to the nearest hundred
[b] One day's receipts missing
[c] Data not available

APPENDIX 34
RANGES IN NUMBER OF BOLETOS SOLD DAILY
FOR SELECTED MONTHS

Months	Weekday lows	Saturday highs
January 1959	1,086	4,452
July 1959	856	4,652
September 1959	1,216	3,743
January 1966	1,127	5,711
July 1966	981	6,168*
September 1966	1,186	5,723

* Sales were higher on Monday, July 25, 1966, the day of the Fiesta of *Lunes del Cerro:* 6, 626.

APPENDIX 35

NUMBER OF BOLETOS SOLD BY PRICE, FOR SELECTED DAYS, JANUARY 1966

Date	Day			Price			
January		$0.20	$0.40	$0.50	$1.00	$5.00	Total
3	Monday	181	196	184	1066	101	1728
8	Saturday	344	594	1147	3082	0	5167
11	Tuesday	150	207	429	970	0	1756
15	Saturday	342	531	1553	3079	15	5520
19	Wednesday	175	223	234	667	0	1299
22	Saturday	355	547	1057	3286	28	5273
27	Thursday	144	207	229	640	0	1220
29	Saturday	314	579	1386	3425	7	5711
Ranges for January 1966:		85–355	142–594	168–1553	617–3425	0–101	1127–5711

APPENDIX 36

NUMBERS ENGAGED IN SPECIAL OCCUPATIONS, MITLA, 1929-1933 AND 1968
(Farmers and traders excluded)[1]

Occupation	Number listed by Parsons	Number listed by Ramirez	Comments
Adobe maker	3	2	
Baker	8	—	
Bandmaster	2	—	
Barber	2	10	The ten barbers listed by Ramirez were employed in five barber shops.
Beekeeper	Unspecified	—	
Blacksmith	1	—	
Bonesetter-veterinarian	1	—	
Brewer of *tepache*	3-4	—	
Butcher	5	3	Ramirez also lists eight beef vendors and five pork vendors in addition to *matanceros*.
Candlemaker	2	1	In 1933 there were five or six candlemakers specializing in candles for religious festivals.
Carpenter	3	4	
Carter	4	10-12	
Charcoal processor	3	—	
Clothing manufacturer	Unspecified	10	In 1933 makers of clothing were small-scale seamstresses. Presently there are ten shops employing three to four workers each, and two small sewing schools.
Curer, traditional, male	3	—	One of the curers was also a barber.
Fireworks maker	1	—	
Flower maker (artificial flowers)	1	—	
Hunter	Unspecified	None	
Image maker	2	15-20	

APPENDIX 36 *(continued)*

Jeweler	—	2	One jeweler employs five workers.
Knotter (of rebozo ends)	—	See "Comments"	Approximately 45 percent of the population is now engaged in this new occupation related to the much-expanded weaving industry
Laborer	98	—[2]	
Master mason	6	18	
Milk vendor	—	6	
Miller of *nixtamal*	1	7	
Pot-still operator (producer of mescal)	3	2[3]	
Rope maker	6, possibly more	25	In 1933 rope making was a secondary occupation of farmers.
Sandalmaker	1	4	
Silversmith	—	1	
Spokesman, traditional (*huehuete*)	Unspecified	—	
Storekeeper	8	39	
Tailor	2	4	In 1933 one of the tailors was also the sandalmaker.
Tanner	2	None	
Taxicab owner-operator	—	7	
Thatcher	1	—	
Weaver	10	About 300	There now are approximately 100 large-scale weavers and 200 small-scale weavers.
Woodchoppers	2	—	

[1] Farmers and traders are dealt with elsewhere.
[2] It is obvious that the occupation of laborer existed in 1968 but it is not specificaly listed.
[3] Large-scale mescal operations existing in 1968 were not investigated.

APPENDIX 37
Sources of Goods Handled in Mitla Trade, 1933[1]

Product	Sources
Alfalfa	Tlacolula* (Valley).
Animals	
Domestic, generally	Hacienda de Narro, Lachixila, Largasia, Nejapa, Quiavicuzas, Tavela (eastern Zapotec Sierra)
Burros, goats, oxen	San Lorenzo Albarradas (northern Zapotec Sierra)
Horses	San Lorenzo Albarradas; Tlacolulita (Isthmus)
Avocados	Tepantlali (Mixe Sierra)
Bags (*costales*)	San Mateo Cajonos (northern Zapotec Sierra)
Baskets	San Lorenzo Albarradas (northern Zapotec Sierra), Tlacolula,* Miahuatlan* (Valley)
Beans	Santa Catarina and San Miguel Albarradas, Betaza, Yalalag* (northern Zapotec Sierra), Tepuxtepec, Ayutla,* Zacatepec, Cacalotepec, Tepantlali, Quetzaltepec, Mazatlan, Juquila Mixe, Ixcuintepec (Mixe Sierra), Coatlan, Santiago Guevea, Lachiguiri, San Pedro Quiatoni (eastern Zapotec Sierra), San Dionisio Ocotepec, Tlacolula,* Mitla, Xaagá (Valley).
Beeswax	Matatlan, Mitla (Valley)
Bread	Tlacolula* (Valley)
Bricks	Tlacolula*
Bridles	San Mateo Cajonos (northern Zapotec Sierra)
Brooms	San Miguel and San Lorenzo Albarradas (northern Zapotec Sierra)
Buckskin and/or buckskin coats	Ixcuintepec (Mixe Sierra), Santiago Guevea, Coatlan, Lachiguiri (eastern Zapotec Sierra), Tlacolulita (Isthmus), Mitla (Valley)
Castor beans	Mitla
Castor oil	Tepuxtepec (Mixe Sierra)
Cacao	Oaxaca* (Valley)
Cheese	Tanive (Valley)
Chick-peas	Tlacolula* (Valley)
Chile	Betaza, Yalalag* (northern Zapotec Sierra), Ayutla,* Zacatepec, Cacalotepec, Tepantlali, Quetzaltepec, Mazatlan (Mixe Sierra), San Pedro Quiatoni (eastern Zapotec Sierra)
Chocolate	Tlacolula* (Valley)
Cinnamon	Oaxaca* (Valley)
Coconut	Isthmus of Tehuantepec*
Coffee	Betaza, Yalalag* (northern Zapotec Sierra),

APPENDIX 37 *(continued)*

	Ayutla,* Zacatepec, Cacalotepec, Tepantlali, Quetzaltepec, Mazatlan, Juquila Mixes, Ixcuintepec (Mixe Sierra), Santiago Guevea, Coatlan, Lachiguirí (eastern Zapotec Sierra)
Cornstalks	Matatlan, San Dionisio Ocotepec (Valley)
Dress goods and dry goods	Oaxaca*
Dye of the cascalote nut	Tabela (eastern Zapotec Sierra)
Eggs	Santa Catarina, San Miguel and San Lorenzo Albarradas (northern Zapotec Sierra), Tepuxtepec (Mixe Sierra)
Fire fans (palmleaf product)	San Lorenzo Albarradas (northern Zapotec Sierra)
Fish, dried	Isthmus of Tehuantepec*
Flour of wheat	Oaxaca*
Flowers	
General	San Sebastian de Abasolo (Valley)
Lilies	San Pedro Quiatoni (eastern Zapotec Sierra)
Manzanilla and marigolds	San Bartolome Quialana (Valley)
Fowl	Santa Catarina, San Miguel and San Lorenzo Albarradas (northern Zapotec Sierra), Tepuxtepec (Mixe Sierra), Lachixila, Quiavicuzas and Hacienda de Narro (eastern Zapotec Sierra)
Fruit	Tepuxtepec (Mixe Sierra), San Juan, Santa Ana and San Luis Quiatoni (eastern Zapotec Sierra), San Sebastián Abasolo (Valley)
Apples	San Sebastián Abasolo and Tlacochahuaya (Valley)
Bananas	Cacalotepec (Mixe Sierra)
Cherries	San Miguel Albarradas (northern Zapotec Sierra)
Custard apples	San Miguel Albarradas
Lemons	Santa María Albarradas
Mamey	Quetzaltepec (Mixe Sierra)
Mangoes	San Juan, Santa Ana and San Luis Quiatoni (eastern Zapotec Sierra)
Oranges	Betaza, Yalalag,* Santa María Albarradas (northern Zapotec Sierra), Ayutla,* Zacatepec, Cacalotepec, Tepantlali, Quetzaltepec, Mazatlan, Tepuxtepec (Mixe Sierra)
Peaches	San Miguel Albarradas
Plums	San Sebastián Abasolo, Tlacochahuaya
Prickly pear fruit *(tuna)*	Mitla
Tamarinds	Tlacolulita (Isthmus)
Zapote	San Juan, Santa Ana and San Luis Quiatoni (eastern Zapotec Sierra)
Grass for brooms	San Lorenzo Albarradas (northern Zapotec Sierra)

Hammocks	San Mateo Cajonos (northern Zapotec Sierra)
Husk tomatoes	San Bartolome Quialana (Valley)
Ixtle	Santo Domingo Albarradas (northern Zapotec Sierra)
Jícama	Zaachila* (Valley)
Lime, mineral	San Lorenzo Albarradas (northern Zapotec Sierra), Matatlan, San Antonio de la Cal (Valley)
Magpies	San Lucas Quiavini (Valley)
Maguey	Matatlan (Valley)
Maize	Betaza, Yalalag* (northern Zapotec Sierra), Tepuxtepec, Ayutla,* Zacatepec, Cacalotepec, Tepantlali, Quetzaltepec, Mazatlan (Mixe Sierra), San Dionisio Ocotepec, Tlacolula,* Xaagá (Valley)
Mats (palm-leaf products)	Santa Catarina, Santo Domingo, San Lorenzo and San Miguel Albarradas (northern Zapotec Sierra), San Baltasar Guelavila (Valley)
Meat	Tlacolula* (Valley)
Metal goods	Oaxaca* (Valley)
Milk	Xaagá (Valley)
Net containers	San Mateo Cajonos (northern Zapotec Sierra)
Nuts	San Sebastián Abasolo, Tlacochahuaya (Valley)
Oil	San Pedro Quiatoni (eastern Zapotec Sierra), Matatlan (Valley)
Pack straps (ixtle product)	Santo Domingo Albarradas, San Mateo Cajonos (northern Zapotec Sierra)
Peanuts	San Sebastián Abasolo, Tlacochahuaya (Valley)
Pixtle (mamey nut)	Mazatlan (Mixe Sierra)
Pottery	San Marcos Tlapazola, San Bartolo Coyotepec, Santa María Atzompa, San Sebastián Abasolo, Tlacochahuaya, Oaxaca* (Valley)
Pulque	Matatlan (Valley)
Rawhide	Juquila Mixes, Ixcuintepec (Mixe Sierra), Santiago Guevea, Coatlan, Lachiguirí (eastern Zapotec Sierra), Isthmus of Tehuantepec*
Rope (ixtle product)	Santo Domingo Albarradas (northern Zapotec Sierra), Mitla
Saddles	Nejapa (eastern Zapotec Sierra)
Salt	San Miguel Albarradas (northern Zapotec Sierra), Isthmus of Tehuantepec*
Sandals, plaited	Betaza, Yalalag* (northern Zapotec Sierra)
Shrimp	Isthmus of Tehuantepec*
Squash seeds	San Pedro Quiatoni (eastern Zapotec Sierra), San Dionisio (Valley)
Starch	Oaxaca* (Valley)

APPENDIX 37 *(continued)*

Sugar, brown	Zacatepec (Mixe Sierra)
Sugar, white, refined	Oaxaca* (Valley)
Sugarcane	San Antonio de la Cal, Zaachila,* Oaxaca* (Valley)
Thatching plant *(cucharilla)*	San Miguel Albarradas (northern Zapotec Sierra)
Tiles for roofing	Tlacolula* (Valley)
Tomatoes	San Lucas Quiavini, San Bartolome Quialana (Valley)
Vegetables	San Sebastián Abasolo (Valley)
Wood products	
General	Matatlan (Valley)
Bamboo	Matatlan
Bark	San Pedro, San Juan, Santa Ana and San Luis Quiatoni (eastern Zapotec Sierra)
Beams, posts, and timbers	San Miguel Albarradas (northern Zapotec Sierra)
Charcoal	Matatlan
Copal	San Pedro Quiatoni (eastern Zapotec Sierra)
Pine wood (torch pine)	San Miguel and Santa María Albarradas (northern Zapotec Sierra), Tepuxtepec (Mixe Sierra)
Wool	Matatlan, San Dionisio, San Lucas Quiavini (Valley)
Woven goods	Mitla

* Towns with important marketplaces *(plazas)*.

[1] Includes goods sold in Mitla by vendors from elsewhere or handled by Mitla *viajeros*. Sources given are not always places where goods are produced; this is especially true of towns with marketplaces. To products mentioned by Parsons, Beals adds dried shrimp, salt, and coconuts as important Isthmus exports carried by Mitla traders in 1933.

APPENDIX 38
Sources or Places of Purchase of Major Goods
Handled by Mitla Traders (including truckers), 1968[1]

Product	Sources
Arms and ammunition	Oaxaca*
Avocados	Cacalotepec, Juquila Mixes, Ayutla,* Tamazulapan, Tepantlali, Tepuxtepec, Tlahuitoltepec (Mixe Sierra)
Bags made of ixtle	Mitla
Beans	Cacalotepec, Ayutla,* Tepuxtepec (Mixe Sierra)
Beer	Oaxaca*
Bread	Mitla, Oaxaca*
Bricks	Tlacolula*
Candles	Mitla
Castor beans	Tepuxtepec, Ayutla*
Chile, fresh	Tamazulapan
Chile, tinned	Mitla
Cigarettes	Mitla, Oaxaca*
Clothing	Oaxaca,* Mexico City
Coconuts	Isthmus of Tehuantepec*
Coffee	Ayutla,* Alotepec, Cacalotepec, Cotzocón, Juquila Mixes, Ocotal, Ocotepec, Quetzaltepec, San Isidro, Tamazulapan, Zacatepec, Camotlán Choapan, Santa María (Mixe Sierra), Mitla
Construction materials	Mexico City
Fish, fresh and dried	Isthmus of Tehuantepec*
Flour	Mexico City
Fruit	
Fruit generally	Oaxaca*
Bananas	Cacalotepec (Mixe Sierra)
Oranges	Tepantlali, Ayutla* (Mixe Sierra)
Tamarinds	Isthmus of Tehuantepec*
Gasoline	Oaxaca*
Goats	Tepuxtepec, Ayutla* (Mixe Sierra)
Grains	Oaxaca,* Mexico City, Isthmus of Tehuantepec*
Groceries	Oaxaca,* Mexico City
Kerosene	Oaxaca*
Lime, mineral	Isthmus of Tehuantepec*
Liquors	Oaxaca,* Mexico City
Maize	Mitla, Oaxaca,* Isthmus of Tehuantepec*
Marble	Northern Zapotec Sierra near San Lorenzo Albarradas

APPENDIX 38 (continued)

Meat	Tlacolula*
Milk, powdered	Mexico City
Milk, whole	Tanivé, Loma Larga (Valley)
Rice	Oaxaca*
Salt	Mitla, Oaxaca,* Isthmus of Tehuantepec*
Sardines, tinned	Mitla, Oaxaca*
Soap	Mitla
Sugar, brown	Mitla, Oaxaca,* Isthmus of Tehuantepec*
Sugar, refined, white	Oaxaca,* Mexico City
Sweets, cookies	Mitla, Oaxaca*
Tiles for roofing	Tlacolula*
Vegetables, generally	Oaxaca*
Wax	Oaxaca*
Wood products	
Charcoal	San Lorenzo Albarradas
Firewood	San Lorenzo Albarradas, Xaagá, Corral del Cerro (Valley)
Beams	San Miguel Albarradas

* Towns with major marketplaces (*plazas*) serving out-of-town buyers.

[1] It will be noted that appendix 38 is not as extensive as appendix 37. Ramirez was more concerned about products handled in quantity by Mitla traders than he was about accounting in detail for all goods entering Mitla.

APPENDIX 39

CENSUS OF TEN MAJOR COMERCIANTES OF MITLA, 1968

	Years in business	Investment	Products handled and product sources	Where or to whom products sold	Trucks owned	Reported income
Case 1.	14 (formerly a farmer)	$10,000	Coffee and avocados purchased from *viajeros* to Mixe region. Groceries, plastics, aluminum articles, etc. from Mexico City.	Mexico City. Sold to Mitleños, Mixes, etc. from Mitla store. Some barter with Mixes.	1	$900/month*
Case 2.	25 (formerly a farmer)	$50,000	Groceries, clothing, *semillas* (usually maize, beans, garbanzos), liquors, purchased in Oaxaca and Mexico City. Avocados, coffee trucked from the Mixería. Tamarinds trucked from the Isthmus.	Clientele of Mitla store; Ayutla Mixes. Products traded between Mexico City, the Isthmus, and Ayutla.	3	$2000/month
Case 3.	20 (formerly a farmer)	$10,000	Clothing, *semillas*, school supplies, and groceries purchased in Oaxaca.	Sold from Mitla store primarily to Mitleños.	—	$400/month*

APPENDIX 39 (*continued*)

Case 4.	12 (formerly a farmer)	$30,000	Beer, bought in Oaxaca. Sold from truck in Mitla. Coffee and maize, purchased in Mitla. Sold in Oaxaca.	1	$1500/month*
Case 5.	12 (formerly a *viajero*)	$ 6,000	Groceries, clothing, maize and *semillas*, purchased in Oaxaca (clothing made by seamstresses under contract). Sold from Mitla store to Mitleños and Mixes.	—	$600/month
Case 6.	? (formerly a *viajero*)	$10,000	Purchased groceries and *semillas* in Oaxaca and on the Isthmus. Sold from Mitla store to Mitleños and residents of Xaagá, and San Lorenzo and Santa María Albarradas. Coffee from Mitla. Trucked to the Isthmus. Salt from the Isthmus. Trucked to Oaxaca.	1	$300/month*
Case 7.	40 (formerly a farmer and *viajero*)	$ 9,000	Groceries, paper products, clothing, *semillas*, purchased in Oaxaca and Mexico City. Sold from Mitla store to Mitleños and residents of surrounding communities.	1	$900/month

Case		Investment	Products purchased	Where sold	Employees	Income
Case 8.	5 (formerly a *viajero*)	$10,000	Groceries, *semillas*, paper products, purchased in Oaxaca, the Isthmus, Mexico City, Puebla, and Tuxtla Gutierrez.	Sold from Mitla store to Mitleños and residents of surrounding communities.	2	$600/month*
Case 9.	4 (formerly a baker)	$ 600*	Groceries and *semillas* purchased in Oaxaca and Puebla.	Sold from Mitla store and trucked to Ayutla.	1	$300/month*
			Coffee and avocados from Ayutla Mixe.	Trucked to the Isthmus, sometimes to Puebla.		
Case 10.	4 (formerly a baker)	$ 2,300	Groceries, *semillas* and hats purchased in Oaxaca.	Sold from Mitla store.	1	$2,400/6 months
			Fruits, greens, etc. from Oaxaca.	Sold in small Mitla marketplace.		

* Investment or income appears to be understated.

APPENDIX 40
Mitla Trucks Serving Ayutla

	Goods Carried to Ayutla	Goods Bought in Ayutla
1.[1]	Maize	Coffee and avocados
2.[2]	Groceries	Coffee and avocados
3.	Bread	Coffee and avocados
4.[2]	Groceries, pottery, plastic and metal containers, cement, lime, corrugated roofing and other construction materials	Coffee
5.	Maize, white sugar, brown sugar	Coffee and avocados
6.[1]	Groceries	Coffee and avocados
7.	Maize, brown sugar	Avocados
8.	Maize	Coffee
9.[1,2]	Soft drinks, maize, crackers, soap, beer	Coffee and avocados
10.[2]	Maize, brown sugar, white sugar, cookies, soap	Coffee
11.[1]	Maize	Coffee and avocados
12.[2]	Maize	Coffee and avocados
13.[1,2]	None (travels empty)	Avocados
14.[1]	Ices and ice cream (own factory)	Coffee and avocados
15.	Bread, pottery, groceries, household articles	Coffee and avocados
16.	Goods for travelers with animals in Ayutla	Coffee and avocados

[1] Drives own truck.

[2] Owns store.

APPENDIX 41

Sellers in Ayutla Plaza, March 1968 Census[1]

Town of Origin	Number of People	Products
AYUTLA	4	Tepache
	5	Turkey eggs, toasted squash seeds
	6	Rope, beans
	3	Rope, nets
	1	Notions (purchased in Mitla)
	7	Black maize, white maize (very little), beans, peas
	3	Salt (purchased in Mitla)
	3	Prepared food
	2	Clothing
	12	Meat
	2	Salt (purchased in Mitla), dried fish (purchased in Oaxaca)
	2	Salt (purchased in Mitla)
	2	Refreshments, soap, thread
	1	Pineapple (purchased in Oaxaca), brown sugar (purchased in Mitla), onions, empty bottles
	1	Brown sugar (purchased in Mitla), bread (from Juchitán), soap, ice water
	1	Bread (purchased in Mitla), pottery (from Oaxaca)
	6	Salt, kerosene (purchased in Mitla)
	2	Bread, brown sugar
	4	Bread (from Ayutla)
	1	Brown sugar, bread
	2	Candles, candle holders
	3	Refreshments, brown sugar
	2	Brown sugar (purchased in Mitla)
	2	Brown sugar, bread, refreshments
	1	Groceries
	2	Pottery (from Oaxaca)
	1	Kerosene (purchased in Mitla)
	3	Soap, brown sugar, bread (from Mitla)
	1	Groceries
	1	Prepared food
CAJONOS	1	Chile, garlic, fish
	3	Dried fish, chile

APPENDIX 41 *(continued)*

Díaz Ordaz	1	Woolen blankets (purchased in Puebla)
Mitla	3	Hardware, notions
	4	Notions, clothing
	6	Cloth, clothing
	8	Bread[2]
	1	Groceries[3]
Oaxaca	4	Melons, tomatoes, chile[2]
	3	Tomatoes, onions, garlic, lettuce, mineral lime, ollas[2]
	3	Hats, groceries
	2	Cloth remnants
	1	*Huaraches,* rubber soles, tin cans, cloth dolls
San Pedro Cajonos	10	Dried fish, chile, hats, nets, soap, groceries, hardware, belts, plastic objects, cookies, sacks[2]
	1	Sacks, dried fish, chile, nets
	2	Chile, dried fish
Tamazulapan	3	Beans, some maize
	3	Turkeys
	1	Rebozos
	1	Coffee (very little)
	2	Blue cloth for skirts (purchased in Juchitán)
	1	Cloth (purchased in Oaxaca)
	5	Ollas, hens
	4	Dried fish (purchased in Oaxaca)
	3	Dried fish (purchased in Oaxaca)
	1	Dried fish, sweets, bread (from Juchitán)
	2	Dried fish
Tepantlali	3	Bananas
	3	Oranges and bananas
	6	Oranges and bananas
Tepuxtepec	5	Gaskets, mats, *guaje* beans
	3	Eggs, peas, broad beans
	1	Rope, mats
	2	Wool (very little)
	2	*Guaje* beans, small tomatoes

TLAHUITOLTEPEC	8	Pulque, tomatoes, zapotes, *guaje* beans, rope, nets, "*palo de* pulque"
	2	Nets
	4	*Guaje* beans, zapotes
	5	Zapotes, rope, hammocks, leather sheaths for machetes (purchased in San Pedro Cajonos)
	4	Belts, leather straps, and other leather articles
	2	Cloth (made in Tlahuitoltepec)
	2	Groceries
YALALAG	5	*Huaraches,* clothing

[1] Based on census by Ramírez (50 ff.).

[2] Brought by truck. The two groups of vendors from Oaxaca rent a truck together. The San Pedro Cajonos group rents a truck for the trip every Sunday.

[3] The vendor, a store operator, is a Mitleño with three years' residence in Ayutla.

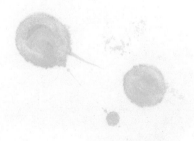

APPENDIX 42
Estimated Numbers of Mixe Traders Dealing With
Mitla Traders in the Ayutla Marketplace, and Their Products[1]

Village of Origin	Numbers of Traders	Products Sold
Tamazulapan	25	Coffee, chile, avocados[2]
Cacalotepec	10	Beans, avocados, coffee, bananas
Juquila Mixes	15	Coffee, avocados
Tlahuitoltepec	20	Avocados[3]
Zacatepec	5	Coffee
Tepantlali	20	Oranges and avocados
San Isidro	5	Coffee
Tepuxtepec	10	Beans, castor beans, avocados, goats
Ocotepec	10	Coffee
Alotepec	15	Coffee

[1] These estimates were given to Ramírez by a knowledgeable informant he encountered at Ayutla.
[2] The coffee must be assembled; it is not produced in Tamazulapan.
[3] Carried in by human transport only.

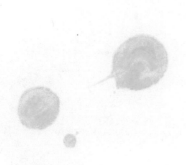

APPENDIX 43
Case Histories of Traders

Case 1

This trader travels by bus to the Ayutla marketplace. He buys goods in Oaxaca, including soap, crackers, brown sugar, salt, and vegetables (mainly lettuce, radishes, onions, garlic, and tomatoes), which he sells to dealers in Ayutla or to buyers from other Sierra towns. His purchase and selling prices are as follows:

Article	*Purchase Price*	*Selling Price (Mitla)*
Coffee	$55 per *arroba* (25 lbs.)	Not given.
Avocados	$80 per basket of 100–110 (varies from $25 to $100)	Purchase price plus 25 percent.
Beans	$8 per almud	$11 per almud
Castor beans	$5 per almud	$6 per almud
Oranges	$15 per 100	$18–$19 per 100
Goats (infrequent items)	$60 per head	Purchase price plus 25 percent

Expenses for the round-trip journey (transportation and meals) average $40. Profits for each trip are ordinarily about $250, and under favorable circumstances they may reach $350 *(39–43)*.

Case 2

This trader goes from Ayutla to Cotzocón, a five-day journey, remains two days in Cotzocón, and returns. He ordinarily travels with his brother (but accounts are apparently separate). Between them they own 12 mules that are left in Ayutla with a *mozo* while they take goods to Mitla by bus. They purchase all their goods in Mitla from one storekeeper, mainly brown sugar, salt, soap, bread, small chiles, canned sardines, sweets, matches, cigarettes, candles, and maguey fiber sacks (presumably for coffee). These are all sold to a storekeeper in Cotzocón. The trader buys only coffee in Cotzocón, selling in Mitla at $300 per 60-kilogram sack. His expenses per round trip he estimates at $100; the value of the merchandise he carries is around $1,500. His estimated profit is $500 per trip. The interviewer notes that he has a large and well-kept house and is always well dressed. He has been traveling to Cotzocón for 10 years, his brother for 20 years *(44–45)*.

Case 3

This trader travels with mules from Santa María Albarradas via Tepuxtepec, Juquila, and Ocotepec to Ocotal (near Quetzaltepec). He began as a *mozo* or assistant to another trader, later bought burros and began trading on his own. He replaced the burros with mules. From a Mitla storekeeper he buys brown sugar, candles, matches, cigarettes, and whatever else he is commissioned to buy. In Ocotal he buys coffee, which he sells to a dealer in Mitla. He estimates the cost of the goods he carries at $300 to $400, the expenses of his journey at $200, and his profits for each trip at from $300 to $400 (46–47).

Case 4

This trader travels to Alotepec (and sometimes to Cotzocón if he cannot buy enough coffee in Alotepec) with ten burros. On his outward trip he carries no goods except occasionally when something is specifically requested. He buys only coffee, which he sells in Mitla. He has traveled this route "since he was a child" (he is now 39 years old) and has never had any other occupation. Formerly he brought his burros to Mitla, now he uses the bus from Ayutla to Mitla (53–55).

Case 5

This traveler is 55 years old and has had no other occupation. At present he carries only beer from Mitla by truck to Ayutla, thence by burros to Zacatepec. In Zacatepec he buys coffee, which he sells in Mitla. Although the traveler was cooperative, the public nature of the interview made it impossible to discuss costs and profits (54–55).

Case 6

This father and son team (ages 39 and 18) travels to Quetzaltepec, the father for five years, the son for three. On outgoing trips they carry nothing but maize for feeding their eight mules. In Quetzaltepec they buy coffee, bringing it to Ayutla, whence it is shipped to Mitla by a public for-hire truck and sold. The journey takes between five and seven days, expenses for each trip are $100, and profits are about $400. They travel only during the dry season. Although the father owns lands, he does not cultivate them; during the three or four months of the rainy season they simply rest. Before becoming a trader, the father cultivated his lands and worked as a day laborer (56–57).

Case 7

This trader visits Quetzaltepec via Ayutla. He has followed this route for nearly five years. Before that he bought maize in Chiapas and shipped it to Mitla by public carrier. He travels only during the best part of the dry season, six or seven months. The rest of the year he rests and plants a little maize. He carries no goods to Quetzaltepec "because six or seven local traders go to Ayutla to buy for the town." In Quetzaltepec he buys coffee, which he carries on ten mules to Ayutla, transshipping by truck to Mitla where he sells his coffee. He estimates expenses as $300 per trip, his profits as $1,000. Discussion with this informant suggests that there is considerable cooperation among relatives: one stays in the region to buy coffee, the other transports the coffee to Mitla and sells it 58–59).

APPENDIX 44

SUMMARY OF MITLA TRUCKERS, 1968, BY DESTINATION

Totals[1]	Drivers	Products exported and number of trucks carrying each product	Products imported and number of trucks carrying each product
Trucks to Mixe region: 16	Owner drives, 6; owner's son drives, 1; hired driver, 9.	Maize (8 trucks) groceries (4), bread (2), household articles (2), construction materials (1), sugar (2), brown sugar (3), soft drinks (1), beer (1), cookies (2), soap (2), homemade ices (1), passengers with their cargo[2] and mail (1), nothing (1).	Coffee (14), avocados (13).
Trucks to Isthmus: 7	Owner drives, 4; owner's son or nephew drives, 3.	Lard (1), wheat flour (2), sugar (3), candles (1), soaps and detergents (2), coffee (1), construction materials (2), powdered milk (1), cooking oil (1).	Salt (6), maize (4), mineral lime (1), brown sugar (1), coconuts (1). [3]
Trucks to Mexico City: 9	Owner drives, 5; owner's son drives, 1; hired driver, 3.	Marble (2), coffee (6), avocados (5).	Groceries (8), construction materials (3), flour (1), powdered milk (1), sugar (1).
Trucks to Oaxaca: 2	Owner drives, 1; hired driver, 1.	—	Fruits and greens (1), beer (1).

[1] One truck which travels to the Isthmus also goes to the Mixe region; two trucks which travel to Mexico City also go to the Isthmus of Tehuantepec, and two others go to the Mixe region. The net total of trucks in operation is therefore 29, and since two truckers each own two trucks, the number of truck owners represented is 27.

[2] Traveling vendors with animals in Ayutla.

[3] The salt is sold in Oaxaca and the maize is stored in Mitla. About 20 tons of each are imported monthly from the Isthmus.

SAMPLE OF SEVEN MAJOR LOOM OWNERS OF MITLA: BACKGROUND AND BUSINESS OPERATIONS

Owner's former occupation	Number of years in weaving industry	Number of looms owned	Where goods are sold	Work hours	Employees Number	Employees Salary/day
Farmer, *viajero*	8	5	Mitla, Oaxaca,[1] Mexico City[2]	9 hours daily	7	$10 for (five) regular employees, $3 for (two) apprentices
Farmer	10	4	Oaxaca,[1] Mexico City[3]	9 hours daily	4	$8.00
Viajero	6	3	Mitla, Oaxaca, Mexico City[2]	8 hours daily	3	$10.00
Farmer	12[4]	10	Mitla, Oaxaca, Mexico City, U.S.A.	9 hours daily	8	$12.00
Day laborer, farmer	12[4]	5	Mitla, Oaxaca, Mexico City	9 hours daily	4	$10.00
Farmer, *bracero*	8[5]	4	Mitla, Oaxaca, Mexico City	?	1	$9.00
Farmer, *viajero*	7	4	Oaxaca, Mexico City[2]	?	3	$8.00

[1] Sells at the Saturday *plaza* in Oaxaca.
[2] Travels to Mexico City.
[3] Son travels to Mexico City.
[4] Brothers who apprenticed with Frissell.
[5] Has two working partners who are brothers.

Bibliography

AHRIN, KWAME
  1970 Aspects of the Ashanti northern trade in the nineteenth century. *Africa*
       40:4:363–373.
BEALS, RALPH L.
  1945 Ethnology of the Western Mixe. University of California Publications in
       American Archaeology and Ethnology 42:1.
  1946 Cherán: A Sierra Tarascan village. Smithsonian Institution, Institute of Social
       Anthropology Publication 2. Washington, D.C.
  1967 The structure of the Oaxaca market system. *Revista Mexicana de Estudios
       Antropológicos* 21:333–342.
  1970 Gifting, reciprocity, savings and credit in peasant Oaxaca. *Southwestern Journal of
       Anthropology* 26:3:231–241.
  1971 Estudio de poblados en la sierra zapoteca de Oaxaca, México. *América Indígena*
       31:671–691.
BELSHAW, MICHAEL H.
  1967 A village economy: land and people of Huecorio. New York: Columbia
       University Press.
BERG, RICHARD L., JR.
  1968 The impact of modern economy on the traditional economy in Zoogocho, Oaxaca,
       Mexico, and its surrounding area. Ph.D. dissertation, University of California, Los
       Angeles.
  1971 The Zoogocho "plaza"-market system in the Sierra Zapotec of Villa Alta, a
       peripheral unit of the greater Oaxaca market system. Paper presented at the 1971
       Annual Meeting of the Southwestern Anthropological Association, Tucson,
       Arizona. Unpublished.

BOHANNAN, PAUL, and LAURA BOHANNAN
    1968 Tiv economy. Evanston, Ill.: Northwestern University Press.
BRAND, DONALD D.
    1951 Quiroga: a Mexican municipio. Smithsonian Institution, Institute of Social
    Anthropology Publication 11. Washington, D.C.
CALNEK, EDWARD E.
    1972 Settlement pattern and chinampa agriculture at Tenochtitlan. *American Antiquity*
    37:104–115.
CARRASCO, PEDRO
    1961 The civil-religious hierarchy in Mesoamerican communities: pre-Spanish back-
    ground and colonial development. *American Anthropologist* 63:483–497.
CASSADY, RALPH, JR.
    1962 Competition and price making in food retailing. New York: Ronald Press
    Company.
    1968 Negotiated price-making in Mexican traditional markets: a conceptual analysis.
    América Indígena 28:1:51–79.
    1974 *Exchange by Private Treaty.* Studies in Marketing. No. 19. Bureau of Business
    Research, Graduate School of Business, University of Texas at Austin.
COE, MICHAEL D.
    1969 Photogrammetry and the ecology of Olmec civilization. Paper presented at the
    Conference on Aerial Photography and Anthropology, Cambridge, Massachusetts.
COOK, H. SCOTT
    1968 Teitipac and its metateros: an economic anthropological study of production and
    exchange in a peasant-artisan economy in the Valley of Oaxaca, Mexico. Ph.D.
    dissertation, University of Pittsburgh.
    1970 Price and output variability in a peasant artisan stoneworking industry in Oaxaca,
    Mexico. *American Anthropologist* 72:4:776–801.
    1971 Aspects of marketing in a peasant-artisan stoneworking industry in the Valley of
    Oaxaca, Mexico: the metateros. Paper presented at the 1971 Annual Meeting of
    the Southwestern Anthropological Association, Tucson, Arizona. Unpublished.
CORTÉS, HERNANDO
    1962 Five letters. J. Bayard Morris translation. New York: Norton Library.
COWGILL, U. M.
    1971 Some comments on *manihot* subsistence and the ancient Maya. *Southwestern Journal
    of Anthropology* 27:1:51–63.
DAHLGREN, BARBRO DE JORDAN
    1963 La grana cochinilla. Mexico City: José Porrua e Hijos.
DAVIS, WILLIAM GEORGE
    1969 Interaction and sociability in a Philippine market: the dynamics of personal
    economic relations. Ph.D. dissertation, University of California, Berkeley.
DE LA FUENTE, JULIO
    1947 Los zapotecas de Choapan, Oaxaca. Mexico City, *Anales del Instituto Nacional de
    Antropología e Historia* 2:143–206.

1949 Yalalag, una villa zapoteca serrana. Mexico City: Museo Nacional de Antropología.

DESHLER, WALTER W.
1971 Urbanization in Africa: some spatial and functional aspects. *Items* of the Social Science Research Council 25:3:25–29.

DIAZ DEL CASTILLO, BERNAL
1956 The Bernal Diaz chronicles: the true history of the conquest of Mexico, translated and edited by Albert Idell. Garden City, New York: Doubleday and Company.

DIRECCION GENERAL DE ESTADISTICA (DGE)
1963 VIII Censo General de Población, 1960. Mexico City: Secretaría de Industria y Comercio.
1970 IX Censo General de Población, 1970; datos preliminares, sujetos a rectificación. Mexico City: Secretaría de Industria y Comercio.

DISKIN, MARTIN
1967 Economics and society in Tlacolula, Oaxaca, Mexico. Ph.D. dissertation in Anthropology, University of California, Los Angeles.

DOWNING, THEODORE
1971 Field fragmentation in Zapotec land inheritance. Paper presented at the 1971 Annual Meeting of the Southwestern Anthropological Association, Tucson, Arizona. Unpublished.

EASBY, DUDLEY T., JR., EARLE R. CALEY, and KHOSROW MOAZED
1967 Axe-money: facts and speculation. *Revista Mexicana de Estudios Antropológicos* 21:107–148.

FIRTH, RAYMOND
1939 Primitive Polynesian economy. London: Routledge and Sons.

FLANNERY, KENT V., ANNE V. T. KIRKBY, MICHAEL J. KIRKBY, and AUBREY WILLIAMS, JR.
1967 Farming systems and political growth in ancient Oaxaca. *Science* 158:3800:445–454.

FORMAN, SHEPARD, and JOYCE F. RIEGELHAUPT
1970 Market place and marketing system: toward a theory of peasant economic integration. *Comparative Studies in Society and History* 12:2:188–212.

FOSTER, GEORGE M.
1948 Empire's children: the people of Tzintzuntzan. Smithsonian Institution, Institute of Social Anthropology Publication 6. Washington, D.C.
1965 Peasant society and the image of limited good. *American Anthropologist* 67:2:293–315.
1967 Tzintzuntzan: Mexican peasants in a changing world. Boston: Little, Brown and Company.
1972 The anatomy of envy: a study in symbolic behavior. *Current Anthropology* 13:165–202.

GAY, JOSÉ ANTONIO
1950 Historia de Oaxaca, 2 tomos. Mexico City: Biblioteca de Autores y de Asuntos Oaxaqueños.

GRABURN, NELSON

  1969 Eskimos without igloos: social and economic development in Sugluk. Boston: Little, Brown and Company.

HERSKOVITS, MELVILLE J.

  1940 The economic life of primitive peoples. New York and London: A. A. Knopf.

HILL, POLLY

  1970 Studies in rural capitalism in West Africa. Cambridge, England: Cambridge University Press.

HINTON, THOMAS B.

  1961 The village hierarchy as a factor in Cora Indian acculturation. Ph.D. dissertation, University of California, Los Angeles.

JIMÉNEZ MORENO, WIGBERTO, and SALVADOR MATEOS HIGUERA

  1940 Códice de Yanhuitlan, estudio preliminar. Mexico City: Instituto Nacional de Antropología e Historia.

KAPLAN, DAVID

  1965 The Mexican marketplace then and now. *In* Essays in economic anthropology, proceedings of the annual spring meeting of the American Ethnological Society, pp. 80–94, edited by June Helm. Seattle: University of Washington Press.

LESLIE, CHARLES M.

  1960 Now we are civilized: a study of the world view of the Zapotec Indians of Mitla, Oaxaca. Wayne University Press.

LEWIS, OSCAR

  1963 Life in a Mexican village: Tepoztlán restudied. Urbana, Illinois: University of Illinois Press.

MCBRYDE, F. WEBSTER

  1933 Sololá: a Guatemalan town and Cakchiquel market center. New Orleans: Tulane University, Middle American Research Publication 5:45–152.

MCKERN, W. C.

  1922 Functional Families of the Patiwin. University of California Publications in American Archaeology and Ethnology 13:7.

MALINOWSKI, BRONISLAW

  1922 Argonauts of the Western Pacific: an account of native enterprise and adventure in the archipelagos of Melanesian New Guinea. London: Routledge and Sons.

MALINOWSKI, BRONISLAW, and JULIO DE LA FUENTE

  1957 La economía de un sistema de mercados en México. *Acta Antropológica*, Epoca 2, vol. 1, no. 2.

MARROQUIN, ALEJANDRO

  1957 La ciudad mercado: Tlaxiaco, México. Mexico City: Instituto Nacional Indigenista, Imprenta Universitaria.

MARSHALL, ALFRED

  1920 Principles of economics, 8th edition. London: Macmillan and Company, Limited.

MARX, KARL

  1936 Capital, a critique of political economy. Edited by Friederich Engels, translated by

Samuel Morse and Edward Aveling. New York: Modern Library. Originally published 1867.

MILLON, RENÉ

1970 Teotihuacan: completion of map of giant ancient city in the Valley of Mexico. *Science* 170:3962:1077–1082.

MINTZ, SIDNEY

1955 The Jamaican internal marketing pattern: some notes and hypotheses. *Social and Economic Studies* 4:1:95–103.

1957 The role of the middleman in the internal distribution system of a Caribbean peasant economy. *Human Organization* 15:2:18–23.

NADER, LAURA

1964 Talea and Juquila: a comparison of Zapotec social organization. University of California Publication in American Archaeology and Ethnology 48:3:195–296.

NAHMAD, SALOMON

1965 Los Mixes. Mexico City: Ediciones del Instituto Nacional Indigenista.

NASH, MANNING

1966 Primitive and peasant economic systems. San Francisco: Chandler Publishing Company.

1967 Indian economies. *In* Handbook of Middle American Indians 6:87–102. Austin: University of Texas Press.

O'NEALE, LILA

1932 Yurok-Karok basket weavers. University of California Publication in American Archaeology and Ethnology 32:1:1–184.

ORELLANA, CARLOS L.

1972 Mixtec migrants in Mexico City: a case study of urbanization and social development. M. A. thesis in Anthropology, University of California, Los Angeles.

PARSONS, ELSIE CLEWS

1936 Mitla: town of the souls. Chicago: University of Chicago Press.

PORTILLO, ANDRES

1910 Oaxaca en el centenario de la independencia nacional. Oaxaca de Juárez: Imprenta del Estado.

POSPOSIL, LEOPOLD J.

1963 Kapauku Papuan economy. New Haven, Connecticut: Yale University Publication in Anthropology 67.

RAMIREZ OCHOA, MIGUEL

1968 Field notes for Mitla study. Typescript.

REES, JOHN D.

1971 Forest utilization by Tarascan agriculturalists in Michoacan, Mexico. Ph.D. dissertation in Geography, University of California, Los Angeles.

RELACIÓN DE LOS PUEBLOS DE PEÑOLES (1579)

1956 Biblioteca de Historiadores Mexicanos, Mexico City.

RELACIÓN DE TEUTITLAN DEL CAMINO

1905 Papeles de Nueva España, Segunda Serie, 4:213–223, edited by F. del Paso y Troncoso. Madrid: Sucesores de Rivadeneyra.

RELACIONES DE SANTA CRUZ Y DE TETIQUIPA, OAXACA (1581)
  1955 Biblioteca de Historiadores Mexicanos, Mexico City.

ROJAS, BASILIO
  1962 Miahuatlan: un pueblo de México 2. Mexico City: Monografía del Distrito de
      Miahuatlán.
  1964 Miahuatlan: un pueblo de México 3. Mexico City: Monografía del Distrito de
      Miahuatlán.

SAHAGÚN, FR. BERNARDINO
  1950 General history of the things of New Spain; Florentine Codex, Book 9, The
      Merchants, translated and edited by Arthur J. O. Anderson and Charles E. Dibble.
      Santa Fe, New Mexico: School of American Research.

SHILS, EDWARD
  1971 Tradition. *Comparative Studies in Society and History* 13:122–159.

SKINNER, G. WILLIAM
  1964 Marketing and social structure in rural China. *Journal of Asian Studies* 24:1:3–43.

STEWART, GEORGE R.
  1957 N. A. 1, the North South continental highway: looking South. Boston:
      Houghton-Mifflin.

TAMAYO, JORGE L.
  1950 Geografía de Oaxaca, México. Ediciones de El Nacional.

TAMAYO LOPEZ PORTILLA, JORGE
  1960 Proyecto de integración vial en el Estado de Oaxaca. Mexico City, Universidad
      Nacional Autónoma de México, Escuela Nacional de Economía.

TAX, SOL
  1953 Penny capitalism: a Guatemalan Indian economy. Smithsonian Institution,
      Institute of Social Anthropology Publication 16. Washington, D.C.

TAYLOR, WILLIAM B.
  1972 Landlord and peasant in colonial Oaxaca. Stanford, California: Stanford University
      Press.

VAN DE VELDE, PAUL, and HENRIETTE R. VAN DE VELDE
  1939 The Black Pottery of Coyotepec, Oaxaca, Mexico. Los Angeles: Southwest
      Museum Paper 13.

VAN ZANTWIJK, R. A. M.
  1970 Las organizaciones social-económica y religiosa de los mercaderes gremiales
      aztecas. Boletín de Estudios Latinoamericanos 10:1–20. University of Amsterdam.

WAITE, WARREN C., and RALPH CASSADY, JR.
  1949 The consumer and the economic order. New York: McGraw-Hill Book Company.

WATERBURY, RONALD G.
  1968 The traditional market in a provincial urban setting, Oaxaca, Mexico. Ph.D.
      dissertation, University of California, Los Angeles.
  1971 The traders of a Zapotec peasant community: a quantitative analysis. Paper
      presented at the 1971 Annual Meeting of the Southwestern Anthropological
      Association, Tucson, Arizona. Unpublished.

WELTE, CECIL

    1965 Mapa de las localidades del Valle de Oaxaca (cuenca superior del Rio Atoyac), según el censo de población de 1960. Oaxaca de Juárez, Mexico: Oficina de Estudios de Humanidades del Valle de Oaxaca.

WEST, ROBERT C.

    1948 Cultural geography of the modern Tarascan region. Smithsonian Institution, Institute of Social Anthropology Publication 7.

    1964 Surface configuration and associated geology of Middle America. *In* Handbook of Middle American Indians, 1:33–83. Austin: University of Texas Press.

WHITECOTTON, JOSEPH W.

    1968 The Valley of Oaxaca at Spanish contact: an ethnohistorical study. Ph.D. dissertation, University of Illinois.

WOLF, ERIC

    1953 La formación de la nación. *Ciencias Sociales* 4:20:50–61. Washington, D.C.: Unión Panamericana.

    1955 Types of Latin American peasantry. *American Anthropologist* 57:452–471.

    1956 Aspects of group relations in a complex society. *American Anthropologist* 58:1065–1078.

    1959 Sons of the shaking earth. Chicago: University of Chicago Press.

    1966 Peasants. Englewood Cliffs, New Jersey: Prentice-Hall.

Index

Mixtec (language and region), 3, 29; emigrants from, 224; relations of with Oaxaca system, 12, 43, 46; silk production in, 36; Valley society similar to, 35

Mobility, peasant, 24, 272, 379

Modern, definition of term and use, 10, 11, 12

Modernity of peasants, indicators of, 100–106 *passim*

Mole, festival food, 99

Money: and currency shortages, 220–221; past use of, 220; pre-Columbian forms of, 31

Moneylenders: interest charged, 102; use of, 102–103, 185

Moneylending, surplus cash used for, 103, 105

Morgan, Lewis H., influence on Karl Marx, 3

Mozos, 68, 69; in marketplace, 22, 23. *See also* Laborers

Mules, rarity of, 65

Municipio: as closed corporate community, 32; definition of, 7–8; as integrated cultural and social system, 8; numbers of in State, 32; as political administrative units, 8; resistance to consolidation of, 32; self-governing character of, 32

Nahua language, spoken in Isthmus, 44. *See also* Pochutla

Nochistlan (Mixtec town), marketing relations with Valley, 43

Nucleated settlements, 8

Oaxaca City: cattle markets in, 64; commercial importance of, Colonial, 35–36; enterprises in, commercial, 127, founding of, 35; Indian population of, 8; industries in, 33–34; neighborhood businesses in, 127; population of, 7, 33, 39; rainfall in, average, 30. *See also* Marketplaces, Oaxaca; Plaza, City

Oaxaca State: comparative studies on, importance for, 277–278; cultural characteristics of, 34–37; geography of, 26–31; as locale of study, 1, 2, 4–5; maize deficits in, 57–59 *passim;* population growth of, 33; society of, 2

Oaxaca Valley: Aztec trading center in, 34; differing definitions of, 29; geography of, 26–29; as marketing subsystem, 44, 46; prehistoric settlements and culture in, 34–35; rainfall variations in, 30

Occupations: diversity of nonfarm, 16; in Mitla, 1933–1968, 377–378; open structure of, 16; in San Juan Teitipac, 289–290; in Tlacolula, 291. *See also* Roles

Ocelot, ancient trade in skins of, 31

Ocote. *See* Pitch pine

Ocotlan (town): cattle market in, 64; marketplace described, 128; rainfall, average in area, 30. *See also* Marketplaces, secondary; Plaza

Onions, trade in, 147

Operational budget, effects on selling strategies, 113. *See also* Budgets

Opportunities. *See* Mobility

Oxen, ownership problems of, 64, 69–70; purchase of in markets, 64; rental of, 64, 74; replacement of, 70

Pan American Highway, 10; construction dates of, 34; economic impact of, 240; effects on Oaxaca City marketplace, 243; and isthmian trade, 43–44. *See also* Transportation

Partnerships, uses of, 103

Peasants: as buyers in market, 117; characteristics of, 2n, 13–14; credit not advanced by, 276; dependence of on market for subsistence, 14; economic planning by, 101–103; language of inadequate to define, 33; market orientation of, 2n; nonfarming, 15; preoccupation with market, 277; production strategies of, 113; selling strategies of and price, 207–208; studies of economics of, 3; subsistence economies of, 13–14. *See also* Propios; Villages

Pecan cultivation in southern Valley, 62–63

Peddlers, in villages, 20. *See also* Ambulantes; Traders; Viajeros

Peons, virtual disappearance of, 23

Perfect competition. *See* Competition, perfect

Periodic market. *See* Plaza

Phaseolus, 59. *See also* Beans

Piedmont soils. *See* Soils

Pigs: economics of raising, 81–83; raising, methods and problems of, 64; and marketing alternatives, 144

Pitch pine: as basic item, 92n; economic complexities of, 55–56 *passim;* modern replacements for, 56; production and marketing of, 56; uses of, 55–56, 109

Plaza: absence of cyclical types of on southern coast, 44; basis for inclusion of in system, 42; classified and listed by subsystem and days held, 47–48; common characteristics of in Valley, 132–133; continuing importance of, 244; defined, 8–9; economic usefulness of, 210; employment opportunities in, 22; food items sold, varied sources of, 56; hierarchical

276–277; farm, variations among, 139–144; as fruit sellers, 140–143; in handicraft marketing, 144–145; importance of plazas to, 151; maize sales by, 140; perishables limit sales options of, 141; pricing methods of, 200–201; sales by to mercado stalls, 157; selling activities and strategies of, 118–119, 138–145, 207–208; supply and demand effects on limited, 140–141. *See also* Price; Vendors

Public offices: declining interest in holding, 99, 104; description of, 99; economic aspects of holding, 87, 88, 99; prestige aspects of, 99

Puestos. *See* Mercados

Railroad, limitations of, 11n

Rainfall: deficiencies in, 74; local variations in, 30. *See also* Geography

Rattlesnake, ancient cult associations of, 31

Raw materials, sale of, 66

Real estate: as basis of wealth ranking, 108; investments in, 108. *See also* Housing; Land

Reciprocity, 4; kinds and importance of, 137; labor, 73; relation of to gifting and guelaguetza, 137–138. *See also* Gifting; Guelaguetza Redistribution, 4; through mayordomía, 262–263

Regatones: ambulantes in plazas, 152; as buyers and sellers, 117–118, 119; customer relations of, 206–207; definition, types and operations of, 9, 146–152; importance of to system, 151–152; part-time, 118, 119, 151; and price differentials, interplaza, effects on strategies, 204; village based, operations of, 119, 146–148, 149. *See also* Buyers; Marketing system; Mitla traders; Traders; Vendors

Religious institutions, economic aspects of, 104, 262–263. *See also* Budgets, public; Cargos; Cofradias; Mayordomias

Repartimientos, 3

Research planning, problems and methods, 1–7, 14

Resources, natural, 6; varied distribution of, 31

Revolution, Mexican, 32

Rio Verde, 29

Roles: ascription of, rare, 22; changes in, 23–25; criteria used for identification of, 17; definition of and use of term, 16, 17; diversity of, 14, 15, 16, 25; entrance restrictions for, 16, 22; multiple, and effects of, 20–22 *passim*, 24–25; new, created by modern sector, 23, 24; numbers of found in villages studied, 19–20; occupancy of, varied patterns, 16, 17, 22–23;

performance standards for, 16; in production and exchange, listed, 283–288; sex distinctions in, 16; structure of, openness of, and consequences of, 16, 22–23; subdivisions of for special purposes, example, 17–19; types of and distribution of in Atzompa (pottery village), 18–19, 20, 21–22; types of in Diaz Ordaz (village), 20; types of in Magdalena Ocotlan (village), 21; types of in San Juan Teitipac, 19, 289–290; types of in Tlacolula (town), 20. *See also* Occupations; Status

Rural settlements, 13. *See also* Villages

Sacamisa, festival, prestige of, 97

Salesmen, kinds of, 119–120

Salina Cruz, modern town on Isthmus of Tehuantepec, 49

San Antonino Ocotlan (village), 7, 51–52, 59, 66–67, 74, 79, 109, 146–147

San Ildefonso de Villa Alta (Sierra town). *See* Villa Alta

San Juan Teitipac (village), 7, 9, 289–290

San Lazaro Etla (dairying village), 7, 20, 105, 106, 313–314

San Marcos Tlapazola (village), pottery from, 130

San Pablo Guila (village), agave production center, 61, 131

San Pablo Huitepec (village), tertiary plaza in, 132

San Pedro Apostol (village), tertiary plaza in, 132

San Sebastian Teitipac (village), roles in, 19

Santa Ana Zagache (village), bean specialization in, 59

Santa Maria Atzompa. *See* Atzompa

Savings, forms and uses of, 6, 64, 101–102, 103, 270–271

Scale of economic operations, problems of, 270–272 *passim*

Schools, expenditures connected with, 96

Sears, Roebuck and Co., 12, 168, 169

Secondary marketplaces. *See* Marketplaces, secondary

Self-sufficiency of peasants, 56–57

Sellers. *See* Propios; Regatones; Wholesalers; Vendors

Semidurable goods, 89. *See also* Budgets

Serape vendors, 147–148.

Service occupations: as alternative sources of income, 66–67; economics of, 6, 84; sellers of as propios, 138. *See also* Roles